To George,

Here's to years of fantast

I love you.

Lisa
xo

Aircraft Wrecks
THE WALKER'S GUIDE

Aircraft Wrecks

THE WALKER'S GUIDE:
HISTORIC CRASH SITES ON THE MOORS
AND MOUNTAINS OF THE BRITISH ISLES

Nick Wotherspoon,
Alan Clark and Mark Sheldon

Pen & Sword
AVIATION

First published in Great Britain in 2009 by
PEN & SWORD AVIATION
An imprint of
Pen & Sword Books Ltd
47 Church Street
Barnsley
South Yorkshire
S70 2AS

ISBN 978 1 84415 9109

A CIP catalogue record for this book is
available from the British Library

Set in ITC Century Book Condensed 10pt on 12pt
Printed and bound in England by CPI

Pen & Sword Books Ltd incorporates the Imprints of Pen & Sword
Aviation,
Pen & Sword Family History, Pen & Sword Maritime, Pen & Sword
Military, Wharncliffe Local History,
Pen & Sword Select, Pen & Sword Military Classics, Leo Cooper,
Remember When, Seaforth Publishing and Frontline Publishing

For a complete list of Pen & Sword titles please contact
PEN & SWORD BOOKS LIMITED
47 Church Street, Barnsley, South Yorkshire, S70 2AS, England
E-mail: enquiries@pen-and-sword.co.uk
Website: www.pen-and-sword.co.uk

Contents

Acknowledgements

The authors would like to extend their thanks to the many individuals and organisations that have assisted us with our research, provided information and accompanied us on our forays into the hills in search of aircraft remains. Therefore we would like to offer our thanks to the following: Richard Allenby, Avro Heritage Group, Russell Brown, Jim Corbett, David W. Earl, Aldon P. Ferguson, Craig Fuller (AAIR), Mark Gaskell, David Hanson, Brian Lunn, John Molyneux, Peter Moran, Kevin Mount (Deceased), Matt Rimmer, David J Smith, David Stansfield, Mike Stowe (Accident-Report.com), M. Wheatley, Kevin Whittaker, Peter Wilkinson.

Inevitably searching for and researching the sites listed in this book has involved many different individuals, organisations, archives and published and unpublished written sources. We have tried to acknowledge those that have contributed over the years here and the sources we have consulted in the Bibliography at the end of this book. However, naming everyone is difficult, so to anyone we have inadvertently omitted, please accept our sincere apologies, but you can be sure your contribution was appreciated.

Introduction

The past has always held a fascination for mankind and it seems as society becomes more advanced, we become increasingly interested in the tangible evidence left by our ancestors. Indeed discoveries of shipwrecks, lost civilisations and buried treasure etc are always newsworthy and make popular subject material for a host of books, magazines and documentary programmes. For most of us, taking part in archaeological discoveries can only be a vicarious experience, as such activity is closely regulated and requires serious training, experience and sophisticated equipment. However, as this book shows, relics from important historical events in our more recent past are still lying accessible on high ground and in remote areas throughout the UK and Ireland.

As technology advances, machines that were once at the forefront of man's achievement are viewed as ancient relics in the light of today's high-tech computer controlled marvels. This comparison is perhaps most obvious in the field of aviation and we look back with amazement at the flying machines of the past and often wonder at the bravery of the men and women who flew such basic and potentially dangerous machines, let alone the heroism of those who went to war and fought in them. Whilst it is perfectly possible to gain some insight into this through visiting museums and viewing intact examples of these vintage machines, it is quite a different experience to stand on some remote spot where a life or death struggle was played out, surrounded by the twisted evidence of an aircraft's demise. To some this interest may seem a little morbid and if it was just a matter of gawping at the destruction wrought, then this accusation may have a ring of truth. It is true that human nature also seems to give us a fascination for past disasters, the *Titanic* being a prime example, but by taking the time to learn the circumstances behind a crash and to find the names of those involved, we can gain an insight into the past and an understanding and respect for what they went through.

The authors of this work all began with a keen interest in historic aviation and combined this with a love of hill walking to search out and visit as many of these sites as we could find. This has, with a combined experience of over 50 years, developed into a passion for recording these sites and researching the details of the individuals and machines involved. We have always believed in sharing information and the results of this research have been shared with others through talks, displays and our websites. Through these means, we have realised that there is a wide range of people with an interest in these crash sites and a shortage of up to date and accurate information on them. Certainly when we started out there were almost no books available, other than a few self-published works, concentrating on specific areas of the country and the original 'comprehensive' guide, *High Ground Wrecks* by David J. Smith. Though this was certainly the best (and essentially the only!) work available at the time and gave us a head start on our quest, in the early days it also led to more than one frustratingly fruitless trek into the hills! Some books could also lead to disappointment when finally reaching some sites to find that the photographed remains had long since disappeared, at best now preserved in a museum or at worst hauled off for scrap. In producing this book the authors aim to share the knowledge of these sites that they have gained, to provide the reliable guide we wish had been available to us when we started out. Though not all the sites in this book feature major aircraft remains, many still do and the photographs we have used feature remains that we know or believe to still be present. Some sites are, however, little more than a scar on the landscape that might otherwise be overlooked, but are none the less important for the story that they can tell. Also a more recent phenomenon is the erecting of new memorials at remote crash sites, often to provide a more permanent marker as the last scraps of wreckage have disappeared. As long as there is some identifiable feature at a crash site, virtually all those that we have visited have been included in this book.

We hope this book will fill a gap, not only in many aviation enthusiasts' bookshelves, but also on those of hill walkers whose curiosity may have been aroused by the chance finding of fragments on a lonely hillside or are looking to add a new experience to their exploration of remote areas. Whilst we hope that many readers will be able to share our experience of the thrill of discovery and the unique insight that visiting these sites can bring, as well as the opportunity for reflection on sacrifices made in wartime and to pay our respects to those who lost their lives. For those visiting a site, each entry gives a verified grid reference for the main site, together with additional references for significant pieces, where the wreckage is scattered and we have attempted, as far as is possible, to give an up-to-date, accurate description of what may be expected to be seen today, together with notes on how to locate the remains. Many entries are accompanied by recent photographs, taken by the authors, most framed to show landmarks and terrain that also aid in the location of the remains. The inclusion of this illustrative material, whilst intended to provide a guide to what may be seen at individual sites, will also hopefully allow armchair enthusiasts and those unable to travel to the actual sites to share in the experience and gain a sense of the nature of these sites.

Finally, over the years much material has disappeared from many of the crash sites listed and although the reasons for this are discussed elsewhere in this book, we would like to draw readers attention to the notes on visiting crash sites before they set off into the hills in search of aircraft remains. Human nature, it seems, has given many of us a natural acquisitiveness and in the first instance on reaching a site, our instinct may be to take a souvenir, but we ask visitors to pause and think again – What will happen to it? Who else will see it? Will it later be discarded once your interest has waned? Our personal view is that unless recovered material is to be used in a restoration project or placed on display where it is accessible to the public, then these artefacts are best left where they are, as a memorial. Many readers of this book will no doubt be enthusiasts themselves and understand this point of view, but we ask all visitors to these sites to consider others who will come after them and will also expect to be able to see these artefacts in situ – if everyone took a souvenir, what will be left to see?

Notes on visiting the sites in this book

An important criterion when selecting the sites for inclusion in this book has been their accessibility in respect of public rights of access and unless any particular restrictions are noted in the individual entries, this factor, at least, should not be an issue. However there are of course many other things to consider before setting off to look for aircraft crash sites and the information in this section should help when planning such trips and we hope, make readers aware of the unique issues surrounding these sites.

Using this book

The sites listed in this book have been selected by the authors as those where some form of physical evidence of the loss of the aircraft remains at the crash site. This may vary from only a small scar on the landscape to virtually the whole aircraft, in pieces, scattered across a mountainside. In a few cases a memorial is all that remains to commemorate the event, but virtually all have been visited by at least one of the authors and we have endeavoured to ensure the accuracy of all the grid references and site descriptions in this book.

The individual sections of the book divide these listings into a number of broad geographical areas, each accompanied by a key map, intended to provide an overview of each site location for ease of reference. All the entries within each section of this book are arranged uniformly, with aircraft listed by manufacturer, then type and finally by serial number, if more than one example of a type is included. Each entry then includes; details of the aircraft type, parent unit and air force/owner along with the date of the loss and an individual map number, referring to the map which accompanies that section. Below this is a full Ordnance Survey map reference, including grid identification letters and six figure grid reference, an approximate altitude and the place name location for the site. Full details of all those onboard the aircraft and their fates are also given, followed by a brief narrative of the circumstances behind the loss and a description of the crash site today and what may be found there, including any relevant notes to aid its location.

Planning a Trip

It is envisaged that most readers will probably have considerable experience of hill walking and may already have visited a number of crash sites, either intentionally or by chance. It is certainly not within the scope of this work to give detailed instructions on walking skills and equipment, there are plenty of books that do this. However, to those novices tempted by photos of some of the more intact wreck sites, a few words of warning are required. Even to those who consider themselves to have a fair level of experience, some of the areas covered in this book feature the most demanding conditions for hill walking. The extreme terrain, remoteness and often hostile environment created by rapidly changeable and extreme weather conditions, should never be underestimated. It is often these very factors that have ensured the aircraft remains are still there!

When planning any trip always ensure that maps and guidebooks used are up to date and be prepared to take note of local information, as there may be restrictions in place while work is carried out and during breeding or shooting seasons etc. For navigation, map reading and compass skills are essential, for although GPS units might provide a useful means of checking your position, they should not be relied upon as a primary means of navigation, even if you know how to use them correctly. Ensure you are properly equipped and prepared for the conditions likely to be encountered, don't underestimate duration of the trip or try to tackle excessively long or difficult routes for your experience. Check weather forecasts, but be prepared for changes in the weather and as far as possible for the unexpected – wear appropriate footwear and take suitable clothes, including a waterproof outer layer, adequate food and drink, a first aid kit, survival bag, whistle and torch etc. Note: Be prepared to give up! If conditions deteriorate have a contingency plan to cut short a trip. Don't rely on mobile phones in case of emergency – In many remote areas signal coverage may be unreliable – make sure someone knows where you are going and when to expect you back.

Obviously this is only a very general overview, anyone venturing to any of the sites in this book is responsible for their own safety and for those they may take with them. There are many books that go into far more detail, but there is no substitute for experience and we would suggest that anyone new to walking starts off by going along with someone more experienced or a guided group. Additionally there are various organisations that can offer advice, such as the Ramblers Association and Mountain Rescue Council.

Open Access – Right to Roam

In England and Wales the Countryside and Rights of Way Act 2000 (CRoW) created new rights for people to walk on areas of open country and registered common land. The Government introduced the new access rights in stages, on a regional basis, with the act coming into full effect on the 31 October 2005. Commonly known as the 'right to roam' this right covers mapped areas of mountain, moorland, downland, heathland and registered common land, giving the public the chance to explore legally away from the beaten track for the first time. All new editions of Ordnance Survey Explorer series maps have been updated to show these areas and this is indicated by the inclusion of a symbol on the front cover.

Most recreational activities that are carried out on foot, such as walking, bird-watching, climbing, running and of course, visiting aircraft wreck sites are all permitted on access land. However there are restrictions, some only applicable to protected areas and others only enforced at certain times. Full details of these would require a substantial chapter in this book and are published by the Countryside Agency and Natural England, or the equivalent bodies in Wales and Scotland. However by following the Countryside Code and taking note of any signs and warnings you may come across, visitors should not have any problems. A number of general restrictions are in force and activities that are specifically not allowed on access land under the Act include: Camping, cycling, horse riding, driving or riding of any vehicle, lighting or tending a fire and using a metal detector. However any of these activities may be carried out with the consent of an individual landowner on their land. It should also be noted that metal detecting is not permitted on all National Trust land, unless under exceptional circumstances, and only ever under a Licence Agreement issued by a National Trust Archaeologist.

The *Countryside Code*

The *Countryside Code* has been around for many years and is simply a basic advisory code for anyone wanting to visit and enjoy the countryside in England and Wales. The full code is published by the Countryside Agency, or in Wales, the Countryside Council for Wales and has recently been updated to cover the changes brought about by CRoW and the full code differs slightly between England and Wales. The code is not in any way draconian, but is a simple set of common sense reminders to consider others and help protect the countryside for the future. To most walkers it is second nature and its contents are summarised under five distinct headings:

1. **Be safe, plan ahead and follow any signs**
2. **Leave gates and property as you find them**
3. **Protect plants and animals and take your litter home**
4. **Keep dogs under close control**
5. **Consider other people**

More recently the *Countryside Code* has been joined by the *Moorland Code*, published by the Moorland Access Advisory Group and based on the *Countryside Code*, but with additional information for those visiting heather moorland areas. The main additions are with regard to the protection of wildlife, particularly ground nesting birds and the prevention of uncontrolled moorland fires.

Outdoor Access Code (Scotland)

In Scotland the situation is slightly different, but still gives individuals a right of access established by the Land Reform (Scotland) Act 2003. These rights may be exercised, provided an individual behaves responsibly, over most land and inland water in Scotland, including mountains, moorland, woods and forests, grassland, margins of fields in which crops are growing, paths and tracks, rivers and lochs, coastal areas and most parks and open spaces. As with England and Wales, most recreational activities that are carried out on foot, such as walking, bird-watching, climbing, running and of course, visiting aircraft wreck sites are all permitted. Additionally in Scotland more active pursuits, such as horse riding, cycling and lightweight wild camping are permitted. Again there are some restrictions, particularly at times when shooting or deer stalking (which may affect access to a number of sites in this book) and land management work is taking place or in specifically protected areas – noting any signs and warnings you may come across, should ensure these do not cause any problems. The Act states that both land managers and walkers must behave responsibly and that access should take into account land management needs. Both parties must also respect the environment, including wildlife and historic features and metal detecting is not permitted on any 'cultural heritage sites'.

The *Scottish Outdoor Access Code*, was approved by the Scottish Parliament in 2004 and outlines what is considered responsible behaviour for both the public and land managers. Again this code is largely common sense and the visitor's responsibilities may be summarised under the following headings:

1. **Take personal responsibility for your own actions and act safely**
2. **Respect people's privacy and peace of mind**
3. **Help land managers and others to work safely and effectively**
4. **Care for your environment and take your litter home**
5. **Keep your dog under proper control**
6. **Take extra care if you're organising an event or running a business**

Ireland

In the Republic of Ireland, there is no 'Right to Roam' for remote areas and the CRoW Act does not extend to Northern Ireland either. There are relatively few rights of way and therefore, walkers can only enjoy the countryside through the goodwill and tolerance of landowners. In the Republic of Ireland, the rights of walkers and ramblers are specified in the 'Occupiers' Liability Act 1995', which includes 'recreational user' as a category of users of privately owned lands. Under the Act, a recreational user is a person present on the premises or land of a private citizen, without charge (other than a reasonable charge for parking facilities) for the purposes of engaging in a recreational activity. Under this act, the owner of the land is only obliged not intentionally to injure or harm the recreational user or act with reckless disregard for their welfare! This act has however removed many of the insurance issues often cited by landowners in the past for restricting access to their land. Walking has certainly increased in popularity in recent years, leading to to a number of schemes for walking route development resulting in an increasing number of established paths. Also access is permitted within the national parks and state owned forests, but most popular walking areas are still on, or require access through private property. The situation in Northern Ireland is broadly similar, where again landowners fearing liablity issues have used this as a reason not to allow access to the public. Again legislation has been put in place to limit this liability, but many landowners are still reluctant and the government is apparently looking into ways of easing the situation, particularly in light of the growth of tourism in the area. Much of Northern Ireland's public land is also accessible, including Water Service and Forest

Service land, as well as land owned and managed by organisations such as the National Trust and the Woodland Trust.

The Mountaineering Council of Ireland (MCI) is the representative body for walkers and climbers in Ireland and is working to promote access to remote areas through cooperation and negotiation with landowners and in fact, the vast majority of rural landowners have traditionally granted access to upland/mountain areas as well as general countryside areas and continue to do so. Those areas where this is not the case, restrictions are generally well marked with signs and may be enforced by landowners. In order to keep this goodwill, the MCI promotes responsible behaviour amongst walkers has issued a wide-ranging countryside code based on the 'Leave No Trace Principle of Outdoor Ethics', summarised as follows:

1. Plan Ahead and Prepare
2. Be Respectful of Others
3. Respect Farm Animals and Wildlife
4. Keep to Durable Ground
5. Leave What You Find
6. Dispose of Waste Properly

The MCI's advice to walkers also includes parking safely and with regard to access to property, being courteous towards landowners and locals, keeping noise to a minimum, respecting conservation issues, removal of litter and using local shops and filling stations etc.

Conduct at Crash Sites

As mentioned elsewhere in this book, the removal of aircraft remains and artefacts from crash sites can be a contentious issue, with various parties having differing viewpoints leading to this being a topic that can generate strong feelings. The purpose of this section is not to debate these views, but to increase the reader's awareness of the ethical, practical and legal considerations when visiting these sites and to promote responsible behaviour.

Many people, it seems, regard aircraft crash sites as war graves, whereas in fact only a surprisingly small number of sites have this status. Despite wartime conditions, inadequate equipment and the remoteness of many lost aircraft, great efforts were often made to ensure the recovery of deceased aircrew and only very rarely were their remains interred at crash sites. Such sites are clearly marked as war graves and this is noted in the entries concerned in this book and I should hardly need to say that they must be treated with the utmost respect. However, many aircraft losses sadly involved fatal casualties and although these airmen may be buried elsewhere, the crash sites still have a sombre atmosphere that most visitors are sensitive to and may still wish to pay their respects. The authors would ask that whatever your interest in these sites, be it the individuals involved, the machines themselves or the landscape, you take the time to remember this and act accordingly.

Protection of Military Remains Act 1986

Whilst these on conduct at crash sites represents a request for respectful behaviour when visiting the sites in this book, there are are also important legal implications to be aware of that could otherwise lead to individuals finding themselves liable to prosecution, resulting in a fine or even imprisonment.

All military aircraft crash sites in the United Kingdom, whether wartime or otherwise, are classified as 'controlled sites' under the Protection of Military Remains Act 1986, regardless of whether there was any loss of life involved or not. Under this Act it is an offence to tamper with, damage, move, remove or unearth any items at such sites, unless the Ministry of Defence has issued a licence authorising such activity. Clearly this Act leaves little room for misunderstanding and any individual wishing to remove anything from a crash site will require a licence, and these are only issued subject to a number of conditions. These include: that the applicant must, through demonstratable research, be able to identify the aircraft and the fate of the crew. Signed consent of the landowner, on the appropriate form, must be provided. Special requirements may have to be met, if imposed by local councils or heritage agencies. Official witnesses may be required to attend an excavation/recovery and no licence will be issued if a site is believed to contain human remains or unexploded ordnance. This licensing procedure is managed by the Service Personnel & Veterens Agency, located at the; Joint Casualty and Compassionate Centre (Historic Casualty Casework), Room 14, Building 182, Innsworth Station, Gloucester. GL3 1HW and full details are included in their 'Notes for guidance of recovery groups', which may be obtained from this address.

Though the Act extends to Northern Ireland, in the Republic of Ireland and the Isle of Man the situation is less clear, although in The Republic of Ireland there certainly appears to be provision within the National Monuments (Amendment) Act, 1987 to protect designated sites less than 100 years old, including aircraft crash sites. Though no such sites seem to have been designated historic monuments as yet. This act also places very strict restrictions on the use of metal detectors within The Republic of Ireland.

Ownership of aircraft remains

The actual ownership of military aircraft remains within the UK has in the past been a source of some confusion, as, despite stating in 1973 that they had abandoned all claim to crashed aircraft remains, the Ministry of Defence later declared that all crashed UK military aircraft and their equipment remained the property of the Crown until such time as the Ministry of Defence decides to dispose of them. This position was given a legal basis under the Protection of Military Remains Act 1986 and in the aforementioned 'Notes for guidance of recovery groups', it has been extended to include all crashed enemy aircraft and their equipment, as these may be regarded as captured enemy property which has been surrendered to the Crown. This document further states that crashed United States military aircraft and their equipment remain the property of the United States Government, but the Ministry of Defence acts on behalf of the US authorities.

Under the terms of a licence to recover military aircraft remains, full details of all material removed must be provided in order for the transfer of ownership to take place and the Ministry of Defence reserves the right to retain items considered of historical importance, under the guidance of the Royal Air Force Museum. Though in practice this is rarely an issue. However all items of personal property, or any official documents that may be found have to be passed to the Ministry of Defence. In the case of personal items, such as watches, rings, keys etc these remain the property of the families concerned and efforts are then made to identify the original owner, so that the next of kin may be traced and they might be returned.

Civilian aircraft are not covered by the aforementioned legislation, though even if they are considered to have been abandoned by their original owners, then ownership of any remains is likely to revert to the landowner. Personal property, once belonging to passengers or crew may well remain at such crash sites and again these remain the property of the original owner, if they survived, or their families if deceased.

Dangers specific to aircraft crash sites

Finally a few words of warning regarding the possible dangers likely to be encountered when visiting aircraft crash sites. Some may be considered obvious and some are just common sense, but to those unfamiliar with the likely assortment of artefacts that may be encountered at these sites, it is all too easy, during the excitement of discovery, to unintentionally put themselves or others in danger.

Most aircraft wreckage is metal and likely to be twisted and torn, it is all too easy to cut yourself whilst handling such items. Torn stainless steel is often particularly sharp and as it retains its shiny appearance despite many years of exposure to the elements, it often catches visitors attention. As well as a nasty cut, it may be worth bearing in mind that such metal may be contaminated with animal droppings, increasing the chances of infection.

Many aircraft components may be hazardous in their own right – undercarriage oleos were highly pressurised, as were oxygen bottles, accumulator bottles and fire extinguishers (which can also contain toxic chemicals). Asbestos was widely used and being fireproof, as intended, is often still found at crash sites in a variety of forms. Also instrument dials may still bear traces of toxic and radioactive radium paint. A more recent danger that has been identified following crashes of modern aircraft constructed using carbon fibre materials, is the release of carbon fibres following a severe impact. These can become mixed in with the debris left at a crash site and although they are not toxic, they have a strong affinity to dirt and as they can easily penetrate human skin and tissue, they may carry the often highly toxic dirt of the crash site into the unprotected skin of anyone visiting the crash site.

Ammunition is perhaps the most obvious danger likely to be encountered at military crash sites, yet many people, it seems, underestimate the danger and a bullet may be seen by some as a suitable souvenir. However, all ammunition contains explosives that may have degraded and become unstable. Even small calibre rounds may well be incendiary or tracer bullets that contain phosphorus, which can spontaneously ignite and larger calibre rounds may well have high explosive heads with highly sensitive detonators. It cannot be stressed too highly that all ammunition should be treated as potentially dangerous and left well alone. A few crash sites may even contain bombs or depth charges and at least two are listed in this book where this is known to be the case. With previously buried wreckage regularly being revealed at sites where erosion is taking place, there is always the possibility such dangerous items may be revealed. There are plenty of other potentially explosive items that may remain at crash sites including: flame floats, smoke floats, target markers, flares, incendiary devices, demolition charges and on more recent aircraft, ejector seat parts. Also many high ground areas were used for military training during wartime and finds of live mortar shells and other munitions on the moors around crash sites are not unknown. Hopefully common sense should indicate to the reader that there is a clear case for leaving all unfamiliar objects at crash site well alone!

Chapter One

South-west Moors

Clearly, as the purpose of this work is to provide a guide to the aircraft remains and crash site memorials likely to be encountered by hill walkers, this largely excludes much of Southern England, as there are relatively few areas of high ground where such remains lie. Obviously there are many scattered aviation related memorials, often at the sites of old airfields, but those commemorating individual crash sites are few and far between and unlikely to be encountered by chance. Most are easily accessible by car and are covered in other works (see Bibliography), so have not been included. This leaves the moors of South-west England where the combination of high ground, frequent poor visibility and navigational errors, all too often combined with fatal results for the crews involved. Additionally, due to their particular interest to enthusiasts, the two Heinkel He111 crash sites on Lundy have also been included in this section.

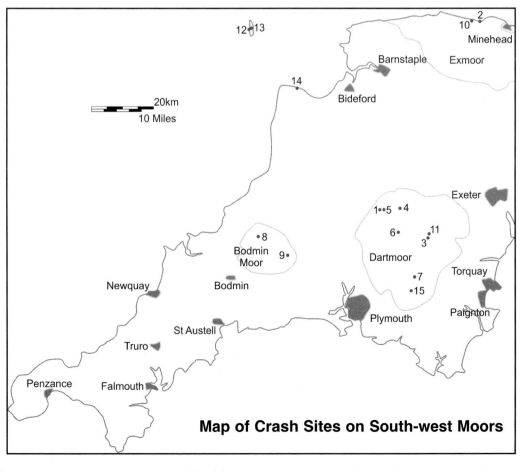

Map of Crash Sites on South-west Moors

The majority of the sites covered lie within the Dartmoor National Park, created in 1951 and covering an area of 368 sq. miles of mostly open moorland. Dartmoor rises to a height of 2,039ft above sea level and the landscape has formed as a result of its underlying geology, being the largest of the six exposed granite domes which form the 'backbone' of the West Country. The resulting landscape features include the famous 'Tors' and their associated boulder, 'clitter' slopes, as well as extensive peat deposits, up to seven metres thick. The impervious igneous rock combined with the high rainfall, means this peat forms extensive wetland areas, such as the large blanket bogs found on the higher, central parts of the north moor and the higher northern part of the south moor. Also common are the valley mires, which are areas of waterlogged, deep peat in valley bottoms, following the rivers and streams that drain the moor. To the west, the high ground of Bodmin Moor has also claimed its share of aircraft and the moor is a designated Area of Outstanding Natural Beauty covering some 80 sq. miles of granite uplands, averaging at 800ft, and rising to 1,375ft at its highest point. The terrain shares many of the features of Dartmoor and is well known for its megalithic monuments and remains of prehistoric habitation. Finally, the Exmoor National Park, created in 1954 and covering an area of 267 sq miles, with its highest point at 1,704ft, features a quite different landscape, this time overlying largely red sandstones, slates and shales, giving rise to large areas of high, heather covered moorland, interspersed with wooded valleys. The Exmoor shoreline is the most remote in England, due to the height and steepness of the cliffs, meaning that there is no landward access to long stretches of shoreline. With a diverse range of landscapes and the usual changeable weather conditions over high ground, including the infamous Dartmoor mists, all the usual warnings apply to visiting the sites listed in this section.

Many of the remoter areas in this region have seen much use for military training activity, dating back to the early 1800s and continuing to the present day. During WW2 this activity was expanded and many of the areas of high ground saw extensive use for this purpose, though perhaps surprisingly less so for aircrew training, than many other parts of the country, hence relatively few of the incidents recorded here involved training flights. During WW2 there were no airfields located within the actual areas outlined, though there were one or two in their immediate vicinity, with most of those in the region being concentrated along the Northern coast of Cornwall and in the area to the east of Dartmoor. Some of these airfields were home to Coastal Command and US Navy squadrons involved in Air Sea Rescue, U-Boat hunting and anti-shipping patrols. Others were home to the USAAF, forming part of the North Atlantic route for the long distance ferrying of aircraft from the USA and later as staging posts for the delivery of replacement aircraft to North Africa and then Europe. There were also Fleet Air Arm stations and Fighter stations for local defence, as well as the usual air traffic passing to and from airfields outside the area, all adding to the wide variety of aircraft likely to be overflying these areas of high ground. Even though these crews would invariably be highly experienced, the combination of changeable British weather conditions and an unfamiliar landscape, often proved more dangerous than enemy action, though there were also losses due to combat damage. A number of aircraft returning from raids over Europe were lost in this area, but again possible fatigue, navigational error and the weather seem to have been more critical factors. The presence of high ground so near to the coast was also a major danger to crews returning from long flights over the sea, where relatively small navigational errors could unknowingly place aircraft on a collision course with the high ground or facing an unexpected early landfall against high sea cliffs.

Though the majority of losses occurred on less accessible and largely uninhabited high moorland areas, it seems that unlike other areas of the country, many were subject to thorough recovery operations by the RAF Maintenance Unit at Taunton and almost completely cleared soon after they crashed. This coupled with high ground crash sites being something of a scarce commodity in the South of England and therefore, their being subject to the recovery activities of enthusiasts from an early date, means that relatively little remains to be seen at these sites, when compared with other parts of the country. One or two wrecks are recorded as having been broken up and buried on site, but it seems these were the first to attract attention and sadly, as with many early high ground recoveries in other areas, little is known of the ultimate fate of the recovered parts in most cases.

Boeing B-17G 42-37869: Meteorological Flt, USAAF.   25-12-1943
Map No.1
SX 552884 (1,675ft), Tigers Marsh, Corn Ridge, Dartmoor, Devon.

1st Lt E.H. Patterson	Pilot	Survived
2nd Lt R.A. Coats	Co-pilot	Survived
2nd Lt R.T. Neary	Nav	Killed
T/Sgt S.R. Renner	Eng	Killed
T/Sgt S.L. Craig	Radio Op	Killed
S/Sgt M.A. Panetti	Radio Op	Killed
S/Sgt A.J. Blanchard	Gunner	Killed
Sgt B. Brown (RAF)	Met Obs	Survived

Following a meteorological reconnaissance sortie the aircraft landed at RAF St. Eval in Cornwall and later departed to return to its base at Cheddington Air Station in Hertfordshire. Flying on a north-easterly track the pilot attempted to maintain visual contact with the ground, but having cleared a lower hill on the edge of Dartmoor, the aircraft entered cloud hanging over the valley beyond. A climb, with reference to instruments, was commenced, but the rate of climb was too low, and the aircraft struck the hill, bounced up the gentle slope and then caught fire as the fuel tanks ruptured.

A large scar remains on the boggy hilltop where the aircraft burned out, and contains a few pieces of armour plating and lumps of melted aluminium.

The area where B-17 42-37869 burnt out is littered with fragments including melted alloy and steel fittings, as well as a few sheets of armour plate.

Consolidated B-24D 41-23712 / R: 330th BS / 93rd BG, USAAF. 29-10-1942
Map No.2
SS 880479 approx., Porlock Marsh, Somerset.

Capt W.J. Williams II	Pilot	Killed
2nd Lt T.W. Lewis	Co-pilot	Killed
1st Lt J.G. Simpson	Nav	Killed
2nd Lt C.G. Sorrell	BA	Killed
T/Sgt W.D. Uffleman	Eng	Killed
Pvt S.C. Prekel	Radio Op	Killed
S/Sgt J. DiMuzio	Gunner	Killed
S/Sgt S.V. DeMaroney	Gunner	Killed
S/Sgt E.R. Purdy	Gunner	Killed
PFC J.J. Odell	Gunner	Killed
S/Sgt H.B. Thorpe	Gunner	Survived
1st Lt L.C. Riess Jr	Pass	Killed

On a training flight from RAF Holmsley South in Hampshire, the aircraft was flying low over the sea in poor visibility, when the pilot noticed high ground on the coast ahead, and attempted to take evasive action. However, during this manoeuvre, the aircraft stalled and crashed onto the marshland.

A memorial stone was originally erected at the crash site on the marsh, but was later relocated slightly, to a more prominent position where it is currently marked on Ordnance Survey 1:25000 scale maps at SS 880480. However, in 2006 the memorial stone was relocated once again, this time to the edge of the fields bordering the marsh.

Consolidated B-24D 42-40474: 36th BS / 482nd BG, USAAF.   27-12-1943
Map No.3
SX 709794 (1,600ft), Hamble Down, Dartmoor, Devon.

Capt R.L. Williams	Pilot	Killed
2nd Lt J.W. Hanley	Co-pilot	Killed
1st Lt M.L. Remling	Nav	Killed
2nd Lt L.F. Peterson	BA	Killed
T/Sgt J.A. Wallace	Eng	Killed
T/Sgt G.O. Wichner	Radio Op	Killed
S/Sgt H.D. MacMillan Jr	Gunner	Killed
S/Sgt E.P. Rush	Gunner	Killed

Airborne from Alconbury Air Station in Cambridgeshire, the aircraft was on the third leg of a cross-country training flight. This part of the route was intended to take the aircraft from over Taunton to Bude Bay, but the aircraft deviated south and was 20 miles off the planned route when it flew into the cloud covered hill and burned out.

A grassy patch on the heather covered slope contains a few pieces of melted aluminium from the aircraft.

Consolidated PB4Y-1 32014 / B-2 (G): VB103, USN.   03-12-1943

Map No.4

SX 618888 (1,700ft), Steeperton Tor, Dartmoor, Devon.

Lt T.A. Lucas Jr	Pilot	Killed
Lt JG J.H. Alexander Jr	Co-pilot	Killed
Ens D.B. Shea	–	Killed
Ens F.J. Buckley	–	Killed
AMM1c T.L. Ray	–	Killed
ARM2c W.A. Bean	–	Killed
AOM1c W.H. Davidson	–	Killed
AOM2c J.W. Laubinger	–	Killed
AMM2c R.J. O'Leary	–	Killed
AMM3c E.A. Shubert	–	Killed

Aircraft was on a training flight from Dunkeswell in Devon. While flying in cloud it struck the top of the tor and disintegrated scattering wreckage down the steep western slope and into Steeperton Gorge.

No.67 MU spent 9 days salvaging the aircraft, and had to borrow several vehicles from the US Army that were more suited to the boggy terrain. As a result only a few fragments now remain on the upper slopes.

Consolidated PB4Y-1 63926 / B-5 (E): VB110, USN.   28-12-1943

Map No.5

SX 565884 (1,800ft), Slipper Stones, Dartmoor, Devon.

Lt W.W. Parish	Pilot	Killed
Ens D.M. Lyons	Co-pilot	Killed
Ens R.W. Lovelace Jr	Nav	Killed
AMM2c A.J. Stork	Eng	Killed
AMM2c J.E. Shaffer	Eng	Killed
ARM2c L.M. Davenport	Radio Op	Killed
ARM3c J.F. Benson	Radio Op	Killed
AOM3c A.J. Roddy Jr	Ord Op	Killed
AMM3c C.A. Reynard	Gunner	Killed
AMM3c D.E. Nash	Gunner	Killed

In order to locate and attack a group of enemy destroyers in the Bay of Biscay, USN Fleet Air Wing 7, based at Dunkeswell in Devon., launched fifteen PB4Y-1 Liberators from VB103, VB105 & VB110. While on patrol PB4Y-1 B-5 engaged with two enemy aircraft. PB4Y-1 B-12 was close by and also fired at the enemy aircraft, which then broke off the attack and disappeared into cloud. On finishing the patrol the two PB4Y-1s exchanged headings to base and returned individually. On reaching the coast of south-west England, B-5 descended into cloud and having turned onto an easterly track, struck the hilltop and then dropped onto the rocky ground below where it disintegrated and burned out.

Large pieces of burnt airframe remain from PB4Y-1 63926, probably originally buried by the recovery team and since uncovered.

Quite large pieces of burnt airframe and sections of armour plating can be found on the rocky slope where the aircraft disintegrated. It appears that the wreckage was partially buried by the salvage team in a series of pits between SX 568885 and SX 569886, just outside the Okehampton Range Danger Area.

de Havilland Sea Vixen F.A.W. Mk.1 XN648 / 716-VL: No.766 Sqn, RN. 31-05-1961
Map No.6
SX 613813 (1,675ft), Flat Tor, Dartmoor, Devon.

Sub Lt D.J. Cottrill	Pilot	Survived
Sub Lt M.R. Kenward	Nav	Survived

During a training flight, from Yeovilton in Somerset, the aircraft entered a spin and unable to regain control the crew ejected, leaving the aircraft to dive into the ground creating a sizeable crater.

The water-filled crater in the boggy moorland hides the bulk of the aircraft's remains. However, a few metres out from the northern side of the crater small fragments of wreckage can be seen.

The large water filled crater where Sea Vixen XN648 impacted probably contains the bulk of this aircraft.

Douglas C-47A 42-100640: 484th ASG, 9th AFSC.   13-10-1945
Map No.7
SX 665671 (1,425ft), Huntingdon Warren, Dartmoor, Devon.

2nd Lt R.H. Mara	Pilot	Killed
2nd Lt F.C. McCutchin	Co-pilot	Killed
T/Sgt M.J. Kack	Eng	Killed
Lt/Col C.R. Rasmussen	Pass	Killed
PFC D.I. Klapps	Pass	Killed
PFC R. Flower	Pass	Killed
PFC V.E. Whiting	Pass	Killed

Inbound from Villacoubley in France the aircraft arrived over RAF Exeter in Devon. at 4,000ft, but was unable to land as planned due to the weather conditions. While holding over the airfield the pilot asked if an alternative airfield was available and the controller recommended RAF Western Zoyland in Somerset. The pilot then requested a QDM and distance to RAF Western Zoyland, along with a description of the terrain on the route. The requested information was provided, however, the course passed to the aircraft was the reciprocal of the required QDM. As a result the aircraft turned onto a south-westerly track, and whilst flying in cloud at an altitude that allowed minimal clearance over terrain on the intended route, hit the hillside and disintegrated.

On impact the aircraft struck the north-east corner of a stone-walled enclosure, with the broken remains of the wings and fuselage then coming to rest on the slope close to the south-west corner of the enclosure. To date, the section of stone wall demolished on impact has not been rebuilt, and a few tiny fragments of wreckage are be found in the rubble.

Douglas C-47A 43-30733: 9th USAAF.   23-12-1943
Map No.8
SX 158798 (1,300ft), Brown Willy, Bodmin Moor, Cornwall

1st Lt T.E. Garland	Pilot	Killed
2nd Lt D.C. Larkin	Co-pilot	Killed
Sgt C. Miller	Eng	Killed
S/Sgt P.W. Weltner	Radio Op	Killed

The pilot, from the 310th Ferry Squadron, 27th ATG, and three other crew members were assigned to fly the aircraft from RAF St. Mawgan in Cornwall to Grove Air Station in Oxford. After take-off the aircraft failed to climb to a suitable altitude and flew into the cloud covered summit of the tor on an easterly track.

A scar containing a few pieces of wreckage remains, where the aircraft burned out by a rock outcrop.

The scar containing pieces of C-47 42-30733 lies just below this distinctive rock outcrop on Brown Willy.

Douglas C-54A 42-72249: Flt 1, 2nd Ferry Gp, ATC, Ferry Div, USAAF. 18-10-1944
Map No.9
SX 253739 (1,200ft), Langstone Downs, Bodmin Moor, Cornwall.

Capt C.J. Norton	Pilot	Survived
1st Lt R.E. Givens	Co-pilot	Survived
Capt D. Holt	Check Pilot	Survived
1st Lt F.C. Ratchford Jr	Nav	Survived
T/Sgt J.G. Moucha	Eng	Survived
Sgt C.J. Dambeck	Radio Op	Survived
Pvt J. Obiol	Flt Clerk	Survived
Capt W.E. Ropp	Pass	Survived
1st Lt G. Morris	Pass	Survived

Inbound from Lagers in the Azores to RAF St. Mawgan in Cornwall, on a transport flight, the aircraft crossed the coast and was authorised to descend to 3000ft and position for an approach. After overflying the airfield in cloud the aircraft flew out to the east and attempted to acquire the approach beam. However, the liaison radio equipment onboard was being adversely effected by the weather conditions and the radio compass was inoperative, making acquisition of the beam difficult. After receiving a QDM to RAF Exeter the aircraft turned to the north to intercept the beam. At this point the navigator and check pilot realised a barometric pressure setting received previously, and selected on the altimeters, was incorrect and the aircraft was too low. Before they were able to inform the pilot, the aircraft flew into a downdraught and as the pilot tried to recover airspeed the aircraft hit the ground, skidded across the hilltop and then caught fire.

No.67 MU salvaged the burnt-out remains of the aircraft using a tractor and sledge, and now only a boggy scar containing a few tiny fragments of wreckage can be seen at the site.

Handley Page Halifax B. Mk.V Srs.I EB132: No.295 Sqn, RAF. 11-06-1943
Map No.10
SS 853480 (675ft), Ashley Combe, Porlock Weir, Somerset.

F/O B.L. Tomkins	Pilot	Survived
F/Sgt F.C. Schultz (RAAF)	Co-pilot	Killed
F/O A.D. Gardner	Nav	Killed
Sgt Rogers	Flt Eng	Survived
Sgt W.A.B. Stokes (RCAF)	WO/AG	Killed
W/O J.N. Hansen	AG	Killed

Flying from RAF Holmsley South in Hampshire the aircraft flew in off the sea in poor visibility, struck the wooded hillside and burned out.

A memorial has been built into a rock bank, at the side of a track round the hillside, close to where the aircraft impacted and a few pieces of wreckage remain nearby.

The memorial to the crew of Halifax EB132 is sited closed to where the aircraft impacted on the wooded hillside.

The imposing monument close to the crash site of Hampden X3054 on Hamble Down.

Handley Page Hampden Mk.I X3054/EA-S: No.49 Sqn, RAF. 21-03-1941
Map No.11
SX 713807 (1,525ft) Hamble Down, Dartmoor, Devon.

P/O The Hon R.D. Wilson	Pilot	Died of injuries 21-03-1941
Sgt R.L.A. Ellis	Nav	Killed
Sgt C.J. Lyon	WO/AG	Killed
Sgt R. Brames	WO/AG	Killed

Descended below cloud at night and flew into hillside. Aircraft was returning to base at RAF Scampton in Lincolnshire, following a bombing raid on Lorient in France.

In the years following the accident the mother of P/O Wilson arranged for a large inscribed standing stone to be erected close to the site, and in 1991 the stone was cleaned and a plaque attached. The aircraft struck the hillside approximately 50 metres SSE of the standing stone but no wreckage is visible.

The remains of an engine from He111 3837 lies on the steep slope below the rocky outcrop where the aircraft impacted.

Heinkel He111H-5 3837 / 1G+FL: III/KG27, *Luftwaffe*.   01-04-1941
Map No.12
SS 129453 (300ft), Earthquake, Lundy.

Ufz G. Nikolai	–	Killed
Ufz H. Kunze	–	Killed
Ufz H. Krozer	–	Survived
Ufz F. Keuchel	–	Survived
Gfr A. Hohenbaum	–	Survived

While over the Bristol Channel on a day bombing sortie the aircraft suffered an engine failure. Attempting to force land on the island the aircraft flew into the cliffs on the west coast.

   The remains of both Junkers Jumo engines can be seen at the site, one being wedged in a gap between rocks where the aircraft impacted at the base of a large rock outcrop. Small pieces of melted aluminium alloy are scattered down the steep slope, and sections of armour plating lie just above where the slope drops off into the sea.

Heinkel He111H-5 3911 / 1G+AL: III/KG27, *Luftwaffe*.   03-03-1941
Map No.13
SS 136457 (400ft), Halfway Wall, Lundy.

Fw H. Scharrschuch	–	Survived
Ufz E. Bottcher	–	Survived
Fw H. Bongers	–	Survived
Fw H. Ludwig	–	Survived
Gfr P. Timmermann	–	Survived

Airborne on a day bombing sortie the aircraft suffered an engine failure, possibly as a result of an attack by fighters, and force landed on the island virtually intact. The aircraft was then set on fire and destroyed by the crew who became prisoners of war.

   At the site where the aircraft burned out, there is a sizable scar containing the crankshafts and pieces of casing from the Junkers Jumo engines and numerous lumps of melted aluminium.

The area where He111 3911 burnt out still contains the crankshafts from both Junkers Jumo engines, as well as a cylinder block and other fragments of mainly melted aluminium.

Vickers Wellington Mk.VIII Z8721: No.172 Sqn, RAF.   13-04-1942
Map No.14
SS 284267 approx., Beckland Bay, Devon.

P/O H.W. Russ (RCAF)	Pilot	Killed
F/O E.A. Blair (RNZAF)	Pilot	Killed
P/O L. Noble	Nav	Killed
P/O F.C. Le Bon	AG	Killed
Sgt C.T. Daniel	WO/AG	Killed

Aircraft hit the cliffs during a positioning flight from RAF Chivenor in Devon to RAF St. Eval in Cornwall, and remained officially missing until the wreckage was spotted by a pilot from No.5 OTU on 21-04-1942.

An engine from the aircraft was recovered from the beach below the cliffs by a Wessex from No.22 Sqn in 1987, and the following year a memorial plaque was erected on the coast path above the site.

Vickers Wellington B. Mk.X LN775: No.3 OADU, RAF.   01-03-1944
Map No.15
SX 654627 (1,500ft), Three Barrows, Dartmoor, Devon.

P/O F.J. Cook	Pilot	Killed
F/Sgt W.M. Jack	Nav	Killed
Sgt A.G. Beeston	WO/AG	Killed
Sgt J.J. Yeates	WO/AG	Killed

After leaving the Overseas Aircraft Dispatch Unit at RAF Hurn in Dorset for transfer to Mediterranean Air Command, the aircraft drifted 25 miles off the briefed route to Rabat Sale in Morocco. Flying in cloud on a westerly track, the aircraft struck the side of the hill and burned out. It was three days after the crash before the remains of the aircraft were located.

At the crash site, within sight of the central barrow of Three Barrows, can be found a scar containing a few small pieces of melted aluminium and heat discharged 0.303 in. cartridge cases.

Chapter Two

Wales

Despite its relatively small size, at only 170 miles from north to south and 60 miles east to west, Wales has seen a large number of aircraft accidents on its high ground. It features a varied and dramatic, often mountainous landscape, bordered on three sides by the sea. The underlying geology is mostly older sedimentary rocks, believed by many experts to have been uplifted and folded by the tectonic collisions responsible for the joining of what is now Scotland to England. Volcanic activity was largely confined to the Snowdonia region and continued tectonic movements and weathering, culminating in glacial erosion during the ice ages, finally shaped the landscape we know today. The result is a series of upland areas stretching from the Brecon Beacons (highest point Pen-y-Fan – 2,907ft) in the south of the country, which merge into the Cambrian Mountains (highest point Plynlimon – 2,468ft). This chain of hills and mountains runs the entire length of Wales to the Snowdonia region in the north, its highest point being Snowdon (3,560ft), the mountain, which gave its name to the Snowdonia National Park. It is the area in and around Snowdonia that saw the highest concentration of high ground aircraft losses, particularly one small area of the range, the Carneddau, a ridge of high ground to the west of the River Conway which has a number of peaks above 3,000ft and features in a separate inset map to the main map for this section.

Almost all the aircraft, which came to grief in Wales, were on training flights either from airfields in England or the few that were sited within the country itself. To the north, there were navigation training schools stationed on the coast, at Llandwrog near Caernarfon, and Mona on Anglesey and both lost aircraft in the mountains of Snowdonia. Clearly the problem was taken seriously as Llandwrog also became the home of one of the first RAF Mountain Rescue teams, tasked with saving survivors from such incidents, but all too often crew members had been killed and they had the grim task of recovering bodies as well. Many of their rescue operations were carried out at night and in appalling weather conditions with little more than the standard issue equipment that was issued to servicemen of the time. The USAAF also lost aircraft in this area, the 495th Fighter Training Group, at Atcham near Shrewsbury lost a number of their P-47 Thunderbolts, which are included here, and in Snowdonia a C-47 of the 27th Air Transport Group flew into the cliffs above Llyn Dulyn in November 1944 while flying from an airfield in France to RAF Valley on Anglesey. The area around this small lake in the Carneddau became infamous as an aircraft 'graveyard' during the mid 1940s. This particular site is both difficult and very dangerous to approach as it is located someway down the cliffs approximately 500ft above the lake. Civilian aircraft have not been immune from the dangers of the high ground here either, a number of light aircraft are included and an Aer Lingus DC-3 lost in bad weather in Snowdonia, where a memorial near to the crash site commemorates the accident and marks the graves of a number of

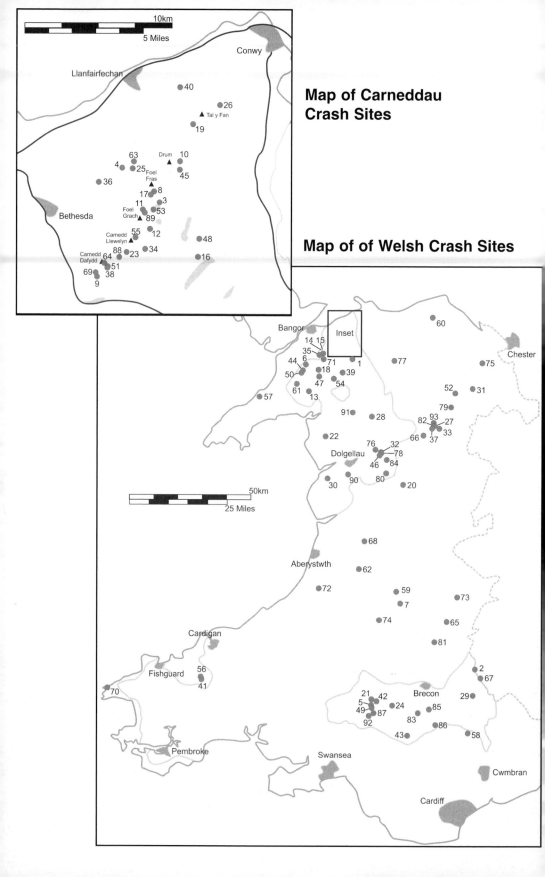

Map of Carneddau Crash Sites

Map of of Welsh Crash Sites

the occupants of the aircraft whose remains were never found.

Other airfields were scattered along the south coast, or to the west in Pembrokeshire and they lost a handful of aircraft on the high ground of the Brecon Beacons. But most aircraft that were lost in this area came from across the border, many being trainee bomber crews on night navigational training flights which crossed this area on regularly used routes. Other casualties came from the US forces, with a number of bomber and transport aircraft in south Wales. These included some that were returning from operations such as a B-17 that crashed in the Black Mountains while returning with a damaged engine from a raid over France. In the same region a US Navy PB4Y-1 Liberator maritime patrol bomber flew into a hill while returning to its base in Devon. More recently the RAF have lost several jet aircraft on low level training sorties, including an Avro Vulcan near Brecon and an F-4J (UK) near Aberystwyth. The latter is commemorated with a memorial plaque dedicated to the two crewmen who were killed in the crash.

Finally, two crash sites, numbers 2 & 67 on the map, in this section are actually over the border in England, in both cases by less than half a mile, but it seems appropriate to include them in this section. The first aircraft, an Airspeed Oxford from No.21 (P)AFU at Wheaton Aston in Shropshire crashed virtually on the border on Hay Bluff above Hay-on-Wye, this is also the highest crash site in England south of Wellington N2848 on Buckden Pike in North Yorkshire. The other was a USAAF P-38, which flew into the eastern face of the same mountain a couple of miles further south.

With a relatively high proportion of sites containing substantial remains of aircraft and the closer proximity of Wales to the more populated areas of Britain than, say, the Highlands of Scotland, it is not surprising that many sites in this area have attracted the attention of enthusiasts over the years. This has resulted in a number of major recoveries taking place, as well as the usual gradual piecemeal disappearance of other sites. However, this activity has not gone unnoticed and with differing viewpoints emerging amongst enthusiasts as to whether these remains should be left where they crashed or recovered for preservation, which has led to strong feelings developing over the fate of crash sites in this area. Two particular sites have created quite heated debate; the Boston Mk.III, Z2186 on Carnedd Dafydd and F-5E Lightning 44-24229 on Plynlimon, both having been complete wrecks. Although neither aircraft was particularly rare, with surviving examples already in museums, they both attracted the attentions of groups of enthusiasts. In the 1980s the outer wings, centre section, main undercarriage legs and both engines were removed from the Boston site by a group intending to recreate one of these aircraft. However one wing was reputedly damaged during the recovery and the controversial decision was taken to scrap this piece. Later other parts were apparently sold and their ultimate fate is obscure to say the least. Much of the F-5E disappeared in a more piecemeal fashion, with a couple of major operations to remove the larger pieces, as well as the removal of many smaller pieces by various visitors over a period of time. Again the ultimate fate of the major parts is unclear, though as with the Boston, much effort was put into these recoveries, presumably by individuals who felt that what they were doing was at the time in the best interests for the preservation of these remains. Further controversy resulted from an operation, which resulted in the removal of larger remains, including several engines from crash sites within the Snowdonia National Park area. Apparently this was carried out with the approval of the park authorities, as the wreckage was considered detrimental to the appearance of the landscape, though the details of exactly who was responsible and to what extent are still unclear. Again it would seem that the motives of those involved were considered reasonable, both for the environment and the preservation of the remains. However, the recovered parts have ended up being split up and changing hands, until once again their fate is unclear. Though these examples are extreme and unfortunate in their outcomes, they are often cited as demonstrating poor practice and this has left recovery groups with a very poor reputation in this area. It is easy to make such judgments with the benefit of hindsight, forgetting that for many years, before enthusiasts became interested in these crash sites, they were regularly the target of scrap metal merchants, who were probably regarded as providing a service by clearing such eyesores, until only the most inaccessible wrecks were left intact.

Airspeed Oxford Mk.I LB537: No.418 Sqn, RCAF.   13-01-1945
Map No.1
SH 746599 (1,200ft), Cornel Min, Llyn Craftnant, Conwy.

F/Lt T. Matthew	Pilot	Killed
P/O J. Firth (RCAF)	Pass (Pilot)	Killed
F/O G. Day	Pass (Nav)	Killed
F/O W.P. Retzer (RCAF)	Pass (Nav)	Killed

Flying from RAF Blackbushe in Hampshire to RAF Woodvale in Merseyside, on the first stage of a trip to Abbotsinch in Renfrewshire, the aircraft descended through cloud while over high ground and crashed. The wrecked aircraft lay undiscovered until the 6th February 1945, when it was spotted by a Shepherd.

A few tiny pieces of wreckage remain amongst heather, on the slope overlooking Llyn Craftnant.

Airspeed Oxford Mk.I PH242: No.21 (P)AFU, RAF.   07-01-1946
Map No.2
SO 255358 (2,250ft), Hay Bluff, The Black Mountains, Herefordshire.

F/O A. Hopewell	Pilot (Inst)	Survived
W/O E.G.S. Monk	Pilot (u/t)	Survived
F/Sgt G. Robinson	WO	Killed

During a night beam approach training flight from RAF Seighford in Staffordshire the aircraft failed to receive a recall signal from flying control for adverse weather. Trying to obtain a QDM to the airfield, while flying through snow showers and buffeted by strong winds, the aircraft lost altitude and hit the hill. W/O Monk was able to make his way down off the hill to New Forest Farm, and as a result F/O Hopewell was then rescued.

A scar near the top of the ridge, containing small pieces from the aircraft, remains at the site where there is evidence of wreckage having been burnt. Approximately 50 metres off the Offa's Dyke footpath, the site is actually in England, but has been included in this chapter for convenience. In 1972 the two Cheetah engines and other items from the aircraft were recovered by No.2478 Air Training Corps Sqn.

Armstrong Whitworth Whitley Mk.V BD232: No.24 OTU, RAF. 25-09-1942
Map No.3
SH 702671 (2,150ft), Craig-y-Dulyn, The Carneddau, Conwy.

Sgt C.A. Stuart (RNZAF)	Pilot	Killed
Sgt V.R. Smith	Nav	Killed
Sgt W.R. Hughes	BA	Killed
Sgt J.P. Hookey	WO/AG	Killed
Sgt J. Hassall	AG	Killed

Aircraft had drifted 12 miles off the planned route, during a night cross-country navigation exercise from RAF Honeybourne in Worcestershire, when it flew into the mountainside and burned out.

Following the recovery of wreckage from the site, using an RAF Chinook helicopter in 2005, only small pieces remain where the aircraft burned out, and scattered south-east down the slope.

The view towards Llyn Dulyn from the crash site of Whitley Mk.V BD232.

Auster A.O.P. Mk.6 VF554 /G: No.663 Sqn, RAuxAF.   21-10-1956
Map No.4
SH 676692 (1,475ft), Bera Mawr, The Carneddau, Gwynedd.

Capt H. Morris (Army)   Pilot   Survived

While conducting an air search of Cwm yr Afon Goch, for two Army Cadets overdue from an exercise, the pilot attempted to turn in the valley. However, the aircraft flew into a downdraught and came down steeply into boggy ground adjacent to the Afon Goch.

The framework and engine remained in situ for several years, however, now nothing is visible at the site. In the 1990s pieces of framework, thought to originate from this Auster, were noted in the Afon Goch further downstream, close to the sheepfolds above Aber Falls.

Avro Anson Mk.I L9149: No.9 E&RFTS, RAF.   17-01-1939
Map No.5
SN 826213 (2,475ft), Fan Brycheiniog, The Black Mountain, Powys.

F/O E.R.H. Coombes	Pilot	Died of Injuries 18-01-1939
LAC A.D. Mabbett	Obs (u/t)	Killed
LAC J.M.M. McDonald	Obs (u/t)	Survived
Mr L.A. Prescott	WO	Survived

Aircraft flew into the cloud-covered mountain top while returning to its base at Ansty in Warwickshire, following a cross-country navigation flight routed via Hamble and Cardiff. Mr Prescott made his way down off the mountain to obtain assistance and eventually reached Tir-y-Cwm farm. A group of local men then set out and searched for the wreck through the night, finally locating it at 06:00 in the morning. F/O Coombes and LAC McDonald were then rescued, but F/O Coombes died later in the day in hospital.

Only small fragments remain in a scar where the aircraft actually crashed, but pieces of undercarriage framework and aluminium alloy panels lie lower down the hill at SN 826212 amongst a group of stones. In Glyntawe Church yard at SN 848169 there is a plaque dedicated to the local men who participated in the search and rescue operation, erected by Air Services Training (Southampton Training Aviation Company) who operated No.9 E&RFTS for the RAF.

Wreckage from Anson L9149 lies scattered on the edge of a boulder field on Fan Brycheiniog.

Avro Anson Mk.I N4981: No.9 (O)AFU, RAF.   20-11-1942
Map No.6
SH 551569 (1,450ft), Moel Eilio, Betws Garmon, Gwynedd.

Sgt A.E. Clay	Pilot	Killed
Sgt F.H.G. Trimmer	Obs (u/t)	Killed
Sgt B.H. Walter	Obs (u/t)	Killed
Sgt A. Walton	WO/AG	Killed
LAC A.C. Lever	WO/AG (u/t)	Killed

During the initial stage of a cross-country navigation exercise from RAF Penrhos, the aircraft flew into the cloud-covered lower slopes of the mountain. One member of the crew survived the impact, but died of shock and exposure several hours later, just as RAF personnel from the bomb storage depot at Llanberis arrived at the scene.

A small scar on the grass covered slope marks the crash site, and contains a few small pieces of wreckage.

Avro Anson Mk.I N5019: No.15 OTU, RAF.   10-07-1940
Map No.7
SN 942616 (1,875ft), Y Gamriw, The Elan Valley, Powys.

P/O T.C. Watson	Pilot (Inst)	Killed
Sgt A.C. Smith	Pilot (u/t)	Survived
Sgt C.J. Dent	Obs	Killed
Sgt A. Williams	WO	Killed
Sgt H. Hannan	WO/AG	Killed

Hit the hill on descending through cloud while lost during a night navigation exercise from RAF Harwell in Oxfordshire. Sgt Smith was able to make his way down off the hill to Tý-Coch farm.

Aluminium panels remain in a scar on the gentle heather covered slope, close to a small pool.

Avro Anson Mk.I N5371 / AK: No.9 (O)AFU, RAF.   23-08-1943
Map No.8
SH 698678 (2,900ft), Foel Fras, The Carneddau, Conwy.

Sgt A. Bickerdike	Pilot	Survived
P/O O.I.H. Stoeckel (RAAF)	Nav (Inst)	Survived
Sgt G. Martin	Nav (u/t)	Survived
Sgt -	Nav (u/t)	Survived
Sgt L. Tommie	WO	Survived

While flying in cloud on the final leg of a daytime navigation exercise, inbound to RAF Llandwrog in Gwynedd from Shrewsbury, the pilot suddenly saw ground immediately below and pulled back on the control column in an attempt to climb. The aircraft hit the mountainside and slid up the slope, the starboard wing striking a boulder and slewing the aircraft around so it came to rest pointing down the slope. The onboard radio equipment still functioned and with remaining battery power a message was transmitted to base and a Direction Finding fix on the aircraft obtained. The derived approximate position was passed to the RAF Llandwrog Mountain Rescue Unit, who reached the site 4 hours later.

The only remains at the site, adjacent to a distinctive boulder, are a few fragments by a small rock.

Avro Anson Mk.I N9855: No.3 (O)AFU, RAF.   08-11-1943
Map No.9
SH 656620 (3,150ft), Pen yr Ole Wen, The Carneddau, Conwy.

Sgt E.A. Hoagg (RCAF)	Pilot	Killed
Sgt J.H. Lewis (RAAF)	Nav	Killed
Sgt W. Gavin	BA	Killed
Sgt L.J. Hill	WO/AG	Killed
Sgt D.J. Roberts	WO/AG	Killed

Having taken off from RAF Halfpenny Green in Staffordshire, on a night navigation exercise, the aircraft subsequently flew into the mountain close to the summit and disintegrated down the steep north facing slope.

Small pieces of airframe are scattered down the slopes from the point of impact. However, the bulk of the remaining wreckage, including sections from the undercarriage assemblies and large aluminium panels from the engine nacelles, lie close to Ffynnon Lloer at SH 660622.

Main undercarriage and panels from Anson N9855 close to Ffynnon Lloer.

Avro Anson Mk.I AX583: No.2 (O)AFU, RAF.   25-04-1944
Map No.10
SH 717697 (1,975ft), Drum, The Carneddau, Conwy.

Sgt R.W.T. Smith	Pilot	Killed
P/O J.M. Polomark (RCAF)	Nav	Killed
P/O G. Williams	BA	Killed
Sgt N.V.N. Robson	WO	Killed
Sgt W. Jackson	WO/A/G	Killed

While flying in cloud during a navigation exercise from RAF Millom in Cumbria, the aircraft crossed the North Wales coast at approximately 2000ft on a south-south-westerly track and flew into the hillside.

The site is marked by a scar containing many small fragments of wreckage, along with the remains of the undercarriage assemblies and the aircraft's batteries.

Avro Anson Mk.I EF909 / J3: No.5 AOS, RAF.   30-11-1943
Map No.11
SH 691666 (2,850ft), Foel Grach, The Carneddau, Conwy.

Sgt A.J. Knight (RCAF)	Pilot	Survived
LAC Reid	Nav (u/t)	Survived
LAC Thomson	Nav (u/t)	Survived
Sgt R. Gilbert	WO/AG	Survived

Returning to RAF Jurby on the Isle of Man from a night navigation exercise routed via Worcester, the aircraft flew off track and was then forced to alter course due to air defenses. Now flying on a westerly track the aircraft entered cloud, and having descended due to icing, struck the mountain. Fortunately the aircraft remained relatively intact and the crew survived. At first light Sgt Knight and Sgt Gilbert went the short distance up the slope onto the ridge and then made their way down off the mountain to Bethesda. The RAF Llandwrog Mountain Rescue Unit were then contacted and set out to rescue the other crew members, but despite searching well into the night in poor visibility, they were unable to locate the wreck. The search resumed at 07:30 the following day, but at 11:00 LAC Reid turned up in Bethesda having made his own way down off the mountain. Based on information he provided, the search area was revised, and at 15:30 the wreck was located and LAC Thomson rescued.

The remains of the undercarriage assemblies from the aircraft and a few pieces of airframe lie at the head of a shallow gully.

Section of undercarriage from EF909 on Foel Grach. Other pieces lie scattered downhill from this point.

Avro Anson Mk.I EG110: No.9 (O)AFU, RAF.   14-01-1943
Map No.12
SH 696654 (2,825ft), Foel Grach, The Carneddau, Conwy.

P/O K. Archer (RNZAF)	Pilot	Survived
Sgt F. Paterson (RNZAF)	Nav	Survived
Sgt W.H. Barnett (RNZAF)	Nav	Killed
Sgt E.T. Brocklehurst	WO/AG	Killed

During a night navigation exercise from RAF Llandwrog in Gwynedd, the aircraft turned onto a north-westerly track over Shrewsbury for the initial leg of the return route, which was intended to take the aircraft to Great Ormes Head. However, flying in broken cloud the aircraft diverged to the south of the planned route and flew into the snow covered mountainside. As the aircraft had failed to return to Llandwrog, two aircraft set out at first light to conduct an air search, but were unsuccessful due to the cloud cover. Later at 15:50 a report was received that P/O Archer had turned up at Rolwyn Uchaf farm, having made his way down off the mountain. The RAF Llandwrog Mountain Rescue Unit immediately set out to rescue the other crew members, who had survived the accident but were seriously injured. The search continued long into the night, but when the weather suddenly deteriorated the search parties were forced to take shelter. At 10:00 the following morning the search was resumed and at 11:15 the wreck was located on the slopes of Foel Grach above Melynllyn. Sgt Barnett and Sgt Brocklehurst were found to have died of their injuries or exposure, but Sgt Paterson was rescued.

A small piece of magnesium alloy, from part of the engine cooling system, and a few tiny steel fragments lie in a small group of stones at the site. A length of steel tube also remains, the end protruding from the grass on the slope below.

Avro Anson Mk.I EG472 / CW: No.9 (O)AFU, RAF.   13-06-1944
Map No.13
SH 568470 (1,950ft), Moel Hebog, Bedgelert, Gwynedd.

F/O R.A. Dawson	Pilot	Killed
P/O J.E. Gunning	Nav	Killed
P/O D.A. McFadyen (RCAF)	BA	Killed
Sgt H. Howard	WO (Inst)	Survived
Sgt J.F. Potts	WO/AG (u/t)	Killed

During a night navigation exercise, from RAF Llandwrog in Gwynedd, the aircraft descended due to the level of turbulence at 6000ft and flew into the mountain. The navigator had thought the aircraft was in the vicinity of Hawarden and clear of high ground. The accident was witnessed by villagers in Bedgelert and the RAF Llandwrog Mountain Rescue Unit was called out. As the team was guided up the mountain by a farmer they came across Sgt Howard crawling down the mountain. He had been thrown from the aircraft on impact before it skidded up the slope into a rock outcrop and caught fire.

At the site are quite a few pieces of airframe, including the panels from the engine nacelles and also the remains of the undercarriage assemblies. These lie scattered on the slope below the rock outcrop where the aircraft burned.

Avro Anson Mk.I LT116: No.9 (O)AFU, RAF.   08-06-1944
Map No.14
SH 626623 (2,300ft), Mynydd Perfedd, Bethesda, Gwynedd.

F/Sgt P.S. Sullivan (RAAF)	Pilot	Killed
F/O M.J. Mott (RAAF)	Nav	Killed
F/O W.D.N. McKessock (RCAF)	BA	Killed
W/O H.J. Fletcher (RAAF)	WO/AG	Killed
Sgt L.J. Pearce	WO/AG	Killed

Aircraft flew into the mountain approximately 40 minutes after having taken off from RAF Llandwrog on a night navigation exercise.

Anson LT116 hit an escarpment very close to where Anson LT184 had been lost eight months earlier. As a result wreckage from both aircraft lies in the same area. It is possible to trace two trails of wreckage down from the escarpment onto the scree below, where wreckage is then scattered across the slope for several hundred metres. However, there appears to be no means of positively determining the aircraft from which each trail of wreckage originates, but based on the available evidence the details given here are thought to be correct. The trail of wreckage thought to originate from Anson LT116 begins on the escarpment at SH 626623 and can be traced down the scree below to SH 628623 where there are the remains of an undercarriage assembly and fragments of engine casing. The trail of wreckage thought to originate from Anson LT184 begins on the escarpment above a rock face at SH 625622 and on the scree below at SH 627622 are the remains of two undercarriage assemblies, an engine exhaust duct, a number of aluminium alloy panels and pieces of engine casing.

Avro Anson Mk.I LT184: No.7 AOS, RAF.   04-10-1943
Map No.15
SH 625622 (2,300ft), Mynydd Perfedd, Bethesda, Gwynedd.

Sgt J.G. Shepherd	Pilot	Killed.
LAC J. Chrystal	Nav (u/t)	Killed
LAC J.T. Key	Nav (u/t)	Killed
Sgt E.J. Keightley	WO/AG	Killed

While on a night navigation exercise, from RAF Bishops Court in County Down, the aircraft drifted 25 miles off the planned route and hit the mountain while in cloud at 23:00. It is reported that there had been a sudden deterioration in the weather before the aircraft crashed.

For information on the remaining wreckage refer to the entry for Anson LT116 above.

Avro Anson Mk.I LT433 / MI: SPTU, RAF.   20-02-1944
Map No.16
SH 727635 (1,825ft), Craig Ffynnon, Llyn Colwyd, Conwy.

Sgt J.W.F. Grant	Pilot	Killed.
Sgt R. Birch	Nav	Survived
W/O T. Renton	WO (Inst)	Survived
P/O M.J. Byrne (RAAF)	WO (u/t)	Survived

Having taken-off from RAF Cark in Cumbria, on the initial leg of a night navigation exercise, the aircraft flew 20 miles off track and hit the snow-covered hillside. The planned route was intended to keep the aircraft clear of high ground, so the crew had been briefed to fly at 1,500ft in order to remain below cloud and icing conditions. The following morning the wreck was spotted and the three survivors were rescued.

The undercarriage assemblies and a number of aluminium panels from the engine nacelles remain at the site close to the top of the ridge.

As with many of the Ansons that crashed in Snowdonia LT433 was largely cleared by the local Maintenance Unit, leaving only heavier parts, such as from the aircraft's undercarriage. These are seen with Llyn Colwyd in the background.

Undercarriage parts and wing section from Anson MG804 lie close to rocks on Foel Fras.

Avro Anson Mk.I MG804: No.8 (O)AFU, RAF.   12-07-1944
Map No.17
SH 696676 (2,950ft), Foel Fras, The Carneddau, Conwy.

F/Sgt A. Biffin	Pilot	Survived
P/O V.J. Sibthorpe	Nav	Survived
F/Sgt A.F. Standring	WO (Inst)	Killed
Sgt Lorrimer	WO (u/t)	Survived
Sgt Dalton	BA	Survived

During a night navigation exercise from RAF Mona on Anglesey the aircraft entered cloud and flew into the mountainside at 02:00. On impact the staff wireless operator was killed, but the pupil suffered only minor injuries and on checking the onboard radio equipment he found that it was still functioning. A message was transmitted to base and this enabled the bearing of the aircraft to be obtained through Direction Finding. The RAF Llandwrog Mountain Rescue Unit was then called out, and based on the bearing, began a search for the aircraft at 05:45. Despite poor weather the wreck was located at 08:30 and the four survivors rescued.

At the crash site there is an area of stones strewn with small fragments of melted aluminium, where wreckage from the aircraft was burned during the salvage operation. More sizeable pieces of wreckage lie by boulders slightly lower down the slope, level with an isolated section of stone wall. There are parts from the undercarriage assemblies and a 12 ft long section of an aerodynamic surface from the aircraft.

Avro Anson Mk.19 VM407: No.23 MU, RAF.   11-08-1952
Map No.18
SH 609557 (2,775ft), Clogwyn, Snowdon, Gwynedd.

Master Pilot J. Malenczuk	Pilot	Killed
F/Sgt J. Tracey	Pass	Killed
Mr W.J. Elliott	Pass	Killed

En-route from RAF Aldergrove in County Antrim to collect radio spares from RAF Llandow in the Vale of Glamorgan, the aircraft was flying in cloud below safety altitude when it struck the mountain. On impact the aircraft bounced up the steep slope onto the track of the Snowdon Mountain Railway, where it burned out blocking the line while two trains were at the Summit Station. Although the wreckage was cleared from the track later in the day, the wind speed had then increased to the point where the railway manager considered it unsafe for the trains to descend, and 120 passengers and railway staff were stranded overnight in the Summit Station building.

As a result of railway maintenance work there is no trace of wreckage where the aircraft burned out. However, a few pieces of the aircraft have been found on the steep slope below the track.

Avro Anson T. Mk.21 VV955: CCCS, RAF.   20-05-1959
Map No.19
SH 724721 (1,825ft), Foel Lwyd, Tal y Fan, The Carneddau, Conwy.

F/Lt E.A. Hart	Pilot	Killed
F/O P.N. Handa	Nav	Killed
Grp Capt J.E. Preston, AFC	Pass	Killed

The aircraft had taken off from RAF Bovingdon in Herefordshire to transport Grp Capt Preston to RAF Ballykelly in County Londonderry for a maritime exercise. However, while over the North Wales coast the aircraft was instructed to divert to RAF Valley on Anglesey, due to adverse weather. Having turned onto a south-westerly track towards the airfield, the aircraft descended and flew into the cloud-covered hill.

A few tiny fragments of wreckage lie at the site, adjacent to a stone wall running up the hill, while slightly to the west, at the foot of a steep section of slope, lies one of the undercarriage assemblies. Further small pieces of wreckage are scattered to the east of the site at SH 725721.

Avro Lancaster B. Mk.I W4326 / SR-C: No.101 Sqn, RAF.   16-11-1942
Map No.20
SH 954092 (1,325ft), Dolwen Hill, Dolwen, Powys.

W/O2 J.W. Spinney (RCAF)	Pilot	Killed
Sgt S.R. Clarke	Flt Eng	Killed
Sgt H.W.A. Collett (RNZAF)	Obs	Killed
Sgt C.L. Coleman	Obs	Killed
Sgt J.R. Gould (RCAF)	WO/AG	Killed
Sgt A.E. Beach	AG	Killed
Sgt D.A.J. Holloway	AG	Killed

Having taken off from RAF Holme-on-Spalding Moor in East Yorkshire for a night cross-country bombing and photographic exercise, the intended 'target' was St Tudwal's in Gwynedd. However, although the aircraft was observed overhead, the planned release of a photoflash flare was not noted. Subsequently 40 miles to the east-south-east a bright flash in the sky was observed and the aircraft then dived into the moorland. On investigation there was evidence that a photoflash had detonated in the release chute, the explosion resulting in the tail section of the aircraft detaching from the fuselage.

A considerable amount of airframe wreckage, including several sizeable sections from the engine nacelles, can still be seen at the site where a large boggy hollow remains. In 1988 the site was excavated and two of the Rolls-Royce Merlin engines from the aircraft were recovered.

Scattered pieces of No.101 Sqn Lancaster W4326 surrounding the crater at the crash site which have since been gathered into two large heaps.

Avro Lancaster Mk.I W4929 / GP-R: No.1661 HCU, RAF.   05-09-1943
Map No.21
SN 828239 (1,575ft), Garn Las, The Black Mountain, Powys.

P/O N.T. Duxbury	Pilot	Killed
F/O V.R. Folkersen (RCAF)	Nav	Killed
Sgt L. Holding	Flt Eng	Killed
P/O T.F.E. Johnson DFM	BA	Killed
Sgt R. Wilson	BA	Killed
Sgt F.W. Pratt	WO/AG	Killed
F/Sgt E.M. Buckby (RAAF)	AG	Killed
Sgt J.G. Curran	AG	Killed

Airborne from RAF Winthorpe in Nottinghamshire, on a night cross-country training exercise, the aircraft dived into the ground after flying into a storm.

A scar containing distinct depressions made by the fuselage and engines is evident at the site, and indicates the aircraft struck the ground in a steep dive. Parts from the engines and small pieces of aluminium skinning remain in and around the scar. There is also a memorial plaque at the site mounted on a concrete post.

Avro Lancaster B. Mk.III NE132: No.1653 HCU, RAF. 06-02-1945
Map No.22
SH 637288 (1,400ft), Foel Ddu, The Rhinog, Gwynedd.

F/O D.H.R. Evans (RAAF)	Pilot	Killed (Missing)
F/O M. W. Moon (RAAF)	Nav	Killed
Sgt G.E.W. Hodge	Flt Eng	Killed
Sgt C.W. Souden	BA	Killed
Sgt A.E. Oliff	WO/AG	Killed
Sgt H. Nielsen	AG	Killed
Sgt A.D. Gash	AG	Killed (Missing)

During a night cross-country training exercise from RAF North Luffenham in Rutland the aircraft entered a high-speed dive after penetrating cumulonimbus clouds. Structural loading from an attempted dive recovery is understood to have resulted in a section of the port fin and several wing panels separating from the aircraft in flight before it hit the rocky hillside and completely disintegrated. Such was the severity of the impact that two of the crew were never found and their names are recorded on the Runnymede Memorial in Surrey.

The shattered remains of the engines, undercarriage assemblies and armoured plating, along with many pieces of airframe are scattered across the hillside from where the aircraft impacted. In 1997 a memorial plaque was mounted on a rock outcrop at the site.

Mark Sheldon holding up a piece from Lancaster NE132. This is one of the few crash sites with aircrew officially listed as missing.

Section of main wing spar and other parts including two Merlin engine superchargers from Lincoln RF511.

Avro Lincoln B. Mk.2 RF511: No.230 OCU, RAF.   15-03-1950
Map No.23
SH 681637 (2,900ft), Carnedd Llewellyn, The Carneddau, Gwynedd.

S/Ldr J.T.L. Shore MC, AFC	Pilot	Killed
F/Lt C.A. Lindsey	Nav	Killed
Eng2 R.A. Forsdyke DFC	Flt Eng	Killed
Sig3 H.H. Charman	Radio Op	Killed
Gnr2 G.L. Cundy	AG	Killed
Gnr1 R.H.H. Wood	AG	Killed

On completing a night cross-country navigation exercise from RAF Scampton in Lincolnshire, the aircraft was instructed to divert to RAF Valley on Anglesey, due to the weather at base having deteriorated. However, on descending over Anglesey it appears the aircraft turned onto a south-easterly track, rather than out to sea, and subsequently flew into the steep rocky slope at the head of Cwm Llafar.

Pieces of melted aluminium and a plaque mark the spot where the aircraft impacted, while sections of armoured plating are built into a stone shelter nearby. The remains of the undercarriage assemblies and pieces of airframe lie in rocks lower down, while a section of the main spar from one of the wings, an engine mounting frame and two super-chargers from the Rolls-Royce Merlin engines lie in and around the stream at SH 679638.

Avro Vulcan B. Mk.2 XH536: Cottesmore Wing, RAF.   11-02-1966
Map No.24
SN 912214 (1,900ft), Fan Bwlch Chwtyth, The Brecon Beacons, Powys.

F/Lt J.D. MacDonald	Pilot	Killed
F/O G.H. Sutcliffe	Co-pilot	Killed
F/Lt B. Waring	Nav/Plotter	Killed
F/Lt R. Clare	Nav/Radar	Killed
F/Lt G.E. Fuller	AEO	Killed

The aircraft having taken off from RAF Cottesmore in Rutland on a routine training flight, transited south-west at high level before descending to low level over the Bristol Channel. The aircraft then crossed the South Wales coast near Swansea and flew up the Vale of Neath before turning onto a northerly track towards Sennybridge. The visibility at low level in the area was poor and two other aircraft on the low-level route a few minutes ahead of the Vulcan were forced to climb as the snow covered ground merged into the cloud base. The Vulcan, however, which was not fitted with terrain following radar, continued at low level, flew into the top of the hill and disintegrated. The long trail of wreckage from the aircraft was located by a helicopter at first light the following day. The crew in the accident were from 9 Squadron.

Near where the aircraft impacted many small pieces of airframe lie within a patch of stony ground. Other fragments of wreckage are scattered over the summit of the hill.

Blackburn Botha Mk.I L6202 / 6-20: No.11 RS, RAF. 28-08-1943
Map No.25
SH 684692 (2,325ft), Llwytmor, The Carneddau, Gwynedd.

Sgt G.M. Heppinstall	Pilot	Killed
Sgt W. Frearson	WO/AG	Killed
Sgt D.O. Hargreaves	WO/AG	Killed
Sgt W.B. Bettin (RCAF)	WO/AG	Killed

Hit mountainside and burned out, after flying into cloud during a training flight from RAF Hooton Park in Cheshire. Following a prolonged search the wreck was located on the 31st August 1943.

Many pieces of airframe, with paintwork in good condition, are scattered down the mountainside from the impact point. Both Bristol Perseus engines from the aircraft remain, one being wedged above a gap in a rock outcrop at SH 683692, while the other lies in the Afon Goch below the waterfall at SH 678692.

One of the two engines from Botha L6202 on Llwytmor is wedged into rocks on an outcrop at the crash site.

Blackburn Botha Mk.I L6318: No.3 SGR, RAF.   23-08-1942
Map No.26
SH 742734 (1,275ft), Tal-y-Fan, The Carneddau, Conwy.

W/O H.L. Pendal	Pilot	Killed
Sgt R.W. Patrick (RNZAF)	Nav / BA	Killed
Sgt J.B. Wood (RNZAF)	Nav / BA	Killed
AC1 A. Smyth	WO	Killed
AC1 R. Ibbetson	WO	Killed

The aircraft flew into the hillside, after entering cloud, while on a day navigation exercise from RAF Squires Gate in Lancashire.

Only a few small pieces of wreckage are to be found amongst the gorse and heather beside a small stream, just a few metres down the slope from a stone wall.

Note: This area was used for Army training and, as well as cartridge cases, quite a few mortar shells still remain and should not be touched.

Boeing B-17E 41-9098: 340th BS / 97th BG, USAAF.   11-08-1942
Map No.27
SJ 079334 (2,150ft), Craig Berwyn, Berwyn Mountains, Powys.

2nd Lt H.L. Gilbert	Pilot	Killed
2nd Lt R. Beers	Co-pilot	Killed
2nd Lt L.G. Schmitt	Nav	Killed
2nd Lt L.H. Phillips	BA	Killed
S/Sgt R.A. Kemp	Radio Op	Killed
M/Sgt S. Lepa	Gunner	Killed
Sgt K.H. Branum	Gunner	Killed
Sgt W.V. Sidders	Gunner	Killed
Cpl M.A. Koepke	Pass (Crew Chf)	Killed
Cpl S.G. Aldridge	Pass (Aerial Eng)	Killed
Pvt F.A. Villarreal	Pass (Ast Crew Chf)	Killed

On a training flight, from Polebrook Air Station in Northampton to Base Air Depot 1 at Burtonwood near Warrington, the aircraft flew into the mountainside and burned out. A second aircraft following the same planned route returned to base on encountering deteriorating weather conditions. It is reported that the Royal Observer Corps tracked the aircraft flying towards the Berwyn Mountains, and due to its low altitude, lit a pattern of red flares in accordance with the 'Granite' warning system, intended to signal to an aircraft that it should turn onto a reciprocal course. However, even if the flares were visible to the crew their significance would probably not have been realised.

A large patch of bare earth marks the site on the steep grassy slope. However, little wreckage remains from the aircraft, the first USAAF bomber to crash on high ground in Britain.

Boeing B-17F 42-3124 / GN-N: 427th BS / 303rd BG, USAAF.   04-08-1943.
Map No.28
SH 826369 (2,750ft), Arenig Fawr, Gwynedd.

1st Lt J.N. Pratt	Pilot	Killed
2nd Lt W.A. Bowling	Co-pilot	Killed
2nd Lt A.M. Boner	Nav	Killed
S/Sgt W.J. Johnston	Eng	Killed
T/Sgt F.J. Royar	Radio Op	Killed
Sgt W.B. Robinson	Gunner	Killed
Sgt P. Simonte	Gunner	Killed
Pfc A.B. Van Dyke	Pass	Killed

During a night cross-country training flight from Molesworth Air Station in Cambridgeshire, the aircraft flew into the summit of the mountain at 01:00 and caught fire.

After the accident virtually all the wreckage was salvaged by No.34 MU. Now only lumps of melted aluminium lie in a patch of stony ground where the aircraft burned out, from where small pieces are scattered down the slope for some distance. A slate memorial plaque is built into the wall of the stone shelter on the very top of the mountain.

The memorial plaque on the summit of Arenig Fawr in memory of the crew of B-17 42-3124 which crashed there in August 1943.

Boeing B-17F 42-5903 / 'Ascend Charlie': 571st BS / 390th BG, USAAF. 16-09-1943
Map No.29
SO 242254 (1,775ft), Pen Gwyllt Meirch, The Black Mountains, Powys.

1st Lt H.I. Turner Jr	Pilot	Killed
2nd Lt F.M. Broers	Co-pilot	Killed
2nd Lt R.L. Schanen	Nav	Killed
2nd Lt O. Tofte	BA	Killed
S/Sgt P. Catania	Radio Op	Killed
S/Sgt S.B. Mason	Gunner	Killed
S/Sgt A.C. Monson	Gunner	Killed
S/Sgt J.J. Peterson	Gunner	Killed
S/Sgt S.E. Rambo	Gunner	Killed
S/Sgt S.A. Zetterberg	Gunner	Killed

Having taken-off from Framlingham Air Station in Suffolk, to join a force of twenty-one B-17s on an operational mission over France, bombing of the intended target had to be abandoned due to cloud cover and instead an opportunity target at La Rochelle in France was raided. During the attack the aircraft was damaged by anti-aircraft fire with the port-outer engine being put out of action. Returning from the attack the force encountered cloud and rain squalls and on nearing the South West coast of England the aircraft became separated. Around an hour later at 21:20 'Ascend Charlie' flew into the hilltop and burned out.

At the site a metal cross stands on a stone base onto which a memorial plaque is mounted. A large scar where the aircraft burned out contains lumps of melted aluminium and small fragments of airframe.

Boeing B-17G 44-8639: 511th BS / 351st BG, USAAF. 08-06-1945
Map No.30
SH 644122 (1,400ft), Craig Cwm Llywd, Barmouth, Gwynedd.

1st Lt H.R. Hibbard DFC	Pilot	Killed
Capt J.C. Robinson	Co-pilot	Killed
Capt J.A. Glover Jr DFC	Nav	Killed
T/Sgt M. Marksheid	Radio Op	Killed
M/Sgt J.Q. Montgomery	Eng / Crew Chf	Killed
T/Sgt K.W. Craumer	Gunner	Killed
T/Sgt L.A.F. Rhein	Gunner	Killed
Sgt D.I. Rapoport	Gunner	Killed
S/Sgt S.A. Caruso	Gunner	Killed
S/Sgt R.E. Smith	Gunner	Killed
Ten passengers	(See Appendices)	Killed

Aircraft was flying from Polebrook Air Station in Northampton to Valley on Anglesey, in preparation for a transatlantic ferry flight to the United States, following the end of WW2 in Europe. Onboard the aircraft were 20 airmen from the 351st BG. Flying at low level in poor visibility the aircraft was near Barmouth when it contacted Valley and requested a QDM to the airfield. A course was passed, but the aircraft then flew south, away from the airfield, and hit the steep hillside.

A sizeable scar on the steep grassy slope can be seen where the aircraft burned out and this contains small bits of melted aluminium. Below the site, on a stone wall at SH 643124, is a plaque that was unveiled in memory of the crew on 8th June 1995, exactly 50 years after the accident.

Bristol Beaufighter T.F. Mk.X NE203: No.2 FPP, ATA. 03-11-1943
Map No.31
SJ 239482 (1,475ft), World's End, Llangollen, Denbighshire.

F/Sgt J. Shepherd	Pilot	Killed

While en-route to RAF Kirkbride in Cumbria, on the initial stage of a delivery flight from Weston in North Somerset, it appears the pilot lost control while flying on instruments in cloud, and the aircraft dived into the moorland.

The crater made by the aircraft on hitting the rocky ground still contains small pieces of steel and aluminium alloy, but little is recognisable due to the severity of the impact damage.

Bristol Beaufighter T.F. Mk.X RD210: No.1 FU, RAF. 10-02-1945
Map No.32
SH 863226 (2,575ft), Aran Fawddwy, Gwynedd.

F/O A.L. Roe (RAAF)	Pilot	Killed
W/O D.R. Newbury	Nav	Killed

Aircraft was on a flight from RAF Pershore in Worcestershire to assess aircraft fuel consumption when it flew into the mountain while in cloud.

The impact point is in a deep gully on the rock face above Craiglyn Dyfi and climbing up to it is not recommended. The bulk of the remaining wreckage though is scattered on the scree slope below, including the propeller reduction gear units, parts from the undercarriage assemblies and sections of the wing main spar. Other pieces of airframe lie in the lake. The Bristol Hercules engines from the aircraft were still to be seen into the 1990s, but have since been removed.

Bristol Blenheim Mk.IV L4873: No.90 Sqn, RAF. 23-03-1940
Map No.33
SJ 102324 (1,875ft), Foel Wen, Berwyn Mountains, Powys.

Sgt M.C. Cotterell	Pilot	Killed
Sgt R.J. Harbour	Obs	Killed
AC2 K.C. Winterton	WO/AG	Killed

Having departed RAF Upwood in Cambridgeshire, as one of three Blenheims on a cross-country training flight, the aircraft broke formation after entering cloud and subsequently flew into the hillside.

A considerable amount of airframe wreckage, including several large sections of the wing main spar, is still scattered at the site, with much of the paintwork in good condition.

A collection of panels from Blenheim L4873 on Foel Wen in the Berwyn Mountains.

Bristol Blenheim Mk.IV L9039 / LD-Y: No.13 OTU, RAF.   08-04-1940
Map No.34
SH 691641 (2,850ft), Craig-yr-Ysfa, The Carneddau, Conwy.

Sgt A.E. Hall	Pilot	Killed
Sgt F. Graham	Obs	Killed
Sgt A.C. Catton	Obs	Killed
LAC G.H. James	WO/AG	Killed

Having taken-off from RAF Bicester in Oxfordshire for a formation cross-country training flight the aircraft was flying towards Ronaldsway in cloud, on the initial leg of the planned route, when at 11:20 it entered a gentle turn and broke formation. The wrecked aircraft was located the following day and on investigation it appeared to have flown into the mountain in level flight.

Small pieces of wreckage remain at the impact point, which is on rocks above a steep gully close to the top of an escarpment. From this point pieces of wreckage are scattered down into the gully and onto the slope below where both propeller reduction gear units and parts of the engine cowlings can be found. On a small plateau at SH 693641 is the crankshaft from one of the Bristol Mercury engines and a section of undercarriage framework. The rest of the engine from which the crankshaft originated and the other more complete engine lie on a rocky slope near a sizeable collection of airframe wreckage in reeds at SH 696638. These parts fell down the escarpment the aircraft hit, over the cliffs and down the scree slope below coming to rest 1000ft below the impact point. The lowest wreckage is easily accessible and the wreckage on the small plateau can be reached by going around the northern end of the cliffs, but the climb up the gully to the impact point is not recommended.

Bristol Blenheim Mk.IV V6099: No.13 OTU, RAF.   31-03-1943
Map No.35
SH 610616 (2,475ft), Elidir Fawr, Llanberis, Gwynedd.

F/O E.A. Perry (RNZAF)	Pilot (u/t)	Killed
P/O G.I. Gunter	Nav (u/t)	Killed
Sgt H. Applegarth	WO/AG	Killed

Flew into the mountainside in poor visibility during a day navigation exercise from RAF Bicester in Oxfordshire. The aircraft remained missing for twelve days, before it was reported that aircraft wreckage had been spotted on Elidir Fawr. On the 13-04-1943 the RAF Llandwrog Mountain Rescue Unit climbed to the site and identified it as the missing Blenheim.

On the scree where the aircraft impacted there are bits of melted aluminium and parts from the wing main spar. Further wreckage is scattered lower down the slope, including parts from an undercarriage assembly at SH 610618.

Cessna 152 Aerobat G-BHAC: Herefordshire Aero Club.   11-09-2006
Map No.36
SH 661684 (2,100ft), Drosgl, The Carneddau, Gwynedd.

Mr B. Vaux	Pilot	Survived
Mr S. Kingsbury	Pass	Killed

Having flown from Shobdon Airfield in Herefordshire to Caernarvon Airfield (former RAF Llandwrog) in Gwynedd earlier in the day, the aircraft departed on a return flight in the late afternoon. However, on taking off and flying on a direct route towards Shobdon the aircraft encountered poor weather and the pilot opted to return to Caernarvon. After refuelling, the aircraft departed again, the pilot having decided to this time follow the North Wales coast around Snowdonia before turning towards Shobdon. Only eleven minutes later, the aircraft had drifted east of the intended route, and after entering cloud hit the mountainside and turned over.

The wreckage from this comparatively recent accident was cleared within a few days, leaving only a few tiny pieces and a scar from the initial impact to mark the site.

Cessna 172M Skyhawk G-BXLJ: APB Leasing Ltd.   12-02-1999
Map No.37
SJ 070322 (2,575ft), Moel Sych, Berwyn Mountains, Powys.

Mr G. Newton	Pilot	Killed
Mr S. Mole	Pilot (Inst)	Killed
Miss F. McWilliam	Pass	Killed

The aircraft had been hired by the pilot so he could regain his flying currency, and as a result needed to be accompanied by an instructor. After taking off from Welshpool Airfield in Powys the aircraft flew north-west toward the Berwyn Mountains and was observed at relatively low level in the vicinity of Pistyl Rhaeadr waterfall. Having then turned onto a more northerly track, it appears the aircraft was either caught in a downdraught or entered cloud, for it failed to clear the mountainside ahead.

In the col between Moel Sych and Cadair Berwyn, at the base of a small patch of exposed rock, there is a stone cross in memory of Miss McWilliam, a student pilot flying as a passenger on the aircraft. Close by, a narrow track leaves the ridge and cuts north-east across the steep slope to join a more defined path running down off the ridge to Moel yr Ewig. It was on the narrow track approximately 30 metres from where it leaves the ridge that the aircraft impacted, before tumbling down the steep slope and coming to rest at SJ 071319, but in a thorough clear up operation all the wreckage was removed.

The memorial to one of the victims of Cessna 172 G-BXLJ, laid close to the spot where the aircraft flew into Moel Sych.

Cessna 310F G-ARMK: Aircruise (Operating) Ltd.   29-09-1968
Map No.38
SH 670626 (2,800ft), Carnedd Dafydd, The Carneddau, Conwy.

     Mr R.S. Ducker   Pilot   Killed

During a private flight from Leavesden Airfield in Hertfordshire to Blackpool in Lancashire, the aircraft diverged from the planned route while flying in IFR conditions and hit the mountain. The wreckage was found the following day.

    The only sizeable piece of wreckage remaining from the aircraft is an engine block, lying some distance down the slope from the site at SH 666622.

Cessna 337A Skymaster G-ATNY: Ron Webster (Midlands) Ltd. 08-06-1979
Map No.39
SH 710551 (2,600ft), Moel Siabod, Capel Curig, Conwy.

Mr V. Wilson	Pilot	Killed
Mr C. Fletcher	Pass	Killed
Mr R. Gregory	Pass	Killed
Mr J. Gregory	Pass	Killed
Mr T. Greenan	Pass	Killed
Mr T. Hood	Pass	Killed

Airborne from Coventry Airport in Warwickshire, on a private flight to Ronaldsway on the Isle of Man, the aircraft was on the second leg of the route when it flew 12° off track. This part of the route was intended to take the aircraft from Droitwich to Great Ormes Head, but instead the aircraft flew towards Snowdonia and having failed to climb to a safe altitude, on entering cloud the aircraft hit the mountain.

Only small parts remain where the aircraft impacted on a very steep rock face. Lower down the mountain, however, in a bog close to Llyn y Foel, are a few pieces of airframe that are easily accessible.

The two memorials at the crash site of B-24 'Bachelors Baby' above Penmenmawr.

Consolidated B-24J 42-99991 / 'Bachelors Baby': 8th USAAF. 07-01-1944
Map No.40
SH 716744 (1,275ft), Moelfre, Penmenmawr, Conwy.

2nd Lt A.J. Schultz	Pilot	Survived
2nd Lt A.W. Davis	Co-pilot	Died of Injuries 07-01-1944
2nd Lt J.S. Erts	Nav	Survived
2nd Lt N.P. Boyer	BA	Survived
S/Sgt S.L. Offutt	Eng	Killed
S/Sgt J.E. Tymczak	Radio Op	Survived
Sgt J. Nieglos	Gunner	Survived
Sgt H. Alexander	Gunner	Survived
Sgt W.G. Nichols	Gunner	Killed
Sgt W.M. Lorenz	Gunner	Died of Injuries 08-01-1944
T/Sgt N. Cennemo	Pass (Eng)	Killed
'Booster' (Fox Terrier)	Crew mascot	Killed

This aircraft had arrived at Valley on Anglesey via the South Atlantic Ferry Route, and due to poor weather the onward flight to Watton Air Station in Norfolk had been delayed by a day. The crew were simply briefed that the flight was to be in formation with a B-17G piloted by F/O L.L. Borris, who as a ferry pilot was familiar with the intended route to Watton via Rhyl, Chester and Kettering. After taking off at 13:45 the two aircraft initially remained at low level below cloud, but as the fully loaded B-24 attempted to close up on the B-17, it then turned onto an easterly track and commenced a climb. At 700ft having entered the cloud, the B-24 lost visual contact with the B-17, but on informing Flt Off Borris, he reported that he had broken out of the cloud and instructed the B-24 crew to hold their course. However, the B-24 was not on a specific course, so 2nd Lt Schultz commenced a gentle spiral climb to get above the cloud. It was then while on an east-south-easterly heading the aircraft struck the side of Clip-yr-Orsedd, ripping off the bomb doors and scattering baggage over the hillside. Flying on briefly the aircraft hit the ground again on the plateau beyond, before sliding to a halt at the base of Moelfre where it caught fire.

A patch of bare earth remains where the aircraft burned out. Only a few tiny pieces from the aircraft are to be found but there is a memorial plaque mounted on a large slab of slate set vertically into the ground and a metal cross mounted on a large boulder.

Consolidated Liberator G.R. Mk.VI EV881: No.547 Sqn, RAF. 19-09-1944
Map No.41
SN 127316 (1,225ft), Carn Sian, Precelli Mountains, Pembrokeshire.

W/O S.W. Kearey	Pilot	Killed
F/Sgt A.J. Campbell	Co-pilot	Survived
P/O R.N. Shearley (RCAF)	Nav	Survived
F/Sgt J.D. Boyd (RCAF)	Nav / BA	Killed
F/Sgt R. Sellors	Flt Eng	Killed
F/Sgt R. Evans	WO/Flt Mech /AG	Killed
W/O B.W. Soroski (RCAF)	WO/AG	Killed
W/O E.J. Moody	WO/AG	Survived
Sgt A.H. Humphries	AG	Killed

Having returned from an anti-submarine patrol in the early hours of the morning, the crew departed from RAF St. Eval in Cornwall during the evening for an anti-submarine exercise codenamed Oasthouse. The exercise was to involve practising night attack patterns, using Radar and the recently introduced Leigh Light (airborne searchlight), against a Royal Navy submarine. However, outbound to the exercise the aircraft deviated from the briefed route, which was via Smalls Light off the Pembrokeshire coast, flew into the hilltop and caught fire.

In 1985 the Pembrokeshire Aviation Group placed a memorial plaque at the site, where a large scar is evident, containing lumps of melted aluminium and small parts from the aircraft.

Consolidated PB4Y-1 38753 / B-2(F): VB110, USN.   24-08-1944
Map No.42
SN 848228 (1,900ft), Moel Feity, The Black Mountain, Powys.

Lt JG J.G. Byrnes	Pilot	Killed
Lt JG J.N. Hobson Jr	Co-pilot	Killed
Ens A. Manelski	Nav	Killed
AMM1c H.P. Holt Jr	–	Killed
ARM2c F.R. Shipe	–	Killed
AMM3c D.F. Keister	–	Killed

While on a night familiarisation flight, the position of the aircraft was determined as being several miles to the north-west of Brecon by facilities at RAF Fairwood Common. Flying control at RAF Exeter then passed the aircraft a QDM of 220°T, for it to follow back to base at Dunkeswell in Devon. Having turned onto the required track the aircraft was flying in cloud with the auto-pilot engaged and the radar functioning when it struck the very top of the hill, disintegrated and caught fire.

A number of fragments of aluminium skinning are scattered in the tussock grass on the hilltop, while slightly further south in a peat filled hollow there are some spars and other small parts.

De Havilland Hornet F. Mk.1 PX273: No.30 MU, RAF.   30-09-1946
Map No.43
SN 977093 (1,225ft), Mynydd-y-glog, Rhondda Cynon Taff.

| W/Cdr P.M. Bond | Pilot | Killed |

On a cross-country flight, from St. Athan in the Vale of Glamorgan to West Raynham in Norfolk, the aircraft hit the hilltop at high speed and disintegrated.

Fragments of plywood, steel brackets and torn pieces of aluminium are scattered for some distance on the hilltop, but no sizeable parts from the aircraft remain.

De Havilland Mosquito Mk.II W4088: No.51 OTU, RAF.   01-11-1944
Map No.44
SH 543552 (1,900ft), Mynydd Mawr, Rhydd Ddu, Gwynedd.

| Capt J. De Thuisy (FFAF) | Pilot | Killed |
| P/O J.A.G.H. Marchal (Belgian) | Nav | Killed |

While on a night navigation exercise from RAF Cranfield in Bedfordshire, the aircraft was flying at approximately 2000ft when the pilot turned onto the next course on the planned route, prior to reaching the intended turning point. As a result the aircraft subsequently flew into the mountainside and disintegrated across the slope.

Small fragments of wreckage remain in a scar where the aircraft burned out, in the col between Craig Cwmbychan and the summit of Mynydd Mawr. Scattered across and down the heather covered slope from this point are the remains of the undercarriage assemblies and sections of armour plating.

De Havilland Mosquito F.B. Mk.VI HX862: No.60 OTU, RAF.   25-09-1944
Map No.45
SH 716692 (2,125ft), Drum, The Carneddau, Conwy.

| F/Lt F.G. Johnson (RCAF) | Pilot | Killed |
| F/O J. Else | Nav | Killed |

This aircaft flew into the mountainside while on a night navigation exercise from RAF High Ercall in Shropshire. At 00:45 the ROC reported the accident, and following a five hour search by the RAF Llandwrog Mountain Rescue Unit the burned out remains of the aircraft were located.

Sections of armour plating, the remains of the undercarriage assemblies and a propeller hub unit with reduction gear lie on the rough grassy slope below the point of impact, which is marked by a small scar containing burnt plywood and brass woodscrews.

De Havilland Mosquito P.R. Mk.IX LR412 / A: No.540 Sqn, RAF. 09-02-1944
Map No.46
SH 857216 (2,450ft), Aran Fawddwy, Gwynedd.

F/O M.O. Slonski (PAF)	Pilot	Killed
F/Lt P. Riches DFC	Nav	Killed

Having taken off from RAF Benson in Oxfordshire, to air test replacement flaps and also complete a cross-country exercise, the ROC lost track of the aircraft, its last estimated position being roughly 5 miles north-east of Dolgellau. The aircraft had hit the summit of nearby Aran Fawddwy, but it was five days before a farmer came across the wreckage and reported it to the Police.

A propeller hub unit with the badly corroded remains of two blades attached lies close to the impact point, where many small fragments of plywood and aluminium are scattered. Sections of armour plate and parts from the undercarriage assemblies are lower down the slope along with several crumpled fuel tanks, which lie in a hollow by a large boulder. One of the Rolls-Royce Merlin engines from the aircraft is mounted on a stone base by the entrance to Esgair-Gawr farm at SH 816224.

A propeller hub with the heavily corroded remains of of its blades still attached on Aran Fawddwy, this is from LR412, a photo-reconnaissance Mosquito which crashed while on an air test and training flight from RAF Benson.

Tangled sections of undercarriage and armour plating are the few remaining items from Mosquito TV982 on Snowdon.

De Havilland Mosquito T. Mk.III TV982: No.502 Sqn, RAuxAF. 31-07-1948
Map No.47
SH 611530 (1,350ft), Cwm Llan, Snowdon, Gwynedd.

Pilot 2 J. Campbell	Pilot	Killed
Cpl C.E. Walker	Pass	Killed

Returning to RAF Aldergrove in County Antrim, following a unit detachment for a RAuxAF Summer Camp at RAF Horsham St.Faith in Norfolk, the aircraft flew into cumulonimbus clouds and broke-up, the wreckage falling into Cwm Llan. With the aircraft being one of the first group to return from the fortnight-long detachment, it is thought that Cpl Walker, a member of the unit's ground crew, was onboard to allow his return at the earliest opportunity, his wife having just given birth to twins.

Where the bulk of the aircraft impacted, at the base of a rock outcrop, only a few small pieces of wreckage and one piece of armour plating remain. However, scattered approximately 50 metres to the south are parts from the undercarriage assemblies, a propeller hub unit and the remains of the engine mounts and other sections of armoured plating, including the armored backs from the crew seats.

De Havilland Vampire F.B. Mk.5 VV601: No.7 FTS, RAF.   19-04-1956
Map No.48
SH 729647 (1,525ft), Cwm Eigiau, The Carneddau, Conwy.

Msm R.M. Armitage, (RNVR)   Pilot   Killed

This aircraft had taken off from RAF Valley on Anglesey, the pilot having been briefed to conduct medium level aerobatics, but after only 15 minutes it was observed to hit the hill at high speed while in a shallow wings level dive. Amongst the shattered wreckage of the cockpit, investigators later found a 13-inch-long steel bar, which may have jammed the elevator controls, but no firm conclusion was reached.

A rock outcrop forms the upper part of the impact crater made by the aircraft. It lies on the line taken by an old stone wall, approximately 20 metres south-east of where the remains of the wall meet another running down the slope. A few tiny fragments of aluminium are all that remain.

De Havilland Vampire F.B. Mk.5 VZ106: No.233 OCU, RAF.   09-10-1953
Map No.49
SN 827201 (2,025ft), Fan Hir, Glyntawe, The Black Mountain, Powys.

P/O J.R. Baldock   Pilot   Killed

Returning to RAF Pembrey in Carmarthenshire from a training exercise, the aircraft was the lead in a pair. On breaking out of cloud, during a rapid descent, the pilot of the aircraft flying as No.2 saw the ground and immediately commenced a climb. The pilot of the lead aircraft either failed to notice the ground and continued to descend, or did not take evasive action in time for the aircraft to avoid hitting the hillside.

Substantial remains of the aircraft are scattered at the site. Sections of the wings, both tail booms, the tail plane, the undercarriage legs and the jet pipe from the engine are gathered together on fairly level ground. In the stream to the north-east of this wreckage are further pieces of airframe from the wings and fuselage pod along with part of the de Havilland Goblin turbojet engine.

De Havilland Vampire F.B. Mk.5 VZ874: No.7 FTS, RAF.   12-10-1956
Map No.50
SH 539546 (2,150ft), Mynydd Mawr, Rhydd Ddu, Gwynedd.

Sub Lt R. Davies (RN)   Pilot   Killed

Having been briefed to conduct night circuits and roller landings, remaining in the vicinity of the airfield, the pilot had taken off from RAF Valley on Anglesey at 19:01. However, approximately 10 minutes later the aircraft was south-east of Caernarfon flying towards the cloud covered mountains and had just commenced a turn to port when it hit Mynydd Mawr. On impact the aircraft exploded and wreckage was scattered east over the top of the mountain into Cwm Planwydd.

Only small fragments of wreckage, in the scree near the summit of the mountain, mark the point where the aircraft impacted. However, the compressor and several combustion chambers from the aircraft's engine and sections of wing spar lie where they came to rest in Cwm Planwydd at SH 546546.

The large items from Vampire VZ106 have been arranged into a rough representation of its former shape.

Douglas Boston Mk.III Z2186: No.418 Sqn, RCAF.   17-10-1942
Map No.51
SH 669629 (3,125ft), Carnedd Daffydd, The Carneddau, Conwy.

Sgt M. Sims (RCAF)	Pilot	Survived
F/Lt H.F. Longworth (RCAF)	Nav	Killed
Sgt R. Walker	AG	Killed

After taking off from RAF Bradwell Bay in Essex at 11:15 on a day cross-country training flight, the aircraft drifted off the planned route while in cloud, and hit the summit of the mountain. Sgt Sims suffered leg injuries in the accident and remained in the wrecked aircraft for two days, until he was discovered by a couple out hill walking and rescued.

In the 1980s the outer wings, centre section, main undercarriage legs and both Wright Cyclone engines from the aircraft were removed from the site. Now only a few pieces remain, the only one of any size being a section of airframe 4ft x 2ft with armour plating attached.

Following the recovery of the large sections of wreckage of Boston Z2186 this piece of armour and the slate plaque in the background are the main physical reminders of the crash.

Douglas C-47 41-7803: 18th TCS / 64th TCG, USAAF.   23-08-1942
Map No.52
SJ 168464 (1,625ft), Moel-y-Gaer, Llangollen, Denbighshire.

1st Lt C.E. Williams	Pilot	Killed
1st Lt R. Pazder	Nav	Killed
2nd Lt T.F. Furness	–	Killed
2nd Lt M.B. Penner	–	Killed
T/Sgt J.B. Akers	Pass	Killed
T/Sgt R.E. Anderson	Pass	Killed
T/Sgt I. Gross	Pass	Killed
T/Sgt H.A. Hermes	Pass	Killed
T/Sgt G.A. Lesikar	Pass	Survived
T/Sgt R.S. Nash	Pass	Killed
T/Sgt J.L. Patterson	Pass	Died in hospital.
Pfc H.R. Adams	Pass	Killed

Transporting ground crew from the 14th FG to Atcham Air Station in Shropshire, on the final stage of their transfer with the unit from the United States, the aircraft had departed Prestwick in South Ayrshire and subsequently flew off track. On descending through the cloud cover it struck the hilltop and caught fire.

On the north-east side of the hill, just below the earthwork that surrounds the summit, is a small scar containing very small fragments from the aircraft.

Douglas C-47B 43-48473: 86th Fy Sqn / 27th ATG, USAAF.   11-11-1944
Map No.53
SH 698666 (2,300ft), Craig-y-Dulyn, The Carneddau, Conwy.

2nd Lt W.C. Gough	Pilot	Killed
2nd Lt R. Rolff	Co-pilot	Killed
Cpl H. Levitski	Radio Op	Killed
S/Sgt K.N. McLoren	Eng	Killed

Inbound from Le Bourget in France as part of a flight of four C-47s, the aircraft arrived over Base Air Depot 1 at Burtonwood near Warrington, but was unable to land as planned due to the weather conditions. The flight was then instructed by flying control to divert to Valley on Anglesey, this being acknowledged by the aircraft. However, while flying in cloud on a west-south-westerly track towards Valley the aircraft struck the cliffs above Llyn Dulyn. The wreck was located on the 22nd November 1944 when an RAF radio unit climbing Foel Grach, to complete maintenance work on a 'squeaker' aircraft warning beacon located on the summit, spotted aircraft wreckage lodged on the cliffs above the lake.

The aircraft impacted on a narrow ledge at the head of a gully high on the cliffs, and reaching the site without suitable climbing equipment is very dangerous! In the late

1940s the sections of wreckage from the aircraft that had not already fallen into Llyn Dulyn were dislodged from the cliffs, but in 1972 divers from the West Bromwich Underwater Exploration Club brought up several parts of the aircraft from the bottom of the lake for the Warplane Wreck Investigation Group. These included the complete tail section from which the fin was removed, but much of the wreckage that had been raised was then left in the lake close to the outflow. As a result when the level of the lake falls a propeller assembly can be seen, but there are plans for this to be moved and mounted by the side of the lake as a memorial to the crew.

Douglas Dakota EI-AFL / 'St Kevin': Aer Lingus.   10-01-1952
Map No.54
SH 670520 (1,125ft), Cwm Edno, Dodwydelen, Conwy.

Capt J.R. Keohane	Pilot	Killed
1st Officer W.A. Newman	Co-pilot	Killed
Miss D.M. Sutton	Stewd	Killed
Twenty passengers	(See Appendices)	Killed

At 17:15 the aircraft departed Northolt, London on a scheduled passenger service to Collinstown, Dublin. The planned route was via Daventry and Nefyn and the aircraft reported having over flown the radio navigation beacon at Nefyn at 19:10, when in fact it was 20 miles to the east. At this point is it thought that the pilot believed that he was clear of land and having climbed to 6,500ft earlier in the flight due to turbulence, he commenced a descent to 4,500ft and flew into a strong downdraught in the lee of the nearby mountains. The aircraft went into an extremely steep dive, with a section of outboard wing breaking off before it plunged into the boggy hilltop.

Following the accident, several of those killed were buried in a shared grave at Llanbeblig Cemetery in Caernarvon, due to difficulties in identifying the bodies. However, 4 bodies were not accounted for, so a service was held at the site on the 17th January 1952 and the ground consecrated. Trees were planted around the water filled crater, from which the tail section of the aircraft still protruded and the site was enclosed by a fence. In the 1980s, however, the Snowdonia National Park Authority cleared the site, leaving only the boggy crater and a single tree. These can still be seen, along with a slate memorial plaque that has been placed on a nearby rise at SH 669521.

English Electric Canberra B. Mk.2 WK129: RRE, RAF.   09-12-1957
Map No.55
SH 685649 (3,100ft), Carnedd Llwelwyn, The Carneddau, Conwy.

F/Lt W.A. Bell	Pilot	Killed
F/Lt K.C.F. Shelley	Nav	Killed

Flying from RAF Pershore in Worcestershire, the aircraft was taking part in Radar trials involving the Ministry of Supply Radar Station located on the summit of Drum. The circumstances of how the aircraft came to fly into the top of Carnedd Llwelwyn, approximately 4 miles south-south-west of the Radar Station, are unclear. However, while flying on a south-easterly track the aircraft impacted at high speed, the bulk of the wreckage travelling over the top of the ridge and being scattered for some distance in the upper reaches of Cwm Eigiau.

A disrupted patch of boulder field containing small pieces of wreckage marks the impact point on the western side of the ridge top. From this point fragments of wreckage are strewn to the south-east over the ridge and down the rocky eastern slopes of the mountain to Ffynnon Llyffant. Scattered in and around this small lake are sections of wing and fuselage, the remains of the Rolls-Royce Avon engines, the stainless steel jet pipes and both main wheel and tyre assemblies. Further wreckage can be found in the stream that runs out of the lake, with sizeable pieces of wing structure at SH 690644 and other parts being submerged in a deeper section of the stream lower down at SH 694645.

Fairey Battle K7688: No.9 BGS, RAF.   26-02-1940
Map No.56
SN 129328 (1,175ft), Carn Bica, Precelli Mountains, Pembrokeshire.

Sgt T. Forbes	Pilot	Survived
Sgt N.V. Pleno	–	Survived

The aircraft force landed on the hillside after encountering poor weather during a cross country training flight from RAF Penrhos in Gwynedd to RAF Newton Down (later Stormy Down) in the Vale of Glamorgan. No.50 MU dismantled the aircraft, and although the Rolls-Royce Merlin engine was salvaged, a significant proportion of the airframe was burned and then buried on site.

A large hollow containing only a few tiny fragments of aluminium remains where the MU buried the wreckage. However, slightly lower down the slope are the broken up remains of one wing.

These are the larger remaining parts from Battle K7688, and also the largest remaining parts of a Fairey Battle at a crash site in the UK.

Handley Page Halifax Mk.II Srs.Ia JD417: No.1656 HCU, RAF. 03-09-1944
Map No.57
SH 370453 (1,125ft), Yr Eifl, The Rivals, Gwynedd.

P/O L.G. Walker (RAAF)	Pilot	Killed
F/O M. Cox (RAAF)	Nav	Killed
Sgt F.R. Jones	Flt Eng	Killed
W/O J.A. White (RAAF)	WO	Killed
F/Sgt K. Panwick (RAAF)	AG	Killed
F/Sgt R. Walmsley (RAAF)	AG	Killed

The Halifax flew into the cloud covered mountain at 15:00, while on a day cross-country navigation exercise from RAF Lindholme in South Yorkshire. No.34 MU salvaged the burnt out remains of the aircraft and during this operation one of the recovery party, LAC Shallow, escaped with comparatively minor injuries when he fell around 60 ft down a rock face below the site.

The site lies on a heather covered slope not far from a section of stone wall, and is at the top of a spur that runs down between a series of escarpments. A small scar contains a few lumps of melted aluminium and other fragments of wreckage.

Handley Page Halifax B. Mk.III LK835 / MH-U: No.51 Sqn, RAF. 22-05-1944
Map No.58
SO 220104 (1,400ft), Waun Afon, Blaenavon, Torfaen.

Sgt A.S. Jones	Pilot	Survived
Sgt D. Bibby	Nav	Survived
Sgt J. Brown	Flt Eng	Survived
F/O G. Cowd	BA	Survived
Sgt E.W.J. Luff	WO	Survived
Sgt T. Minns	AG	Survived
Sgt A.G. Westbrook	AG	Survived

During a night cross-country training flight from RAF Snaith in East Yorkshire the starboard inner engine began to run hot, probably due to an oil leak, and it was decided to feather the propeller to reduce drag and shut down the engine. However, a fault with the propeller feathering unit resulted in it going into fine pitch, with the engine racing at high RPM and then catching fire. After diving the aircraft in an attempt to extinguish the fire the pilot levelled off and engaged the auto-pilot. The crew then baled out, and a few minutes later the aircraft dived into the ground.

A small fenced enclosure surrounds the site, where sections of airframe protrude from the extremely wet and unstable patch of bog where the aircraft impacted.

While a large of number of parts from Halifax LK835 remain, access is restricted as it lies in a very boggy area which is enclosed by the fence that can be seen in the background.

Handley Page Halifax Mk.V Srs.Ia LL541 / ZU-O: No.1664 HCU, RAF. 12-12-1944
Map No.59
SN 924669 (1,575 ft), Nant-yr-Haidd, The Elan Valley, Powys.

P/O G.L. Lister (RCAF)	Pilot	Killed
F/O E.H. Brautigam (RCAF)	Nav	Killed
F/Sgt D. Levine (RCAF)	BA	Killed
F/Sgt J.H. Preece (RCAF)	WO/AG	Killed
Sgt F. Willmek (RCAF)	Flt Eng	Killed
Sgt A.F. McMurtry (RCAF)	Flt Eng	Killed
Sgt J.S. Overland (RCAF)	AG	Killed
Sgt G.G. Goehring (RCAF)	AG	Killed

Airborne from RAF Dishforth in North Yorkshire on a day cross-country bombing exercise the aircraft was flying at 18,000ft, when another Halifax flying ahead observed it suddenly spiral into an extremely steep dive, from which it appeared to recover briefly at 15,000ft, before diving into the cloud below. A member of the ROC then observed the aircraft dive out of the cloud base and hit the hilltop. Structural failure had occurred in the dive, with several parts of the aircraft having separated in flight.

On the side of a hilltop rise there is a large scar containing many small pieces of wreckage, and further parts are scattered in the heather that surrounds the site.

Handley Page Halifax C. Mk.8 G-AIHU: Lancashire Aircraft Corporation. 05-12-1947
Map No.60
SJ 073767 (1,000ft), Mynydd-y-Cwm, The Clwydian Range, Flintshire.

Capt J.H. Parsonage DFC	Pilot	Killed
Mr A. Brook	Nav	Killed
Mr J. Driver	Flt Eng	Killed
Mr J. Evans	WO	Killed

Transporting three tonnes of cloth bales from Lille in France to Speke in Merseyside, it appears the aircraft had strayed too far west, when it descended to 1,000 ft and turned onto an easterly course towards the airfield. Visibility was poor and the aircraft flew into trees on the summit of the hill and disintegrated.

A cairn and a wooden cross mark the site, on the very top of the hill, which is on private land.

Hawker Henley Mk.III L3334: No.1605 Flt, RAF.   20-11-1942
Map No.61
SH 518502 (2,000ft), Craig Cwm Silyn, Nantle, Gwynedd.

P/O W.J. Havies	Pilot	Killed

During a target-towing flight from RAF Towyn, the aircraft entered cloud and flew into a gully in the near vertical rock face. The sound of the aircraft and the subsequent impact were heard by quarry workers in the valley below and the RAF Llandwrog Mountain Rescue Unit were called out. However, a four-hour search revealed nothing and during this time Anson N4981 had crashed approximately five miles away, with the team being called out to this accident on returning to their base. At dawn the following day the weather had improved and an air search located the wrecked Henley, but due to the inaccessibility of the wreckage it was to be another day before the body of P/O Havies was recovered by quarry workers who were able to scale the rock face.

On the steep and somewhat unstable scree, below the gully where the aircraft impacted, are small bits of torn aluminium skinning and sections of fuel pipe.

Hawker Hunter T. Mk.7 XL575: No.229 OCU.   08-11-1971
Map No.62
SN 775758 (1,350ft), Gelmast, Devils Bridge, Ceredigion.

F/Lt J.R. Metcalfe	Pilot (Inst)	Killed
2nd Lt B. Yong (SAF)	Pilot (u/t)	Killed

Having taken-off from RAF Chivenor in Devon, on a training flight that included live-fire ground attack practice at Pembrey Range in Carmarthenshire, the aircraft flew into the forest covered hillside and exploded. There was thunderstorm activity in the area at the time of the accident and the aircraft struck the ground in a steep nose down attitude at high speed.

Pieces of aluminium alloy, fabric insulation and blue electrical wiring were scattered over the forest floor for some distance in the 1990s, but since then the trees in the area have been felled and only fragments remain.

Heinkel He111H-5 F4801 / IT+EL: III/KG 28, *Luftwaffe*.   14-04-1941
Map No.63
SH 686698 (2,300ft), Llwytmor, The Carneddau, Gwynedd.

Ltn L. Horras	Pilot	Survived
Gfr J. Bruninghausen	Eng	Killed
Fw B. Peronowski	Nav/BA	Survived
Gfr K. Schlender	Radio Op/Gunner	Survived

Having taken off from Nantes in France the aircraft was tasked with bombing the aircraft carrier HMS *Victorious*, which had been sighted by members of the crew the previous night during a reconnaissance of the docks at Barrow-in-Furness in Cumbria. However, on running in to the target at low level the crew discovered HMS *Victorious* had been moved, and only noticed her in a different part of the dock basin after the bomb load had been released on dock buildings. Heavy anti-aircraft fire damaged the navigation equipment onboard the aircraft and after flying out over the Irish Sea the pilot turned onto an assumed southerly heading to return to base. Remaining at low level the aircraft later crossed the North Wales coast, flew into the top of Llwytmor Bach and caught fire. At first light Gfr Schlender made his way down the mountain to Cydcoed in order to obtain assistance for the other two survivors.

In 1970 one of the Junkers Jumo engines from the aircraft was recovered by helicopter, and today only lumps of melted aluminium and a couple of small pieces of airframe remain, scattered in a scar on the slope where the aircraft burned out.

Jodel DR250 Srs.160 G-AVIV: Staverton Flying School Ltd.   22-08-1969
Map No.64
SH 665631 (3,400ft), Carnedd Dafydd, The Carneddau, Conwy.

| Mr J.R. West | Pilot | Killed |
| Mr J.C. Long | Pass | Killed |

Having flown from Staverton to Bristol and then to Birmingham in the morning, the aircraft refuelled before departing on a flight to Dublin later in the afternoon. The planned route via Hawarden and Holyhead was intended to avoid high ground, so the aircraft would be able to fly at 2,500ft and remain below commercial airways. However, in calculating the required course for each leg of the route it is thought the pilot omitted the magnetic variation, and as a result having turned onto the leg from Hawarden to Holyhead the aircraft diverged from the planned route towards Snowdonia, entered cloud and flew into the mountain. The wreck was found the following morning by a climber.

The site lies adjacent to the ridge path, approximately 70 metres east of the summit cairn, but only a few fragments of wreckage remain.

Junkers Ju88A-6 3459 / 5K+DW: IV/KG3, *Luftwaffe*.   25-04-1942
Map No.65
SO 135549 (1,250ft), Gwaunceste Hill, Builth Wells, Powys.

Oltn G. Brixius	Pilot	Killed
Ofw W. Kreinenbrock	BA	Survived
Gfr P. Kochon	Radio Op	Survived
Fw A. Liedig	Gunner	Killed

Taking off from Brussels Evère in Belgium, the aircraft was tasked with attacking RAF airfields in Wiltshire, in order to disrupt night fighter operations while a bombing raid on Bath was underway. While over England the onboard radio direction-finding equipment failed, and the aircraft subsequently became lost. After being fired upon and damaged by anti-aircraft fire from a gun battery on Flat Holm island in the Bristol Channel, the bomb load was jettisoned. Flying north the aircraft was then intercepted by Beaufighter X7933 from No.255 Sqn, RAF, which was equipped with the latest Airborne Interception Radar and crewed by F/O Wyrill (Pilot) and Sgt Willins (Radar Op). They had been practising radar intercepts under the control of the Ground Controller Interception station at Honiley, when control was handed over to the station at Comberton and they were vectored onto an unidentified aircraft. Closing in using the onboard Radar the Beaufighter intercepted the Ju88 and following two bursts of canon fire the Ju88 dived out of control, with only *Ofw* Kreinenbrock and *Gfr* Kochon managing to bale out before the aircraft hit the hillside at 23:50.

At the site, now within a plantation of fir trees, pieces of aluminium are gathered together next to a metal post that has a plaque attached to it in memory of the two crew members who were killed. Note: the woodland is private land but the memorial is on a public right of way.

Lockheed P-38F 42-12579: 27th ATG, USAAF.   15-02-1944
Map No.66
SJ 038295 (1,825ft), Ty'n-y-ffynonydd, Berwyn Mountains, Powys.

2nd Lt W.M. Chapman	Pilot	Killed

The pilot was ferrying the aircraft from Nuthampstead in Hertfordshire to Base Air Depot 3 at Langford Lodge in County Antrim. While descending through low cloud the aircraft struck a hilltop and briefly became airborne again before flying into the adjacent hill.

Very little wreckage remains, but a few pieces can still be found on the heather covered slope.

Lockheed P-38J 42-67859: 402nd FS / 370th FG, USAAF.   12-04-1944
Map No.67
SO 271325 (1,750ft), Olchon Valley, The Black Mountains, Herefordshire.

1st Lt C.C. Richards   Pilot   Killed

The aircraft was on a low altitude navigation exercise from Andover Air Station in Hampshire, when it flew into the cloud covered hillside. The briefed route for the flight consisted of an initial leg to Aberdovey followed by a leg to Bedford, but based on the weather forecast the pilot had been instructed to fly direct to Bedford, avoiding high ground if poor weather was encountered on the initial leg. Two other pilots attempting to fly the same route returned to base as per these instructions, due to the weather on the initial leg being worse than forecast.

The impact point is marked by a patch of bare earth on the steep slope, containing a few fragments of wreckage. Although the site is actually in England, it has been included in this chapter for convenience.

The view from the crash site of P-38J 42-67859 in the Olchon Valley. The small scar that still remains can be seen in the foreground.

Lockheed F-5E 44-24229: 27th PRS / 7th PRG, USAAF.   11-09-1945
Map No.68
SN 798866 (2,150ft), Plynlimon, Ceredigion.

2nd Lt X.E. Eugenedes   Pilot   Killed

While on a ferry flight from Chalgrove Air Station in Oxfordshire to Base Air Depot 1 at Burtonwood near Warrington, the aircraft hit the mountain. The following day a shepherd sighted the wreckage and reported it to the police. When investigators surveyed the scene it was discovered that the aircraft had clipped a slope below the top of a nearby ridge while descending at high speed, shedding the propellers, and then flew on for some distance before impacting inverted and disintegrating. Based on this evidence the investigators concluded the pilot had lost control while flying on instruments, after entering cloud, and was recovering from a dive when the aircraft struck the ground.

Substantial remains, including wing, tail boom and tail-plane sections were recovered in the late 1970s, while one of the Allison engines from the aircraft was recovered in the 1980s. Several sizeable sections of the aircraft still remain, however, including the forward section of the port tail boom with the inboard section of the port wing still attached.

This section of wing and tail boom root containing an engine turbo-charger and ducting from the engine exhausts is the largest remaining item from Lockheed F-5E (P-38) 44-24229 on Plynlimon..

Lockheed Ventura Mk.I AE688 / SB-Q: No.464 Sqn, RAAF.   18-08-1943
Map No.69
SH 658625 (2,950ft), Carnedd Daffydd, The Carneddau, Conwy.

F/Sgt J.A. Johnston (RAAF)	Pilot	Killed
F/Sgt E.J.E. Beaudry (RCAF)	Nav	Killed
F/O L. Fullerton (RCAF)	WO/AG	Killed
F/Sgt A.S. Clegg (RCAF)	AG	Killed

During a night cross-country training flight from RAF Sculthorpe in Norfolk, the aircraft flew into the mountainside and burned out.

Wreckage is scattered down the steep slope from the impact point onto the scree below. One of the main undercarriage legs and numerous small pieces of airframe, with paintwork in good condition, are to be found. Further parts from the aircraft, including a sizeable section of outboard wing, lie amongst the wreckage from Anson N9855 at SH 660622.

Martin B-26C 41-34765 / 'Lil'Lass': 335th BG, USAAF.   04-06-1943
Map No.70
SM 739281 (425ft), Y Lliddi, St. David's Head, Pembrokeshire.

1st Lt R.E. Lawrence	Pilot	Killed
F/O J.G. Jackson	Co-pilot	Killed
2nd Lt H.H. Robertson	Nav	Killed
S/Sgt W.A. Brown	Eng	Killed

On the final stage of a transatlantic ferry flight to St. Eval in Cornwall, the aircraft departed from Port Lyautey in Morroco as part of a formation of eight B-26s at 07:15, and did not receive an instruction issued at 07:30 to cancel the flight due to poor weather at the destination. In due course the formation encountered poor weather and unable to hold formation in cloud, the aircraft became separated. Due to stronger than forecast tail winds, and having been reliant on the Radio Op on the lead aircraft in the formation to obtain any radio position fixes, the crew commenced their descent over the south-west coast of Wales. Having turned onto a westerly track, it is presumed the crew had been trying to get below the fog, which was hanging over the coast, when the aircraft hit the hill and exploded.

The site is on a steep slope below the top of the ridge, to the north-east of the rocky outcrop that forms the summit of the hill. Only a few small pieces of torn aluminium remain, scattered down the slope. In 2005 a memorial, comprising a propeller blade from the aircraft and a plaque, were erected nearby in the Whitesands Bay car park at SM 735272.

Martin B-26G 44-68072: 9th AF, USAAF.   01-02-1945
Map No.71
SH 628598 (2,750ft), Y Garn, The Glyders, Gwynedd.

2nd Lt K.W. Carty	Pilot	Killed
2nd Lt W.H. Cardwell Jr	Co-pilot	Killed
1st Lt N.B. Sowell	Nav	Killed
Cpl R.M. Aguirre	Eng	Killed
Cpl J.D. Arnold	Radio Op	Killed

Having arrived at RAF St. Mawgan via the South Atlantic Ferry Route, the aircraft subsequently departed on a ferry flight to Base Air Depot 1 at Burtonwood near Warrington. Weather conditions on the briefed route were poor, and while flying in cloud on a north-easterly track the aircraft struck the mountain and disintegrated.

Following the initial impact of the aircraft on the western flank of the mountain, the bulk of the wreckage travelled up the slope and fell down into Cwm Cywion. As a result only a few fragments of wreckage are to be found close to the summit of the mountain, while the undercarriage legs, sections of armour plating and pieces of torn aluminium are strewn down the northern face of the mountain. The trail of larger pieces of wreckage runs from on the steep scree slope at SH 631600 down over an escarpment and along the stream in the valley to approximately SH 632603.

McDonnell Douglas Phantom F-4J(UK) ZE358 / H: No.74 Sqn, RAF. 26-08-1987
Map No.72
SN 611682 (1,050ft), Trefenter, Aberystwyth, Ceredigion.

F/Lt E.H. Murdoch	Pilot	Killed
F/O J.L. Ogg	Nav	Killed

Flying as No.2 of three Phantoms, tasked with practising low-level intercepts, the aircraft held with the flight leader to the east of Aberystwyth, while No.3 flew to the south to act as target. During the subsequent intercept, the flight leader commenced a turn to port and lost contact with No.2 which had been to starboard at 3-4 miles range and slightly below. When contact was not regained it was realised that No.2 had crashed. It appears the pilot had misjudged his clearance over the terrain and although evasive action was taken immediately before impact, it was too late and the aircraft struck the ground.

Where the aircraft impacted, at the side of a track, there is a memorial plaque on a concrete base commemorating the crew.

Sections of undercarriage from B-26G 44-68072 on Y Garn.

Miles Martinet T.T. Mk.I HN888: No.595 Sqn, RAF.   21-12-1945
Map No.73
SO 178647 (1,950ft), Great Rhos, Radnor Forest, Powys.

F/O M. Davies	Pilot	Killed
F/L G.H. Hammond	(Equipment Officer)	Killed

The aircraft, normally used for target towing, was flying from RAF Aberporth in Ceredigion to Castle Bromwich in West Midlands in poor visibility, when it flew into the steep slope at the head of Cwm Bwch. Despite an extensive air search the aircraft remained missing until the 2nd February 1946, when a Shepherd came across the wreckage.

A few small pieces of wreckage remain at the site, while the Mercury engine from the aircraft is partially buried in the stream below at SO 176646.

Wreckage from the double Miles Master crash at Abergwesyn.

Miles Master Mk.IIIs W8773 and DL570: No.5 FTS, RAF.   04-10-1942
Map No.74
SN 857556 (1,550ft), Near Afron Gwesyn, Abergwesyn, Powys.

P/O J. Chinery	Pilot (Inst)(W8773)	Killed
Sgt T. Hyndman (RCAF)	Pilot (u/t)(W8773)	Killed
Sgt H.B. Hubbard	Pilot (Inst)(DL570)	Survived
Sgt R. Camsburn	Pilot (u/t)(DL570)	Survived

During a formation cross-country training flight from RAF Tern Hill in Shropshire the two aircraft became lost, descended through cloud to obtain a visual position fix and flew into the hillside in formation. W8873 was leading and on hitting the slope caught fire, while DL570 overturned and remained relatively intact.

Aluminium panels from these aircraft lie on the grassy slope, the majority having been piled together. A section of engine cowling that was amongst the wreckage in the 1990s was marked W8773.

North American Harvard Mk.2B FX249: No.502 Sqn, RAuxAF. 19-03-1951
Map No.75
SJ 280584 (875ft), Waun-y-Llyn Country Park, Hope Mountain, Flintshire.

    Sgt J. Hanna   Pilot   Killed

Returning to RAF Aldergrove in County Antrim after collecting the aircraft from RAF Shawbury in Shropshire, the pilot did not follow the previously planned route and was flying below safety altitude in poor visibility when the aircraft hit the hillside.

    The site lies on the brow of the hill. A few small pieces of wreckage remain, but can be difficult to find.

North American P-51D 44-72340 / WD-K: 335th FS / 4th FG, USAAF. 17-05-1945
Map No.76
SH 841237 (1,025ft), Aran Fawddwy, Gwynedd.

    Capt R.L. Tannehill   Pilot   Killed

While at 29,000ft, on a formation training flight from Debden Air Station in Essex, the aircraft dropped away and dived into the ground. It is presumed that the pilot was overcome by hypoxia following an oxygen system failure.

    Wreckage from the aircraft is scattered on both sides of the Afon Tycerig. The impact point lies to the south of the river within dense forest. However, to the north of the river there are sections of airframe that can be accessed slightly more easily, lying in an area of the forest felled in the 1990s.

Republic P-47C 41-6195: 551st Ftr Tng Sqn / 495th FTG, USAAF. 08-07-1944
Map No.77
SH 916593 (1,275ft), Aled Isaf Reservoir, Denbigh Moors, Conwy.

    2nd Lt O. Wahl   Pilot   Survived

During a training flight from Atcham Air Station in Shropshire, the aircraft was flying as No.3 in formation of four P-47s. Following the formation leader, in line-astern formation, into an Immelman manoeuvre at 12,000ft, the pilot attempted to roll out of the manoeuvre, caught the slipstream of the aircraft ahead and entered a spin. Unable to recover from the spin immediately the pilot baled out, leaving the aircraft to dive into the open moorland.

    Pieces of rubber lining from the fuel tanks and fragments of aluminium lie within an obvious impact crater at the site.

Republic P-47C 41-6246: 551st Ftr Tng Sqn / 495th FTG, USAAF. 16-09-1944
Map No.78
SH 862220 (2,600ft), Aran Fawddwy, Gwynedd.

F/O P. Quinci   Pilot   Killed

During an individual intercept and attack training flight from Atcham Air Station in Shropshire, the aircraft was flying in cloud when it struck the mountain and disintegrated. The aircraft remained missing for a few days, the wreck being found and reported to the police on the 22nd September 1944.

The impact point lies on a very steep rock face high up the mountain, but nearly all the remaining wreckage lies at the base of the slope, where it came to rest. An undercarriage leg, the turbo-charger and supply ducting along with many aluminium panels from the wings and fuselage are to be found.

Republic P-47D 41-7897: 6th FW, USAAF.   18-07-1943
Map No.79
SJ 151409 (1,400ft), Ffrith Dreborth, Glyndyfrdwy, Denbighshire.

2nd Lt R.A. Sprague   Pilot   Killed

Flying in a formation of four P-47s the aircraft was on a low-level navigation exercise from Atcham Air Station in Shropshire. On approaching high ground, poor weather conditions were evident ahead and the formation leader commenced a turn to port. However, the aircraft, which had been flying as No.2 in the formation, dropped away and came down on the hilltop approximately 10 minutes later. On investigation of the wreckage it was discovered the pilot had switched to the main fuel tank from the auxiliary, possibly indicating the engine had been running rough. It also appeared the aircraft was in a glide at a relatively low speed with the flaps down when it contacted the ground near the top of the hill and skidded down the slope for some distance before breaking into several sections.

Only a few tiny fragments of wreckage are to be found, scattered on the heather covered slope where the aircraft came to rest.

Republic P-47D 42-75101: 551st Ftr Tng Sqn / 495th FTG, USAAF. 04-05-1944
Map No.80
SH 884144 (1,350ft), Mynydd Copog, Dinas Mawddwy, Gwynedd.

1st Lt J.W. Beauchamp   Pilot   Killed

Flying from Atcham Air Station in Shropshire, the pilot was performing authorised aerobatics when he drifted over high ground. During a series of rolling manoeuvres the aircraft entered a spin and although the pilot regained control, there was insufficient altitude to recover the aircraft from the resulting dive and it struck the hilltop.

The Pratt & Whitney Double Wasp engine from the aircraft and large quantities of airframe wreckage still lie at the site, on the edge of a plantation of fir trees.

The Pratt & Whitney Twin Wasp engine and other shattered pieces of wreckage from P-47D 42-75101 lie on the edge of the plantation on Mynydd Copog.

Sepecat Jaguar G.R. Mk.1A XZ386: No.226 OCU, RAF.　　　24-06-1987
Map No.81
SO 084467 (725ft), Pantau, Aberedw, Powys.

F/Lt I.D. Hill	Pilot	Killed

The aircraft, flying from RAF Chivenor in Devon, was one of three Jaguars tasked with conducting low-level evasion practice. Acting as the attacking aircraft it hit the ground following a loss of control while making an intercept on the other two aircraft.

A thorough salvage operation was completed a few days after the accident, removing the wreckage, which was scattered over a wide area. However, there is a memorial cairn in memory of F/Lt Hill in trees at SO 084468 and also a plaque in the churchyard wall at Aberedw Church. Note: the impact point is on private land, but the memorial is by a public right of way.

Supermarine Spitfire Mk.IIA P7295: No.61 OTU, RAF.　　　14-12-1942
Map No.82
SJ 076336 (2,575ft), Cadair Berwyn, Berwyn Mountains, Denbighshire/Powys.

P/O P. Degail (FFAF)	Pilot	Killed

When the aircraft departed RAF Mountford Bridge in Shropshire on a routine training flight, the weather conditions were reported as very good, but the aircraft subsequently flew into the snow covered mountain top. P/O Degail survived the impact and the following day, despite poor weather, the wrecked Spitfire was located by F/Lt Walker in Lysander T1655. However, on making a low pass over the wreck, the Lysander flew into a downdraught and came down in the adjacent valley killing F/Lt Walker. When a ground team finally reached the wrecked Spitfire it was discovered P/O Degail had died of exposure.

A few fragments from the aircraft remain in a patch of bog, roughly 20 metres south-south-east of the turn in the ridge top fence, where the boundaries of Denbighshire, Powys and Wrexham merge.

Supermarine Spitfire Mk.I X4588: No.53 OTU, RAF.   23-05-1942
Map No.83
SO 017184 (2,250ft) , Fan Ddu, Brecon Beacons, Powys.

      Sgt D.P. Carruthers (RCAF)   Pilot   Killed

Aircraft entered cloud during normal flying practice from RAF Llandow in the Vale of Glamorgan and flew into the hilltop at high speed and disintegrated.

The remaining pieces of wreckage have been gathered together into a small pile alongside a cairn that also marks the site.

On an otherwise barren area of grassy moorland this cairn and the small pile of wreckage to its left marks where Spitfire X4588 crashed.

Vickers Wellington Mk.IC P9299 / KX-A: No.1429 Flt, RAF.   06-04-1942
Map No.84
SH 886196 (1,200ft), Pistyll Gwyn, Llanymawddwy, Gwynedd.

Sgt A. Keda (Czech)	Pilot	Killed
Sgt R. Vokurka (Czech)	–	Killed
Sgt R. Grimm (Czech)	–	Killed
Sgt J. Horinek (Czech)	–	Killed
F/Sgt J. Stanovsky (Czech)	–	Killed
P/O J. Stefek (Czech)	–	Killed

Airborne on a cross-country training flight from RAF East Wretham in Norfolk, the aircraft descended through cloud and flew into the hillside at 13:12.

A few small pieces of wreckage are scattered on the slope adjacent to Pistyll Gwyn waterfall. Some of these are difficult to spot amongst the scree, and other pieces are covered over by bracken for much of the year.

Vickers Wellington Mk.IC R1465 / Y: No.22 OTU, RAF.   06-07-1942
Map No.85
SO 062201 (2,400ft), Waun Rhydd, The Brecon Beacons, Powys.

F/Sgt J.B. Kemp (RCAF)	Pilot	Killed
F/Sgt E.E. Mittel (RCAF)	Obs	Killed
Sgt K.F. Yuill (RCAF)	Obs	Killed
F/Sgt H.C. Beatty (RCAF)	WO/AG	Killed
Sgt J.P. Hayes (RCAF)	AG	Killed

During a night cross-country navigation exercise from RAF Wellesbourne Mountford in Warwickshire, it appears the crew became uncertain of their position and attempted to obtain a visual position fix. Descending through cloud, below the briefed minimum altitude of 10,000ft, the aircraft struck the hilltop.

The aircraft impacted at the northern end of the Cwar y Gigfran outcrop and disintegrated down the slope. Sections of geodetic wing framework and the remains of the undercarriage assemblies lie below the outcrop adjacent to a stone memorial cairn marked as 'Meml' on Ordnance Survey 1:25000 & 1:50000 scale mapping. A plaque commemorating the crash is built into the cairn, erected in 1980 by staff and pupils from Tredegar Comprehensive School. In the stream running down from the site into the valley are the remains of both Pegasus engines from the aircraft.

A large cairn and pile of collected wreckage mark the crash site of Wellington R1465.

Vickers Wellington Mk.IC T2520 / KO-A: No.115 Sqn, RAF.   09-12-1940
Map No.86
SO 089137 (2,000ft), Cefn-yr-Ystrad, Powys.

P/O A. Tindall	Pilot	Killed
Sgt D. Mills	Co-pilot	Killed
Sgt H.D. Ellis	Obs	Killed
Sgt S.G. Howard	WO/AG	Killed
Sgt D.E. Wallace	AG	Killed
Sgt R. Brown (RNZAF)	AG	Killed

The Wellington descended through cloud at night and flew into the hilltop. The aircraft was returning to base at RAF Marham in Norfolk, following a bombing raid on the docks at Bordeaux in France.

Small pieces of melted aluminium lie in rocks at the site, which is marked by a small cairn.

Vickers Wellington Mk.III BJ697 / G: No.12 OTU, RAF.   26-09-1942
Map No.87
SN 833184 (1,750ft), Fan Hir, The Black Mountain, Powys.

F/Sgt. K.S.H. Bird	Pilot	Died of Injuries 29-09-1942
SgtW.D. Barr	–	Survived
Sgt W.A. Fairweather	–	Survived
Sgt J. Head	–	Survived

BJ697 flew into the hillside and caught fire, after diverging from the planned route and then descending. The aircraft was on a night cross-country training flight from RAF Chipping Warden in Northamptonshire.

A scar on the slope, where the aircraft burned out, contains a few small fragments of wreckage.

Vickers Wellington Mk.IC DV800: No.27 OTU, RAF.   19-07-1942
Map No.88
SH 676635 (2,475ft), The Black Ladders, The Carneddau, Gwynedd.

Sgt E.H. Longbottom (RAAF)	Pilot	Killed
Sgt L.D. Traylen	Obs / BA	Killed
Sgt R.I. Bowen	Obs	Killed
Sgt S.J. Wilson	WO/AG	Killed
Sgt R.T. Bannister (RAAF)	AG	Killed

DV800 descended through cloud to obtain a visual position fix, and flew into the steep mountainside, while on a day cross-country navigation exercise from RAF Lichfield in Staffordshire.

A slate plaque and small collection of parts at the crash site of Wellington DV800 on the Black Ladders.

Small pieces of wreckage, including geodetic framework are gathered together in a pile near where the aircraft impacted. Further pieces from the aircraft can be found lower down the hillside, where there are also a few pieces of wreckage from Lincoln RF511.

Vickers Wellington B. Mk.X HE466: No.30 OTU, RAF.   13-02-1943
Map No.89
SH 692665 (2,800ft), Foel Grach, The Carneddau, Conwy.

Sgt E.G. Frezell (RCAF)	Pilot	Killed
P/O F.K. Thorogood	Nav	Killed
Sgt C.G. Bennett	BA	Killed
Sgt G.N. Rafferty	WO	Killed
Sgt E. Towler	AG	Killed

HE466 flew into the mountain and disintegrated after the aircraft drifted off track during a night cross-country navigation exercise from RAF Hixon in Staffordshire.

Pieces of geodetic framework and aluminium panels are scattered down the rough grassy slope from the impact point, marked by a peat filled scar containing small fragments of wreckage.

Scattered around these two patches of peat high on Foel Grach are the remains of Wellington HE466.

Vickers Wellington B. Mk.X HX433: No.1443 Flt, RAF.   28-05-1942
Map No.90
SH 728138 (2,600ft), Mynydd Moel, Dolgellau, Gwynedd.

F/Sgt W.J.P. Grant (RCAF)	Pilot	Killed
F/Sgt H.L. Davis (RCAF)	Co-pilot	Killed
Sgt G.D. Graham	Obs	Killed
Sgt H.N. Williams (RAAF)	WO/AG	Killed
Sgt J.I. McDowell	WO/AG	Killed
Sgt C.J. Thomas	AG	Killed

Airborne from RAF Harwell in Oxfordshire, the aircraft diverged significantly from the planned route, entered cloud and struck the mountainside. The purpose of the flight had been to complete day cross-country training and also assess fuel consumption, in preparation for the aircraft being ferried overseas.

Small fragments of wreckage are scattered from the point of impact, on an unstable scree slope, all the way down to the foot of the slope.

Vickers Wellington Mk.VIII LB185: No.3 OTU, RAF.   20-11-1943
Map No.91
SH 747386 (1,500ft), Moel y Croeso, Trawsfynydd, Gwynedd

Sgt M.L. Wolman	Pilot	Killed
Sgt H.B. Maxwell	Co-pilot	Killed
F/Sgt L.S. Lauritz (RAAF)	Nav	Killed
Sgt W.T. Muir	WO/AG	Killed
Sgt A. Sinclair	WO/AG	Survived
Sgt F.W. Maskell	WO/AG	Survived

During a night navigation exercise from RAF Haverfordwest in Pembrokeshire, the crew were unable to obtain radio direction fixes in the later stages of the flight and became uncertain of their position. As their fuel ran low, the pilot descended through cloud to obtain a visual position fix and the aircraft struck the hilltop.

A few tiny fragments of wreckage are all that remain below a small outcrop of rock on the southern side of the knoll the aircraft flew into.

Vickers Wellington B. Mk.X MF509: No.22 OTU, RAF.   20-11-1944
Map No.92
SN 817169 (1,725 ft), Carrag Goch, The Black Mountain, Powys.

Sgt C. Hamel (RCAF)	Pilot	Killed
Sgt J.R.R. Villeneuve (RCAF)	Nav	Killed
F/O W.J. Allison (RCAF)	BA	Killed
Sgt J.P.E. Burke (RCAF)	WO/AG	Killed
Sgt J.A.E. Groulx (RCAF)	AG	Killed
Sgt J.L.U. Du Sablon (RCAF)	AG	Killed

This wing from Wellington MF509 is now one of the largest items still at a crash site in Wales.

Flying from RAF Stratford in Warwickshire, on a night cross-country navigation exercise, the aircraft descended after the starboard engine developed a fault, and flew into the hill.

Although the engines from the aircraft were salvaged, the majority of the airframe was abandoned on site, where relatively large sections of geodetic wing framework and the undercarriage assemblies still remain. Other wreckage is scattered west down the slope for a considerable distance. A memorial plaque, mounted on a stone base, is located at the site.

Westland Lysander Mk.III T1655: No.61 OTU, RAF.   15-12-1942
Map No.93
SJ 079338 (2,200ft), Bwlch Maen Gwynedd, Berwyn Mountains, Wrexham.

F/Lt D.H. Walker	Pilot	Killed

Despite poor weather the aircraft departed RAF Montford Bridge in Shropshire to conduct a low level search for Spitfire P7295, lost the previous day. The search was successful, but the wrecked Spitfire was lying close to the edge of an escarpment, and it appears the Lysander flew into a downdraught and came down in the valley below the escarpment.

Following the recovery of the Bristol Mercury engine from the aircraft only a few pieces of airframe remained in the stream below the site. However, flash flooding in the mid 1990s appears to have now removed all trace of wreckage.

Chapter Three

The Peak District

The Peak District was Britain's first designated National Park and lies between the cities of Manchester and Sheffield, which are to the West and East respectively. Forming the southern end of the Pennine hills, the park covers a wide area and variety of landscapes and is the most visited of the country's National Parks, with four dedicated visitor centres and a useful National Park Authority website:

(http://www.peakdistrict.gov.uk)

This site provides information and has downloadable leaflets online.

Walking in the Peak District, particularly on the higher ground can be challenging. Even in summer, the weather can change rapidly and unexpectedly for the worse and navigation can become difficult, especially if the visibility drops. Some of these sites are also on or near cliffs, sink holes, peat bogs etc. – Please make sure that you have the necessary skills, equipment and level of fitness before setting off into the hills.

The northern end of the park is dominated by the high moors of Kinder Scout, Bleaklow and Saddleworth, forming what is known as the Dark Peak, due to the Gritstone rock that forms the hills in the area. Between these high moorland plateaus are steep sided valleys, several of which contain reservoirs. Some aircraft ended up flying up these, in poor visibility and quite simply ran out of valley. Also the western edges of Kinder Scout, Bleaklow and Saddleworth fall away steeply to form escarpments, here the ground rises steeply from about 300ft to between 1,500ft and 2,000ft. These edges claimed their share of aircraft with several unfortunate pilots flying straight into them. While these altitudes may not be as high in terms of those found elsewhere in the more mountainous parts of the British Isles, during WW2 many training flights, particularly from RAF units based in the Midlands, passed over this area and the combination of aircrew inexperience, the proximity of the high ground and night flying often in poor weather, made such accidents inevitable. A number of aircraft returning from operations over Europe to RAF bases in Yorkshire and Lincolnshire also crashed in the area after overshooting their bases at night and eventually being forced to descend as their fuel tanks ran dry. Also the area lay on the busy air route to and from the huge USAAF Base Air Depot repair and supply centres in the North West and the operational bases in the South East, inevitably adding to the toll. The majority of Peak District crashes occurred on the less accessible and largely uninhabited high moorland of the Dark Peak area, leading to fewer sites being cleared at the time and many still feature larger surface remains to this day.

The southern part of the National Park is mainly Limestone and is known as the White Peak, again due to its geology. This area takes the form of a limestone plateau used for grazing, with fields enclosed by dry stone walls and is easily accessed so little if anything survives on the surface at the crash sites of aircraft in this area. However there are some areas of moorland in the south of the Peak District where small remains of some aircraft can be found.

In common with most National Park Authorities, The Peak District Authority do not really publicise the aircraft crashes that occurred within the area that is now covered by the Park (Only the Brecon Beacons Authority publish any material giving the locations and stories of air crashes). However the Ranger Service do run guided walks to some of the crash sites during the course of the year, mainly to the Meteors on Sliddens Moss and the Blenheim on Bleaklow, though in recent years walks to sites on the eastern moors and Kinder have been organised. Details are available from the visitor centres or a programme downloadable from the website – these walks are free, but many need booking well in advance.

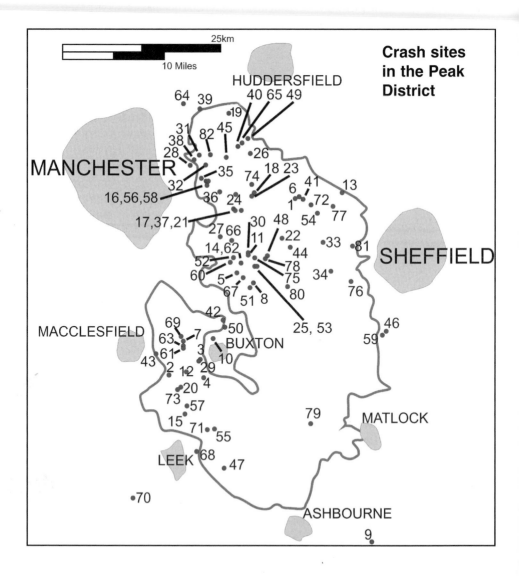

Airspeed Consul TF-RPM: Icelandic Airline.   12-04-1951
Map No.1
SK 174966 (1,600ft), Crow Stone Edge, The Derwent Valley, South Yorkshire.

Mr P. Magusson	Pilot	Killed
Mr A. Watson	Radio Op	Killed
Mr J. Rist	Pass	Killed

Crashed in poor visibility while on a ferry flight from Croydon to Iceland via Liverpool and Prestwick. The aircraft had been in England for renewal of the aircraft's Certificate of Airworthiness. The aircraft was originally built as Oxford Mk.I serial No. HN471 for the RAF and was sold back to Airspeed in March 1946 as G-AHJY for conversion to a Consul.

Both engines are still present, one stripped of all removable parts and the other partially buried and semi-stripped. Many other parts including cowling panels and wooden wing spar sections may also be seen.

Airspeed Oxford Mk.I L4601: No.17 SFTS, RAF.   04-04-1945
Map No.2
SJ 976695 (1,550ft), Shutlingsloe, Macclesfield, Cheshire.

F/O H.K. Shawyer	Pilot	Survived
F/Lt H.G. Featonby	Pilot	Killed
LAC F. Roscoe	Pass	Killed
Cpl A.J. Burd	Pass	Survived
AC1 G. Fishwick	Pass	Killed

The aircraft was on a cross-country flight from RAF Cranwell, Lincolnshire, when it flew into the southern side of Shutlingsloe near Macclesfield.

There is no remaining surface wreckage at this site, other than a few tiny fragments of yellow painted canvas and corroded metal, which have been found in recent years.

Airspeed Oxford Mk.I EB717 / XT: No.11 (P)AFU, RAF.   13-05-1943
Map No.3
SK 026717 (1,600ft), Burbage Edge, Buxton, Derbyshire.

Sgt J.H.L. Wilson	Pilot	Killed

Crashed while carrying out an early morning cross-county navigation flight from RAF Calveley near Nantwich, Cheshire. The aircraft struck a wall on the crest of the ridge while flying in light mist.

Some fragments remain in the wall the aircraft struck and a small pool on the western side of the wall contains pieces of plywood and a few metal items.

Airspeed Oxford Mk.I HN429: No.11 (P)AFU, RAF.   03-11-1944
Map No.4
SK 032692 (1,700ft), Axe Edge, Buxton, Derbyshire.

F/O C.V. Mayhead,	Pilot (Inst)	Survived
F/O A.C. Nullen (RCAF)	Pilot (u/t)	Survived
F/O J.S. Bean (RCAF)	Pilot (u/t	Survived

The crew was on a Beam Approach training flight from RAF Calveley near Nantwich, when the crash occurred in poor visibility, severely injuring the three crew crew members.

The largest items remaining are the stainless steel brackets, which were bolted to the wooden part of the main wing spars, with the undercarriage mounting points still attached.

Airspeed Oxford Mk.I HN594: No.21 (P)AFU, RAF.   28-12-1945
Map No.5
SK 082852 (1,800ft), Brown Knoll, Edale, Derbyshire.

F/O E.A. Croker	Pilot	Survived
F/O J.E. Dowthwaite	Pilot	Survived
W/O G. Robinson	Inst	Survived

This aircraft flew into the ground and broke up while trying to climb clear of high ground in poor weather conditions, close to the summit of Brown Knoll, on a daytime map-reading exercise from RAF Seighford, Staffordshire. The pilot, Edward Croker, managed to reach Lee Farm, despite injuries, to summon help.

This site lies in a large hollow at the head of a gully, close to the summit on the western side of the hill. This contains numerous aluminium panels, mainly from the engine cowlings.

Airspeed Oxford Mk.I LX518: No.21 (P)AFU, RAF.   18-10-1943
Map No.6
SK 180967 (1,700ft), Outer Edge, Derwent Valley, South Yorkshire.

P/O D.P. Kyne (RNZAF)	Pilot	Killed

This aircraft was on a short solo night cross-country navigation exercise from RAF Wheaton Aston, Staffordshire and the pilot failed to respond to a recall to base as weather conditions deteriorated. The aircraft was missing for five days before being found. Described as a very difficult recovery operation, the airframe was broken up on site after the engines had been manhandled by sledge across one and a half miles of very rough moorland.

A number of small parts remain in a gully adjacent to the crash site and this is where the airframe was disposed of by the recovery crew – the actual crash site only has a few tiny fragments on the surface.

Parts from Airspeed Oxford LX518 lie in a gully, where the airframe was disposed of by the recovery team.

Airspeed Oxford Mk.I LX745: No.11 (P)AFU, RAF.　　　　　12-03-1944
Map No.7
SJ 998746 (1,600ft), Shining Tor, Buxton, Derbyshire.

F/O C.S.G. Wood	Pilot	Killed
F/O G.C. Liggett (RCAF)	Pilot	Killed
F/Sgt J.G. Hall	Nav	Killed

The crash occurred while the crew was undertaking a daytime cross-county navigation exercise from RAF Calveley near Nantwich.

Cowling panels, a wheel and other aluminium parts remain in a shallow depression in the peat. Nearby in a similar depression there are many small fragments including wood, aluminium and brass wood screws. Slightly north of the site an oil tank can also be found.

Airspeed Oxford Mk.I NM683: PFFNTU, RAF.　　　　　04-03-1945
Map No.8
SK 110838 (1,200ft), Rushup Edge, Edale, Derbyshire.

F/Lt B. Gipson DFC	Pilot	Survived
F/Lt D.I. Jones DFC	2nd Pilot	Survived
F/Lt W.J. Barclay DFC (RAAF)	Nav	Survived
F/O V.P. Skone-Rees DFC	BA	Survived

This aircraft crashed while the pilot was attempting to fly below cloud on a cross-country navigation exercise from RAF Warboys in Cambridgeshire. It flew into the Edale valley and with the hills on either side obscured by cloud and rising ground directly ahead, the pilot either attempted to climb out or turn within the valley and struck the hillside.

Stainless steel brackets and undercarriage mounts from the main wing-spar lie in a scar on the side of a gully a short way from the Chapel Gate track.

Armstrong Whitworth Whitley Mk.V BD230: No.42 OTU, RAF. 24-07-1944
Map No.9
SK 295434 (550ft), Bullhurst Hill, Weston Underwood, Derbyshire.

F/Sgt J.W.E. Cooper	Pilot	Killed (Missing)
Sgt W.B. Smith	BA	Killed
Sgt H. Cowan	Nav	Killed (Missing)
Sgt W.C. Norcross	WO	Killed (Missing)
Sgt M.M. Lyon	AG	Killed

The crew was returning to RAF Ashbourne from a night cross-country flight when the aircraft dived into a field near the village of Muggington.

This site is on private land and is a designated war grave as three of the crew are still entombed in the wreck. A stone memorial cross bearing the names of the victims marks the crash site, close to the convergence point of two public rights of way.

Avro Anson Mk.I L7968: CNS, RAF.   15-10-1942
Map No.10
SK 046751 (1,450ft), Moss Ridge, Buxton, Derbyshire.

Sgt P.J. Woodcock	Pilot (Inst)	Killed
Sgt J.M. Matheson (RCAF)	Pilot (u/t)	Killed
Sgt R.J. Reay (RCAF)	Pilot (u/t)	Killed
Sgt W.G. Dale	WO/AG	Killed

The Anson flew into the ridge just below the summit while on a night navigation exercise from RAF Cranage near Middlewich, Cheshire.

This site lies at 1,450ft but, whilst there is very little surface wreckage at this site, the exact spot can easily be found as the site is next to an orienteering indicator marked with a letter Y.

Avro Anson Mk.I N9853: No.16 SFTS, RAF.   11-12-1944
Map No.11
SK 101879 (2,000ft), Edale Moor, Kinder Scout, Derbyshire.

F/Lt A. Chelstowski (PAF)	Pilot	Survived
F/Sgt S. Pasinski (PAF)	WO	Survived
F/O J. Kilmczak (PAF)	Pass	Survived
F/Lt A. Melcinski (PAF)	Pass	Survived
F/Lt W. Suida (PAF)	Pass	Survived

The crash occurred while N9853 was on a transit flight from RAF Newton in Nottinghamshire to RAF Millom in Cumbria. The pilot was descending through cloud to obtain a fix on their position when the aircraft struck the ground still in cloud.

Many parts of the aircraft, including the stripped remains of both engines, lie in one of the many shallow gullies which criss-cross the Kinder Plateau.

The memorial marking the crash site of Whitley BD230.

Avro Anson Mk.I N9858: No.10 FTS, RAF.   14-11-1940
Map No.12
SK 003699 (1,600ft), Wildboarclough, Macclesfield, Cheshire.

LAC M.J.W. Taylor	Pilot	Killed

This Anson flew into high ground in poor visibility while on a cross-country navigation exercise from RAF Tern Hill near Market Drayton in Shropshire.

There is no remaining wreckage on the surface at this site. However, on a recent visit, flakes of yellow painted canvas were noted in molehills just to the right of a track leading from the A54.

Avro Anson Mk.I N9912: No.25 OTU, RAF.   31-03-1941
Map No.13
SK 248975 (1,150ft), Bolderstones, Stocksbridge, South Yorkshire.

P/O B.M. Fournier	Pilot	Survived
Sgt D.H. Barrett	Pilot	Survived
Sgt E.R. Palmer	WO/AG	Survived
Sgt D. Watson	WO/AG	Survived

The aircraft crashed on very gently sloping heather moorland whilst on a night cross-country navigation exercise from RAF Finningley near Doncaster. Note: All four men onboard lost their lives during operational flying on the 29th August 1941 while flying with 49 Sqn. Their aircraft Hampden Mk.I AE126 was shot down by a night-fighter of 4/NJG1.

There are only a few tiny fragments left in the heather and these prove increasingly difficult to locate.

The Wool Packs as viewed from the crash site of Avro Anson NL185.

Avro Anson Mk.XI NL185: B.C.C.F., RAF.   23-11-1945
Map No.14
SK 089867 (1,650ft), The Cloughs, Edale, Derbyshire.

      W/Cdr R.D.D. Speare DSO DFC   Pilot   Killed

The aircraft was on a ferry flight from RAF Halton, Oxfordshire, to RAF Feltwell in Suffolk. The pilot became hopelessly lost in poor weather and while descending through cloud flew into the southern side of Kinder.

    Cowling panels and other parts remain at the crash site and these are sometimes confused with the nearby North American Harvard (FT415). A single engine from the Anson lies in a gully some way down the hill towards the Jacob's Ladder path.

Avro Lancaster Mk.I NF908 / PO-C: No.467 Sqn, RAAF.   03-01-1945
Map No.15
SK 002636 (1,600ft), The Roaches, Leek, Staffordshire.

F/O W.V.W. Allamby (RAAF)	Pilot	Killed
Sgt N. Lees	Flt Eng	Killed
F/Lt J.I. Pritchard (RAAF)	Nav	Killed
F/Sgt G.J. Dunbar (RAAF)	BA	Killed
F/Sgt R. Emonson (RAAF)	WO	Killed
F/Sgt T.E.H. Wright (RAAF)	AG	Killed
F/Sgt C.C. Watson (RAAF)	AG	Killed

The aircraft crashed at dusk in poor weather while on a fighter affiliation exercise from RAF Waddington near Lincoln. Note: The entire crew of NF908 was laid to rest at Chester's Blacon cemetery.

Small items, largely burnt aluminium, are scattered about a sizeable scar on the eastern side of the ridge, exploded .303 rounds may also be found, though the number of these has diminished greatly in the last few years. During a recent (Summer 2008) visit only a single example was seen.

Avro Lancaster Mk.I PA411 / A3-U: No.230 OCU, RAF.   21-12-1948
Map No.16
SK 036993 (1,400ft), Rhodes Hill, Tintwhistle, Derbyshire.

F/Sgt J.S. Thompson	Pilot	Killed
F/Sgt V. Graham	Flt Eng	Killed
F/Lt P.M. Maskell	Nav	Killed
F/Lt T.I. Johnson	Inst	Killed
F/Lt D.W.H. Harris	Inst	Killed
F/Sgt R. Smith	Sig	Killed
F/Sgt W.A. Love	Sig	Killed

This Lancaster flew into the western side of Rhodes Hill while on a night cross- country exercise from RAF Lindholme near Doncaster.

Various undercarriage struts, engine reduction gears and sections of propeller hubs can be found strewn down the rocky slope. Until recently sections of armour plate could also be found at the site but these have disappeared over the years.

Avro Lancaster Mk.X KB993 / EQ-U: No.408 Sqn, RCAF.   18-05-1945
Map No.17
SK 079948 (1,800ft), James's Thorn, Bleaklow, Derbyshire.

F/O A.A. Clifford (RCAF)	Pilot	Killed
F/O K. McIvor (RCAF)	Flt Eng	Killed
F/O D. Fehrman (RCAF)	BA	Killed
W/O M.C. Cameron (RCAF)	WO	Killed
F/Sgt C. Halvorson (RCAF)	AG	Killed
F/Sgt L.C. Hellekson (RCAF)	AG	Killed

The crew had been carrying out circuit flying practice and touch-and-go landings at RAF Linton-on-Ouse near York when they departed the area around the airfield, with the intention of engaging in some unbriefed local flying. They became lost as it became dark without a navigator onboard, as none had been required for the designated exercise. Unable to locate their position, the aircraft was heard circling the Glossop area and crashed into the hillside in the dark.

Only small parts of the aircraft remain, most collected together by visitors to the site, though there is a memorial present, which also commemorates the crew of the nearby C-47 (42-108982).

The two large sections of wing that can be found at the crash site of Botha W5103 on Bleaklow.

Blackburn Botha Mk.I W5103: No.7 FPP, ATA.   10-12-1942
Map No.18
SK 111975 (1,800ft), Round Hill, Bleaklow, Derbyshire.

1st Off T.W. Rogers (ATA)	Pilot	Killed

A new aircraft which crashed in bad weather while on a ferry flight from the Blackburn factory at Sherburn-in-Elmet near Leeds to Hawarden near Chester. The pilot was attempting to fly above the cloud which covered the hills and it is thought he was descending thinking that he had cleared the hills, but a head wind may have slowed his progress and therefore meant he was still over the high ground as he descended.

The site lies on fairly level moorland where two large sections of wing and numerous smaller structural parts remain. Both engines were present until the 1960s – 70s, when they were recovered by personnel from RAF Henlow.

Boeing B-17G 43-37667/C: 709th BS / 447th BG, USAAF.   06-04-1945
Map No.19
SE 071095 (1,400ft), Meltham Moor, Huddersfield, West Yorkshire.

1st Lt W.R. Johnson	Pilot	Survived
2nd Lt R.W. Parks	Co-pilot	Survived
2nd Lt W.A. Vukelic	Nav	Survived
Sgt R.J. Schnug	Eng	Survived
Sgt R.J. Woodbeck	Radio Op	Survived

The crew was on an air test from Rattlesden near Stowmarket, Suffolk, to put hours onto new engines which had been fitted to the aircraft. They became disorientated in low cloud and struck the ground to the north-west of West Nab on Meltham Moor. Note: The

The wreckage of B-17G 43-37667 on Meltham Moor near Huddersfield.

pilot died in 1961 due to his injuries

Both undercarriage legs with the wheel hubs still attached and sections of framework from inside the wings and bomb bay remain. Recently part of this site has been incorporated into the overshoot area of the Deer Hill Rifle Range.

Boeing B-17G 43-38944: 398th BG, USAAF.   02-01-1945
Map No.20
SJ 994678 (1,500ft), Birchenough Hill, Wildboarclough, Cheshire.

1st Lt D.J. De Cleene	Pilot	Killed
2nd Lt M. Stravinski	Co-pilot	Killed
Flt Off T. Manos	Nav	Killed
T/Sgt F.E. Garry	Eng	Killed
T/Sgt H.F. Ayers	Radio Op	Killed

The aircraft was on a ferry flight at night from BAD 1 at Burtonwood near Warrington, Cheshire, to Nuthampstead near Royston in Hertfordshire when it flew into the top of Birchenough Hill in fairly clear weather.

A stone marker and wooden memorial with a few fragments of aluminium can be found where the aircraft impacted on the hill. Not far way (SJ 995678) is a scar where the aircraft burned, containing more small parts.

The scar on Birchenough hill containing burnt fragments from B-17G 43-38944.

Boeing RB-29A 44-61999: 16th PRS / 91st RG, USAF.   03-11-1948
Map No.21
SK 090949 (2,000ft), Higher Shelf Stones, Bleaklow, Derbyshire.

Capt L.P. Tanner	Pilot	Killed
Capt H.A. Stroud	Co-pilot	Killed
T/Sgt R.W. Fields	Eng	Killed
Sgt C.R. Wilbanks	Nav	Killed
S/Sgt G.A. Gartner	Radio Op	Killed
S/Sgt D.D. Moore	Radar Op	Killed
Capt H.E. Keel	Photo Advr	Killed
Sgt D.R. Abrogast	Camera Crew	Killed
T/Sgt S.R. Banks	Camera Crew	Killed
PFC W.M. Burrows	Camera Crew	Killed
S/Sgt R.I. Doyle	Camera Crew	Killed
Cpl C.M. Franssen	Pass	Killed
Cpl G. Ingram Jnr	Pass	Killed

This RB-29 crashed on a cross-country flight from RAF Scampton near Lincoln to Burtonwood near Warrington, Cheshire. The pilots, believing they had cleared the Peak District, began their descent too soon and struck high ground while still in low cloud. The passengers had been carrying the payroll for US personnel stationed at Burtonwood and this was quickly recovered following the crash.

This site is one of the best known and most visited crash sites in the area, with large sections of the aircraft, albeit now in poor condition due to the rapid pace of corrosion, remaining at the site including: the aircraft's four engines and huge main undercarriage.

One of the huge main undercarriage units from RB-29A 44-61999 near to Higher Shelf Stones, often to be found today covered with crosses and wreaths in memory of the crew.

Boulton Paul Defiant Mk.I N1766: No.96 Sqn, RAF.   12-04-1941
Map No.22
SK 153905 (1,450ft), Rowlee Pasture, Derwent Valley, Derbyshire.

F/Lt P.W Rabone (RNZAF)	Pilot	Survived
F/O J.M. Ritchie	AG	Survived

Abandoned due to engine seizure while on an air test from RAF Cranage near Middlewich, Cheshire. The aircraft eventually dived into the ground on Rowlee Pasture.

Several sections of aluminium spar litter the bottom of the crater, partly caused by the crash and since enlarged during the recovery of the aircraft's engine in the 1980s. This can now be seen at the Yorkshire Air Museum at Elvington near York.

Boulton Paul Defiant Mk.I N3378: No.255 Sqn, RAF.   29-08-1941
Map No.23
SK 106969 (1,950ft) Near Bleaklow Stones, Bleaklow, Derbyshire.

P/O J. Craig	Pilot	Killed
AC1 G.D. Hempstead	Pass	Killed

The aircraft struck the ground while flying in low cloud. The pilot was returning to duty from leave, which he had spent in Edinburgh and allowed A.C.1 Hempstead to travel as a passenger. They had taken off from RAF Turnhouse on the edge of Edinburgh and intended to follow the coast to Lincolnshire where their destination was to have been RAF Hibaldstow near Scunthorpe. It is often speculated that the aircraft may have come under fire from a Spitfire operating in the Durham area, but this has never been proven. The aircraft was missing for over a month before being located.

Wreckage at the crash site of Defiant N3378 on Bleaklow.

A pile of parts with a number of small crosses marks the highest extent of the site with parts scattered down-hill from there. Approximately 50ft lower down there is an area of bare peat containing small fragments where the aircraft first impacted the moor. Substantial parts including the complete tail section were recovered from the site between the 1970s – 1990s and may be seen at The Boulton Paul Heritage Project museum at Wolverhampton.

Bristol Blenheim Mk.I L1476: No.64 Sqn, RAF. 30-01-1939
Map No.24
SK 083970 (1,700ft), Sykes Moor, Bleaklow, Derbyshire.

P/O S.J.D. Robinson	Pilot	Killed
P/O J.E. Thomas	Pass	Killed

This Blenheim dived into the ground in bad weather while on a familiarization flight from RAF Church Fenton near York. The aircraft remained missing until 12-02-1939 when it was found by a member of a local walking club who was trying to catch up with his group.

A memorial commemorating the two airmen was placed at the site in 1991 by a local ATC unit, both engines, the very battered tail section and numerous other parts also remain.

Cessna F.150M G-BFRP: B.T.J. Aviation Group. 25-10-1983
Map No.25
SK 114861 (1,450ft), Broadlee Bank Tor, Edale, Derbyshire.

Mr B. Bryant	Pilot (Inst)	Survived
Mr J. Bateson	Pilot (u/t)	Survived

The gully on Sykes Moor which contains the shattered remains of Blenheim L1476. In the centre is the memorial constructed in 1991.

The aircraft was on a tuition flight around dusk from Ringway, Manchester, when the aircraft was caught by a strong down draught and crashed on the Edale side of Broadlee Bank Tor part way down a gully above a ruined barn.

Though virtually no wreckage remains, the site was located with the aid of contemporary photographs. This incident shows that pilots may still be caught out by unexpected weather conditions in this area.

Consolidated B-24H 42-94841: 857th BS / 492nd BG, USAAF.   09-10-1944
Map No.26
SE 106034 (1,600ft), Twizzle Head Moss, Holmfirth, West Yorkshire.

1st Lt E.D. Pitsenbarger	Pilot	Killed
2nd Lt J.D. Nendel	Co-pilot	Killed
Flt Off J.M. Bliss	Nav	Killed
Flt Off F. Cser	BA	Killed
T/Sgt P.S. Farris	Eng	Killed
T/Sgt Z.W. Zwinge	Radio Op	Killed
T/Sgt F.A. Villelli	AG	Killed
Cpl C.T. Lowbald	AG	Killed
S/Sgt C. Anderson	Dpr	Survived
Cpl C.S. Watson	Pass	Killed

This B-24 crashed while on a low-level cross-country navigation training exercise from Harrington near Kettering in Northamptonshire. The intended route was Harrington, Goole, Huddersfield, Stafford, Builth Wells, Worcester, Banbury and return to Harrington. The aircraft was less than a mile from its intended track when it hit the ground. Note: A number of the crew were buried at Cambridge American Cemetery and interestingly Cpl Watson is commemorated on the Tablets of the Missing, in spite of the fact that his body is known to have been found and recovered.

This site is marked by a large patch of peat devoid of vegetation and containing numerous small fragments and a single undercarriage leg, while nearby is the other leg, which has at some point been cut in two. Further to the north-east there are more scattered fragments.

Consolidated B-24J 42-52003: 310th Fy Sqn / 27th ATG, USAAF. 11-10-1944
Map No.27
SK 058906 (1,650ft), Mill Hill, Glossop, Derbyshire.

2nd Lt C. Houpt	Pilot	Survived
Sgt J. Najvar	Eng	Survived

The two crew members were ferrying the aircraft from Burtonwood near Warrington to Hardwick approximately 10 miles south of Norwich. The engineer reported that the pilot flew too low following take-off, only beginning a climb shortly before the crash, which occurred in very limited visibility.

This site has a number of widely spread large sections. Two large sections of wing and an engine can be found in a gully next to the path from the Grouse Inn while, a further wing section with undercarriage still attached is at the main site a little to the north along with two engines and the other main undercarriage leg.

Consolidated PB4Y-1 63934: VB-110, USN.   18-12-1943
Map No.28
SE 009016 (1,450ft), Irontongue Hill, Mossley, Greater Manchester.

Lt G. Charno Jr	Pilot	Survived
Lt JG R.G. Wissman	Co-pilot	Survived
Esn C.R. Colyer	Nav	Survived
AOM W.O. Levering	Sig	Survived
ACRM1c B.S. Barber	Radio Op	Survived
AMM3c D.S. Peterson	Radio Op	Survived
AMM3c A.P. Oliver	Radio Op	Survived
ARM3c W.W. Olson	AG	Survived
SM 2 D.M. Clark	AG	Survived
SM 2 W.C. Ketchem	AG	Survived

Abandoned while returning from an operational patrol over the Bay of Biscay. During the flight weather conditions had deteriorated to such an extent that few airfields were open to returning aircraft, additionally the aircraft's radio equipment failed. Upon running low on fuel the crew abandoned the aircraft over Lincolnshire and it continued flying west on the auto-pilot until the fuel ran out.

Much of the remaining wreckage was buried a few years ago, but recently one main undercarriage leg and a few other items have been unearthed again.

Two engines and a main undercarriage oleo from B-24J 42-52003 on Mill Hill.

De Havilland DH-60X G-EBWA: 11-10-1934
Map No.29
SK 024716 (1,550ft), Burbage Edge, Buxton, Derbyshire.

Mr W.J. Alington	Pilot	Survived
Mr H. Ellis	Pass	Survived

This aircraft crashed in poor weather while travelling from Broxbourne in Essex to Stanley Park at Blackpool, Lancashire while en route to Belfast. With poor visibilty over the Peak District, they decided to turn back, but the weather conditions deteriorated and whilst attempting a forced landing in strong winds the aircraft turned over and was wrecked.

No surface wreckage remains at this site, though small parts have been found in the past. It is nevertheless easily located as a shallow depression in the otherwise fairly uniform slope, a feature that caused the aircraft to flip over on impact.

De Havilland Dragon Rapide G-ALBC: Solair Flying Services.   30-12-1963
Map No.30
SK 102882 (2,000ft), Kinder Scout, Edale, Derbyshire.

Mr D. Holmes	Pilot	Survived
Mr J. McWhirter	Co-pilot	Survived

Caught by a down-draught while flying from Middleton St George, near Darlington, to Ringway, Manchester, the aircraft was returning from a photographic survey flight.

A single engine block, stripped of all removable parts, various aluminium panels and parts of the wooden structure of the aircraft remain at the site.

View towards Grindslow Knoll from the crash site of de Havilland Dragon Rapide G-ALBC.

De Havilland Mosquito B. Mk.XVI PF395 / 8K-K: No.571 Sqn, RAF. 22-10-1944
Map No.31
SE 026032 (1,400ft), Dove Stone, Mossley, Greater Manchester.

F/O E.D. Scotland	Pilot	Killed
Sgt H.R.C. Soan	Nav	Killed

Failure of the port engine caused loss of electrical power to radio equipment while returning to RAF Oakington near Cambridge from a raid against Hamburg. As a result the aircraft overshot its base and became lost and was last seen flying in the vicinity of Oldham before eventually flying into high ground.

Some small fragments remain in the rocks where the aircraft impacted with other pieces gathered into a pile, by visitors to the site, on a slightly flatter area nearby.

De Havilland Tiger Moth Mk.II T6464: No.24 EFTS, RAF.   12-04-1945
Map No.32
SE 034016 (1,600ft), Blindstones Moss, Chew Reservoir, Greater Manchester.

F/Sgt M.A. O'Connell (RNZAF)	Pilot	Killed

The aircraft crashed following loss of control in cloud while on a cross-country flight from RAF Sealand near Chester.

The site is marked by a small collection of fragments, mainly cowling panels. These are in the hollow caused by the crash and subsequent recovery efforts.

De Havilland Vampire F.B. Mk.5 WA400: No.102 FTS, RAF.   25-07-1951
Map No.33
SK 218898 (1,150ft), Strines Moor, Sheffield, South Yorkshire.

F/O L.L. Beckford	Pilot	Survived

The pilot made a 'wheels up' forced landing on moorland after becoming disorientated and using up the aircraft's fuel reserves while on a training flight from RAF Finningley near Doncaster. The aircraft was destroyed by fire following the landing.

Only a few lumps of fused aluminium remain amongst the heather, where the aircraft was burned out.

De Havilland Vampire T. Mk.11 XE866: No.4 FTS, RAF.   07-08-1957
Map No.34
SK 224857 (1,400ft), Stanage Edge, Hathersage, Derbyshire.

F/O P.R. Redvers	Pilot (Inst)	Killed
F/O D.J. Brett	Pilot (u/t)	Killed

The crew was on a training flight from RAF Worksop in Nottinghamshire and flew into Stanage Edge while making a controlled descent through cloud at high speed.

Small pieces remain in a large rock fall adjacent to the crash site.

De Havilland Canada Chipmunk T. Mk.10 WB579: No.2 RFS, RAF. 03-07-1951
Map No.35
SK 027999 (1,350ft), Arnfield Moor, Arnfield, Derbyshire.

P4 H.B. Wright	Pilot	Survived

The pilot was on a training flight from Barton airfield to the west of Manchester. He had been carrying out exercises above cloud and had flown further east than he had realised. On descending through the cloud the aircraft struck the ground and turned over trapping the pilot in the cockpit.

A few fragments of aluminium have been gathered together at the site around a wooden stake set into the ground to mark the spot.

De Havilland Canada L-20A 52-6145: 7519th OPRON / 81st FBW, USAF. 05-12-1956
Map No.36
SK 055976 (1,250ft), Bramah Edge, Longdendale, Derbyshire.

1st Lt J.R. Tinklepaugh	Pilot	Killed
1st Lt G.E. Waller	Pass	Killed

Flying from Sculthorpe near Fakenhem to RAF Burtonwood near Warrington on a personnel transfer flight. The aircraft was misidentified on radar by a ground controller at Burtonwood and given directions, which 'guided' the aircraft into the side of Bramah Edge not far from the summit.

This site lies just below the top of the edge, where there is a collection of small fragments. A white painted cross also marks the site of the crash.

Douglas C-47A 42-108982: 32nd TCS / 314th TCG, USAAF.   24-07-1945
Map No.37
SK 081947 (1,750ft), Shelf Moor, Bleaklow, Derbyshire.

1st Lt G.L Johnson	Pilot	Killed
1st Lt E.W. Burns	Co-pilot	Killed
1st Lt B.W. Azlar	Nav	Killed
Sgt T.R. McCrecklin	Crew Chf	Killed
Sgt F.M. Maloney	Radio Op	Killed
Cpl G.R. Alexander	Pass	Killed
LAC J.D. Main (RAFVR)	Pass	Killed

The aircraft flew into Shelf Moor close to the crash site of Lancaster KB993 while on an administrative flight from Leicester East, currently Leicester Airport, to Renfrew, Glasgow.

    Wreckage from this aircraft is very widely scattered with small remains where the aircraft crashed and longer sections strewn down the steep slope down into Ashton Clough. A substantial section of main undercarriage lies near the top and a large section of fuselage can be found slowly being crushed by sand and gravel in the Clough, further down is one of the two engines, the other having disappeared in flash flooding in 2002 and is possibly now buried much lower down. Note: This aircraft was carrying a jeep amongst its cargo and over the years pieces have been found in the area.

Douglas DC-3 Dakota G-AHCY: British European Airways.   19-08-1948
Map No.38
SE 015027 (1,000ft), Wimberry Stones, Mossley, Greater Manchester.

Capt F.W. Pinkerton	Pilot	Killed
1st Off G. Holt	Co-pilot	Killed
Radio Off R.W. Haig	Radio Op	Killed
21 Passengers	(see Appendices)	Killed
8 Passengers	(see Appendices)	Survived

The aircraft was on a scheduled flight from Nutts Corner, Belfast, to Ringway, Manchester, when it flew into Wimberry Stones as it was turning to approach Ringway.

    There is almost no wreckage at the crash site itself SE 015025 though there is a single undercarriage leg in the stream just above the wall bordering the fields lower down.

Fairey Barracuda Mk.III MD963: RNAS Dunino Stn Flt, RN.   29-07-1945
Map No.39
SE 024104 (1,150ft), Redbrook Clough, Marsden, West Yorkshire.

Sub Lt (A) G.H. Ambler (RN)	Pilot	Killed

This RN aircraft crashed while on a cross-country flight from Donibristle near Dunfermline. It appears as though the pilot lost control while attempting to turn the aircraft within the confines of the valley in which it crashed.

Alan Clark at the crash site of Fairey Barracuda MD963 with Redbrook Clough in the background.

A collection of small burnt fragments can be found near to a rough path on the grassy moorland.

Fairey Swordfish Mk.I P4223: No.751 Sqn, RN.   25-01-1940
Map No.40
SE 083048 (1,800ft), Heydon Head, Black Hill, Derbyshire.

Sub Lt G.V. Williamson (RN)   Pilot   Killed

Having become separated from rest of flight while ferrying from Silloth near Carlisle to RNAS Ford in West Sussex, in extremely bad winter weather, the pilot is assumed to have descended to ascertain his position and struck high ground. Note: the aircraft was missing for a month before enough snow cleared for the wreck to be visible from the nearest road.

This site is now somewhat depleted, a small collection of fragments including cowling panels and some steel struts having been gathered in a pile in the gully next to where the aircraft crashed.

Fieseler Fi-103s (V-1 Flying Bombs): *Luftwaffe*.   24-12-1944
Map No.41-43
SK 182970 (1,700ft), Outer Edge, Derwent Valley, South Yorkshire.
SK 062779 (1,600ft), Black Edge, Buxton, Derbyshire.
SJ 955727 (900ft), Five Ashes, Macclesfield, Cheshire.

During Christmas Eve and early into Christmas Day 1944 V-1 flying bombs fell over a wide area of Northern England. They had been air launched by Heinkel He111 aircraft off the East Yorkshire coast with the intention of causing damage to the Manchester area. This aim failed as only a couple of the weapons fell in the Manchester area, and none actually in the city.

There are three easily located sites where V-1s exploded in the Peak District. Two are on open moorland and both are marked by a large bare patch and a pool of water. The third near Macclesfield is on farm land but a public by-way runs adjacent to the field and the crater is clearly visible to the left of the path and next to an electricity pole when heading up hill. Note: a large crater at SK 186965 often reported as being that of this V1 has now been identified as being from a *Luftmine B* parachute mine.

Gloster Meteor F. Mk.4 RA487: No.66 Sqn, RAF.   08-12-1950
Map No.44
SK 166890 (1,150ft), Hagg Side, Derwent Valley, Derbyshire.

Sgt J. Harrington	Pilot	Survived

The pilot was on a night cross-country flight from RAF Linton-on-Ouse near York when he became disorientated. He attempted to force land the aircraft as he ran out of fuel but narrowly missed crashing into a building and then abandoned the aircraft successfully. The Meteor subsequently dived into the ground on Hagg Side leaving a sizable crater close to a wall on the densely wooded hillside above Ladybower Reservoir.

This site lies in woodland, where a pile of aluminium parts can still be found in the distinct depression in the ground caused by the impact of the meteor's fuselage and two engines.

Gloster Meteor F. Mk.8 VZ518 and WA791: No.66 Sqn, RAF.   12-04-1951
Map No.45
SE 066029 (1,650ft), Sliddens Moss, Black Hill, Derbyshire.

F/O A.H. Hauxwell	Pilot (VZ518)	Killed
F/Lt D.M. Leach	Pilot (WA791)	Killed

The two aircraft were taking part in a four-ship interception exercise to the west of the Pennines from RAF Linton-on-Ouse near York. While returning to base the two aircraft descended through cloud too soon and flew into the ground still in formation.

This is one the largest and most widely spread crash sites in the Peak District with two distinct scars on the western side of Sliddens Moss where the aircraft impacted and large sections of wreckage, including tail section, wing parts, undercarriage legs, engine remains and cowling panels etc. are scattered across to the upper reaches of Meadow Clough SE 072029.

Gloster Meteor F. Mk.8 WE904: No.211 FTS, RAF.   12-05-1955
Map No.46
SK 317763 (475ft), Millthorpe, Dronfield, Derbyshire.

P/O R.A. Tritton	Pilot	Killed

The pilot was on a training flight from RAF Worksop in Nottinghamshire; and was to carry out a controlled descent through cloud from 10,500ft. P/O Tritton radioed he was flying at 20,000ft and had just checked his oxygen supply. Shortly after this, and only 7 minutes into the flight, the aircraft was seen diving out of cloud before crashing into a small field behind a farm house in the village of Millthorpe.

The crash site today is the site of a private house. A memorial to the pilot can be

Still recognizable tail section from one of the two meteors to be found on Sliddens Moss.

found on the village green at SK 318764 opposite the crash site, this was unveiled on the 50th anniversary of the crash by the pilot's sister. The only trace of the crash is an old tree missing some branches which the aircraft hit just before impacting the ground.

Handley Page Halifax A. Mk.9 RT922: No.47 Sqn, RAF.   13-02-1947
Map No.47
SK 063553 (1,200ft), Grindon Moor, Grindon, Staffordshire.

S/Ldr D.D McIntyre	Pilot	Killed
W/O R.S. Kearns	Flt Eng	Killed
F/Lt E. Smith	Nav	Killed
W/O G.V. Chapman	Nav	Killed
F/Sgt K.C. Pettit	WO	Killed
Sgt W.T. Sherry (Army)	Obs	Killed
Mr J.J. Reardon (Civilian)	Pass (photographer)	Killed
Mr D.W. Savill (Civilian)	Pass (photographer)	Killed

The crew was attempting to drop relief supplies to the villages of Butterton and Grindon which at the time were cut off by snow. In white-out conditions the pilot brought the aircraft lower than he probably realised and one wing struck the ground near the road across Grindon Moor and cart-wheeled the aircraft.

This site is also on private land and there is no remaining surface wreckage, though a large stone memorial was erected on the site adjacent to a public right of way, that is signposted locally as 47 Sqn Cairn.

Handley Page Halifax Mk.II Srs 1 HR727 / MH-V: No.51 Sqn, RAF. 05-10-1943
Map No.48
SK 131876 (1,900ft), Blackden Edge, Kinder Scout, Derbyshire.

Sgt E.H. Fenning	Pilot	Killed
Sgt E.G. Lane	Flt Eng	Killed
W/O J.G.F. Fortin (RCAF)	Nav	Killed
Sgt V. Garland	BA	Survived
Sgt F. Squibbs	WO	Killed
Sgt J. Mack	AG	Survived
Sgt B.K. Short	AG	Killed

The crew had taken part in a raid against Hamburg from RAF Snaith near Selby in Yorkshire and the aircraft had been attacked over the target by a *Luftwaffe* night-fighter which had caused severe damage to the aircraft's port-inner engine, causing the loss of most of the aircraft's electrical power. This meant the crew was unable to use their radio equipment to aid their return to Snaith. Having overshot their base and while attempting to locate their position, the aircraft flew into the rough moorland on Blackden Edge. The aircraft broke into a number of large sections spread over a wide area.

A large hollow on the edge of a gully contains sections of the aircraft, while there are further small parts spread along a line towards SK 129879. These more widely spread parts have often been confused for the remains of Wellington X3348, which can also be found in this section.

The main collection of wreckage on Blackden Edge from Halifax HR727.

Handley Page Hampden Mk.I L4055: No.83 Sqn, RAF.   23-05-1940
Map No.49
SE 099057 (1,250ft), Black Hill, Holmfirth, West Yorkshire.

Sgt S.W. Jenkins	Pilot	Killed
Sgt A. Marsh	Obs	Killed
AC1 W. Thornton	WO	Killed
Sgt P.W. Josse	AG	Killed

The aircraft crashed in a field adjoining Cliff Road above the village of Holme while returning from an unsuccessful raid against Munchen Gladbach, having overshot its base at RAF Scampton near Lincoln.

There is no remaining surface wreckage as the site is on agricultural land, though it can be located by the craters on each side of the Cliff Road where the Royal Engineers detonated the bombs that were not destroyed in the crash.

Handley Page Hampden Mk.I L4189: No.106 Sqn, RAF.   30-09-1940
Map No.50
SK 064768 (1,550ft), Black Edge, Dove Holes, Derbyshire.

Sgt J.G. Gow	Pilot	Killed
Sgt C.O. Cook	Obs	Killed
Sgt E. Burt	WO	Killed
Sgt N. Powell	AG	Killed

The crew was on a night cross-country navigation flight from RAF Finningley near Doncaster when they flew into the hill in low cloud.

Small pieces of the aircraft, mainly lumps of once molten burnt aluminium remain at the site. Note: this site is on private land.

Handley Page Hampden Mk.I X3154 / ZN-A: No.106 Sqn, RAF. 21-12-1940
Map No.51
SK 104830 (1,600ft), Rushup Edge, Chapel-en-le-Frith, Derbyshire.

P/O M. Hubbard	Pilot	Killed
Sgt K.W.B. Perkins	Nav	Killed
Sgt D.W. Smith	WO/AG	Killed
Sgt D.J. Davey	WO/AG	Killed

As with Hampden L4189 described above, the crew of X3154 was on a night cross-country navigation flight from RAF Finningley near Doncaster, when the aircraft flew into the southern side of Rushup Edge.

Small pieces of the aircraft, consisting of mainly burnt aluminium, remain. Note: this site is on private land.

Handley Page Hampden Mk.I AE381 / VN-J: No.50 Sqn, RAF. 21-01-1942
Map No.52
SK 078875 (2,000ft), Cluther Rocks, Kinder Scout, Derbyshire.

Sgt R.G. Heron (RAAF)	Pilot	Killed
Sgt W.C. Williams (RAAF)	Nav	Killed
Sgt W.T. Tromans	WO	Killed
Sgt S.A. Peters	WO/AG	Killed

The crash occurred while the crew was on a night cross-country navigation flight from RAF Skellingthorpe near Lincoln. After becoming lost the crew made radio contact with Ringway and had flown over the airfield but did not see anything due to the appalling weather. Before they could turn to make another pass the aircraft crashed just below the Pennine way and burned out on the opposite side of the path.

A slate memorial plaque and small parts of the aircraft can be found at the site on the uphill side of the Pennine Way.

Handley Page Heyford Mk.III K6875: No.166 Sqn, RAF.   22-07-1937
Map No.53
SK 111860 (1,700ft), Broadlee Bank Tor, Edale, Derbyshire.

Sgt J.W. Baker	Pilot	Killed
Sgt N.W. Baker	Pilot	Killed
AC1 W.H. Gray	WO	Killed
Sgt C.P.D. McMillan	Crewman	Killed
AC1 E.J. McDonald	Crewman	Killed
AC2 E.J. Musker	Crewman	Killed

This Heyford crashed while on a night cross-country navigation exercise from RAF Leconfield near Beverley in Yorkshire. At the time of the crash the aircraft was approximately 13 miles off course.

Only a few steel struts and small parts remain at the site close to the wall that runs around the edge of the hill. In 1975, Officer Cadets from RAF Henlow recovered, as a training exercise, parts of tailplane structure from this site and these remain in store with the RAF Museum.

Hawker Hunter T. Mk.7 G-BTYL / 78: Cubitt Aviation.   11-06-1993
Map No.54
SK 209943 (1,600ft), Broomhead Moor, Langsett, South Yorkshire.

Mr W. Cubitt	Pilot	Killed

This privately owned aircraft, formerly RAF serial XL595, was being flown from Foulsham airfield in Norfolk to Warton near Preston in Lancashire when it flew into a thunderstorm. Shortly afterwards the aircraft dived into the ground from roughly 14,000ft leaving a large crater in the moorland.

The crater caused by Hawker Hunter G-BTYL. Much of the moor in the area of the crash site is fairly level and otherwise featureless.

The crater, on an otherwise featureless moor, caused by the crash is more evident now than at the time of the crash due to fuel contamination preventing plant growth in a wide area around the crater. There are many pieces of twisted aluminium from the aircraft scattered around the crater and sections of PSP tracking used during the recovery attempts. It is reported that the pilot's body was never recovered but this has not been substantiated.

Hawker Hurricane Mk.I V6793: No.5 (P)AFU, RAF.　　　　27-07-1944
Map No.55
SK 048613 (1,350ft), Merryton Low, Leek, Staffordshire.

　　　　F/Sgt R.H.T. Martin (RNZAF)　　　　Pilot　　　　Killed

The aircraft dived into the ground while the pilot was on a sector reconnaissance exercise from RAF Tern Hill near Market Drayton in Shropshire. It appears the pilot lost control of the aircraft while performing aerobatics.

There is surface wreckage at the site which is otherwise marked by an obvious crater. This lies part way between two trenches which were dug by the Army, who use the area for training exercises.

Hawker Hurricanes Mk.IIC PZ765 + PZ851 + PZ854: No.11 (P)AFU, RAF.
Map No.56　　　　　　　　　　　　　　　　　　　　　22-02-1945
SK 036989 (1,150ft), Tintwhistle Knarr, Tintwhistle, Derbyshire.

　　　　F/Sgt M.H.L. Orban　　　　Pilot (PZ765)　　　　Killed
　　　　Sgt E.M.L. Marien　　　　Pilot (PZ851)　　　　Killed
　　　　Sgt J.V. Robinson　　　　Pilot (PZ854)　　　　Killed

The three aircraft were on a formation flying exercise from RAF Calveley near Nantwich, Cheshire when they flew into Tintwhistle Knarr in formation while in cloud.

Small parts from the three aircraft are scattered on the uphill side of the fence separating the edge of a forestry plantation and the open moor. Most can be found near a wooden pole with a cairn built around it.

Junkers Ju88A-5 6213 / FI+AD: KG 76, *Luftwaffe*.   08-05-1941
Map No.57
SK 004647 (1,050ft), Black Brook, The Roaches, Staffordshire.

Maj D.H. Von Ziehlberg	Pilot	Killed
Olt W. Lemke	Obs	Killed
Ofw R. Schwalbe	WO	Killed
Fw G. Mahl	AG	Killed

The aircraft had taken part in a raid against Manchester and had been damaged by anti-aircraft fire, either from the ground or a night fighter. The crew were in the process of abandoning the aircraft when it flew into the hillside above Black Brook.

A reasonable quantity of small burnt fragments litter the hillside where the aircraft impacted, these are most prominent at its base but extend up amongst the trees above.

Lockheed P-38J 42-67207 / B9-1: 496th FTG, USAAF.   10-05-1944.
Map No.58
SK 039991 (1,500ft), Tintwhistle Knarr, Tintwhistle, Derbyshire.

Flt Off H.A. Jones	Pilot	Killed

The pilot of this P-38 lost control in cloud and struck the hill inverted while on a training flight from Goxhill near Barton-on-Humber.

A pile of fragments collected up by visitors, together with a wooden post marks the crash site.

McDonnell RF-4C 64-1018: 1st TRS / 10th TRW, USAF.   06-05-1970
Map No.59
SK 310757 (550ft), Unthank Plantation, Dronfield, Derbyshire.

Maj D.E. Tokar	Pilot	Survived
Maj P.M. Dunn	Nav	Survived

The aircraft was undertaking a reconnaissance sortie as part of a NATO exercise when it suffered complete engine failure. Both crew members ejected safely, though the pilot was injured when he landed on Curber Edge near to Warren Lodge.

This site lies in woodland where occasionally it is possible to find small fragments on the surface. The crash site is just inside the wood and to the west (uphill), is a shallow bramble-filled depression indicating the now filled-in impact crater.

Miles Hawk Trainer Mk.III G-AJSF: Blackpool Aero Club.   29-07-1957
Map No.60
SK 074867 (1,950ft), Kinderlow, Kinder Scout, Derbyshire.

Mr W.W. Hall	Pilot	Killed

The pilot became lost in cloud and flew into high ground having overshot his intended destination while flying from Squire's Gate at Blackpool to Barton aerodrome on the edge of Manchester.

The only remaining items at the crash site are tiny pieces of silver and yellow painted canvas in a large bare patch of peat to the north of the path from Kinderlow End to Kinder Low.

Noorduyn UC-64A 43-35439: 10th DRS / 10th ADG, USAAF.   29-09-1944
Map No.61
SJ 998736 (1,700ft), Shining Tor, Buxton, Derbyshire.

    2nd Lt A. Fredrickson   Pilot   Survived

The aircraft flew into Shining Tor while flying from RAF Winthorp near Newark on Trent in Nottinghamshire to Burtonwood near Warrington. Most of the flight had been in cloud and against a strong headwind, which had impeded the progress of the aircraft to a much greater extent than was realised and the pilot descended over high ground.

The site is marked by a scar in the heather containing many burnt fragments. Lower down the hill are engine parts which may be from this aircraft or the nearby Harvard (FT442) as both aircraft had the same type of engine and propeller.

Note: This crash site has in the past been misidentified as being that of Defiant T3921, which was thought to have crashed in the area in 1941, though the parts found at the site and archive research have proved the Defiant to be elsewhere.

North American Harvard Mk.IIB FT415: No.22 FTS, RAF.   14-01-1952
Map No.62
SK 089868 (1,800ft), The Wool Packs, Kinder Scout, Derbyshire.

    Msm B. Farley (RN)   Pilot   Killed

This aircraft crashed just to the west of the Wool Packs while on a cross-country flight from RAF Syerston near Newark-on-Trent to RAF Kemble in Gloucestershire. Note: This aircraft was being piloted by a Fleet Air Arm pilot, who was in training at Syerston.

There are no parts to be found in the area of rocks where the aircraft actually crashed, but parts of the aircraft are a little lower down the hill on a level area. There is an undercarriage leg and a few other fragments in an often waterlogged pit in the peat. This site is often mistaken with Anson NL185 a little lower down and parts from the latter aircraft are often found at this site, having been collected by well meaning but misinformed visitors.

North American Harvard Mk.IIB FT442: No.5 (P)AFU, RAF.   30-11-1944
Map No.63
SJ 997737 (1,750ft), Shining Tor, Buxton, Derbyshire.

    Sgt J. Sofranko (Czech)   Pilot   Killed

Sergeant Sofranko flew into Shining Tor in cloud while on a cross-country exercise from RAF Tern Hill near Market Drayton. The aircraft appears to have flown off course and then descended before it was clear of high ground.

Only the odd small pieces remain at the site, though there is a large crater, reputedly caused by an attempt to break up the engine with explosives following the war, clearly it was successful.

North American P-51D 44-72181 / VF-S: 336th FS / 4th FG, USAAF. 29-05-1945
Map No.64
SD 999112 (1,300ft), Castleshaw Moor, Delph, Greater Manchester.

1st Lt H.H. Fredericks	Pilot	Killed

This aircraft, which carried the name 'Sunny VIII', was one of twenty-three P-51s being ferried from Debden in Essex to Speke airfield on the edge of Liverpool, but while descending through dense cloud this aircraft ploughed into the high ground. A second aircraft from the flight crashed on private farmland near to Glossop.

Parts, including three sections from one of the wings, can be found at the site. The moorland at this site consists of quite long grass and at certain times of the year this can make the site fairly hard to locate.

North American Sabre F. Mk.2 19234: No.137 (T) Flt, RCAF. 14-12-1954
Map No.65
SE 091051 (1,750ft), Holme Moss, Black Hill, West Yorkshire.

F/O P.V. Robinson (RCAF)	Pilot	Killed

The Sabre was being flown on a test flight from Ringway prior to delivery to either the Greek or Turkish air forces when it crashed in bad weather scattering wreckage over a wide area.

Substantial sections of aircraft structure and the wings remain. There was once scattered wreckage along the flight path of the aircraft from where it first impacted the hill, though this is now gathered together into a single collection at the eastern end of one of the many exposed sections of peat.

North American Sabres F. Mk.4 XD707 / B and XD730 / X: 66 Sqn, RAF. 22-07-1954.
Map No.66
SK 073903 (1,500ft), Black Ashop Moor, Kinder Scout, Derbyshire.

F/O J.D. Horne	Pilot (XD707)	Killed
F/Lt A. Green	Pilot (XD730)	Killed

The two aircraft were returning to RAF Linton-on-Ouse near York from an unsuccessful interception exercise when they crashed, either due to a mid air collision as they climbed to avoid Kinder or they simply hit the hill during the climb.

As with the Meteors on Sliddens Moss, this is a very widely scattered wreck site with large remains from both aircraft at the given grid reference. The trail of wreckage begins up on Kinder at 1,950ft with wing and engine parts beside the Pennine Way at SK 069896 and continues beyond what is normally seen as the main site to an almost completely sunken engine nearly half a mile away and 500ft lower at SK 075904.

Remains of P-51 'Sunny VIII' on Castleshaw Moor.

The collected remains of RCAF Sabre 19234 on Black Hill with the Holme Moss television transmitter in the background.

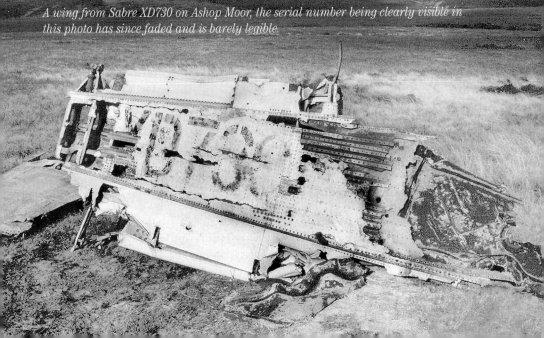

A wing from Sabre XD730 on Ashop Moor, the serial number being clearly visible in this photo has since faded and is barely legible.

Republic P-47C 41-6227 / UN-F: 63rd FS / 56th FG, USAAF.   25-04-1943
Map No.67
SK 093843 (1,650ft), Horsehill Tor, Edale, Derbyshire.

2nd Lt J.E. Coenen	Pilot	Survived

While on a ferry flight from Speke, following maintenance, to Horsham St Faith close to Norwich, the pilot lost control in severe turbulence while passing through a thundercloud. Realising he was unable to recover control of the aircraft, the pilot baled out.

A bare patch containing small parts from the aircraft marks where it dived into the hillside.

Republic P-47C 41-6628 / DQ-M: 552nd Ftr Tng Sqn / 495th FTG, USAAF. 03-10-1944
Map No.68
SK 021578 (1,100ft), Thorncliffe, Leek, Staffordshire.

2nd Lt Q.J. Sella	Pilot	Killed

The pilot was on a formation flying practise flight from Atcham near Shrewsbury that flight entered dense cloud. Shortly after entering the cloud 2nd Lt Sella lost control of the aircraft which then dived at high speed into a very soft patch of ground just off Easing Lane.

The site is close to the spot where a drainage ditch crosses a right of way marked on maps, though it is all but invisible on the ground. There is a white cross at the site with the name of the pilot recorded on it and a few scraps of metal. Note: the crash site is on private land, but is adjacent to a public right of way.

Republic P-47Ds 42-7872 and 42-7898 / VM-H: 2906th Ob. Grp., USAAF. 30-09-1943
Map No.69
SJ 995754 (1,500ft), Cats Tor, Macclesfield, Cheshire.

Capt M. Stepp	Pilot (42-7872)	Killed
S/Sgt L.R. Morrison	Pilot (42-7898)	Killed

The two aircraft were on a training flight from Atcham near Shrewsbury when they flew into the western side of Cats Tor in cloud while still in formation.

While there are only a few small scraps left at the site, there are still two obvious scars on the hillside next to each other, which can be seen from the road near Saltersford Hall.

Republic P-47D 42-74728: 551st Ftr Tng Sqn / 495th FTG, USAAF. 24-08-1944
Map No.70
SJ 919507 (750ft), Greenway Hall Golf Course, Stockton Brook, Staffordshire.

2nd Lt P.R. Fulton	Pilot	Killed

The pilot was on an instrument flying and aerobatics training flight from Atcham near Shrewsbury. During the aerobatics practice phase the pilot lost control of the aircraft.

The view down the vale of Edale from the crash site of Republic P-47C 41-6227 which crashed while returning to East Anglia from Speke after maintenance work.

He abandoned it while in a high speed dive, but opened his parachute too soon which caused severe neck and spinal injuries and damaged the parachute. He landed near Rudyard Reservoir at a higher speed than normal due to the damage to his parachute and this worsened the effects of his injuries from which he died shortly afterwards.

The aircraft came down on the edge of one of the golf course's fairways adjacent to a public right of way. When heading north-west along the path, the site is on the opposite side of the hedge which is to the left, just short a large holly bush. There is no wreckage at the site, though there is a shallow crater which is visible from the footpath.

Shorts Stirling Mk.I N6075 / SR-W3: No.101 Sqn 'C' Flt., RAF. 13-07-1942
Map No.71
SK 038611 (1,350ft), Merryton Low, Leek, Staffordshire.

Sgt R.U. Morrison	Pilot	Killed
Sgt W.A.G. Atkins	Flt Eng	Killed
Sgt J.E. Williams	Flt Eng	Killed
F/Sgt J.R. Griffin (RCAF)	Obs	Killed
F/Sgt T.E. Helgesen (RCAF)	WO/AG	Killed
F/Sgt J.F. Hirst (RCAF)	WO/AG	Killed
Sgt L.J. Regimbal (RCAF)	AG	Killed
Sgt E. Dolphin	Pass	Killed

The Stirling crashed into Merryton Low, some 200ft vertically below the trig point, while on a day time cross-country navigation exercise from RAF Oakington in Cambridgeshire in very low visibility. It is thought that the aircraft had overflown Biddulph shortly before the crash as the passenger was from the town.

Only small pieces of the aircraft can be found at the site which is close to the head of one of the streams that flow down to Upper Hulme and into the River Churnet.

Shorts Stirling Mk.III LJ628: No.1654 HCU, RAF.   21-07-1944
Map No.72
SK 202955 (1,550ft), Upper Commons, Langsett, South Yorkshire.

F/O L.T. Gardiner	Pilot	Survived
F/O J. O'Leary	Pilot (Inst)	Survived
Sgt J. Gittings	Flt Eng	Survived
Sgt McDonald	Nav	Survived
Sgt J. Coulson	BA	Survived
Sgt T. Burroughs	WO	Survived
Sgt Austin	AG	Survived
Sgt L. van Nierkirk	AG	Survived
S/Ldr Hadland	Pass	Survived

The crew was on a cross-country navigation exercise from RAF Wigsley, just inside Nottinghamshire to the west of Lincoln, when they entered thick cloud, while descending to obtain a position fix the aircraft struck high ground.

This was once one of the most impressive sites in the Peak District but much of the remaining wreckage was removed from the site to aid the Stirling Project in January 2005. Today only small pieces remain scattered over a wide area, the site previously was concentrated in the area around a gully containing almost all the remaining wreckage.

Supermarine Seafires F.R. Mk.17 SP325/103 and SX314: No.1831 Sqn, RN. 16-07-1949
Map No.73
SJ 992673 (1,400ft), Tagsclough Hill, Wildboarclough, Cheshire.

Lt E.H.R. Eccles (RN)	Pilot (SP314)	Killed
Lt F.J. Dyke (RN)	Pilot (SX325)	Killed

The two aircraft are believed to have collided in mid-air during a training flight from RNAS Stretton near Warrington.

There are a few parts from both aircraft scattered over a wide area, the largest remaining piece being a section of wing spar.

Vickers Wellington Mk.IC R1011 / M: No.28 OTU, RAF. 30-01-1943
Map No.74
SK 105986 (1,550ft), Birchen Bank Moss, Longdendale, Derbyshire.

F/Lt A.W. Lane	Pilot	Killed
P/O C.L. Grisedale	Nav	Survived
P/O C.D. Brown	BA	Killed
Sgt Miller	WO/AG	Survived
Sgt R.G. Rouse	WO/AG	Killed

The crash occurred while the crew was on a night cross-country navigation exercise from RAF Wymeswold near Loughborough. This was one of three aircraft lost in the region that night due to the weather, though the other two crashed on private land in lower lying areas.

A pile of small parts and sections of geodetic framework from the aircraft have been gathered together at the site, where a post with a ceramic plaque commemorating those who were killed can also be seen.

Vickers Wellington Mk.IC W5719 / JN-S: No.150 Sqn, RAF. 31-07-1941
Map No.75
SK 111875 (1,750ft), Far Upper Tor, Kinder Scout, Derbyshire.

Sgt J.A. Haswell	Pilot	Killed
Sgt P.H.C. Parrot	Pilot	Killed
Sgt J.D. Evelle (RCAF)	Obs	Killed
Sgt F.K. Webber	WO	Killed
Sgt D.A. Monk (RCAF)	AG	Killed
Sgt E. Tilley (RCAF)	AG	Survived

While returning to RAF Snaith near Selby in Yorkshire from a raid against Cologne the aircraft overshot its base and flew into Far Upper Tor. The rear gunner survived because his turret was thrown clear of the burning wreck on impact.

Small pieces of burnt aluminium litter the site and there is a brass plaque attached to the rock outcrop which the aircraft hit just above the wreckage.

Vickers Wellington Mk.IC Z8980: No.27 OTU, RAF. 17-07-1942
Map No.76
SK 262838 (1,350ft), Rud Hill, Ringinglow, South Yorkshire.

Sgt T.F. Thompson	Pilot	Survived
P/O J.W. Moore	Nav	Survived
Sgt J.H. Levett	WO	Survived
Sgt K.J.H. Harris (RAAF)	AG	Survived
Sgt J.H. Roden (RAAF)	AG	Survived

The aircraft flew into the flat moorland on Rud Hill while descending through cloud during a cross-country navigation exercise from RAF Lichfield in Staffordshire.

A bare patch of peat on the otherwise near featureless heather and grass covered moor contains numerous burnt pieces from the aircraft and a few sheets of armour plating.

Vickers Wellington Mk.IC DV810: No.21 OTU, RAF.   09-12-1942
Map No.77
SK 235954 (1,250ft), Broomhead Moor, Langsett, South Yorkshire.

P/O S. Baker	Pilot (Inst)	Survived
F/Sgt A.St.C. Turner (RAAF)	Pilot (u/t)	Survived
F/Sgt D.N. Dawson (RAAF)	Nav	Survived
Sgt R.D. Weeks	AG	Survived
F/Sgt W.S. Sinclair (RAAF)	BA	Survived
Sgt A.G. Allwright	WO	Survived

The crew was on a night cross-country navigation exercise from RAF Edge Hill near Banbury in very poor weather when the pilot became lost. While descending through cloud heading west one engine struck a low rise and caught fire, the pilot immediately carried out a crash landing on the gently sloping moor where the aircraft burned out.

There is a quantity of burnt debris and smaller metal in a scar on the moor and nearby are pieces of geodetic framework and sheets of armour plating.

Vickers Wellington Mk.III X3348 / ZL-Z: No.427 Sqn, RCAF.   26-01-1943
Map No.78
SK 128876 (1,900ft), Blackden Edge, Kinder Scout, Derbyshire.

F/Lt C.A. Taylor	Pilot	Survived
Sgt G.T. Southwood	Co-pilot	Survived
P/O G.A. Martin	Nav	Survived
P/O D. Mortimer	BA	Survived
Sgt A.P. Deane (RCAF)	WO	Survived
Sgt W. Lumsden	AG	Survived

The crew was trying to return to RAF Croft, near Darlington, from a raid against the French port of Lorient. Having missed their base, the aircraft struck the near level moorland not far from Ringing Roger and slid to a halt.

As the aircraft was nearly intact it was easily recovered and consequently only a few small pieces of geodetic framework remain in a bare patch of peat to the south of where Halifax HR727 crashed, not to the west as some sources suggest.

Vickers Wellington Mk.III BJ652 / Z: No.27 OTU, RAF.   21-01-1944
Map No.79
SK 196632 (700ft), Middleton by Youlgreave, Bakewell, Derbyshire.

F/Sgt L.G. Edmonds (RAAF)	Pilot	Killed
F/Sgt F.P. Deshorn (RAAF)	Nav	Killed
F/Sgt J. Kydd (RAAF)	BA	Killed
F/Sgt W.T. Barnes (RAAF)	WO	Killed
F/O K.J. Perrett (RAAF)	Nav	Killed
Sgt T.D. Murton (RAAF)	AG	Killed

The crash occurred while the crew was on a cross-country training flight from RAF Church Broughton near Derby, the crew was returning to the airfield when the aircraft flew into a limestone outcrop.

The crash site is located on private land near Smerrill and is not accessible by public rights of way. In the village of Middleton there is a memorial to the six crew which was placed there in 1995. The memorial is located on a stone cairn which is on the village green.

Vickers Wellington Mk.III HF613 / DD-R: No.22 OTU, RAF.   15-02-1943
Map No.80
SK 161834 (575ft), Peakshole Water, Hope, Derbyshire.

Sgt J.D. Kester (RCAF)	Pilot	Killed
Sgt R.F. Cairns (RCAF)	Nav	Killed
Sgt W.A.B. Marwood	WO	Killed
Sgt W.J. Hackett (RCAF)	AG	Killed
Sgt B.E. Wilkinson (RCAF)	AG	Killed

The crew was on a day cross-country training flight from RAF Wellesbourne-Mountford near Stratford on Avon. The aircraft encountered severe icing conditions in a snow squall and rapidly lost height. While possibly trying to force land the aircraft dived into the ground.

The site of the crash is located on private farm land, however there is a memorial set into a wall beside the A6187 Hope to Castleton road just to the east of Marston Farm.

Vickers Wellington T. Mk.10 MF627: No.6 ANS, RAF.   17-10-1952
Map No.81
SK 264892 (1,100ft), Rod Moor, Sheffield, South Yorkshire.

Sgt R. Keith	Pilot	Survived
P/O J.B.S. Thirkell	Nav (u/t)	Survived
P/O D.E. Ward	Nav (u/t)	Survived

The two trainee navigators became disorientated while on a night cross-country navigation exercise from RAF Lichfield and the pilot was lead to believe they were further south than they actually were.

No surface wreckage remains at this site, which is on a grassy slope above Hall Broom, but a secion of demolished wall on the brow of the hill is evident. Note: this site is on private land.

Westland Lysander Mk.IIIA V9403: No.6 AACU, RAF.   18-08-1941
Map No.82
SE 041032 (1,700ft), Slate Pit Moss, Chew Reservoir.

P/O F.W. Hoddinott	Pilot	Survived
LAC A.M. Chadwick	WO	Died of Injuries 24-08-1941

The aircraft was to take part in a night-time anti-aircraft co-operation exercise near Rhyl on the North Wales coast, but on take-off from Ringway, near Manchester, the pilot flew on the reciprocal course to the one he should have flown and crashed on the moor near Chew Reservoir. The upturned aircraft was not found until the 20th August.

A few pieces of wood and a couple of small sections of aluminium are all that remain from this aircraft on what is one of the most bleak areas of moorland in the Peak District.

Chapter Four

The Pennines

Often called the 'backbone of England', the Pennines are a low mountain range stretching from the Peak District in Derbyshire, through the Yorkshire Dales, the West Pennine Moors of Lancashire and Cumbrian Fells to the Cheviot Hills on the Anglo-Scottish border. To the north, they have been designated an Area of Outstanding Natural Beauty, created under the same legislation as the national parks and affording them the same degree of protecton on planning consent and other sensitive issues. To the south they are designated as a Special Protection Area, comprising several Sites of Special Scientific Interest (SSSIs) and parts of the Pennines also lie within the Peak District (Covered in a section on its own), Yorkshire Dales and Northumberland National Parks. But perhaps they are best known to walkers through the Pennine Way, which was Britain's first long-distance footpath and runs the full length of the Pennine chain at nearly 270 miles long. Covering several counties and a wide variety of terrain, this area is generally associated with high moorland, often covering large areas and with few landmarks or paths and a distinct atmosphere of remoteness. This is certainly true, especialy of the northern sections, where many summits exceed 2,000ft (Cross Fell being the highest summit of the Pennines at 2,930ft) and searching for wreck sites requires perseverence, correct equipment and good navigational skills. The landscape is however largely dictated by the underlying Carboniferous limestone and deltaic sandstones (locally referred to as Millstone Grit), depending on the area. The moors may also include distinctive geological features, including limestone pavements, sink holes and underground cave systems. The central area also encompasses the Forest of Bowland, an area dominated by grit stone fells with summits above 1,500ft and large areas of heather-covered and often boggy peat moorland. Clearly with such a diverse range of landscapes and the usual changeable weather conditions over high ground, all the usual warnings apply to visiting the sites listed in this section.

During WW2 the Pennines formed a natural barrier across the centre of the north of England as far as aircraft were concerned, particularly for those on ferry or training flights, attempting to stay below the cloud for navigation purposes. Many such flights were routed through gaps, such as those formed by the rivers Tyne and Aire, avoiding the highest ground, but basic navigational equipment, lack of experience and prevalent poor weather conditions all too often combined with tragic results. The aircraft involved in these incidents originated from many parts of the country, as no airfields were actually located within this area, though there were many around the immediate periphery. The need to train aircrew in navigational skills, particularly when flying at night, meant a huge increase in the numbers of aircraft in the air during wartime and such training was often carried out over such remote areas. The combination of aircrew inexperience, the proximity of the high ground and night flying often in poor weather, often proved lethal and the reader will note that on more than one occasion incidents in this section occurred on the same night involving different aircraft from the same unit. Though pilots ferrying aircraft over the Pennines might be regarded as more experienced, it was still this combination of high ground and deteriorating weather that proved lethal in most cases. Especially vulnerable it seems were American crews travelling between their operational bases to the east and the huge USAAF Base Air Depot repair and supply centres in the north-west. Though their crews were often experienced, it seems that the rapidly changeable British weather conditions and difficulty navigating over such an unfamiliar landscape could catch out the unwary. Very few losses were in fact as a direct result of combat, even the only German loss listed was more likely as a result of attempting to descend below cloud to confirm their position, though a number of Allied aircraft on operational missions became lost and overshot their Yorkshire bases, eventually being forced to descend as their fuel ran low. Winter Hill to the western edge of the range has perhaps caught out more flyers than any other Pennine peak, rising, as it does, above the relatively flat Manchester plain and was the scene of Britain's worst high ground crash in 1958 when Bristol Freighter G-AICS came to grief with the loss of thirty-five lives.

The majority of the Pennine losses occurred on the less accessible and largely uninhabited high moorland areas, leading to a number of occasions where aircraft remained undiscovered for some time. Despite this a good many were subject to seemingly unprecedented major recovery operations and completely cleared, such as the Wellington at Anglezarke and unless marked with a memorial, as this example is, they have not been included. However, this approach was far from consistent and many of the sites listed were cleared by the simple expedient of chopping the remains up and burying them and it is a combination of natural erosion and the activities of enthusiasts and curious walkers over the years that have uncovered the remains that can be seen today.

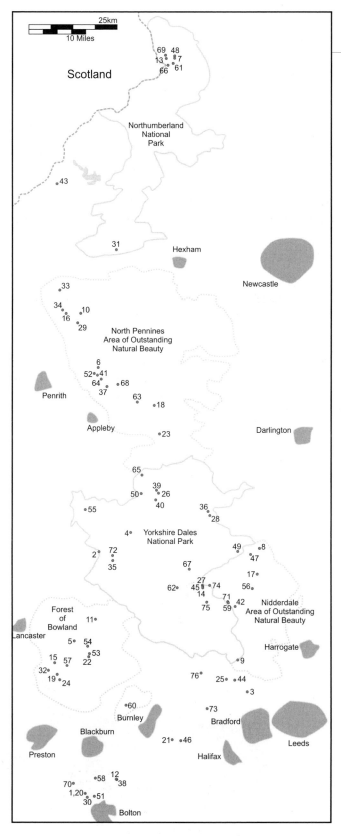

Crash Sites in the Pennines.

Airspeed Oxford Mk.I BM837: No.410 Sqn, RCAF.   24-12-1943
Map No.1
SD 663149 (1,450ft), Winter Hill, Bolton, Lancashire

F/Lt	M.A. Cybulski (RCAF)	Pilot	Survived

F/Lt Cybulski was flying from Acklington in Northumberland to Coleby Grange near Lincoln and had flown off course by up to 90 miles, though there is a possibility he was flying to another airfield en route. While descending through cloud, the aircraft struck the eastern face of Winter Hill.

A small scar on the hill, containing a few fragments of the aircraft and traces of yellow painted fabric and wood, marks where the wreck was probably burnt by the local Maintenance Unit following the crash.

Note: Flt. Lt. 'Cy' Cybulski was awarded the DFC in November 1943 – earlier that year he had become something of a celebrity when the Mosquito he was flying was photographed after he successfully landed it with most of its control surfaces and markings burnt away, when a Do 217 he had been attacking exploded close to his aircraft.

Airspeed Oxford Mk.I DF471: No.427 Sqn, RCAF.   29-08-1943
Map No.2
SD 702828 (2,025ft), Great Coum, Dent, Cumbria

Sgt R.L. Henry (RCAF)	Pilot	Killed
Cpl W.P. Holt (RCAF)	Pass	Killed
Cpl J.E. Keighan (RCAF)	Pass	Killed
LAC D.W. Davies (RCAF)	Pass	Killed

DF471 was on a transport flight from the squadron's base at Leeming, North Yorkshire to RAF Ford, Sussex, with the pilot and three ground crew, on their way to repair one of

The largest remaining section from Oxford DF471 is this section of wing spar with part of the main undercarriage still attached.

the Squadron's Halifax aircraft there. In poor weather conditions and without a navigator on board, the aircraft flew into high ground at 15:00 hrs.

Where the aircraft struck the brow of the hill, there is an area of peat in a dip containing a few fragments of wreckage, while nearby are several small sections of wing structure and parts from an undercarriage assembly. At the foot of the steep slope below the site, several aluminium alloy panels from the aircraft lie in a hollow.

Armstrong Whitworth Whitley Mk.V T4225: No.4 FPP, ATA.   16-10-1940
Map No.3
SE 130433 (1,025ft), Horncliffe Well, Bingley, West Yorkshire

F/O T.D. Trouncer	Pilot	Killed

This aircraft was on a ferry flight to Prestwick, Ayrshire with only an RAF pilot who was assigned to the ATA on board. The aircraft entered cloud and subsequently flew into the high ground and burned out.

Small pieces of aluminium remain at the site, scattered in the heather at the base of a rise in the moorland, where the aircraft crashed. Recently these have been made more visible by moorland fires.

Armstrong Whitworth Whitley Mk.V T4234: No.10 Sqn, RAF.   23-08-1941.
Map No.4
SD 793882 (2,050ft), Widdale Fell, Dent, Cumbria.

P/O K.W. Liebeck (RCAF)	Pilot	Killed
Sgt G. Fletcher	Pilot	Killed
Sgt R. Silver	Nav	Survived
Sgt M. McLaughlin	WO	Survived
Sgt R. Speer	AG	Survived

On a return flight to RAF Leeming from a raid against the French port of Le Havre the pilot became lost in cloud and attempted to descend to locate his position, hitting high ground at 01:41hrs.

A few small pieces of the aircraft remain on the Cumbrian (western) side of the dry stone wall which marks the county boundary.

Avro Anson Mk.I N4919: No.2 (O)AFU, RAF.   09-02-1944
Map No.5
SD 630577 (1,675ft), Wolfhole Crag, Forest of Bowland, Lancashire

F/Sgt A. Dobson	Pilot	Survived
Sgt Edwards	1st Nav	Survived
Sgt Enoch	2nd Nav	Survived
2 Unnamed crewmembers		Survived

Aircraft encountered adverse weather conditions during a cross-country navigational exercise flying with No. 2 (Observer) Advanced Flying Unit based at Millom in Cumbria. Although the pilot knew he was still some 6 miles from the estimated position where it

Pieces from the wings of Anson N4919 and a couple of crumpled engine cowling panels, still bearing traces of their yellow painted finish, lie amongst the rocks.

was safe to descend, he was forced to lose altitude over high ground due to icing up of his aircraft. Despite the lack of visibility he managed to effect a forced landing on the moors.

Today the site can be somewhat tricky to find as the main impact area, where much of the aircraft was later burnt to effect its disposal, is now largely being reclaimed by the plant life. The few larger panels remaining appear to have been collected up and hidden amongst nearby rocks, perhaps in an effort to tidy up the appearance of the moor.

Avro Anson Mk.I DJ453: No.4 AOS, RAF. 18-03-1943
Map No.6
NY 699345 (2,700ft), Cross Fell, Appleby, Cumbria.

Sgt V.H. Hill	Pilot	Survived
4 Unnamed	Crew Members	Survived

On a cross-country navigational exercise when the aircraft began to ice-up in cloud. The pilot descended over high ground and carried out a crash landing on the southern side of Cross Fell.

The site lies partly in a patch of scree and small pieces, some still bearing yellow paint, can be found amongst the rocks. The actual impact point is close by on the grass between the scree and the fence, which runs across that part of the hill.

Avro Lancaster Mk.X KB745 / VR-V: No.419 Sqn, RCAF. 04-10-1944
Map No.7
NT 917215 (2,025ft), Mid Hill, The Cheviot, Northumberland

F/O G.R. Duncan (RCAF)	Pilot	Killed
F/O W.G. Layng (RCAF)	Nav	Killed
P/O W.R. Karstens (RCAF)	WO	Killed
F/O A. Gaddess (RCAF)	BA	Killed
P/O J.W.F. Hall	Flt Eng	Killed
P/O D.A. Trott (RCAF)	AG	Killed
P/O T.B. Tierney (RCAF)	AG	Killed

This aircraft crossed the English coast some 90 miles north of its intended route and crashed whilst returning to Middleton St George from a raid against U-Boat pens at Bergen. It had possibly been attacked by a nightfighter, as undercarriage parts recovered from the site have obvious damage from 20mm and 7.92mm ammunition.

Only small pieces remain today, where the aircraft burned out.

Avro Lancaster B. Mk.I NF963 / BQ-A: No.550 Sqn, RAF. 04-10-1944
Map No.8
SE 164837 (900ft), Ellingstring, Masham, North Yorkshire

F/O S.H. Hayter	Pilot	Survived
F/O R.R. Bradshaw (RNZAF)	BA	Killed
F/O T.Y. Thomas	Nav	Killed
Sgt L.A. Bassman	Flt Eng	Killed
Sgt A.J. Pearce	WO	Killed
Sgt J. McVey	AG	Killed
Sgt J.P. Sheridan	AG	Killed

This aircraft broke up in mid-air whilst in a dive, during which the cockpit section broke free, allowing the pilot to escape. Other crew members are reported to have also escaped the aircraft but were too low for their parachutes to be effective.

A collection of wreckage and a piece of armour plate can be found next to a track.

Avro Lancaster B. Mk.I RA571: No.429 Sqn, RCAF, 05-11-1945
Map No.9
SE 101523 (1,200 ft), Beamsley Beacon / Howber Hill, Ilkley, West Yorkshire

F/O W.F. Conley(RCAF)	Pilot	Killed
F/Sgt A.E. Stinson (RCAF)	Flt Eng	Killed
F/O A. Coleman (RCAF)	Nav	Survived
F/O W.E. Lang (RCAF)	BA	Killed
F/Sgt F.J. Moran (RCAF)	WO/AG	Survived
Cpl W.J. Ellis (RCAF)	AG	Killed
Sgt J.P. Balenger (RCAF)	AG	Survived
LAC R.E. Henderson (RCAF)	AG	Survived

Whilst on a training flight from RAF Leeming, near Northallerton, in poor weather conditions, the pilot became lost flying in cloud and descended in order to obtain confirmation of their position. The aircraft struck the southern side of the hill, just below the summit, disintegrating and immediately catching fire. One of the four survivors, who was less injured than his comrades, managed to make his way down to a nearby farm and summon help.

A small collection of burnt alloy fragments remains at the site today, though these can be difficult to find as they are well hidden amongst the heather.

Avro Tutor Mk.I K3422: No.16 Gp Communications Flight, RAF. 15-01-1940
Map No.10
NY 649498 (1,350 ft), Green Hill, Slaggyford, Northumberland

Name not known	Pilot	Survived

During a formation ferry flight from RAF Linton-on-Ouse in North Yorkshire to RAF Kirkbride in Cumbria, the aircraft entered cloud and became separated from the formation. Rather than attempt a forced landing, which would have necessitated descending through the cloud, the pilot baled out of the aircraft, leaving it to dive into the moorland. Tutor K4820 which was also in the formation force landed successfully near Alston.

A few small pieces of airframe still remain at the site, partially buried in a sink hole. In 1986 the Armstrong Siddeley Lynx engine from the aircraft was recovered from the site for the North East Aircraft Museum.

Blackburn Skua [L2929]: No.4 FPP ATA.   12-09-1940
Map No.11
SD 691638 (1,175ft), Cantsfield Dyke Nook, Burn Moor, High Bentham, Lancashire

PO D.R. Strachan	Pilot	Survived

The serial number of this aircraft is unconfirmed and probably incorrect, but its engine failed on a ferry flight from Hullavington to Donbristle and with no where suitable to attempt a forced landing, the pilot baled out leaving the aircraft to crash on open moorland.

A slight hollow with a bare patch of peat marks the impact point, where the shattered engine, propeller and undercarriage were recovered in 1980s, but small fragments may still be found widely scattered amongst the peat groughs that are a feature of this moor. Parts may also be seen near a ruined bothy, possibly left there by curious beaters.

Boeing B17G 42-31581: BAD1, USAAF.   13-01-1944
Map No.12
SD 751188 (1,100ft), Crowthorn, Edgeworth, Lancashire

2nd Lt D.E. Harris	Pilot	Survived
Lt MacDonald	Co-pilot	Survived
1stLt L.E. Tracy	Gnd Eng	Killed
S/Sgt T. Kristin	Pass	Killed
T/Sgt L.B. Woodall	Pass	Killed
Mr W.H. Killough	Pass	Killed

This was a routine test flight of a newly delivered B-17 from the USAAF Base Air Depot 1 at Burtonwood. On board was the usual crew of three, required for such a flight and also three passengers – two enlisted men and a civilian engineer. After several minutes flying through the cloud, the pilot decided to turn for home and began to descend, expecting at any moment to break out of the cloud over the lowland plain west of Manchester. However the aircraft had drifted further to the east than had been anticipated and at around 1,100ft the plane slammed into the hillside above the village of Edgeworth. The three passengers, sight-seeing in the glazed bombardiers compartment and the Ground Engineer, in the Co-pilot's seat, were killed instantly. The aircraft disintegrated and the fuel tanks exploded scattering wreckage over a wide area. The pilot managed to free himself and pulled the only other, seriously wounded, survivor clear.

No surface remains are normally visible at this site, though small fragments may occasionally be seen due to erosion around the still demolished wall where the fuselage came to rest and burned out, or by the partially rebuilt wall where the aircraft first impacted.

Boeing B-17G 44-6504 / PU-M: 360th BS / 303rd BG, USAAF.   16-12-1944
Map No.13
NT 895213 (2,325ft), Braydon Crag, The Cheviot, Northumberland

2nd Lt G.A. Kyle	Pilot	Survived
Flt Off J.H. Hardy	Co-pilot	Survived
Sgt E.G. Schieferstein	Flt Eng	Survived
Flt Off F. Holcombe Jr	Nav	Killed
Sgt F. Turner	Togglier	Killed
Sgt J.A. Berly Jnr	Radio Op	Survived
Sgt G.P. Smith	Gunner	Survived
Sgt H.F. Delaney	Gunner	Survived
Sgt W.R. Kaufmann	Gunner	Survived

Returning from an unsuccessful raid against Ulm, 2nd Lt Kyle became disorientated in low cloud during a snowstorm and flew into high ground, skidding across the moor and burst into flames. Two crew members died in the crash and the rest, with varying injuries managed to free each other from the wreckage and were led from the moor by locals before the bomb load exploded.

A scar on the moor contains a large number of parts including undercarriage and structural remains, nearby a gully contains an engine nacelle and other pieces.

Boeing B-17G 44-8683/'Dear Mom': 561st BS /388th BG, USAAF. 17-05-1945
Map No.14
SE 001727 (1,950ft), Great Whernside, Kettlewell, North Yorkshire

1st Lt H.M. Cole	Pilot	Killed
2nd Lt V.L. Ferguson	Co-Pilot	Killed
2nd Lt J.M. Young	Nav	Killed
Sgt H.E. Dixon	Eng	Killed
S/Sgt D. Battista	Radio Op	Killed

From Station 136 Knettishall, Suffolk, this B-17 was on a 1,000 mile night navigation training flight from base to Newcastle, then Lands End and back to base. On the second leg from Newcastle to Lands End the weather deteriorated and the pilot is believed to have abandoned the flight and was turning back towards their base when at 15:50, the aircraft struck the mist shrouded side of Great Whernside at cruising speed, killing all on board.

Tiny fragments may be found where the aircraft impacted on the hillside and numerous scattered small aluminium airframe remains lie on the surface at the bottom of the slope below this point, together with some steel components from the undercarriage operating system.

Boulton Paul Defiant I N1651 / JT-Z: No.256 Sqn, RAF.   18-08-1941
Map No.15
SD 574516 (1,350ft), Hawthornthwaite Fell, Forest of Bowland, Lancashire

  P/O N.J. Sharpe   Pilot   Killed

The Defiant was on a practice night flight, from Squires Gate, Blackpool with the only occupant being the 20 year-old pilot. At approx. 22:30 hours the aircraft was flying straight and level when it struck rising moorland, just below the summit of the fell. The unfortunate pilot was found the next day, having crawled about a mile from the wreck before losing consciousness due to his injuries. He was taken to Lancaster Infirmary, but sadly died that evening. Locals strongly believe to this day that he would have survived had help reached him sooner.

The crash site lies on an area of moorland that has suffered severe erosion over recent years. A small collection of parts, mainly wing spar remains and corrugated aluminium fragments from this aircraft, lies exposed on the bare peat, where the aircraft was dismantled.

Fragments of Defiant N1651, left where the largely intact aircraft was dismantled on an area now subject to dramatic erosion of the peat.

Bristol Beaufighter T. F. Mk.X JM223: No.9 OTU, RAF.   04-07-1943
Map No.16
NY 606497 (1,800ft), Croglin Fell, Carlisle, Cumbria

F/O H.J Carver RCAF	Pilot	Killed
F/O R.A. Sedgley	Nav	Killed

The aircraft dived into moorland on the top of Croglin Fell when the pilot lost control in cloud while on a cross-country navigation training flight from RAF Crosby-on-Eden near Carlisle.

The site is marked by a crater containing a few pieces of the aircraft. This is located near to one of many drainage ditches, which run across the top of the fell.

Bristol Blenheim Mk.I K7076: No.54 OTU, RAF.   27-01-1941
Map No.17
SE 158765 (1,075ft), Arnagill Moor, Pateley Bridge, North Yorkshire

P/O R.M. Graham	Pilot	Survived

On a training flight from Church Fenton, North Yorkshire. In poor weather conditions, the pilot attempted to descend below cloud to establish his position, believing he was over water and at 04.50 the aircraft flew into high ground.

A collection of smaller broken airframe parts mark the crash site today lying together in a boggy shallow depression on the moor.

Bristol Blenheim Mk.I L1252: No.34 Sqn, RAF.   26-10-1938
Map No.18
NY 861238 (2,000ft), Hargill Beck, Middleton-in-Teesdale, County Durham

P/O J.O. Sowerbutts	Pilot	Killed
AC1 W. Ashbridge	Fitter (II)/AG	Killed
AC2 H. Redfern	WO/AG (u/t)	Killed

The crew was taking part in a cross-country navigation exercise from RAF Upper Heyford in Oxfordshire to RAF Kingstown near Carlisle with another Blenheim. The two aircraft became separated in cloud and L1252 dived into moorland southeast of Mickle Fell, possibly following loss of control in the overcast.

Wreckage is located in two gullies and a hollow where the shattered remains of the aircraft were buried after the crash. Remaining wreckage consists of sections of skinning, though the partial remains of the tail wheel oleo, crew access door and a cylinder from one of the engines may be seen.

One of the larger pieces of Blenheim L1252 remaining at the site today.

Fragments from Blenheim K7076 remaining on Arnagill Moor.

Bristol Blenheim Mk.V BA246: N0. 12 (P)AFU, RAF. 09-04-1944
Map No.19
SD 579483 (1,475ft), Bleasdale Fell, Forest of Bowland, Lancashire

F/Sgt D.L. Edmonds	Instructor	Killed
F/Sgt J.C. Stones	Pilot (u/t)	Killed

This Blenheim was from No.12 (Pilot) Advanced Flying Unit and took off from RAF Woodvale near Southport on the evening of the 9 August 1944 for a night training exercise when weather conditions began to deteriorate. Despite this the crew apparently decided to continue with the exercise and sometime between 23:40 and 23:59 hours the aircraft struck the summit of Bleasdale Fell, bursting into flames and killing both occupants instantly. A surprising amount of wreckage still lies at the scene of the crash today, though the condition of many parts is poor, probably due to the effects of the fire and the exposed position of the site on open moorland. The most obviously

The main undercarriage legs from Blenheim BA246 lying where the aircraft burnt out.

recognisable components are the two main undercarriage legs lying close to the partially buried main wing-spar which has remnants of the engine nacelles still attached. Nearby in a gully lie many larger pieces of alloy, mainly comprising what appear to be aluminium fuel cells. The engines themselves were no doubt recovered at the time of the crash, as there is no evidence of them at the scene today.

Bristol 170 Freighter Mk.21E G-AICS: Silver City Airways.   27-02-1958
Map No.20
SD662149 (1,450ft), Winter Hill, Lancashire

Capt M. Cairns	Pilot	Survived
1st Off W. Howarth	Co-Pilot	Survived
Ms J. Curtis	Stwd	Survived
33 Passengers	See Appendices	Killed
5 Passengers	See Appendices	Survived
1 Passenger	See Appendices	Died of Injuries

This aircraft was on a flight from the Isle Of Man to Manchester with thirty-nine passengers and three crew. The pilot had accepted a clearance to fly at 1,500ft prior to take-off in order to avoid delay. During the flight, the first officer set the radio compass on an incorrect navigation beacon and as the mistake went unnoticed by the Captain, the aircraft gradually approached high ground. At 09:44, a message from Manchester Control, which had spotted the possible danger, ordered the aircraft to make a right turn immediately on to a new heading. Shortly after, in zero visibility and whilst making the turn as ordered, the aircraft crashed on the north-east slope of Winter Hill, at a height of approximately 1,460ft.

There is little to see at the actual crash site today – a few badly corroded fragments of aluminium may be found amongst the heather, but large flakes of paint, stripped from the transmitter masts by the ferocious winds here, can easily confuse the eye. There is a memorial plaque on the side of the main transmitter station, which acknowledges both those who perished and the survivors in what was the area's worst air disaster.

Consolidated B-24J 42-50668 / 6X-M: 854th BS 491st BG, USAAF. 19-02-1945
Map No.21
SD 912300 (1,450ft), Black Hameldon, Burnley, Lancashire

1st Lt C.A. Goeking	Pilot	Survived
1st Lt G.H. Smith Jr	Co-pilot	Killed
1st Lt F.E. Bock	Nav	Killed
T/Sgt H.E. Denham Jr	Eng	Killed
T/Sgt L.E. Johnson	Radio Op	Survived
2nd Lt E.R. Brater	Pass	Killed
2nd Lt J.B. Walker III	Pass	Killed
Flt. Off G. Procita	Pass	Killed
Flt. Off D.A. Robinson Jr	Pass	Killed
Sgt R.E. Hyett	Pass	Survived
Sgt R.R. Mohlenrich Jr	Pass	Killed

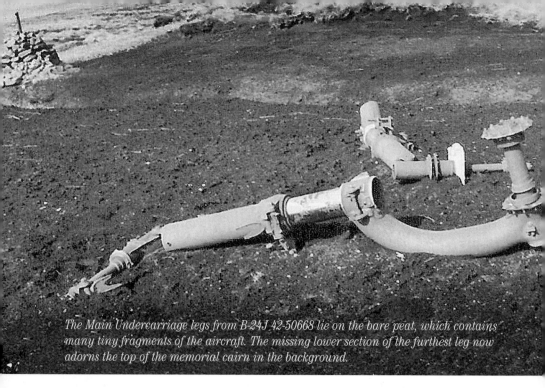

The Main Undercarriage legs from B-24J 42-50668 lie on the bare peat, which contains many tiny fragments of the aircraft. The missing lower section of the furthest leg now adorns the top of the memorial cairn in the background.

The B-24 was being returned to Base Air Depot 1, Burtonwood from its base, AAF Station 143, North Pickenham, Norfolk, but weather conditions deteriorated as they made their way Northwards. In poor visibility the pilot glimpsed towns below and assumed he was over Liverpool and altered heading accordingly. However, the new course in fact headed toward high ground and the aircraft impacted with the hillside in cloud at 16:25, tail-first and under full power, disintegrating as it ploughed on some 100 yards up the slope. Six crew members initially survived the impact, all gravely injured and three died in hospital over the next few days.

A cairn topped by part of the undercarriage marks the crash site today, with the largest remains being the two main undercarriage legs, which together with many tiny fragments lie on a large bare patch of peat on the western side of Black Hameldon.

Note: This aircraft was a veteran of twenty-six combat missions and had been recently overhauled and fitted with two new engines.

Consolidated B-24J 42-100322 / 'Come Along Boys': 714th BS 448th BG, USAAF. 02-01-45
Map No.22
SD 671531 (1,375ft), Burn Fell, Forest of Bowland, Lancashire

2nd Lt C.C. Crandell	Pilot	Survived
2nd Lt A.H. Carey	Co-Pilot	Survived
2nd Lt M.K. Dan	Nav	Survived
Sgt O.W. Olson	Radio Op	Survived
T/Sgt D. Zeldin	Flt Eng	Survived
1st Lt C.H. Holt	Acting Pilot	Survived
4 Passengers	See Appendices	Killed
9 Passengers	See Appendices	Survived

This war-weary aircraft was on a ferry flight, being returned to Base Air Depot 2 at Warton, Lancashire from AAF Station 146, Seething, Norfolk. On board, in addition to a crew of five, was an additional relief crew, who were to fly a new aircraft back to the base, as well as nine servicemen bound for leave in Blackpool. With the pilot of the relief crew, Lt. Holt at the controls, they experienced navigational difficulties in deteriorating weather conditions. Shortly after 14:30 the pilot attempted to descend in order to obtain a more accurate fix, but as visibility at lower altitude was apparently non-existent he pulled back on the control column in order to regain height. With the aircraft in this tail-down attitude, it struck the summit ridge of Burn Fell, tearing the fuselage apart as the bomber skidded across the moor and then erupted in flames. Despite their injuries, those that survived quickly vacated the shattered bomber and it was realised that by some miracle fifteen of their number had in fact survived.

Until recently the site was marked by two huge main undercarriage legs, which have now been removed. Today there are only a few scraps of aluminium amongst the heather on one side of the wall that runs along the crest of the fell and a large bare burnt area on the other side, with numerous small scraps, including exploded .50 in calibre cases. The wall was completely rebuilt and now weathered it is difficult to tell where the four-engine bomber smashed its way through.

Note: This aircraft flew some fifty-six combat missions, all with the 448th BG, from February 1944 through to the end of August 1944, often as a lead or deputy lead aircraft and returned damaged on several occasions. Additionally it is believed to have flown on another twenty-four combat missions for which records are not available.

Curtiss Tomahawk Mk.I AH744: No.1472 Flt, RAF.   10-02-1943
Map No.23
NY 876159 (1,500ft), Red Gill Moss, Bowes, County Durham

F/O H.E. Wright	Pilot	Killed

F/O Wright was a newly arrived pilot on local flying practice from the RAF Station at Catterick, in North Yorkshire. The aircraft was last seen near Barnard Castle flying in a westerly direction at 5,000 feet by the Royal Observer Corps. The crash site was located three days later, after a search hampered by persistent low cloud. The aircraft had apparently struck high ground in cloud and broken up over a wide area.

The site is located at 1,500ft on an almost flat patch of moor. Large portions of the aircraft remained at the site until 1979 when the complete starboard wing was recovered by the North East Aircraft Museum from Sunderland. Also around this time the Allison engine was removed from the site. Today a reasonable amount still remains with a large number of panels, mainly from the wings, in three distinct collections of parts.

De Havilland DH-84 Dragon II G-ADEE: Railway Air Services Ltd. 26-10-1935
Map No.24
SD 589467 (1,475ft), Fairsnape Fell, Forest of Bowland, Lancashire

Capt C.R. Crow	Pilot	Killed
Mr R. Swales	Pass	Killed

This aircraft was on a scheduled service from Manchester (Barton) to Ronaldsway on the Isle of Man, via Liverpool (Speke) and Blackpool. The pilot had been advised to fly at lower than normal altitude due to deteriorating visibility, which should have presented no problem as the intended route followed the coast. The aircraft was fifteen miles off course when it struck the 1,700ft high fell, in a steeply climbing attitude, killing both occupants instantly and bursting into flames.

Only very small fragments remain at this site jammed amongst rocks some 200ft below the summit of the fell and most are in very poor condition from the effects of the fire, plus over seventy years exposure to the elements on this bleak fell.

This large wing section from Tomahawk AH744, held up for the camera by Mark Sheldon, is the largest piece at the site today.

De Havilland Mosquito N.F. Mk.II DD750: No.25 Sqn, RAF.   23-03-1943
Map No.25
SE 069469 (1,200ft), White Crag, Silsden in West Yorkshire

Sgt Staples, J.H.	Pilot	Killed
Sgt Andrews R.E.	Nav / WO	Killed

This aircraft had been deployed from its home base at RAF Church Fenton near York to RAF Coltishall in Norfolk during the afternoon of the 22nd March 1943, in preparation for a 'Ranger' operation against opportune ground targets over occupied Europe that night. However, the operation was cancelled and on their return flight to their home base, the pilot flew too far west and while descending through cloud struck the gently sloping hillside not far from White Crag Plantation, where the aircraft broke up and burst into flames.

A bare patch in the heather marks the crash site, where only a handful of brass wood screws and other tiny fragments including burnt pieces of wood can be found – these brass screws are a common feature of Mosquito crash sites.

De Havilland Mosquito N.F. Mk.30 NT544: No.54 OTU, RAF.   10-01-1946
Map No.26
SD 873993 (1,800ft), Blackburn Edge, Keld, North Yorkshire

F/Lt T.A. Roskilly	Pilot	Killed
F/Sgt S.A. Whiting	Nav	Killed

This aircraft was on a night cross-country training exercise from East Moor, Helmsley, Yorkshire, when it struck high ground west of Keld at around 20:00 hours and exploded. The aircraft appeared to have flown straight into the fell at cruising speed and was largely destroyed by the impact and the ensuing fierce fire. The accident was attributed to the crew having failed to maintain a minimum clearance altitude of 2000ft as they had been briefed.

Only a few scattered parts remain to mark the crash site today – most of the wooden airframe was no doubt consumed in the fire. A section of armour plate is the largest item, lying on a bare patch of peat covered with many small fragments, including many brass screws.

De Havilland Mosquito N.F. Mk.36 RL197: No.228 OCU, RAF. 13-12-1948
Map No.27
SE 000734 (2,000ft), Great Whernside, Kettlewell, North Yorkshire

P/O A.G. Bulley	Pilot	Killed
F/Lt B.O. Bridgman	Nav	Killed

Flying from RAF Leeming for a night cross-country navigation exercise, the crew was slightly off course in deteriorating weather conditions. In dense cloud they descended to approximately 2,000ft and struck the west face of 2,300ft Great Whernside at cruising speed at 22:00hrs. The aircraft exploded on impact and scattered parts over a wide area.

It was not until late the following day that a local shepherd made the grim discovery, ending a nation-wide search for the missing aircraft.

Little remains on the crash site of RL197 today and what is left is well scattered, some parts even mixed with those of other victims of this peak. Undercarriage remains, cowling panels and flap parts may be identified as from this aircraft, but rumoured engine remains no longer seem to be present.

De Havilland Mosquito F.B. Mk.VI TA525: No.13 OTU, RAF.   14-02-1946
Map No.28
SE 021930 (1,300ft), Rowantree Park, Castle Bolton, North Yorkshire

Sgt G. La Hei (RNLAF)   Pilot   Killed

The pilot was on a solo training flight from RAF Middleton St George, the current Teeside Airport, when he lost control of the aircraft in cloud and dived into the ground.

Parts from the aircraft are scattered over a wide area, with a collection of wreckage in a shallow pit and the smashed parts of one of the engines lying partially buried nearby. There are also a few pieces near the mouth of one of many potholes in the area.

Parts from Mosquito TA525 lying where they have been collected together in a shallow pit on the moor.

De Havilland Venom F.B. Mk.4 WR557: No.22 MU, RAF.   04-03-1957
Map No.29
NY 640473 (1,925ft), Farlam Currick, Croglin Fell, Cumbria

F/L W.F. Marshall   Pilot   Killed

During a routine test flight from RAF Silloth, Cumbria, the pilot contacted flying control to report an elevator problem and a few minutes later he requested to return to the airfield, suggesting he still had control of the aircraft. He then remained in contact with Flying Control for a while without making any further reference to any control issues, before they lost contact. The investigators concluded that while inbound to the airfield

A large section of wing from Venom WR557, with the aircraft's serial number and roundel still just discernable. In the foreground is one of the combustion chambers.

the pilot had simply descended through cloud while still over high ground.

The crash site is well scattered, illustrating the high speed nature of the impact. The main wreckage lies in a pit on the top of the ridge adjacent to a section of boundary wall and contains many pieces of airframe, including a section of wing. In a peat grough to the north-west are further pieces of wreckage including a substantial portion of the other wing with the serial number and roundel still visible. Parts of the engine are scattered in a debris trail leading much further to the north-west with the last notable item being the stainless steel jet pipe, still attached to the rear section of the engine.

De Havilland Canada Chipmunk T. Mk.10 WP968: Manchester UAS, RAF. 22-12-1965
Map No.30
SD 669138 (1,275ft), Winter Hill, Bolton, Lancashire

F/Lt G. Webb	Pilot	Survived
Cdt A. Barnes	Pupil	Survived

The two men were on a training flight from RAF Woodvale near Southport in Lancashire when the aircraft developed engine trouble. The Instructor carried out a downhill forced landing on Smithills Moor, resulting in the undercarriage being torn off and engine cowling being damaged by the crash, but leaving the rest of the aircraft intact.

Only a handful of tiny fragments remain where the aircraft crashed. These are mainly broken stainless steel nuts and bolts left behind when the aircraft was dismantled.

Dornier Do217E-4 1182 / Coded U5+KP: 4/KG 2, *Luftwaffe*.   24-03-1943
Map No.31
NY 752678 (800ft), Steel Rigg, Haltwhistle, Northumberland

Ufz Willi Schneider	Pilot	Killed
Ltn Rudolf Frase	Obs	Killed
Obgfr Alois Ille	WO	Killed
Obgfr Siegfried Hartz	AG	Killed

The aircraft was one of some fifty *Luftwaffe* aircraft that took off from their Dutch bases for what turned out to be a disastrous night attack on Edinburgh, with only fourteen reaching the city and ten aircraft being lost. U5+KP was flying at low altitude when it hit high ground at a shallow angle and under power at 00:20. The aircraft disintegrated on impact, scattering burning wreckage over a wide area and killing all the crew instantly, leaving little of use to RAF Intelligence. Local reports of machine-gun fire in the area shortly before the crash have never been substantiated.

No visible wreckage remains at this site, which remains uninvestigated to date, as metal detecting is strictly forbidden due to the site's proximity to Hadrian's Wall.

Douglas C-54G 45-543: 14th TCS (H)/61st TCG, CALTF. USAFE   07-01-1949
Map No.32
SD 556495 (1,125ft), Stake House Fell, Garstang, Lancashire

1st Lt R.M. Wurgel	Pilot	Killed
1st Lt L.A. Wheaton Jr.	Co-pilot	Killed
Sgt B.J. Watkins	Eng	Killed
Cpl N.H. Theis	Radio Op	Killed
Capt W. A. Rathgeber	Pass	Killed
Pvt R. E. Stone	Pass	Killed

This aircraft was taking part in Berlin Airlift operations and took off from Rhein Main AFB near Frankfurt, Germany en route for Burtonwood for its 'Vittles' 200 hour service. In bad weather conditions and poor visibility, a strong signal from a commercial radio station interfered with the radio compass, leading the crew to believe they were on final approach. At 16:45 the aircraft descended through the cloud and flew into the face of the fell, exploding on impact. Following this incident the frequency of the radio beacon was changed and the problem did not reoccur.

The aircraft impacted the steep scree-covered face of the fell and many small fragments, including pieces of broken medicine bottles from the cargo are jammed between the rocks here. The bulk of the remains were burned on the site and the heavier steel forgings, including the massive undercarriage legs, engine firewalls and propeller hubs now lie at the base of the slope.

The large main undercarriage legs from C-54 45-543 lie at the base of the slope where the aircraft impacted. Also visible is one of the stainless steel engine firewalls and behind it mainly hidden in the bracken is the smashed nosewheel oleo.

Douglas Dakota Mk.II KG502 : No.1383 TCU, RAF. 03-02-1946
Map No.33
NY 588562 (1,500ft), Cold Fell, Castle Carrock, Cumbria

F/O J.D. Taylor	Pilot (Inst)	Killed
W/O W.D. Reeve	Pilot (u/t)	Killed
F/O F.W. Knowles	Nav (Inst)	Killed
Sgt G.T. Wardle	Nav (u/t)	Killed
W/O A.G.F. Gravestock	WO (Inst)	Killed
F/Sgt D. Thomas	WO (u/t)	Killed

The crew was returning to the RAF Station at Crosby-on-Eden from a night cross-country exercise and whilst descending in cloud, the aircraft struck a rise on the western edge of the fell, broke up and burst into flames.

Pieces of melted aluminium alloy are scattered amongst the rocks of the outcrop struck by the aircraft. Other small pieces of wreckage lie in a hollow at the base of the outcrop.

Douglas Dakota G-AMVC: B.K.S. Air Transport. 17-10-1961
Map No.34
NY 596507 (1,600ft), Croglin Fell, Carlisle, Cumbria,

Capt H.L. Mose,	Pilot	Killed
1st Off A. Francis,	Co-pilot	Killed
2nd Off C.N. Wildman,	Sup Pilot	Killed
Ms V. Christian,	Stwd	Killed

The aircraft had been chartered from Woolsington, now Newcastle International Airport, to fly a group from Crosby-on-Eden near Carlisle to North Wales. The crew had flown the aircraft via Yeadon (now Leeds Bradford Airport) and while descending on approach to Crosby, it struck cloud-obscured high ground in poor weather conditions.

The site is located on the northern side of the hill, where the remaining pieces were disposed of by being collected together and placed in a series of holes where they are partially hidden from view – pieces of airframe, engine exhaust piping and seat frames may be seen.

Fairey Barracuda Mk.II DR306: 769 Naval Sqn, RN. 15-12-1945
Map No.35
SD 741804 (1,625ft), Whernside, Ingleton, North Yorkshire

PO J.R. Crevier	Pilot	Survived

On the return leg of a routine cross-country navigational excercise from RNAS Rattray near Crimond, Scotland, the pilot encountered cloud and is believed to have attempted to descend through it to confirm his position. Unfortunately at this point he was over high ground, but fortunately the aircraft struck the lower slopes of the hill some 500ft below the summit and it skidded to a halt largely intact. The lucky pilot vacated the cockpit with only minor cuts and bruises and was able to walk to the nearest farm to raise the alarm.

For many years this was one of the most intact wreck sites in the area. However a series of excavations uncovered the remains and piece-by-piece it gradually disappeared. Unfortunately the whereabouts of the major sections recovered is unknown at the present time. Only a few corroded small panels remain at the site today, these being well scattered – possibly dropped during recovery attempts or picked up and later abandoned by curious walkers.

Gloster Javelin F.A.W. Mk.5 XA662: No.228 OCU, RAF.   29-09-1959
Map No.36
SE 016941 (1,500ft), East Bolton Moor, Castle Bolton, North Yorkshire

Capt R.E. Nietz (USAF)	Pilot	Survived
F/O C.P. Cowper	Nav	Survived

During a training flight from RAF Leeming, the aircraft suffered an engine fire and then lost power in its second engine. Following this the two crew ejected safely from the aircraft, which then fell onto open moorland and was completely destroyed.

Badly twisted parts from Javelin XA662 on East Bolton Moor, with the 9ft long stainless steel jet pipe lying towards the background.

Large section of the port wing from Meteor WD778 lying with other parts in one of the peat groughs on Knock Fell.

A large amount of wreckage, much of which is shattered almost beyond recognition, still lies at the site. The largest piece, and one of easiest to recognise, is a complete, albeit flattened, jet pipe (approximately 9ft long!).

Gloster Meteor N.F. Mk.11 WD778: No.228 OCU, RAF.   24-03-1954
Map No.37
NY 725291 (2,350ft), Knock Fell, Appleby, Cumbria.

P/O J.D. Briggs	Pilot	Killed
F/O D. Walker	Nav	Killed

On return from a navigation training exercise to his base at RAF Leeming near Northallerton, the pilot became lost in cloud and running low on fuel, he descended in an attempt to establish his position. The aircraft struck the rough moorland at a shallow angle, breaking up and killing both crew members instantly.

The site is located on moorland criss-crossed with gullies and large pieces of the aircraft are still present, strewn over a couple of hundred yards, with substantial parts of both engines and a large section of the port wing remaining.

Gloster Meteor F.Mk.8 WH383 and WH384: No.610 Sqn, RAuxAF. 14-11-1953
Map No.38
SD 754186 (1,250ft), Scholes Height, Edgworth, Lancashire

F/O A.M. Fletcher	Pilot (WH383)	Killed
F/Lt A.B. Mercer	Pilot (WH384)	Killed

The two pilots were on a weekend training flight from Hooton Park near Ellesmere Port when they flew into the hill above Crowthorne Farm, destroying a dry stone wall and spreading wreckage over a wide area.

There is no surface wreckage at this site, which is located at the lower of the two walls, which run across the hill, though the site can be identified as the wall appears not to have been rebuilt since the crash.

Handley Page Halifax II L9619 / ZA-E: No.10 Sqn, RAF.   16-02-1942
Map No.39
NY 867001 (1,525ft), Ashgill Side, Keld, North Yorkshire

F/Sgt E.O.S. Lloyd	Pilot	Survived
P/O L.D. Hillier (RCAF)	Co-pilot	Survived
Sgt Thain	Flt Eng	Survived
Sgt Mapes	Obs	Survived
F/Sgt Guertin	WO	Survived
Sgt Mathias	AG	Survived
Sgt Gifford	AG	Survived

The pilot took off at 18:00 hours from Leeming for a night bombing operation against St. Nazaire. Due to cloud cover the aircraft spent too long trying to locate the target. Then the pilot elected to return home with his bomb load intact. Unable to locate his base, the pilot believed he had overshot Leeming and with fuel appearing to be critical, he ordered the crew to abandon the aircraft. All the crew members made successful parachute descents, landing near to Appleby. The aircraft, however, continued on, eventually diving into high ground at 01:40 hours and was completely wrecked.

Only a few small corroded panels still remain to mark the crash site of L9619, though live .303 in. ammunition has also been seen recently and should not be touched. Note: The bomb load was apparently deemed too deeply buried and was left at this site, marked with a warning notice! The old post, which once carried the warning about unexploded bombs also remains – as no doubt do the bombs!

Handley Page Halifax Mk.II W1146 / H: No.1659 HCU, RAF.   28-01-1943
Map No.40
SD 865974 (1,900ft), Great Shunner Fell, Thwaite, North Yorkshire

P/O E.R.Y. LeFebvre (RCAF)	Pilot	Survived
Sgt H. McGeach (RCAF)	Flt Eng	Survived
Sgt R.E. Drago	BA	Killed
F/Sgt J.H.A. Beliveau (RCAF)	Nav	Killed
Sgt J.D. Stone	WO	Killed
Sgt C.L. Pudney (RCAF)	AG	Survived
F/Sgt J.R. Askew (RCAF)	AG	Survived

The aircraft was on a cross-county navigation exercise and was returning to its base at Leeming near Northallerton, when it flew into the north-eastern side of Great Shunner Fell while in cloud. The aircraft caught fire during the crash and Sgt Pudney, having escaped the burning aircraft, re-entered the wreck to extricate the other injured crewmen. Despite his injuries, he entered the blazing aircraft several times and finally succeeded in bringing all his companions out, before then walking the two miles to Thwaite to summon help.

Note: Following this incident Sgt Pudney was awarded the George Medal for his actions but sadly he never received it as he was killed while serving with 405 Squadron when Halifax Mk.II HR832, broke up in mid-air following a lightning strike and crashed some two miles west of Kings Lynn on the 16 June 1943. His award was published in the *London Gazette* issue 36089, 13 July 1943.

At the crash site today, small pieces of the aircraft can be found at the head of a gully. The upper most part is characteristically bare of vegetation where the aircraft burnt and contains very small pieces of wreckage. Some slightly larger pieces can be found a little lower down the hill.

Handley Page Halifax Mk.II BB310: No.1674 HCU, RAF.   12-04-1944
Map No.41
NY 697324 (2,100ft), Great Dun Fell, Appleby, Cumbria

F/O S. Brooks	Pilot,	Killed
F/O P.B. Stevens (RCAF)	Pilot,	Killed
F/Sgt R.J. Littlefield	Flt Eng	Killed
Sgt W.J. Morrison	Nav	Killed
Sgt H. Dunningham	WO/Mech/AG	Killed
F/Sgt W.A. Johnson DFM	WO/AG	Killed
F/Sgt F. Pess (RCAF)	WO/AG	Killed
Sgt H.S. Seabrook (RCAF)	WO/AG	Killed
Sgt D.W. Swedberg (RCAF)	WO/AG	Killed

The crew was on a cross-country navigation training exercise from RAF Longtown to the north of Carlisle when the Halifax flew into the western side of Great Dun Fell on Middle Tongue in low cloud.

Numerous small pieces of the aircraft may be found scattered amongst an area of boulders. There is also a small stainless steel memorial plaque fixed to one of the rocks nearby. This can be seen from just north of Silverband Mine, a little lower down toward Middle Tongue.

Handley Page Halifax Mk.V DG404 / OO-A: No.1663 HCU, RAF.   12-07-1943
Map No.42
SE 096675 (1,400ft), Heathfield Moor, Pateley Bridge, North Yorkshire

F/O J.S. Barber	Pilot	Survived
Sgt W.D. Hall	Flt Eng	Survived
Sgt T.H. Woollard	Nav	Killed
Sgt T. Reid	BA	Killed
Sgt J. Godley	WO	Killed
P/O A.J. Walker	AG	Survived
Sgt D.W. Batten (RAAF)	AG	Survived

One of the collections of parts from Halifax DG404 lying on Heathfield Moor.

The aircraft was on night cross-country navigation exercise, when the crew encountered bad weather conditions and the aircraft suffered a loss of power in one engine. It is believed that the pilot may have attempted to force land the aircraft on the moor at 02:00. The flight engineer managed to walk some distance from the crash site to summon help at the nearest farm.

Note: None of the four surviving crew members from this aircraft lived to see the end of the conflict.

Scattered remains are still to be found over a fairly wide area, the largest being the remains of an engine firewall. There are a couple of water-filled holes containing wreckage in the area of the crash site and these were pits dug to dispose of smaller parts, which have been uncovered over the years.

Handley Page Halifax Mk.V Srs.I DK116 / GG-Z: No.1667 HCU, RAF. 15-10-1944
Map No.43
NY 579862 (1,350 ft), Glendhu Hill, Kielder Forest, Northumberland

P/O H.G. Haddrell	Pilot	Killed
F/Sgt J. Mahoney	Nav	Survived
Sgt J. Neilson	Flt Eng	Killed
Sgt Hammond	BA	Survived
Sgt Reid	WO	Survived
W/O M.F. James	AG	Killed
W/O G. Symonds	AG	Killed

Whilst on a cross-country navigation exercise from RAF Sandtoft, Lincolnshire, the port inner engine of this Halifax caught fire and it began losing altitude. Attempts to extinguish the fire failed, so a decision to abandon the aircraft was made. However, only three of the crew had baled out successfully when the aircraft hit the hillside and disintegrated.

A substantial quantity of the wreckage from the aircraft remains at the site, within a clearing in the forest. A wooden memorial cross was erected at the site in 2000.

Handley Page Halifax Mk.V DK185: No.1664 HCU, RAF.   31-01-1944
Map No.44
SE 093467 (1,150ft), Crawshaw Moss, Ilkley, West Yorkshire

P/O D.G. McLeod (RCAF)	Pilot,	Killed
Sgt F. Byrne	Flt Eng	Killed
W/O L. Riggs (RCAF)	Nav	Killed
Sgt R.H. Rahn (RCAF)	BA	Killed
W/O W.G. King (RCAF)	WO/AG	Killed
Sgt G. Martin (RCAF)	AG	Killed
Sgt A.L. Mullen (RCAF)	AG	Killed

The aircraft had taken off from Dishforth in the Vale of York on a night-navigation exercise. The pilot was flying some 40 miles to the south of his intended track, when at about 17:30 the aircraft struck the ridge above Ilkley and the aircraft disintegrated and burst into flames killing all seven of the crew.

A memorial stone marker and commemorative plaque was placed at the crash site on the anniversary of the crash in January 2006, making the site easy to find. Smaller parts may be found at the base of this and around the crash site itself.

Wreckage from Halifax DK116 lies in a clearing in Kielder Forest, with the memorial cross in the background and wreaths from a recent memorial service held at the site.

Handley Page Halifax Mk.II DT578: No.1658 HCU, RAF.   23-11-1943
Map No.45
SE 001730 (1,975ft), Great Whernside, Kettlewell, North Yorkshire

Sgt S. Chadwick	Pilot	Killed
Sgt F.W. Robson	Flt Eng	Killed
Sgt F.J. Robinson	Nav	Killed
Sgt N. Martin	BA	Killed
Sgt D.P. Aitken	WO	Killed
Sgt E. Stabler	AG	Killed
Sgt K. Vincent	AG	Killed

This aircraft was one of six Halifax's of No.1658 HCU, which were tasked with night cross-country training exercises on this night. Despite very bad weather being forecast the exercises were allowed to continue and only two completed their flights while three crashed. DT578 was heard circling the area, before going into a dive from which it did not recover, crashing vertically into Great Whernside killing all on board. Loss of control through icing of the control surfaces and instruments was given as the probable cause and suggestions of a possible collision with Halifax JB926, also lost that night, were discounted.

Many parts of DT578 remain on Great Whernside today, some lying in what appear to have been pits, where they were buried and mixed with parts from other aircraft that have been lost on this hill. The largest concentration lies in what appears to be the impact crater. Recognisable parts include oxygen bottles, armour plate and hinge assemblies from wing flaps, though most are badly broken up, showing evidence of the violent impact, as well as having suffered badly from exposure to the elements and arouse little more than idle curiosity from the many walkers who frequent this area.

Handley Page Halifax Mk.II DT581 / MH-Y: No.51 Sqn, RAF.   21-01-1943
Map No.46
SD 936297 (1,275ft), Hoarside Moor, Todmordon, West Yorkshire

P/O R.D. Getliffe	Pilot	Survived
Sgt A.Campbell	–	Survived
P/O E.B.Chatfield	–	Survived
Sgt A.Campbell	–	Killed
Sgt G.H.Whyte	WO	Killed
Sgt G.J.Merritt	–	Survived
Sgt E.R.Smart	–	Survived

The Halifax took off at 17:10 from Snaith near Selby, Yorkshire to lay mines off the Friesian Islands (Code name: Nectarines). Returning on dead reckoning navigation, the pilot strayed off course and missed base, crashing at 22:25. The aircraft was completely destroyed by the ensuing fire, possibly additionally so by mines still being on board detonating, as cradles from these were visible at the site at one time.

The site of the crash today can be difficult to find, as it lies in a shallow depression on an otherwise relatively flat moor, making it difficult to see until you are almost upon it. The only visible reminders of the demise of DT581 today are a couple of sections of very weather-worn armour plate, a few scattered fragments of fused alloy and a 90ft long section of missing dry-stone wall on the edge of the moor, where the aircraft initially struck.

Handley Page Halifax Mk.II JB926: No.1658 HCU, RAF.   24-11-1943
Map No.47
SE 139819 (950ft), Slipstone Crags, Agra Moor, North Yorkshire

Sgt R.E.C. Bacon	Pilot	Killed
Sgt G.H. Manley	Flt Eng	Killed
Sgt J. Titterington	Flt Eng	Killed
F/O H. McCarthy	Nav	Killed
F/Sgt J.J. MacGillivray (RCAF)	BA	Killed
Sgt B.F. Taylor	WO	Killed
Sgt A.J. Winton	AG	Killed
Sgt D.E. Phillips	AG	Killed

The informal memorial to the crew of Halifax JB926 incorporating collected fragments from the aircraft with Slipstone Crags in the background.

This aircraft was one of six Halifax' aircraft of 1658 HCU, which were tasked with night cross-country training exercises on this night. Despite very bad weather being forecast the exercises were allowed to continue and only two completed their flights and three crashed. JB926 was heard over the area, shortly before going into a power dive, during which structural failure occurred with the port outer-wing and both outer engines, as well as control surfaces being torn away in flight. Loss of control through icing of the control surfaces and instruments was given as the probable cause and initial suggestions of a possible collision with Halifax DT578, also lost that night, were discounted.

A memorial was erected at the site some years ago and the majority of the pieces of wreckage have been collected together in front of this stone. Smaller parts may be found scattered over a wide area but the majority of the remains are very small and all show evidence of the post-crash fire.

Hawker Hart K6482: No.152 Sqn, RAF.   10-10-1939
Map No.48
NT 919221 (1,775ft), The Cheviot, Northumberland

Sgt T. Mycroft	Pilot	Killed

The pilot was ferrying the aircraft from RAF Turnhouse near Edinburgh to RAF Acklington in Northumberland when he flew too far west and struck high ground while in low cloud.

A small cairn and a scatter of burnt pieces marks the spot where the aircraft crashed, while lower down the hill there is a depression where pieces of the engine, aluminium panels and steel framework from the aircraft were dumped.

Hawker Hurricane Mk.I P3522: No.213 Sqn, RAF.   10-01-1941
Map No.49
SE 102828 (1,300ft), Caldbergh Moor, Caldbergh, North Yorkshire

Sgt. E.G. Bruce	Pilot	Killed

The pilot became lost and flew into snow covered moorland while on a training flight from Leconfield in East Yorkshire.

Note: This aircraft served with No.32 Sqn, coded GZ-V, during the Battle of Britain.

A prominent stone memorial with an attached brass plaque marks the spot where the aircraft crashed, placed at the site after the war by the pilot's mother. Otherwise, only a shallow depression and a few small pieces of alloy, occasionally found amongst the heather, remain at this site.

Hawker Hurricane Mk.IIB AG680: No.5 FPP, ATA.   12-06-1942
Map No.50
SD 823991 (1,850ft), Great Sled Dale, Keld, North Yorkshire

1st Off A.R. Leslie-Melville (ATA)	Pilot	Killed

The pilot was ferrying the aircraft from RAF Henlow to RAF Silloth near Carlisle when he became disorientated in low cloud and flew into high ground.

Wreckage including several panels from Hurricane AG680 lies collected together on Great Sled Dale.

The remaining wreckage has been gathered into a shallow pit. There are numerous panels, including a cowling panel which still has AG680 stencilled on the inside, and sections of the distinctive tubular steel framework from the fuselage.

Hawker Hurricane PG472: No.11 (P) AFU, RAF.　　　　02-02-1945
Map No.51
SD 688141 (975ft), Whimberry Hill, Belmont, Lancashire

　　　F/Sgt T.S. Taylor　　　　　　Pilot　　　　Killed

This aircraft was one of two Hurricanes that took off approximately at 13:40 from the unit's base at RAF Calverley, Cheshire. The two pilots were cleared for local flying exercises only, but some 20 minutes later they were flying over the high ground to the north of the Lancashire mill town of Bolton. The subsequent inquiry noted that the two aircraft must have flown to the north, in formation, directly after take-off to have reached the area in this time. Whilst flying in formation at some 6-7000 feet over the Smithills area, they collided in cloud and both dived into the ground, out of control. Note: The second aircraft, PZ848 piloted by W/O N.T. Huckle, who was also killed, crashed on private farmland less than a mile away.

Although a distinct crater marks the crash site, it can be difficult to spot and in summer is invisible from as little as 10ft away, due to the terrain, long grass and bracken. Smaller parts from the aircraft remain in the crater and a few larger pieces may be found hidden in the long grass on the plateau below.

Lockheed Hudson Mk.I N7325: No.1 (C)OTU, RAF.   06-09-1942
Map No.52
NY 690331 (2,075ft), Cross Fell, Appleby, Cumbria

P/O P.A. Bourke	Pilot	Killed
Sgt J. Bumpstead	Nav	Killed
Sgt R. Band	WO/AG	Killed
Sgt L.T. Griffin	WO/AG	Killed
Sgt R.W. Hewitt	WO/AG	Killed

This Hudson was on a night-navigation training exercise taking place almost entirely over the Irish Sea. The last leg of the flight was from Skerries Lighthouse off Anglesey to the aircraft's base at RAF Silloth on the Solway Firth. For some reason the aircraft ended up flying off course by nearly 40 miles and flew into the southern side of the hill in cloud.

The site above Crowdundle Beck is marked by a cairn and small pieces of airframe lie within an area of scree that was darkened by the post-crash fire.

Lockheed P-38G 42-12905: 83rd FS / 78th FG, USAAF.   26-01-1943
Map No.53
SD 674543 (1,375ft), Dunsop Fell, Forest of Bowland, Lancashire

1st Lt H.L. Perry	Pilot	Killed

The relatively sparse remains of Lockheed P-38G 42-12905 lie amongst thick heather in a hollow on Dunsop Fell. Author's son, Sam Wotherspoon, displays a fragment bearing the aircraft's serial number.

This aircraft was one of a group of forty-five P-38s being ferried from Goxhill, Lincolnshire to Base Air Depot 3, Langford Lodge in Northern Ireland for modification, before they were flown on to North Africa. The group encountered heavy cloud over the North of England and whilst struggling to maintain formation in deteriorating visibility, two of the aircraft collided over high ground.

The crash site can be difficult to spot as the ground is boggy and covered in heather. The main impact point lies in a dip and is now marked by only a few small corroded parts, though other caches of small items of wreckage are spread over a large area of the moor, suggesting that 42-12905 may have broken up in the air.

Note: It is still possible to find live ammunition on this site and care should be exercised before picking up unfamiliar items.

The crash site of P-38G 42-12928 on Baxton Fell contains substantial parts of the aircraft, in sharp contrast to its sister ship only one and a half miles away.

Lockheed P-38G 42-12928: 83rd FS / 78th FG, USAAF.　　　　26-01-1943
Map No.54
SD 668564 (1,450ft), Baxton Fell, Forest of Bowland, Lancashire

　　　　2nd Lt S.L. White　　　　　　　Pilot　　　　　Killed

This aircraft collided with 42-12905 on a ferry flight as detailed in the previous entry. Neither pilot made any apparent attempt to escape their stricken aircraft, perhaps due to injury, or having been killed in the initial collision and the two aircraft crashed within a mile and a half of each other.

　　　The crash site on Baxton Fell is the more substantial of the two P-38s with a couple of fairly large sections of wing structure present and pieces from the tail booms etc, surrounding an area where part of the aircraft clearly burnt out.

Miles Master Mk.III W8479: TFPP, RAF.　　　　　　19-12-1941
Map No.55
SD 662946 (1,975ft), Arant Haw Fell, Sedburgh, Cumbria

　　　　2nd Off A.H. Gosiewski (ATA)　　　Pilot　　　　　Killed

The pilot was on the second stage of a ferry flight from RAF White Waltham, Berkshire to RAF Lossiemouth on the north-east coast of Scotland via RAF Shawbury, Shropshire when the aircraft hit high ground whilst flying in cloud.

　　　On top of the hill, only a few metres south-west of the small summit cairn, is a characteristic stony bare patch, where the aircraft burnt out on the hillside, containing tiny fragments from the aircraft.

North American Mustang Mk.I AG586: No.613 Sqn, RAF.   15-12-1942
Map No.56
SE 144725 (1,300ft), Fountains Earth Moor, Pateley Bridge, Yorkshire

P/O W.J. Bodington   Pilot   Survived

On a formation flying exercise from base at Ouston, Northumberland, the pilot became separated from the flight and lost in poor weather conditions. Being low on fuel, he was unable to find anywhere suitable to try to land and elected to bale out. He landed safely whilst the aircraft dived into moorland nearby.

The crash site is marked by a large boggy and often water filled depression – the result of a number of recovery attempts over the years. This is surrounded by various small pieces of the aircraft, including the remains of the undercarriage legs, which were apparently dug from the crater and then discarded.

North American Mustang Mk.I AP208: No.4 Sqn, RAF.   29-11-1942
Map No.57
SD 608508 (1,175ft), Holdron Moss, Forest of Bowland, Lancashire.

F/O S.P. Marlatt(RCAF)   Pilot   Killed

This Squadron was assigned to Army co-operation duties and the pilot was undertaking a photographic sortie. The aircraft was on course when only some 20 minutes into the flight it struck mist-shrouded moorland at cruising speed, killing the pilot instantly and leaving fragments of wreckage strewn over a wide area.

A surprising amount of wreckage for a single-engine fighter aircraft still lies at the crash site, most probably having been uncovered, from where it was originally buried by the recovery crew, by recent enthusiasts. Larger pieces include part of the centre section, parts of flaps and self-sealing fuel cells, lying amidst many scattered smaller fragments of aluminium aircraft structure.

North American Mustang Mk.III SR411: No.316 Sqn, RAF.   29-07-1945
Map No.58
SD 691192 (1,150ft), Wives Hill, Darwen, Lancashire

W/O. H. Noga   Pilot   Killed

This Mustang was on a routine ferry flight from base at Coltishall, Norfolk, and was apparently on course, when at approximately 15:45 hours it hit mist and industrial haze shrouded, high ground at cruising speed, disintegrating on impact and killing the 24 year old pilot instantly.

Wreckage from the aircraft lies in an often water filled, boggy crater caused by the crash and enlarged by subsequent excavations by several groups of enthusiasts. However many smaller parts of aluminium airframe and stainless steel structure remain to be seen, some partly submerged in the crater and others scattered around the site.

Several substantial parts of Mustang AP208 are scattered around the crash site on Holdron Moss, along with numerous smaller fragments hidden amongst the heather.

Despite several recovery operations over the years, some quite substantial pieces of airframe from Mustang SR411 still protrude from the boggy crater.

Pieces of the wreckage of Piper Cherokee G-AVYN rearranged into their correct position in relation to each other, show that virtually the complete fuselage is present at the crash site.

Piper Cherokee G-AVYN: Newcastle Aero Club,   23-09-1969
Map No.59
SE 075684 (1,650ft), Ashfold Gill Head, Pateley Bridge, Yorkshire

   A.P. Teare   Pilot   Killed

This private light aircraft was being flown by a student pilot on a Visual Flight Rules (VFR) flight from Leeds Bradford Airport to Newcastle Airport, when he encountered bad weather with low cloud en route, after straying some 8 miles off course and flew into high ground at 1,640ft, sometime between 15:05 and 15:20. The aircraft cartwheeled into the ground under power, killing the pilot instantly and the wreckage was finally located after a two-day search.

Note: The pilot was a police constable and had been awarded a Queens Award for Bravery.

Today most of the aircraft remains at the crash site, in pieces, with wings, fuselage and tail all being easily recognisable and still bearing markings. The engine was recovered by local air cadets a number of years after the crash.

Republic P-47D 42-22758 / IV-O: 310th FS / 27th ATG, USAAF. 06-02-1944
Map No.60
SD 780399 (1,100ft), Pendle Hill, Clitheroe, Lancashire

   Flt.Off J.R. Runnells   Pilot   Killed

This aircraft was one of a flight of five P-47s being ferried from Station 133, East Wretham in Norfolk to BAD2 Warton for modification. Despite reports of poor weather over their destination, the Flight Leader decided to proceed with the flight. As conditions deteriorated along the route the other pilots became separated and turned back or landed elsewhere and it appears that Flt. Off Runnells became lost in cloud and continued until his fuel ran out, then crashed during an attempted forced landing.

The crash site is marked by an obvious small bare patch of rock and exposed peat, in an area of otherwise dense bracken and occasionally small fragments of aluminium may be found where they have eroded out of the peat or been exposed amongst the undergrowth.

Note: Pendle Hill was a live firing range during WW2 and unexploded ordnance is still regularly found – DO NOT TOUCH any unfamiliar items you may find in this area.

Shorts Stirling Mk.III EE972 / OG-C: No.1665 HCU, RAF.   25-09-1944
Map No.61
NT 911207 (1,975ft), The Cheviot, Langleeford, Northumberland

F/O J.H. Verrall	Pilot	Survived
F/O E.F. Insley (RCAF)	Pilot	Survived
Sgt R.C. Bisgrove	Flt Eng	Survived
Sgt T.K. Hatfield	Flt Eng	Survived
F/Sgt P.S. Coronel (RAAF)	Nav	Killed
F/Sgt D.C. McLackland	BA	Killed
W/O J.A. Hay (RCAF)	WO/AG	Survived
W/O P.A. Allen	AG	Survived
Sgt Williams	AG	Survived

The aircraft flew into the southern side of the Cheviot while on a cross-country navigation exercise from RAF Tilstock in Shropshire. Although W/O Allen initially survived the crash, he died of his injuries on 29 September 1944.

Only a few small pieces of the aircraft mark the crash site today, perhaps the most interesting being a complete oil cooler. Other parts lie lower down the slope.

Short Stirling Mk.III EE975: No.1660 HCU, RAF   14-08-1944
Map No.62
SD 927727 (1,050ft), Old Cote Moor, Kettlewell, North Yorkshire

P/O D.M. Bowe (RAAF)	Pilot	Killed
F/Sgt R.J. Douglas (RAAF)	Nav	Killed
Sgt I.K. Frazer	Flt Eng	Survived
Sgt F.G. Nelson	Flt Eng	Survived
F/Sgt C.P. O'Neil (RAAF)	BA	Survived
F/Sgt G.I. Maloney (RAAF)	WO	Survived
Sgt C.M. Davies	AG	Survived

This aircraft was on a night cross-country training flight from RAF Swinderby in Lincolnshire when two engines overheated and had to be shut down. The pilot was unable to maintain height and ordered his crew to bale out at 4,500ft. All managed to do so, with the possible exception of the pilot, but the navigator was killed, because he jumped late, over Firth Fell and hit the 1,600ft summit before he could open his parachute.

Many smaller fragments of airframe remain at the crash site; some are scattered, but most parts have been piled together into a couple of collections making them easy to find.

One of the collections of wreckage from Stirling EE975 on Old Cote Moor.

Short Stirling Mk.III LK488: No.1651 HCU, RAF.   19-10-1944
Map No.63
NY 810247 (2,500 ft), Boot of Mickle Fell, Mickle Fell, Teesdale, County Durham

F/Sgt P.D. Young (RNZAF)	Pilot	Killed
F/Sgt N.C. Burgess (RNZAF)	Nav	Killed
Sgt B.G. Davies	Flt Eng	Killed
F/Sgt J.M. Stack (RNZAF)	BA	Killed
F/Sgt R.P. Furey (RNZAF)	WO	Killed
F/Sgt G. Child (RNZAF)	AG	Killed
W/O A.G. Small (RNZAF)	AG	Survived

The crew was on a night cross-country navigation exercise from RAF Wrattling Common in Norfolk when the aircraft flew into the southern side of the ridge of Mickle Fell in low cloud, though the bulk of the aircraft eventually came to rest on the northern side of the ridge.

Probably one of the most famous (or possibly infamous) high ground crash sites in the UK! The aircraft was originally disposed of by being cut up and dumped in a series of sinkholes or pits, where it remained until attracting the attention of enthusiasts as early as the 1960s. The RAF removed the more substantial sections in the late 1970s for a potential reconstruction project, though this never materialised and many parts are rumoured to have been later scrapped. Despite this, a surprising amount of wreckage still remains at the site, including many smaller airframe pieces, armour plate and a propeller hub. The remains of the main undercarriage assemblies and several sections of airframe lie close to where the aircraft initially impacted on the southern side of the ridge. Further wreckage is scattered on the northern side of the ridge where there is a scar at NY 809248. A sizeable section of airframe and a mainwheel tyre are the only significant parts of the aircraft now in the sinkholes at NY 808249, where much of the wreckage was originally dumped.

Note: This crash site lies within MOD firing ranges and access is restricted and by written consent only.

Supermarine Spitfire Mk.I K9888: No.41 Sqn, RAF.   18-07-1939
Map No.64
NY 708313 (2,400ft), Silverband Great Dun Fell, Cumbria

Sgt K. Mitchell   Pilot   Killed

During a cross-country flight from RAF Catterick in North Yorkshire across the Pennines to RAF Kingstown near Carlisle, the pilot entered cloud and began heading east back towards Catterick, when the aircraft struck Great Dun Fell near to the Silverband Mine.

Small pieces of the aircraft, some collected together, lie towards the head of one of many gullies which run down the hillside towards the track to the mine.

Note: The Silverband mine is a baryte mine owned by Silverband Barytes Co. and the steep winding track up to it is in regular use by large lorries transporting mined material to the valley below.

Substantial parts of Stirling LK488 still remain on Mickle Fell.

Supermarine Spitfire F.R. Mk.14 NM814: No.611 Sqn, RAuxAF. 03-07-1948
Map No.65
NY 825043 (1,950ft), Coldbergh Edge, Keld, North Yorkshire

F/O P. Geldart	Pilot	Survived

The pilot was on a cross-country navigation flight from RAF Woodvale near Southport to Morpeth in Northumberland and back. While on the outward leg, the aircraft encountered severe turbulence and the pilot lost control. Realising that he had insufficient altitude to recover, he managed to abandon the aircraft with some difficulty.

Much of the remaining wreckage was recovered during an excavation in the 1980s. A few small parts remain in the large crater left by the excavation, though this does have the appearance of a natural gully from a distance.

Vickers Warwick A.S.R. Mk.I HG136: No.280 Sqn, RAF. 23-07-1946
Map No.66
NT 899196 (2,425ft), Cairn Hill, The Cheviot, Northumberland

F/Lt K.F. Wyett	Pilot	Killed
F/O H.A. Cody	Nav	Killed
F/Lt D.T. Chadd	WO	Killed

The crew was ferrying the aircraft from RAF Thornaby near Middlesbrough to RAF Brackla in Fife where it was to be broken up for scrap. While flying in low cloud the aircraft struck high ground and was destroyed.

A large amount of wreckage remains at the site, this includes the aircraft's two Pratt & Whitney engines, fuel tanks and geodetic framework from the fuselage and wings.

Vickers Wellington Mk.IC N2848: No.18 OTU, RAF. 30-01-1942
Map No.67
SD 962779 (2,275ft), Buckden Pike, Buckden, North Yorkshire

F/Lt C. Kujawa (PAF)	Pilot	Killed
P/O J. Polczyk (PAF)	Co-pilot	Killed
F/O T.J Bieganski (PAF)	Nav	Killed
Sgt J. Sadowski (PAF)	WO	Killed
Sgt J.A. Tokarzewski (PAF)	AG	Killed
Sgt J. Fusniak (PAF)	AG	Survived

The pilot took off from Bramcote, Warwickshire for a night cross-country training flight. Encountering heavy snow and severe icing, it is thought that the pilot began to descend in order to establish his position, and whilst doing so, the aircraft struck high ground, just below the ridge. Two crew members survived the crash, the rear gunner and the wireless operator and the former, despite his injuries, went to try to get help. Sadly in spite of his heroic efforts, his comrade had succumbed to his injuries by the time locals were able to reach the wreck the following morning.

A well-known memorial cross marks the crash site. The original was placed at the crash site by the sole survivor in 1972, but fell into disrepair and the present one was created some years ago. It features a bronze fox's head as the injured airman was able to find his way off the frozen moor by following the footprints of this animal in the snow. The few remaining pieces of the aircraft at the site were collected together and are to be found concreted into the base of the cross.

The memorial cross to the crew of Wellington N2848, seen in rather appropriate conditions, considering the circumstances of the crash.

Vickers Wellington Mk.IC T2715: No.25 OTU, RAF.   20-08-1942
Map No.68
NY 756297 (2,300ft), Dufton Fell, Appleby-in-Westmoreland, Cumbria

Sgt B.G. Crew (RCAF)	Pilot	Survived
Four unnamed crewmembers	–	Survived

The aircraft struck Dufton Fell two thirds of the way between Knock Old Man and Meldon Hill while on a night cross-country exercise from RAF Finningley near Doncaster. The aircraft burst into flames, but all the crew managed to escape uninjured, hence only the pilot's name was recorded on the accident record.

The site may be recognised as a bare patch of the moor, where the aircraft burned out, on the very crest of the hill. This area contains many small fragments, which survived the fire, being mainly brass and steel, though some aluminium parts are also present.

Vickers Wellington Mk.IC Z1078: No.150 Sqn, RAF.   15-01-1942
Map No.69
NT 893223 (1,575ft), West Hill, The Cheviot, Northumberland

Sgt L.W. Hunt (RNZAF)	Pilot	Killed
P/O B.A. MacDonald (RCAF)	2nd Pilot	Survived
Sgt T.W. Irving (RNZAF)	Obs	Killed
Sgt F.G. Maple	WO/AG	Killed
Sgt W.H. Allworth	WO/AG	Survived
Sgt C.F. Glover	AG	Survived

The crew had taken part in a raid against Hamburg and while returning to Snaith in Yorkshire the aircraft flew into the high ground of the Cheviot.

Only small sections of geodetic framework, some armour plate and other smaller parts from the aircraft remain at the crash site.

Vickers Wellington Mk.IC Z8799: No.28 OTU, RAF.   16-11-1943
Map No.70
SD 628175 (975ft), Hurst Hill, Anglezarke Moor, Horwich, Lancashire

F/Sgt J.B. Timperon (RAAF)	Pilot	Killed
Sgt E.R. Barnes	Co-pilot	Killed
Sgt J.B. Hayton	Nav	Killed
Sgt R.S. Jackson	WO/AG	Killed
Sgt G.E. Murray	AG	Killed
Sgt M. Mouncey	AG	Killed

This Wellington was on a night training exercise (Bullseye) from Wymeswold, Leicestershire when, four hours into the flight, severe icing is believed to have caused loss of control, resulting in the aircraft entering a steep high-speed dive resulting in eventual structural failure and the break up of the aircraft. At some point during the last minutes of Z8799, the dinghy broke free from its stowage compartment and is believed to have become entangled with the tail of the aircraft, damaging the control surfaces before breaking free. Whether the ice build up or the damage to the tail was the critical factor behind the loss of this aircraft will remain a matter for conjecture. Wreckage was scattered over a wide area, with one engine apparently being only found 12 months later, some 10 miles away!

An impressive stone pillar memorial at SD 630165 commemorates the crew of this aircraft, placed by Horwich Rotary club in 1955, at a local beauty spot known as Lead Mine Valley, close to where the aircraft crashed. The crash site itself is on an area of moorland known as Hurst Hill, higher up on the moors beyond a conifer plantation planted in recent years, though there is no visible evidence of the tragedy today.

Note: Since 1993 an open air Remembrance Sunday service has been held each year, at this memorial attracting up to 160 ramblers.

Vickers Wellington Mk.IC Z8808: No.11 OTU, RAF.   03-09-1942
Map No.71
SE 073688 (1,650ft), Ashfold Gill Head, Pateley Bridge, North Yorkshire

F/Lt P.R. Coney (RNZAF)	Pilot	Survived
Sgt J. Wilding (RNZAF)	Co-pilot	Survived
Sgt M.B. Grainger (RNZAF)	Obs	Survived
Sgt J.H.F. Kemp	BA	Survived
F/Sgt J E Burrel	WO	Survived
Sgt G. W Wilford	WO/AG	Survived
Sgt W.G. Reading	AG	Survived

One of several aircraft from the same training unit, based at Bassingbourn, Cambridgeshire, taking part in a night cross-country training flight which took them over the north of England, where they encountered deteriorating weather conditions. In poor visibility, due to heavy rain and low cloud, the pilot struggled to retain control of the aircraft, which struck high ground at 00:30, fortunately at a very shallow angle on the relatively flat, boggy moor. Note: Wellington DV718 listed in this section, was lost on this same exercise.

The crash site lies on a particularly featureless moor and the boggy nature of the ground can make walking difficult with numerous water-filled holes and channels hidden by the heather. Though some parts have been recovered in recent years, some large sections of geodetic framework remain at the site to this day, as much of the airframe was disposed of by being chopped up and buried on site, before being uncovered again by erosion and the actions of visitors to the site.

Vickers Wellington Mk.III BK347 / -Q: No.30 OTU, RAF.   21-04-1944
Map No.72
SD 741817 (2,075ft), Greensett Moss, Whernside, Ingleton, North Yorkshire

F/O E.M. Barrett	Pilot	Killed
F/Lt E. Alderson	Co-pilot	Killed
Sgt P.E. Lomas	Nav	Killed
F/O R.G.C. Brodie	BA	Killed
Sgt R.C. Holmwood	WO	Killed
Sgt N. Skirrow	WO/AG	Killed
Sgt J. Marks	AG	Survived

Wellington BK347 crashed on a daytime cross-country training flight 150 miles from its designated route. It descended through cloud and at 16.15, flew into the hillside. All but the rear gunner perished in the crash. Note: This aircraft appears in a photograph that is published in numerous books coded BT-Z, however at the time of the crash the aircraft was carrying the code letter Q.

Only a few tiny fragments and a patch of disturbed ground remain at the impact point just below the ridge of the hill. The remaining wreckage lies at one end of a large sink-hole, at the base of the slope, where much of the aircraft was buried after the crash, but has been uncovered and much removed, leaving little to see today. The largest parts visible for many years were the two circular exhaust collector rings from the front of the engine nacelles, but recently these gradually 'walked' from the site a few hundred yards at a time over several months and eventually disappeared – obviously acquired by a very determined enthusiast!

Vickers Wellington Mk.III BK387: No.82 OTU, RAF.   02-01-1944
Map No.73
SE 013386 (1,050ft), Tewitt Hall Wood, Oakworth, West Yorkshire.

W/O E.I. Glass (RCAF)	Pilot	Killed
W/O J.E. Dalling (RCAF)	BA	Killed
W/O J. Henfrey (RCAF)	WO/AG	Killed
F/O J.J. McHenry (RCAF)	Nav	Killed
Sgt E. Savage (RCAF)	AG	Killed
Sgt N.W. Crawford (RCAF)	AG	Killed

On a night training exercise from Ossington, Nottinghamshire, Wellington BK387

The memorial to the crew of Wellington BK387 at Tewitt Hall Wood, with the pond just visible beyond the wall.

descended through cloud and at 22:40, flew into a hillside, striking first in an open field, then demolishing a dry-stone wall, exploding and continuing on through a wood disintegrating as it went, before finally the fuselage came to rest in an old quarry.

No surface remains are to be seen today at the crash site, though evidence of the crash is still visible in the wood with several damaged trees discernable along the path the aircraft carved through the wood. In 1992 an inscribed memorial stone was placed in the wall along the bridleway that borders the southern edge of the wood, close to a pond where a few remnants of the aircraft were at one time visible. A bench has since been placed next to the stone and each year a memorial service is held at the site, close to the anniversary of the crash.

Vickers Wellington Mk.IC DV718: No.11 OTU, RAF.   03-09-1942
Map No.74
SE 021733 (1,950ft), Blake Hill, Kettlewell North Yorkshire

Sgt G.F. Ridgway (RNZAF)	Pilot	Killed
P/O D.H. Lyne	Nav	Survived
Sgt W. Allinson	BA	Killed
Sgt H.W. Spencer	WO	Killed
Sgt P. McLarnon	AG	Killed

Alan Clark lends scale to a large section of wing lying close to the main crash site of Wellington Mk.IC.

One of several aircraft from the same training unit, based at Bassingbourn, Cambridgeshire, taking part in a night cross-country training flight which took them over the north of England, where they encountered deteriorating weather conditions. In poor visibility, due to heavy rain and low cloud, the aircraft is thought to have attempted to descend whilst over high ground and struck the moor at just after midnight, bursting into flames and killing all but one of those on board.

Note: Wellington Z8808 was lost on this same exercise.

Large sections of this aircraft remained at the crash site until the 1970s when they were recovered for preservation, though their ultimate fate is unknown. The site where the aircraft burnt out is still easily distinguishable by the lack of vegetation and numerous smaller parts, most showing the effects of the intense fire. Scattered nearby are smaller pieces of the geodetic structure and a substantial section of wing.

Vickers Wellington Mk.X HE226: No.17 OTU, RAF.   28-05-1945
Map No.75
SE 012688 (1,350ft), Bycliffe Moor, Conistone, North Yorkshire

W/O E.C. Cole	Pilot,	Killed
Sgt J. Mann	Nav	Killed
F/Sgt A.J. Griffiths	BA	Killed
Sgt J. Duncan	WO/AG	Killed
Sgt H.H. Rawnsley	AG	Killed

Whilst on a cross-country training flight from Turweston, Northants this Wellington missed its turning point and some 39 miles west of this, the pilot descended through cloud to try to pinpoint his position. The aircraft struck high ground at 15:50 whilst in a dive, banked to port and disintegrated, killing all on board instantly.

A large amount of this aircraft remains at the site, including remains of both engines, main undercarriage assemblies and tyres etc. Most of the wreckage has been gathered into collections in a series of sink-holes. However, the level of destruction of the airframe parts is very severe, as the impact area has only a limited soil covering over solid limestone.

Note: Live ammunition is still present at this site and unfamiliar items should not be touched.

Vickers Wellington Mk.XI HZ251: No.6 (C)OTU, RAF.   23-09-1943
Map No.76
SD 999477 (350ft), Bradley, Skipton, North Yorkshire

F/Sgt F. Ciaston (PAF)	Pilot,	Killed
Sgt W. Ostrowski (PAF)	Co-pilot	Killed
F/Lt J. Wolnik (PAF)	Nav(Inst)	Killed
Cpl B.J. Swieca (PAF)	WO/AG	Killed
Cpl B. Rychel (PAF)	WO/AG	Killed
Cpl J. Czyzewski (PAF)	AG	Killed
Sgt A. Kawenocki (PAF)	WO/AG	Killed

Though this unit's base was at Silloth, Cumbria, this aircraft is believed to have taken off from Skipton-on-Swale, North Yorkshire, for a routine training flight. It was seen at approximately 13:00 flying very low to the south of Skipton, Yorkshire and shortly after this the aircraft lost a wing and crashed close to the Leeds Liverpool Canal.

Note: F/Lt Jozef Wolnik then just 31, had completed forty-six missions over enemy territory and received the Virtuti Militari, Poland's highest military decoration.

Though this site was completely cleared, the crash site is now marked by a particularly impressive memorial unveiled in April 2007 on the bank of the Leeds Liverpool Canal near bridge No.183.

The main collection of the shattered remains of Wellington HE226 at Bycliffe Moor, note engine in the foreground and main undercarriage leg just beyond.

Chapter Five

Lake District

The Lake District area includes England's largest National Park, established in 1951 and covering some 885 square miles, which attracts some 14 million visitors each year. It is an area well known for its dramatic and wild scenery and the park contains all the peaks in England that rise higher than 3,000ft above sea level, including Scafell Pike, at 3,210ft – its highest mountain. It also includes sixteen main lakes, including the deepest in England, Wastwater and the largest, Windermere, although very few aircraft have actually been lost in them.

The Lake District is formed around the Cumbrian Mountains, which are a mixture of volcanic and metamorphic peaks that are around 400 million years old. They rise to over 3,000ft above sea level and through the dome-like uplift they underwent, have weathered and been shaped by glacial erosion to form a radial pattern with valleys spreading outward from around the highest mountains. Scafell Pike is one of these central peaks and it, together with the neighbouring peaks of Sca Fell to the southwest, and Broad Crag along with Ill Crag to the northeast, account for six of the aircraft included in this chapter.

Around the mountains, or fells as they are known locally, the upland landscape gives way to a flatter coastal strip that was utilised during WW2 for the construction of airfields. Moving clockwise from the south-east there were airfields at Cark, Walney Island, Millom, Anthorn, and Silloth. There were also a handful of airfields around the city of Carlisle. Finally at White Cross Bay on the shores of Windermere, Short Brothers set up a temporary factory for the production of Sunderland flying boats. Of the thirty-five that were built here, none came to grief locally and despite rumours to the contrary; none are believed to lie on the bottom of the lake! Although one, Sunderland DP197, is included in the Highlands & Islands section of this book.

Both Cark and Millom were used by the RAF for navigation training, mainly operating the venerable Avro Anson, though in its early stages the school at Millom also operated the Blackburn Botha and the Airspeed Oxford. A number of their aircraft crashed on the fells of the Lake District, all too often with fatal consequences. The result was that Millom, like Llandwrog in North Wales, became home to one of the initial RAF Mountain Rescue Units. There is an interesting display at the continually growing museum at the former RAF Millom detailing the history of the RAF Mountain Rescue Service, and the museum also holds many artefacts recovered from Lake District sites over the years. Walney Island, a thin strip of land to the west of Barrow-in-Furness was the home of an Air Gunners School, though many of their losses were over water and only one of their aircraft appears in this chapter. Silloth, on the Solway Firth west of Carlisle, was used by No.1 and later No.6 (Coastal) Operational Training Unit flying Hudsons and Wellingtons and they too lost aircraft in the mountains of Cumbria. The final airfield was at Anthorn (HMS *Nuthatch*), which was used by the Fleet Air Arm and on the whole they stayed clear of the high ground. However an aircraft from this station can be found in the Scottish Lowlands section of this book.

As with other areas, it was not just locally based aircraft that were lost, as crews stationed elsewhere often found themselves over Cumbria, either intentionally or whilst lost. Several Wellingtons from Bomber Command OTUs in the Midlands crashed in the area, as did aircraft from Fighter Command OTUs stationed in the north-east and Scottish borders. Unlike other areas there are no aircraft listed in this section that were lost while on operational sorties, even those aircraft from operational squadrons that were lost in the area being either on training or ferry flights. Also there is a surprisingly high proportion of post-war losses, with almost a third of the aircraft in this section falling into this category, these being a mixture of civilian and military aircraft. One of the more recent and certainly unusual of these is the General Dynamics F-111, lost as the result of a bird strike while on a low-level training flight. Its two-man crew used their escape capsule and separated from the aircraft, landing near the village of Shap on the eastern extremity of the National Park.

With such a high number of visitors to this area, it is probably inevitable that the amount of wreckage at many sites has diminished over the years. Yet surprisingly much still remains and there have been relatively few large-scale recoveries, though two notable ones are the controversial removal of the bulk of the remains of a Spitfire by a private individual for a proposed restoration project and the recovery of parts from the Halifax on Great Carrs. As with other areas of the country, memorials have been placed at some crash sites to provide both a focal point and a more permanent reminder of the sacrifice. Over time some of these have become weathered, with one already having been replaced and plans underway to replace another in the near future.

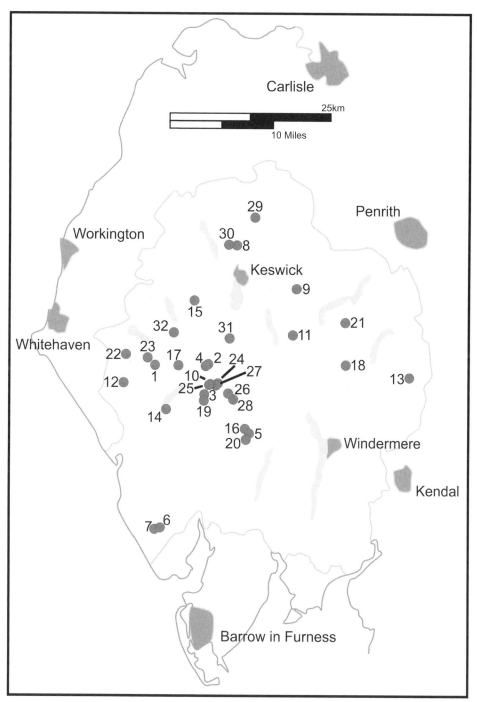

Crash Sites in the Lake District

Airspeed Oxford Mk.I AT486: No.2 AOS, RAF.   02-11-1941
Map No.1
NY 131107 (2,100 ft), Hanging Stone, Caw Fell, Cumbria

Sgt C. Des Baillets (RCAF)	Pilot	Killed
LAC H. Hodgkinson	Obs (u/t)	Killed

Flying in poor visibility whilst on a cross-country navigation exercise from RAF Millom in Cumbria, the aircraft struck the hillside at 09:53.

The remains of the undercarriage assemblies, pieces of wing structure, aluminium panels and a few parts from the engines lie in a scar on the grassy slope.

Avro Anson Mk.I DJ222 / A2: No.10 (O)AFU, RAF.   09-08-1943
Map No.2
NY 215106 (2,625 ft), Green Gable, Cumbria

Sgt W. Panasik	Pilot	Killed
Sgt E.A. Loppe	BA	Died of injuries
P/O C.E. Peake	Nav	Survived
F/O J.P.S. Calder	Nav	Survived
Sgt G.M. Chowney	WO	Survived

This Anson flew into the mountain top, after encountering adverse weather, while on a night navigation exercise from RAF Dumfries in Dumfries & Galloway. Two other Ansons from the unit also flew into high ground in the Lake District that night, one being Anson DJ275 which is included as a separate entry.

Fragments of wreckage remain, mainly within two small areas of stony ground, not far from the path over the top of the mountain.

Avro Anson Mk.I DJ275 / A1: No.10 (O)AFU, RAF.   09-08-1943
Map No.3
NY 209062 (2,900 ft), Sca Fell, Cumbria

Sgt S. Kowalczyk (PAF)	Pilot	Killed
Sgt T.W. Pickering (RCAF)	BA	Killed
Sgt J.T. Chadwick	Nav/BA	Killed
Sgt R.S. Deason	Nav/BA	Killed
Sgt T.S.W. Lawson	WO/AG	Killed

Flying from RAF Dumfries in Dumfries & Galloway, on a night navigation-exercise, the aircraft encountered adverse weather conditions and subsequently flew into the mountain top. Unlike the other two Ansons from this unit, which flew into high ground in the Lake District that night, in this case there were no survivors.

The aircraft struck the mountain high on the ridge, where many small parts from the aircraft remain strewn amongst the rocks. Immediately below is a crag and further pieces of wreckage lie on the scree slope at its base, while lower down, a trail of scattered aluminium panels can be found.

Avro Anson Mk.I DJ410: No.4 AOS, RAF.   01-10-1942
Map No.4
NY 213106 (2,200 ft), Stony Cove, Green Gable, Cumbria

W/O F.O. Cadham (RCAF)	Pilot	Killed
Four crewmembers, names not known		Survived

During a night navigation exercise, from RAF West Freugh in Dumfries & Galloway, the aircraft diverged to the south of the planned route by approximately 14 miles. Having been flying in cloud, it broke out of the cloud base and the pilot saw the high ground ahead. However, it was too late to take evasive action and a crash landing had to be made.

The site lies approximately 10 metres off the path through Stony Cove, at the base of the scree slope below the summit of Green Gable. Only tiny fragments from the aircraft remain, including wood screws and bits of plywood, which are scattered amongst rocks.

Avro Anson Mk.I EG686: No.1 SPTU, RAF.   20-03-1944
Map No.5
NY 274002 (2,100 ft), Swirl How, Coniston, Cumbria

Sgt K.M. Snelling	Pilot	Killed
Sgt K.J. Brettell	Pilot	Killed
Sgt W. Younger	WO/AG	Killed

Following a night navigation exercise this aircraft was returning to base at RAF Cark in Cumbria when it flew too far to the north and hit the mountain. The following day the wreckage was located by the RAF Millom Mountain Rescue Unit.

One of the remaining Cheetah engines from Anson EG686 on Swirl How.

Where the aircraft hit the mountainside there are a few fragments of wreckage, while small pieces of airframe are scattered on the slope below. Lower down on more level ground at NY 277002 are the remains of both Armstrong Siddeley Cheetah engines, one lying hidden in a hollow, while the other is lying on the grass near a stream.

Avro Anson Mk.I LT741: No.10 AGS, RAF.   02-01-1945
Map No.6
SD 140859 (1,880 ft), Blackcombe Screes, Black Combe, Cumbria

F/Sgt A.J. Wood	Pilot	Killed
W/O T.W. Johnson	AG	Killed
Sgt J.L. Turner	WO/AG (u/t)	Killed
Sgt K.D. Jenkins	WO (u/t)	Killed

Having taken-off from RAF Walney Island in Cumbria, on a air gunnery training flight, the aircraft failed to rendezvous with a Martinet Target Tug as planned. It is understood the aircraft then returned towards its base and whilst flying in cloud it hit the hill. Once the aircraft was posted missing, air and sea searches were conducted, but it was not until the 10 January 1945 that the wreckage was located.

The remaining wreckage from the aircraft, consisting of a few parts from an undercarriage assembly and bits of airframe, lies scattered on the Blackcombe screes, below where the aircraft impacted the mountain.

Beech C-45F 44-47194: 371st ASG, USAF.   12-03-1947
Map No.7
SD 130857 (1,650 ft), Black Combe, Cumbria

Capt W.J. Daner	Pilot	Survived
1st Lt A. Garner	Co-pilot	Survived

Having taken-off from Prestwick in South Ayrshire at around 14:00, for a flight to Bovingdon in Hertfordshire, approximately one hour later the aircraft had drifted off track. Flying at 2,000ft in a heavy snow shower it struck the snow covered hillside and slid to a halt. The aircraft remained relatively intact, but although the onboard radio equipment still received messages it would not transmit, so the crew were unable to send a distress call. Remaining in the aircraft overnight, the following morning they set out and made their way down to Holeghyll Farm.

Several sections of steel framework from the aircraft remain at the site, along with one of the main undercarriage legs, a section of firewall and a number of aluminium panels.

Steel framework from Beech C-45F 44-47194 on the top of Black Combe.

Boeing B-17E 41-9051 / UX-O 'Flaming Mayme': 813th BS / 482nd BG, USAAF.

14-09-1943

Map No.8

NY 258287 (2,625 ft), Skiddaw, Cumbria

Capt W.C. Anderson	Pilot	Killed
1st Lt R.J. Sudbury	Co-pilot	Killed
Capt R.R. Oeftiger	Nav	Killed
2nd Lt R.F. Diltz	BA	Killed
S/Sgt B.R. Hills	Eng	Killed
S/Sgt R.L. Jacobsen	Radio Op	Killed
Maj T.C. Henderson	Pass	Killed
Maj H.B. Williams	Pass	Killed
1st Lt C.H. Ballagh	Pass	Killed
1st Lt T.R. Doe	Pass	Killed

This Boeing aircraft flew into the mountainside while in cloud during a navigation training flight from Alconbury Air Station in Huntingdonshire. The aircraft was en route to RAF Turnhouse near Edinburgh, and on investigation it was thought that the crew had commenced a descent at their Estimated Time of Arrival for this destination, but due to drift the aircraft was actually still a long way to the south.

No.83 MU, RAF was tasked with salvaging the wreckage from the aircraft and lowered sections of it down the mountain using ropes. However, scattered on the steep scree slope where the aircraft burned out are many bits of melted aluminium and small pieces of airframe.

Bristol Beaufighter Mk.VIC EL285 / E: No.9 OTU, RAF.   15-11-1943
Map No.9
NY 351223 (1,675 ft), Wolf Crags, Matterdale Common, Cumbria

F/Sgt I.S. Sollows (RCAF)	Pilot	Killed
Sgt M.J. Lahausse	Nav	Killed

This aircraft hit the hillside while on a night navigation-exercise from RAF Crosby-on-Eden in Cumbria.

A rather indistinct hollow, on the tussock grass covered slope, marks the impact point, while a couple of small pieces of wreckage scattered in the vicinity are all that remain of the aircraft.

De Havilland Dominie X7394 / 'Merlin V': No.782 Sqn, RN.   30-08-1946
Map No.10
NY 217077 (2,650 ft), Broad Crag, Cumbria

Sub Lt (A) S.K. Kilsby	Pilot	Killed
CPOA H.J. Clark	–	Killed
Cdr Sgn W.T. Gwynne-Jones	Surgeon	Killed
SBA L.H. Watkinson	Sick Berth Attendant	Killed
CWM C.R Allwright DSM	Pass (Patient)	Killed

Serving as an air ambulance, based at Donibristle (HMS *Merlin*) in Fife, the aircraft was on an urgent flight from Abbotsinch (HMS *Sanderling*) in Renfrewshire to Stretton (HMS *Blackcap*) in Cheshire, where it was to refuel before continuing on to Rochester in Kent, where the seriously ill patient onboard was being taken for treatment. However, whilst flying in cloud the aircraft failed to clear the high ground along the route and hit Broad Crag. The following day an Anson from Anthorn (HMS *Nuthatch*) in Cumbria conducted an air search and located the burned out Dominie.

Amongst the rocks where the aircraft impacted are small fragments of wreckage and several steel interplane struts from the wing structure. On the slope immediately below is one of the de Havilland Gypsy Queen engines, while the other engine lies in rocks, on a wide ledge to the north-east where a few aluminium panels from the engine nacelles are also scattered.

De Havilland Mosquito N.F. Mk.XII HK141: No.51 OTU, RAF.   10-02-1945
Map No.11
NY 350151 (2,500 ft), Red Tarn, Helvellyn, Cumbria

W/O W.D.G. Frost (RAAF)	Pilot	Killed
F/Sgt C.F. Marshall (RAAF)	Nav	Killed

It appears that the aircraft flew off track while on a night cross-country exercise from RAF Cranfield in Bedfordshire and subsequently hit the side of Striding Edge at 20:20. The aircraft disintegrated and the bulk of the wreckage fell down the snow covered slope and into Red Tarn.

On the side of Striding Edge, around where the aircraft impacted, there are a few brass woodscrews and tiny fragments of aluminium. Similar items lie at NY 349152 at the edge of Red Tarn, while more sizeable pieces of wreckage, possibly including both Roll-Royce Merlin engines, are believed to lie submerged in the tarn.

Mark Sheldon views parts from Domine X7394 collected together on a rock below Broad Crag, whilst further down the slope is one of the aircraft's two de Havilland Gipsy Queen engines.

English Electric Canberra P.R. Mk.7 WT505: No.58 Sqn, RAF. 21-01-1956
Map No.12
NY 080067 (925 ft), Ponsonby Fell, Cumbria

F/O W.F.W.N. Gough	Pilot	Killed
F/O D. Cornforth	Nav	Killed

The aircraft was on a day cross-country flight from RAF Wyton in Huntingdonshire, when the Port engine began to lose thrust. Eyewitnesses observed the aircraft flying relatively slow at low-level, as if the pilot was intending to force land, but it then accelerated away, entered the cloud that obscured the high ground and hit the hilltop on a north-easterly track, leaving a long trail of wreckage.

At the site, on the grassy hilltop, there is almost no evidence of the accident, a few small fragments scattered in the grass being all that remained following a thorough operation by the salvage team.

General Dynamics F-111E 68-0081: 20th TFW, USAF.   05-03-1975
Map No.13
NY 529086 (1,700 ft), Saddle Crags, Shap Fells, Cumbria

Maj R.A. Wolf	Pilot	Survived
Maj J.K. Miller	WSO	Survived

Flying from Upper Heyford in Oxfordshire, the aircraft was engaged in low-level flying practice when a bird strike occurred, resulting in part of the cockpit windshield being shattered. Due to the level of damage the crew operated the ejection system, with the cockpit capsule separating from the aircraft and descending by parachute, while the aircraft then flew into the hillside.

A large bog-filled crater marks the impact point, but contains only small fragments of wreckage. A few other parts from the aircraft remain though, lower down the hillside.

The distinct crater caused by the crash of F-111E 68-0081 contains only small pieces scattered about.

Grumman Avenger T.R. Mk.II JZ390: No.763 Sqn, RN.   16-01-1945
Map No.14
NY 151037 approx, Great Gully, Wastwater, Cumbria

Lt B.J. Kennedy (RCNVR)	Pilot	Killed
Msm (A) G. Fell	Nav	Killed
LAM P.R. Mallorie	WO	Killed

Returning to base at Inskip (HMS *Nightjar*) in Lancashire from a night navigation-exercise, the aircraft flew into the crag above Wastwater and disintegrated.

Small parts from the aircraft are scattered on the scree slope below Great Gully at NY149039. The core of the engine from the aircraft remained at the side of Wastwater for many years, but is now thought to lie submerged in the lake, along with the tail section of the aircraft.

Handley Page Halifax Mk.II Srs.Ia JP182: No.14 FPP, ATA.   24-01-1944
Map No.15
NY 193204 (2,625 ft), Crag Hill, Newlands Fells, Cumbria

Flt Capt B. Short (ATA)	Pilot	Killed
Snr Flt Eng A. Bird (ATA)	Flt Eng	Killed

Departing from RAF Kinloss in Moray the aircraft was on a ferry flight to RAF Kemble in Wiltshire, where it was to be delivered to No.5 MU. However, having encountered cloud the aircraft descended and then flew into the crag close to the top of the mountain.

The bulk of the wreckage was salvaged by No.83 MU and although only a few fragments remain on the crag where the aircraft struck, many small pieces of airframe lie on the steep scree slope below. Further wreckage, consisting mainly of torn aluminium panels can be found in the valley at NY 195206, near to and also within the sheepfold below Scot Crag.

Note: Flt Capt Short had been involved in a previous accident on high ground, when he successfully force landed de Havilland Leopard Moth AV986 on the top of Rushup Edge in the Peak District, in deteriorating visibility. However, an attempt to take-off when the weather improved resulted in the aircraft being written-off when it failed to clear a stone wall.

Handley Page Halifax Mk.V Srs.Ia LL505 / FD-S: No.1659 HCU, RAF.   22-10-1944
Map No.16
NY 270009 (2,550 ft), Great Carrs, Furness Fells, Cumbria

F/O J.A. Johnston (RCAF)	Pilot	Killed
F/O F.A. Bell (RCAF)	Nav	Killed
Sgt W.B. Ferguson	Flt Eng	Killed
Sgt H.E. Pyche (RCAF)	Flt Eng	Killed
F/O R.N. Whitley (RCAF)	BA	Killed
Sgt C.G. Whittingstall (RCAF)	WO/AG	Killed
Sgt D.F. Titt (RCAF)	AG	Killed
Sgt G. Riddoch (RCAF)	AG	Killed

During a night navigation-exercise from RAF Topcliffe in North Yorkshire, the crew of Halifax LL505 became uncertain of their position and after circling for a while they decided to descend through cloud to obtain a visual position fix and in doing so hit the mountain top.

Probably the most visited crash site in the Lake District lies on the ridge, where the aircraft partially burned out. There is a cairn with a memorial cross mounted on it, alongside which are the two main undercarriage assemblies. However, most of the remains from the aircraft lie in Broad Slack, where the bulk of the wreck was dumped by the salvage team. On the scree slope at NY 272008 are two substantial wing sections and three of the propeller hub and reduction gear units. The one remaining Rolls-Royce Merlin engine lies slightly lower down, and other pieces of wreckage are scattered down the valley for quite a distance, the fourth propeller hub being at NY 275013. Two of the other engines from the aircraft were removed in 1997 using an RAF Chinook helicopter, and one is now displayed outside the Ruskin Museum in Coniston Village.

A broken up section of wing from Halifax LL505 on the scree slope below Great Carrs.

The remains of the 24 Cylinder Napier Dagger engine from Hawker Hector K8096

Hawker Hector K8096: No.1 SAC, RAF.   08-09-1941
Map No.17
NY 168103 (2,200 ft), Red Pike, Wasdale Head, Cumbria

   F/Lt J.A. Craig DFC   Pilot   Killed

Having taken-off from RAF Binbrook in Lincolnshire on a ferry flight to RAF Dumfries in Dumfries & Galloway, the aircraft subsequently hit the mountain. It appears the pilot, from No.18 MU, did not route via Catterick and refuel as he had been instructed, but attempted to fly direct to the intended destination. Investigators concluded that the accident occurred while the pilot was searching for somewhere to force land after the aircraft began to run low on fuel.

 A scar between a series of rock outcrops marks the impact point, and contains the remains of the 24-cylinder H-block air-cooled Napier Dagger engine from the aircraft, along with some pieces of framework. Other small parts, including the engine oil cooler, are scattered down the slope below the scar.

Hawker Hind K6614: No.98 Sqn, RAF.   05-06-1937
Map No.18
NY 428106 (1,975 ft), Threshthwaite Cove, Cumbria

Sgt S. Mitchell	Pilot	Killed
LAC G. Murray	Obs	Killed

The Hind flew into the mountainside while in cloud, en route from RAF West Freugh in Dumfries & Galloway to RAF Hucknall in Nottinghamshire.

Amongst the rocks where the aircraft burned out there are tiny fragments of wreckage, while in a narrow rocky gully on the steep slope below the site there are a few small pieces of airframe. The remains of the Rolls-Royce Kestrel engine from this aircraft are at the Aviation and Military Museum at Millom.

Hawker Hurricane Mk.Is V6565 and V7742: No.55 OTU, RAF.   12-08-1941
Map No.19
NY 209051 & NY 209050 (2,400 ft), Slight Side, Sca Fell, Cumbria

P/O Z. Hohne (PAF)	Pilot (V7742)	Killed
Sgt S. Karubin DFM (PAF)	Pilot (Inst) (V6565)	Killed

During a training flight, from RAF Usworth in Durham, the two aircraft struck the mountain while diving through cloud in formation. The two aircraft impacted approximately 100 metres apart, and there are two distinct trails of wreckage. At the northern site there is a memorial plaque commemorating both pilots, a cross made from two pieces of wreckage, the remains of the Roll-Royce Merlin engine and sections of wing structure. This wreckage has been identified as originating from Hurricane V6565, as several pieces of wreckage carry Gloster Aircraft inspection stamps, the aircraft having been built by this company under subcontract. Whereas Hurricane V7742 was built by Hawker and this company's inspection stamps can be found on wreckage at the southern site. The impact point here is on a crag, where evidence of a fire can still be discerned on the rocks, and a few small fragments of wreckage remain. Much more wreckage lies on the rocky slope below, including part of the propeller gearing, both main undercarriage legs, sections of wing structure and the broken-up engine oil cooler.

Hawker Hurricane Mk.Xs AG264 and AG275: No.55 OTU, RAF.   23-04-1943
Map No.20
SD 272989 (2,300 ft), Brim Fell, Furness Fells, Cumbria

Sgt H.M. Atherton (RAAF)	Pilot (AG264)	Killed
Sgt L.T. Cook (RAAF)	Pilot (AG275)	Killed

Flying from RAF Annan in Dumfries & Galloway, the two pilots had completed an hour of formation flying training with an instructor, before breaking away over Maryport and being ordered to carry out low-flying training individually in the local area and practise using Direction Finding for homing back to base. However, it is understood that the two

Wreckage from Hurricane V6565: a section of wing spar, shattered remains of the aircraft's Merlin engine and the memorial plaque with an improvised cross.

pilots remained together, in loose formation and then flew off to the south, entered cloud and subsequently hit the mountain.

Hurricane AG264 struck the mountain on a ledge between two crags, and climbing to the impact point, where only a few fragments remain, is not recommended. However, on the scree slope below the crags are small parts from the airframe and pieces of shattered engine casing. The core of the engine, which remained in the stream at the base of the slope for many years, is no longer on site. The impact point of Hurricane AG275 is thought to be on the ridge near to the summit of the mountain, but has not been located by the authors at this time.

Note: There have been reports that wreckage from a Hurricane lies in nearby Low Water, but any wreckage in the tarn is more likely to originate from another aircraft, which hit the ridge close to the summit of The Old Man of Coniston on the 14 October 1942. The type of aircraft involved has not been positively determined, being either a Beech or Lockheed built twin-engine cargo aircraft. It was flying from RAF Ayr in South Ayrshire to Hendon in Greater London via Limavady in Co. Londonderry and the pilot, F/O G.B. Grenfell (RAF) plus two civilian pilots flying as passengers, Mr O.B. Keith (American) and Mr G.W. Branson (American), were killed in the accident.

Lockheed Hudson Mk.V AM680 / B-68: No.1(C) OTU, RAF.   10-11-1942
Map No.21
NY 427171 (1,550 ft), Beda Head, Martindale Common, Cumbria

F/Sgt J.F. Saunders	Pilot	Killed
F/O D.I. Jones	Nav	Killed
Sgt S.A. Veasey	WO/AG	Killed
Sgt H. Dickinson	WO/AG	Killed

Having taken-off from RAF Silloth in Cumbria at 00:50, the aircraft was one and a half hours into a night-navigation exercise, when the ROC lost track of the aircraft in the vicinity of Ullswater. After the aircraft failed to return to base, air and ground searches were commenced, but the cloud covering the high ground hindered the operation. In the afternoon of the 11-11-1942 police involved in the ground search came across the burnt out wreck on the western slopes of Beda Head.

At the site, on the rough grass covered slope, there are two scars containing small pieces of wreckage.

Miles Hawk Trainer G-ALGJ. (Privately Owned).   22-07-1952
Map No.22
NY 085121 (1,350 ft), Lank Rigg, Cumbria

Mr W.L. Foster	Pilot	Survived

During a private flight from Blackpool in Lancashire to Carlisle in Cumbria the aircraft flew into cloud, hit the hillside and overturned. After extricating himself from the wrecked aircraft, Mr Foster made his way down off the hill.

A few small pieces of wreckage from the aircraft, including parts from the undercarriage, lie scattered on the rough grassy slope near to the site.

North American Sabre Mk.6 23380 / BB-380: No.421 Sqn, RCAF. 26-06-1959
Map No.23
NY 122120 (2,075 ft), Iron Crag, Ennerdale, Cumbria

F/O R.G. Starling (RCAF)	Pilot	Killed

Having taken-off from Prestwick in South Ayrshire the aircraft was en route to Wethersfield in Essex, when the pilot descended before clearing the high ground on the route and struck the cloud covered hilltop at 13:11. On impact the aircraft disintegrated leaving a trail of wreckage well over half mile in length.

Pieces of wreckage are scattered south over the hilltop from the point of impact. In rocks at NY 121116 there are many small pieces of airframe, while slightly lower down the slope is the almost complete port wing and a small section of the fuselage with part of the unit code discernable. Another substantial section of wing structure lies in rocks at NY 121114, while engine remains and other wreckage can be found south of Bleaberry Gill close to the sheepfold at NY 120111.

The port wing from RCAF Sabre 23380 on Iron Crag, although sections have been cut out the remains of the Canadian roundel is visible.

Piper Cherokee G-ASEK: J.B. Wimble (Aviation) Ltd.   17-09-1966
Map No.24
NY 230079 (2,550 ft), Esk Hause, Cumbria

Mr G.D. Massy	Pilot	Killed
Mr L. Aitchison	Pass	Killed

On a pleasure flight from the disused RAF Milfield in Northumberland, the aircraft proceeded to the Lake District and flew south along Borrowdale. Cloud was hanging on the mountain tops and it appears the pilot tried to remain below it and fly through the col at Esk Hause in order to get into Eskdale. However, on reaching the col the aircraft entered cloud and then struck a large rock outcrop which tore off the complete starboard wing, leaving the rest of the aircraft to drop onto the rocks below.

There are a few fragments of wreckage where the aircraft struck the rock outcrop, but most of the remaining wreckage is below the outcrop. Gathered together amongst rocks are several aluminium panels and sections of engine exhaust, while approximately 10 metres to the south is the Avco Lycoming engine from the aircraft.

Piper Cherokee G-AWBD: Southport Aviation Company Ltd.   19-04-1978
Map No.25
NY 213077 (2,450 ft), Scafell Pike, Cumbria

Mr R. Bentley	Pilot (Inst)	Survived
Mr A. Thornton	Pilot (Pass)	Survived
Mr K. Charles	Pilot (Student)	Survived

The Cherokee flew into the mountain while in cloud, during a pilot training flight from RAF Woodvale in Merseyside to Carlisle in Cumbria. It was 30 hours after the accident

The remains of panels and exhaust piping from Piper Cherokee G-ASEK on the Knotts of Tongue, some pieces still have paint on them. The piece in the foreground is part of a door with the lock still in place.

when the wrecked aircraft was found and the three men rescued, being airlifted to Whitehaven hospital.

The aircraft came to rest on top of rocks on the steep slope, where following a thorough clear-up operation all that can be found are a few bits of plastic trim from the aircraft.

Piper Saratoga G-BNJS: M.M. & G. Aviation.   29-11-1987
Map No.26
NY 245063 (2,750 ft), Bow Fell, Cumbria

      Mr A.R. Hiscox   Pilot   Killed

The Saratoga hit the mountain close to the summit while flying in cloud. The aircraft was on a private flight, the details of which are not known.

From the impact point wreckage is scattered down the mountain, through one of the gullies on Bowfell Lings and onto the scree below. In the gully is a substantial section of wing, while on the scree is the Avco Lycoming engine and numerous other small parts from the aircraft.

Supermarine Spitfire Mk.XVI SL611: No.603 Squadron, RAuxAF.   20-11-1947
Map No.27
NY 225077 (2,750 ft), Ill Crag, Scafell Pike, Cumbria

F/Lt D.J.O. Loudon AFC   Pilot   Killed

Having flown from RAF Hullavington in Wiltshire to RAF Hawarden in Cheshire, on the first stage of a cross-country flight to RAF Turnhouse near Edinburgh, the aircraft was refuelled and departed on the second stage shortly before mid-day. It subsequently failed to arrive at the intended destination and once it was established the aircraft had not diverted to another airfield, it was posted missing and a search was commenced. Continuing poor weather hindered the search, which was scaled down after a couple of days and eventually called off. It was more than five months later on the 1 May 1948 when the wreckage of the aircraft was finally discovered, when a shepherd boy came across it on the mountainside.

Only a few pieces of wreckage now remain, scattered down the steep scree slope from the impact point, where a small memorial plaque is fixed to an adjacent rock outcrop. A significant quantity of wreckage, including the Rolls-Royce Merlin engine, which had remained on the mountainside for several decades, was removed in the late 1990s.

A badly damaged section of wing from Piper Saratoga G-BNJS on Bow Fell.

Vickers Vildebeast Mk.III K4607: No.42 Sqn, RAF. 04-06-1937
Map No.28
NY 251051 approx., Crinkle Crags, Langdale, Cumbria

Sgt F. Wilkinson	Pilot	Killed
LAC A. Mitchell	Obs	Killed

The aircraft hit the mountain while flying in cloud, during a cross-country flight from RAF Filton near Bristol to RAF Donibristle in Fife.

The aircraft struck the crags near the top of the ridge, the wreckage falling onto the steep slope below, where it appears there is no longer any evidence of the crash. However, lower down the mountain on the northern bank of the stream at NY 255053 (as marked on a sketch map in A. Wainwright's Central Fells Pictorial Guide) are several parts from the engine and a couple of struts from the undercarriage.

The remaining wreckage from Vickers Vildebeast K4607 below Crinkle Crags.

Vickers Wellington Mk.IC T2714 / DD-C: No.22 OTU, RAF.   08-02-1942
Map No.29
NY 287330 (1,950ft), Burn Tod, Uldale Fells, Cumbria

Sgt L.G. Mizen	Pilot	Killed
Sgt J.G. Hardie	Co-pilot	Killed
P/O D.J. Richardson (RCAF)	Obs	Killed
F/Sgt L.J.R. Bechard (RCAF)	WO/AG	Killed
F/Sgt E.G. Jenner (RCAF)	WO/AG	Killed
Sgt Rutherford	AG	Survived

During a navigation exercise from RAF Wellesbourne Mountford in Warwickshire the onboard radio equipment failed and the aircraft subsequently altered track having overshot the intended turning point on the planned route. As a result it then flew into the cloud-covered hill side. Although seriously injured Sgt Rutherford was able to make his own way down off the hill.

Tiny fragments from the aircraft lie at the site, in a small scar running down the slope.

Vickers Wellington Mk.III X3336: No.23 OTU, RAF.   16-12-1942
Map No.30
NY 250284 (2,300ft), Longside Edge, Carl Side, Cumbria

F/Sgt R.V.W. Bellew	Pilot	Killed
P/O A. Higgins (RCAF)	Nav	Killed
P/O R.S. Goodwin	Nav	Killed
F/Sgt A.J. Dubben	Obs	Killed
F/Sgt G.W. Hicks	WO/AG	Killed
F/Sgt R.W. Lawton (RCAF)	AG	Killed

Flying from RAF Pershore in Worcestershire on a night navigation exercise, the aircraft diverged from the planned route, struck the mountain and disintegrated.

Where the aircraft initially struck the mountain, high on the ridge, only fragments of wreckage are to be found. Quite a few small pieces of airframe remain on the steep scree slope down into Southerndale, and as the scree is unstable it has undoubtedly buried further wreckage.

Vickers Wellington Mk.IC DV600 / L3: No.25 OTU, RAF.   04-09-1942
Map No.31
NY 249145 (775ft), High Doat, Borrowdale, Cumbria.

Sgt W.B. Sage (RCAF)	Pilot	Killed
F/Sgt G.E. Derbyshire (RCAF)	Nav	Killed
Sgt J.L. Brovender (RCAF)	BA	Killed
F/Sgt J. Anderson (RCAF)	WO/AG	Killed
Sgt H.B. Burnett	WO/AG	Killed

During a night cross-country training flight from RAF Finningley in South Yorkshire, the aircraft descended into Borrowdale and flew into the tree covered crag at 22:30. It is understood that the weather conditions in the area were particularly bad at the time.

A few small pieces of wreckage are scattered in the woodland near the impact point, but are difficult to spot due to the undergrowth. The steep rocky tree-covered slopes surrounding the site also mean reaching it is not straightforward.

Vickers Wellington Mk.III HZ715: No.22 OTU, RAF. 16-06-1944
Map No.32
NY 160156 (2,200 ft), Red Pike, Buttermere, Cumbria

P/O A.D. Cooper (RCAF)	Pilot	Killed
F/O F.A. Dixon (RCAF)	Co-pilot	Killed
F/Lt E. Unterseher (RCAF)	Pilot (Inst)	Killed
P/O D. Titleman (RCAF)	Nav	Killed
Sgt G.M. Anderson (RCAF)	BA	Killed
F/O R.E. Simonson (RCAF)	WO/AG	Killed
W/O G.R. Coatup (RCAF)	WO/AG	Killed
Sgt C.M. Hodges (RCAF)	AG	Killed

While conducting a dual flying instruction and day cross-country navigation exercise from RAF Stratford in Warwickshire, the aircraft flew into the cloud covered mountainside, disintegrated and burned out.

The impact point lies on a steep scree slope. Only small fragments of wreckage remain and these are scattered from the impact point down the rocky slope and into Ling Comb.

Chapter Six

North Yorkshire Moors

The North Yorkshire Moors area has at its centre the National Park of the same name, established in 1952 and covering some 554 square miles. The landscape is characterised by an upland plateau, with its highest point being Urra Moor at 1,489ft and features the largest continuous expanse of heather moorland in England and Wales, as this plant apparently thrives on the acidic peaty soils and relatively low rainfall here. Surprisingly this is also the most wooded of our National Parks, with over a fifth of the landscape under tree cover. However, this is mainly due to new conifer plantations which have been established on moorland reclaimed since the Second World War and a few crash sites, once on open moors, are now to be found deep in such forests. The upland landscape here is formed mainly by Jurassic era sandstones, shales and mudstones, which have been uplifted and tilted, then exposed by glaciation and weathering. To the south younger calcareous sandstones and limestones form tabular hills, giving way to the lowland areas of the Vale of Pickering and Ryedale with undulating land formed from deposits of glacial till, sand and gravel.

During the Second World War, Yorkshire was home to No.4 (Bomber) Group, Bomber Command, whose headquarters was until April 1940, at Linton-on-Ouse, before moving to Heslington Hall, near York. From January 1943 they were joined by No.6 (Royal Canadian Air Force) Bomber Group who took on a number of the No.4 Group airfields. The Canadians also initially used Linton-on-Ouse as their headquarters, but soon moved to Allerton Park near, Knaresborough. These two groups eventually comprised twenty-five operational squadrons operating from airfields throughout the region, but mostly concentrated in the Vale of York area. With the high ground of the North Yorkshire Moors lying between these bases and the east coast it is perhaps unsurprising that this section, contains the highest percentage of Bomber Command losses of any high ground area. As in other areas many of these aircraft were lost as they returned from operational sorties, with fatigue, battle damage, low fuel and navigational errors all contributing. The squadrons of No.4 Group were involved in operational sorties from the earliest days of WW2 and a number of the losses listed in this section reflect this. As the war progressed the two groups were at the forefront of the Bomber Command night bombing campaign and earlier aircraft such as the Whitley and Wellington gave way to the Halifax and Lancaster and again this is reflected in the listings. Not all the losses were operational sorties, as training of bomber and nightfighter crews also took place in the area and this included frequent night cross-country flights to prepare crews for operational flying. Sadly, accidents on such flights seem to have been almost inevitable. Two Coastal Command aircraft returning from patrols over the sea came to grief here, including an Air Sea Rescue Warwick. These were equipped to drop airborne lifeboats and must have been the last hope for many of their Bomber Command counterparts who came down in the North Sea. Finally a number of *Luftwaffe* aircraft became victims of the high ground of North Yorkshire, perhaps as they considered much of Britain's east coast to be low lying and thus were caught out by the moors that rise to nearly 1,500ft above sea level. Only one is included in this section, however, as the crash sites of enemy aircraft were usually completely cleared for intelligence purposes, making them difficult to identify today.

With so many airmen, including those from outside Britain's shores, serving in Yorkshire during WW2, special arrangements were made for the burial of the inevitable casualties in the early months of the conflict. At Harrogate (Stonefall) Cemetery areas were set aside for service war burials in Sections 20E and 21E and in July 1943, the Air Forces Section was opened at the eastern side of the cemetery for burials from airfields in Yorkshire and the north-eastern counties. Many of the casualties from the aircraft listed in this section and from some of those listed in the Pennines section may be found here and for those wishing to pay their respects or wishing to understand the scale of the sacrifice involved, a visit here is recommended. The cemetery contains 988 Second World War burials, almost all airmen, with 665 of them being Canadian, 97 Australian, 23 New Zealand and 170 from the United Kingdom.

Recovery of crashed aircraft from the North Yorkshire Moors area during WW2 was the responsibility of No.60 MU, based at RAF Shipton, a few miles north west of York and they certainly appear to have been diligent in their task. Dismantling aircraft at remote crash sites, constructing wooden sledges to drag the sections away and bridging ditches, as well as enlisting the help of local army units with tracked vehicles, all appear regularly in their records. Recoveries often took place over several weeks and it is surprising that they left anything at all! Those remains that they did leave also seem to have suffered more than most from the attentions of scrap dealers in the past and a number that were noted as having substantial remains after the war, soon disappeared. Though today most of the sites listed in this section only contain small scraps and therefore can be challenging to find, a few are now marked by memorials that will hopefully provide a more permanent reminder to visitors and passers by.

Fire alert: during the summer months the heather can become very dry and susceptible to fire. Accidental fires damage the moors and their wildlife as the peaty soils can burn for months. If you visit the North York Moors please take great care not to start fires. Please don't drop matches, cigarettes or glass and please don't light fires or use barbecues on the moors.

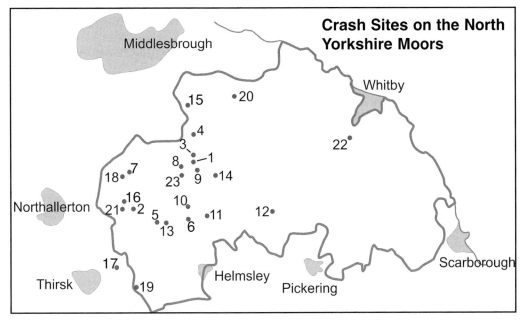

Crash Sites on the North Yorkshire Moors

Middlesbrough

Whitby

•15   •20

•4

3
8.   •—1
18• •7
23• 9 •14

•16
21• •2   10.
Northallerton   5.   •11   12•
        13 6.

17.

Thirsk   •19

Helmsley   Pickering

Scarborough

22•

Airspeed Oxford Mk.I LW903: No.18 (P)AFU, RAF.   08-01-1945
Map No.1
NZ 597010 (1,425ft), Urra Moor, Ingleby Greenhow, North Yorkshire

F/O O.M.W. Clarson (RCAF)	Pilot (Capt)	Killed
F/O N.G. Riley (RCAF)	Pilot	Killed
F/O J.D.S. Barkell	Pilot	Killed

The three crewmembers were flying the aircraft from RAF Snitterfield, used as a satellite airfield by the unit, to their main base at RAF Church Lawford, Warwickshire. In poor weather conditions they had obviously strayed too far north, when the aircraft struck the moor. The aircraft may have crashed due to loss of control in icing conditions rather than it having simply flown into high ground.

A collection of panels and the crushed remains of fuel tanks lie in a pile in the heather.

The pile of wreckage from Oxford LW903 on the otherwise featureless Urra moor.

Armstrong Whitworth Whitley Mk.V T4138 / KN-H: No.77 Sqn, RAF.   15-12-1940
Map No.2
SE 499936 (1,275ft), Arden Great Moor, Osmotherley, North Yorkshire

P/O H.H.J. Miller	Pilot	Survived
Sgt D.H. Gilbert	Co-pilot	Survived
Sgt G. Thorpe	Obs	Survived
Sgt A.E. Hammond	WO/AG	Survived
Sgt C. Williams	WO/AG	Killed

The crew was taking part in operations against Berlin from RAF Topcliffe, when one of the aircraft's engines failed while on the outward leg. The pilot turned back towards England and while circling the Vale of York flew into high ground.

A large burnt scar containing many small fragments of the aircraft remains on the uphill side of a track, which runs around the edge of the moor.

Armstrong Whitworth Whitley Mk.V T4171 / GE-O: No.58 Sqn, RAF. 21-10-1940
Map No.3
NZ 598021 (1,250ft), Greenhow Moor, Ingleby Greenhow, North Yorkshire

P/O E.H. Brown	Pilot	Killed
Sgt L.F.P. Adlam	Co-pilot	Killed
Sgt C.S.G. Green	Obs	Died of Injuries 23-10-1940.
Sgt M.C. Caryll-Tilkin	WO/AG	Killed
Sgt R.E. Langfield	AG	Survived

The crew had taken part in a raid against the Skoda factory at Plzen in Czechoslovakia and was on the final leg of the flight back to RAF Linton on Ouse near York when the aircraft crashed close to Botton Head on the northern edge of Greenhow Moor. The

Sparse remains of Whitley T4171 at the crash site, with the forestry plantation where other parts may be found below.

aircraft has been reported to have been shot down by a German nightfighter on an intruder flight, however the RAF records indicate that it flew into the high ground when the aircraft had all but run out of fuel.

A small number of parts still remain at the crash site and in the forestry plantation that now exists below the site.

Armstrong Whitworth Whitley Mk.V Z6663 / MH-D: No.51 Sqn, RAF. 09-06-1941
Map No.4
NZ 598055 (1,100ft), Bank Foot, Ingleby Greenhow, North Yorkshire.

P/O J.R. Pertwee	Pilot	Killed
F/Sgt G. Stubbs	Pilot	Killed
Sgt W.C.G. Roper	Obs	Killed
Sgt C.F. Ranson	WO/AG	Killed
F/Sgt J. Cousins	AG	Killed

The aircraft flew into high ground in poor visibility while returning to RAF Dishforth from a raid against Dortmund.

A few pieces remain in a disused quarry within a forestry plantation.

Avro Lancaster B. Mk.I ED481 / WS-N: No.9 Sqn, RAF.   30-01-1943
Map No.5
SE 538915 (700ft), Moor Gate, Hawnby, North Yorkshire.

W/O F.G. Nelson (RCAF)	Pilot	Killed
Sgt M. Allan (RCAF)	Flt Eng	Killed
Sgt G.F. Done	Nav	Killed
Sgt A.A.F. Williams	BA	Killed
Sgt H.S. Jones	WO/AG	Killed
Sgt A.W. Butcher	AG	Killed
Sgt W.G. Murton	AG	Killed

The aircraft crashed after having been diverted to RAF Leeming near Northallerton, rather than its normal base of RAF Waddington near Lincoln, while returning from a raid against Hamburg.

The crash site of Lancaster Mk.I ED481 near Hawnby, small pieces remain scattered in the tussocky grass.

Small pieces of the aircraft remain scattered in the tussocky grass between Moor Gate and Hawnby Hill.

Avro Lancaster B. Mk.X KB701 / VR-B: No.419 Sqn, RCAF.   16-05-1944
Map No.6
SE 589920 (875ft), Helmsley Moor, Helmsley, North Yorkshire

F/O J.G. McMaster (RCAF)	Pilot	Killed
P/O E.M. Parsons (RCAF)	Pilot	Killed
Sgt G.T. Jones	Flt Eng	Killed
W/O H.G. Grice (RCAF)	WO/AG	Killed
Sgt N.F. Alsop (RCAF)	AG	Killed
Sgt F.A. Milne (RCAF)	AG	Killed
2nd Lt E.N. Fordham (USAAF)	Pass	Killed

The crew was on a night bombing training flight from RAF Middleton St George, now Teeside Airport, when it crashed while flying in low cloud.

Small pieces of the aircraft still remain scattered across the moor where it crashed.

Avro Lancaster B. Mk.I NF961 / LE-L: No.630 Sqn, RAF.   18-10-1944
Map No.7
SE 492995 (900ft), Far Moor, Swainby, North Yorkshire

F/O D.A. Brammer	Pilot	Killed
Sgt L.G. Cook	Flt Eng	Killed
W/O G.J. Davis	Nav/BA	Killed
F/Sgt W.A. White	Nav/BA	Killed
F/Sgt D.G. Holyoak	WO/AG	Killed
Sgt J.C. Fitzpatrick	AG	Killed
Sgt C.J. Evans	AG	Killed

The crew was on a night cross-country training flight from RAF East Kirkby in Lincolnshire when the aircraft crashed on Far Moor and was destroyed.

Only small pieces of the aircraft still remain at the site, though until the 1960s large pieces of the aircraft were still present, but these are believed to have been removed for scrap.

Bristol Beaufighter Mk.IF R2152: No.2 OTU, RAF.   28-04-1943
Map No.8
NZ 578004 (1,200ft), Broad Ings, Urra, North Yorkshire

F/O P.E. Davison	Pilot	Killed
Sgt E.N. Sykes	Nav	Killed

The two crew were undertaking a cross-country navigation flight from RAF Catfoss near Beverley when they flew into the high ground in poor visibility.

A bare patch in the heather moorland contains a quantity of melted aluminium and exploded 20mm ammunition. The largest remaining items are a couple of pieces of alloy

Sparse remains from Beaufighter R2152 lie in a bare patch amongst the heather on Urra Moor.

aircraft structure, approximately 1ft square.

Note: Explosive 20mm cannon projectiles may be found here and cannot be assumed to be safe, so should not be touched.

Bristol Blenheim Mk.I L1449: No.54 OTU, RAF.   18-07-1941
Map No.9
SE 604998 (1,200ft), Bransdale, Cockayne, North Yorkshire.

P/O E.J. Woodhead   Pilot   Survived

The pilot was on a solo searchlight homing exercise from RAF Church Fenton near York. He was vectored out to the north-east and while descending through low cloud to gain a visual fix on the searchlights back towards York, the aircraft struck the ground.

Little remains at the site, which is now in a wooded area close to a waterfall in Badger Gill that has flooded over the years and remaining pieces have been moved considerable distances each time.

Bristol Blenheim Mk.I L8729: No.54 OTU, RAF.   18-07-1941
Map No.10
SE 590941 (1,000ft), Coniser Howel, Bilsdale, North Yorkshire

P/O A.D. McMurtie   Pilot   Killed

This pilot was undertaking a very similar exercise to the pilot of Blenheim L1449 when he descended into the high ground through cloud. The aircraft burst into flames on impact and was completely destroyed.

A bare patch containing pieces of melted aluminium and small fragments from the aircraft can still be found on the moor.

De Havilland Mosquito N.F. Mk.30 NT266: No.54 OTU, RAF.   08-11-1946
Map No.11
SE 620924 (775ft), Pockley Moor, Kirkbymoorside, North Yorkshire

S/Ldr N.D. Hallifax	Pilot	Killed
F/O R.E. Chater	Nav / Radar Op	Killed

The two airmen were on a training exercise from RAF Leeming, in the Vale of York near Northallerton, in poor weather conditions which were recorded in the unit's records as fit only for restricted flying for most of the day. At some point in the flight the aircraft at high speed dived into the moor leaving a large crater.

The crater, which stands out clearly on current aerial photographs, remains to mark the crash site and is usually filled with water, but is surrounded by many small fragments of the aircraft.

De Havilland Tiger Moth N6793: No.4 EFTS, RAF.   06-09-1945
Map No.12
SE 727932 (875ft), Spaunton Moor, North Yorkshire

F/Sgt J.S. Carter	Pilot	Survived
Sgt P.W. Barsby	Nav	Survived

One of the few sites in the North Yorkshire Moors with a reasonable amount still remaining. This is the crater marking where Mosquito NT266 dived into the ground.

DISCOVER MORE ABOUT MILITARY HISTORY

Pen & Sword Books have over 1500 titles in print covering all aspects of military history on land, sea and air. If you would like to receive more information and special offers on your preferred interests from time to time along with our standard catalogue, please complete your areas of interest below and return this card (no stamp required in the UK). Alternatively, register online at www.pen-and-sword.co.uk. Thank you.

PLEASE NOTE: We do not sell data information to any third party companies

Mr/Mrs/Ms/Other.................Name...

Address...

....Postcode......................

Email address...
if you wish to receive our email newsletter, please tick here ❑

PLEASE SELECT YOUR AREAS OF INTEREST

Ancient History ❑	Medieval History ❑	English Civil War ❑
Napoleonic ❑	Pre World War One ❑	World War One ❑
World War Two ❑	Post World War Two ❑	Falklands ❑
Aviation ❑	Maritime ❑	Battlefield Guides ❑
Regimental History ❑	Military Reference ❑	Military Biography ❑

Website: www.pen-and-sword.co.uk • Email: enquiries@pen-and-sword.co.uk
Telephone: 01226 734555 • Fax: 01226 734438

Pen & Sword Books

FREEPOST SF5

47 Church Street

BARNSLEY

South Yorkshire

S70 2BR

The navigator of the aircraft was undertaking a pilot refresher course at No.4 EFTS, which was stationed at Brough near Hull in East Yorkshire. The pilot had been instructed to avoid poor weather but instead of returning to base on encountering deteriorating conditions, he flew above the low cloud and while subsequently trying to descend through the cloud layer the aircraft struck the ground.

Only a few small pieces of the aircraft still remain at the site and most appear to have been affected by fire, possibly due to the aircraft having been burnt by the recovery unit.

Dornier Do217E-4 4342 / U5+GR: KG2, *Luftwaffe*.　　　17-12-1942

Map No.13

SE 554915 (800ft), Easterside Hill, Hawnby, North Yorkshire

Olt R. Hausner	Pilot	Killed (Missing)
Ufz S. Erd	Obs	Killed (Missing)
Ofw H. Hupe	WO	Killed
Ofw E. Weiderer	Eng	Killed

This aircraft was one of a number taking part in a night raid against York and was flying from its base at Deelan in Holland. While on the inbound leg, flying at low level in cloud, it struck the gently rising moor, ploughed through a wall and exploded. Such was the destruction that only the remains of two of the crew were ever found.

No remains of the aircraft are visible at this site and the only evidence of the crash is an obvious missing section in the wall, which runs roughly west to east.

Note: This crash site is effectively the last resting place for two of the crew, please respect it accordingly.

Handley Page Halifax Mk.II JD106 / ND-T: No.1666 HCU, RAF. 23-06-1944

Map No.14

SE 634990 (1,300ft), Rudland Rig, Church Houses, North Yorkshire

P/O L.B. Lemon	Pilot	Survived
F/O A.P. Haacke (RCAF)	Pilot (u/t)	Killed
Sgt P.R. Davis	Flt Eng	Killed
Sgt R.W.L. Lucas	Flt Eng	Survived
F/O M.A. Foy (RCAF)	Nav	Killed
F/O H.W. Garwood (RCAF)	BA	Killed
W/O J.M.C. Plante (RCAF)	WO/AG	Killed
P/O L.A. Scutt (RCAF)	AG	Killed

The crew was flying from RAF Wombleton, located on the southern edge of the North Yorkshire Moors, having been tasked with a night cross-country navigation exercise. While returning to base after completing the exercise the aircraft strayed too far to the north and while descending through cloud struck the high ground.

A few small pieces of the aircraft can still be found scattered on the moor where the aircraft crashed.

Handley Page Halifax Mk.III LK878: No.1659 HCU, RAF.   15-01-1945
Map No.15
SE 472843 (525ft), Catcliffe Wood, Felixkirk, North Yorkshire

F/Sgt G. Walton	Pilot (Inst)	Killed
F/O F.W. Mooney (RCAF)	Pilot (u/t)	Killed
Sgt M.R. O'Sullivan	Flt Eng (Inst)	Killed
Sgt A.R. Robson (RCAF)	Flt Eng	Killed
F/O J.A. McCrea (RCAF)	Nav	Killed
F/O D.P. McGregor (RCAF)	BA	Killed
Sgt J.A. Savy (RCAF)	WO/AG	Killed
Sgt A.J. MacDonnell (RCAF)	AG	Killed
Sgt L.C. Stavenow (RCAF)	AG	Killed

The crew had just taken off from RAF Topcliffe near Thirsk when the aircraft suffered an engine failure and crashed after the pilot lost control.

At the site of the crash there is a large boulder with a memorial plaque dedicated to the crew. A few small pieces of the aircraft can also be found scattered about the wood close to the memorial.

Handley Page Halifax Mk.II Srs 1a LW334 / FD-T: No.1659 HCU. 18-01-1944
Map No.16
SE 484948 (1,150ft), Black Hambleton, Osmotherley, North Yorkshire

F/O J.P. Lavallee (RCAF)	Pilot	Killed
F/O W.L. Boisvert (RCAF)	Flt Eng	Killed
F/O W. Phillips (RCAF)	Flt Eng	Killed
Sgt R.G. Kimball (RCAF)	Nav	Killed
W/O G.E. Giff (RCAF)	BA	Killed
Sgt G.H. Hivon (RCAF)	WO/AG	Killed

The aircraft flew into the eastern side of Black Hambleton in poor visibility while on a daytime cross-country flight from RAF Topcliffe near Thirsk. The aircraft was flying in a

The crash site of Halifax LW334 is marked by this memorial to its Canadian crew.

westerly direction at the time and well below the briefed minimum safe altitude.

A memorial plaque mounted on a wooden cross marks the site, where there is also a collection of fragments from the aircraft. Other small pieces can be found scattered amongst the heather close by.

Hudson N7294 flew into Easby Moor close to this point and small pieces have been found both in the foreground and the area behind where this photograph was taken from.

Lockheed Hudson Mk.I N7294 / NR-E: No.220 Sqn, RAF.   11-02-1940
Map No.17
NZ 588103 (1,025ft), Easby Moor, Great Ayton, North Yorkshire

F/O T.M. Parker	Pilot	Killed
Sgt H.F. Bleksley	Pilot	Killed
Cpl N.R. Drury	WO	Killed
LAC A. Barker	AG	Survived

The aircraft had taken off from RAF Thornaby, on the edge of Middlesbrough to conduct a convoy protection patrol when the crew encountered a snow squall and the cockpit windows became covered with ice. This prevented the pilots from seeing where the aircraft was heading and shortly after this the aircraft struck high ground. It crashed through a dry stone wall and broke up across the moor beyond it.

Very little of the aircraft remains on the moor where it crashed, near to Captain Cooks Monument. However, during 2003 a memorial was unveiled close to the site. Finding the location of the remaining fragments from the aircraft is made more difficult by the presence of much litter to be found around this popular tourist spot.

Lockheed Hudson Mk.II T9371: No.220 Sqn, RAF.　　　　22-01-1941
Map No.18
SE 481988 (800ft), Pamperdale Moor, Osmotherley, North Yorkshire

Sgt L.B. Scase	Pilot	Killed
Sgt C. Smith	Pilot	Survived
Sgt W. Parfitt	WO/AG	Killed
Sgt T.J. McHugh	AG	Survived

This aircraft was being ferried by its crew from RAF St Eval in Cornwall to RAF Thornaby and the crash occurred while the pilot was descending through cloud towards Thornaby, apparently without taking into account the high ground in the vicinity.

The aircraft came to rest in the bottom of a small valley where there are lumps of melted aluminium and smaller parts amongst the grass and bracken.

North American Sabre Mk.4 XD733: No.92 Sqn, RAF.　　　21-09-1954
Map No.19
SE 504812 (725ft), Hood Hill, Thirsk, North Yorkshire

| F/O C.A. Grabham | Pilot | Killed |

The pilot had been on a night training and cross-country flight from RAF Linton-on-Ouse near York, returning to base he overflew the airfield and minutes later the aircraft dived into the top of Hood Hill.

The aircraft blasted a large crater beside the path towards the southern end of the hill. This remains to this day and a few small fragments of the aircraft may be found in the vicinity.

Supermarine Spitfire F. Mk.22 PK617: No.608 Sqn, RAuxAF.　13-02-1949
Map No.20
NZ 665116 (775ft), Raven Gill, Commondale, North Yorkshire

| P2 K.R. Jeffrey | Pilot | Killed |

The pilot was on a training flight from RAF Thornaby near Middlesbrough when he lost control of the aircraft at low level and crashed.

A crater caused by the crash is still visible at the site and contains a collection of pieces from the aircraft.

Supermarine Spitfire Mk.XVI SM278 / 14-F: No.567 Sqn, RAF.　16-09-1945
Map No.21
SE 481936 (1,250ft), Dodd End, Nether Silton, North Yorkshire

| F/Lt J.B.C. Catterns | Pilot | Killed |

The pilot had been taking part in the Battle of Britain day celebration flypast over London and was flying back to RAF Acklington in Northumberland from RAF Manston in Kent when the aircraft struck high ground while flying in low cloud.

For many years large pieces of the aircraft remained at the site, but are believed to have been removed and scrapped in the 1970s. Today only a few small pieces remain in a deep hollow on the moorland.

Vickers Warwick A.S.R. Mk.I BV336 / YF-P: No.280 Sqn, RAF. 13-11-1943
Map No.22
NZ 854049 (940ft), Sleights Moor, Grosmont, North Yorkshire

S/Ldr E.A. Good (RCAF)	Pilot	Killed
F/O W.W. Coons (RCAF)	Nav	Killed
F/O D.M. Stewart	WO	Killed
W/O W.V. Crockett (RCAF)	WO/AG	Killed
W/O D.A. Payton (RCAF)	WO/AG	Killed
W/O H.G. Richardson	AG	Killed

The crew was returning from an Air Sea Rescue patrol to RAF Thornaby when the pilot lost control of the aircraft after it was possibly struck by lightning whilst encountering severe turbulence in a thunderstorm. The aircraft then dived at a steep angle into the ground.

An elongated crater, not to be confused with a pool, which lies only 150 yards to the south-west, marks the crash site on the near level moorland. This is normally water filled, though a few small fragments of the aircraft can be seen scattered around its edges.

Mark Sheldon beside the crater marking the crash site of Spitfire PK617 on Commondale Moor.

Vickers Wellington Mk.III BJ778 / ZL-A: No.427 Sqn, RCAF.   12-02-1943
Map No.23
SE 581994 (1,075ft), Black Intake Moor, Bilsdale, North Yorkshire.

Sgt O.P.E.R.J. Adlam	Pilot	Killed
F/O B. Dunn	Nav	Killed
Sgt A.C. Clifford	BA	Killed
Sgt W.C.I. Jelley	WO/AG	Killed
Sgt W. Ball	AG	Killed

The crew had taken part in a raid against the French port of Le Havre and was returning to base at RAF Croft, near Darlington, when the pilot strayed from his intended course over the high ground and crashed while in cloud.

For a few years after the crash most of the aircraft remained on the moor, but it was eventually removed for scrap. Today only a few small pieces of the aircraft remain scattered across the moorland, the largest items being a couple of sections of armour plating.

The area where Wellington BJ778 came to grief. Today only small pieces lie scattered across this moor.

Chapter Seven

Isle of Man

This small island nation, fully independent of the United Kingdom, is a little over 30 miles long and less than half that in width and lies in the Irish Sea mid-way between Cumbria and Northern Ireland. Most of the island is fairly high ground, Snaefell being the highest point at 2,037ft, but is criss-crossed by an extensive network of roads and tracks making the vast majority of the hills easily accessible.

The island was home to three airfields, which during the Second World War were used extensively for the training of aircrews. The main RAF units based on the island during the 1940s were No.5 Bombing and Gunnery School, this later became No.5 Air Observer School and then the Air Navigation & Bombing School, and No.11 Air Gunners School. In addition to this, numerous fighter Squadrons spent periods of time at the Island's airfields. The only airfield which is still in large scale use is Ronaldsway, which opened in the pre-war era and was later used extensively by the Royal Navy. The main RAF airfield was at Jurby in the large expanse of flat ground in the north of the island, the site still exists being used as a racing circuit and the island's prison. Its satellite was at Andreas, though this became the home to No.11 AGS and then fully independent of Jurby. There was an earlier fourth airfield at Castletown but this was not used much after the opening of Ronaldsway. There have been approximately 200 aircraft crashes on the island since the 1930s, though most sites were completely cleared and are extremely difficult if not near impossible to locate. Those that remain have very little surface wreckage, but can be found with relative ease. In recent years the remaining parts from many of the sites have been recovered for preservation by the Manx Aviation Preservation Society and are displayed at the Manx Aviation and Military Museum, Ronaldsway Airport, Ballasalla, Isle of Man, making a detour here is a must for anyone visiting the crash sites on the Island.

Due to the location of the Isle of Man it suffers from relatively poor weather, with low levels of sun and a higher average rainfall compared to the majority of the British Isles. The hills are frequently shrouded in mist and low cloud, seemingly more so than other coastal locations around the Irish Sea and it was this weather that was a major factor in most of the crashes on the island. As well as a destination or origin of flights, the island was used as a navigational waypoint on training flights and for flights to or from Northern Ireland. The majority of the high ground crashes did not involve aircraft based on the Island, presumably because living next to the hills, the airmen flying locally were well aware of the dangers and so avoided them. The main casualties were the navigation and bombing schools based in Cumbria and Southern Scotland, which frequently sent their aircraft out over the Irish sea on training flights.

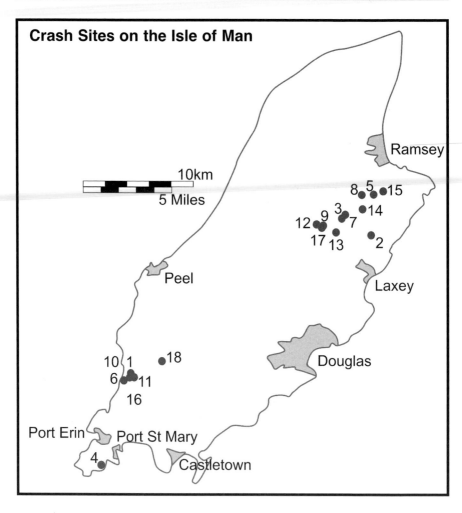

Crash Sites on the Isle of Man

Avro Anson Mk.I AX177: No.1 AOS, RAF.   13-11-1944
Map No.1
SC 224749 (1,100ft), Cronk ny Arrey Laa, Dalby

F/Sgt H.E. McDonald (RCAF)	Pilot	Killed
F/O C.A. Bardwell (RCAF)	Nav	Killed
P/O J. Darlington	BA	Killed
F/O P.H. Hoyle	WO (Inst)	Killed
F/Sgt J.D. Pratt (RAAF)	WO (u/t)	Killed

The crew was on a night navigation exercise from RAF Wigtown in Dumfries and Galloway. The route took them over the Isle of Man on a northerly heading and the aircraft was heard to overfly Ronaldsway but shortly afterwards the aircraft crashed into the western side of Cronk ny Arrey Laa while heading south. It was concluded that the aircraft had entered icing conditions and the pilot had turned back for Ronaldsway but had lost too much height.

The aircraft crashed at the intersection of two walls to the south of the footpath off the top of the hill. Only a couple of pieces of steel remain built into the wall as a few years ago all the other remaining items were recovered to the museum at Ronaldsway by the Manx Aviation Preservation Society.

Avro Anson Mk.I MG445: No.5 ANS, RAF.   03-01-1946
Map No.2
SC 441871 (1,275ft), Slieau Ruy, Laxey

F/Sgt W.H. Beller (PAF)	Pilot	Killed
Sgt B.B. Komkommerman (RNLAF)	Nav	Killed
W/O R.C. Jones	WO	Survived
Mr J. Williams	Pass	Killed
Mr P. Fachire	Pass	Killed

The three airmen onboard had flown from RAF Jurby to Hawarden in Flintshire to collect two civilian contractors who were to carry out repairs on an aircraft at Jurby. During the return flight the aircraft entered cloud and strayed a little to the south-west of its intended track, which put the Anson in line with the high ground which it struck while still in cloud. The aircraft was declared missing until the injured crewman was found by a sheep dog part way down the hill.

The site is marked by a sizeable scar which can be found not far to the south of a track which runs up onto the hill. This contains many burnt parts from the aircraft; the wreck was destroyed by fire during the recovery operation.

The scar containing the remains of Anson MG445 on Slieau Ruy above Laxey.

Avro Anson T. Mk.20 VM418: No.1 ITS, RAF.   06-09-1953
Map No.3
SC 415887 (1,600ft), Clagh Ouyr, Laxey

G/Cpt F.R. Worthington	Pilot	Killed
G/Cpt G.A. Richmond	Pass	Killed
W/Cdr F.J. Fenton	Pass	Killed
S/Ldr R.P. Charter BEM	Pass	Killed

The aircraft which was the station flight for RAF Jurby had been flown by G/Cpt Worthington to RAF Millom in Cumbria to collect his passengers. During the return flight the aircraft struck high ground while flying in dense cloud.

Today nothing remains at this crash site as it is on a fairly gentle grassy slope, having been identified with the aid of photographs taken shortly after the crash.

Boeing B-17G 42-37840 / GY-Y: 367th BS / 306th BG, USAAF.   14-04-1945
Map No.4
SC 197669 (330ft), The Chasms, Glen Chass

1st Lt R.A. Vieille	Pilot	Killed
2nd Lt C.E. Liersch	Co-pilot	Killed
Flt Off H.E. Lecompte	Nav	Killed
T/Sgt E.E. Gallion	Flt Eng	Killed
S/Sgt C.F. Smailczewski	Radio Op	Killed
Capt W.B. Butterfield	Pass	Killed
Capt G.E. Cubberly	Pass	Killed
T/Sgt W.C. Starbuck	Pass	Killed
S/Sgt D.S. Jone	Pass	Killed
Miss E.H. Rea (ARC)	Pass	Killed

The aircraft was being used for a cross-country navigation exercise from Thurleigh in Bedfordshire but was to land at Langford Lodge in Northern Ireland to drop off the passengers who were travelling onboard. The pilot was making a turn to port to avoid the hills when the crash occurred.

The aircraft impacted at about 330ft above sea level and wreckage was spread over a fairly large area. Burnt fragments can be found in the bed of the track from Fistard to the Chasms just before it enters the Manx National Heritage Trust land. There is also a bare patch where the fuselage burned in the field above the track..

The memorial on North Barrule dedicated to the memory of the crew and passengers of B-17 43-38856 which crashed at the spot with the loss of 31 lives.

Boeing B-17G 43-38856: 534th BS / 381st BG, USAAF.   23-04-1945
Map No.5
SC 443907 (1,600ft), North Barrule, Corrany, Isle of Man

Capt C.E. Ackerman Jr	Pilot	Killed
Flt Off E.A. Hutcheson Jr	Co-pilot	Killed
1st Lt M. Matyas	Nav	Killed
1st Lt J.P Fedak	BA	Killed
T/Sgt D.H. Lindon	Flt Eng	Killed
T/Sgt W.H. Hagen	Radio Op	Killed
25 Passengers	See Appendices	Killed

The aircraft was being ferried from Ridgewell in Essex to Nutts Corner in Northern Ireland for maintenance. Along with the crew were passengers going for a short period of leave. The pilot had set course for Northern Ireland but was flying too low to avoid the island's high ground. It struck the southern side of North Barrule about 200ft below the summit.

   This site is the best known on the island, and the one with the most remaining wreckage. There is a slate plaque in memory of those who died and a flagpole used during ceremonies around the time of anniversaries of the crash. There are a number of pieces of armour plate and pieces of aluminium scattered around, and pits which the USAAF dug to conceal wreckage still contain some parts.

Blackburn Botha Mk.I L6314: No.3 SGR, RAF.   12-03-1942
Map No.6
SC 218744 (500 ft), Cronk ny Arrey Laa

F/Sgt L.C. Storey	Pilot	Killed
P/O L. Dobson	Nav	Killed
P/O J.A. Williams	WO	Killed
AC2 W.J.S. Heap	WO	Killed

The crew were on a training flight from Squires Gate, near Blackpool, when they flew into the seaward side of Cronk ny Arrey Laa in poor weather.

The aircraft impacted in the vicinity of a rocky outcrop which lies above a small patch of angular scree. No wreckage is obvious in this area, however, fragments of airframe have been found lower down the slope either side of the stone boundary wall close to Lag-ny-Keeilley.

British Aerospace Hawk T. Mk.1 XX166: No.4 FTS, RAF.   24-06-1983
Map No.7
SC 417889 (1,475ft), Clagh Ouyr, Laxey

F/Lt R.F. Lane	Pilot (Inst)	Killed
F/Lt J.M.B. Lewis	Pilot (u/t)	Killed

The two men were on a low-level training exercise from RAF Valley on Anglesey to RAF Lossiemouth near Inverness when, shortly into the flight, the aircraft struck Clagh Ouyr and broke up over a wide area.

Small pieces of the aircraft remain having been gathered together and placed near a large flat rock with a second smaller rock placed upright next to it.

Consolidated B-24H 42-50762: 312th Fy Sqn / 27th ATG, USAAF. 06-07-1944
Map No.8
SC 430905 (1,575 ft), North Barrule, Ramsey

Capt H.B. Lynch	Pilot	Killed
1st Lt R.B. Storrington	Unk	Killed
Cpl J.F. Syron	Unk	Killed
Pvt W.L. Murray	Unk	Killed
Pvt R.J. Meason	Unk	Killed

Unlike other USAAF losses on the island, this aircraft was being ferried to the mainland from Langford Lodge. It was flying south-east when it struck North Barrule while in cloud.

The aircraft crashed on an undulating slope, today small pieces of the aircraft lie scattered in the grass where the aircraft burned out.

The summit of Snaefell where B-24H 42-51202 crashed, striking the electricity pole on the right hand side of the photo and burning out on the path in the centre.

Consolidated B-24H 42-51202: 310th Fy Sqn / 27th ATG, USAAF. 08-06-1944
Map No.9
SC 398880 (1,950ft), Snaefell, Laxey

1st Lt W. Lennon	Pilot	Killed
2nd Lt S. Scharff	Co-pilot	Killed
Sgt A. Bellini	Flt Eng	Killed
T/Sgt S. Joseph	Radio Op	Killed

The aircraft was being ferried from BAD2 at Warton near Preston, Lancashire, to Langford Lodge in Northern Ireland when it flew into Snaefell close to the summit while in cloud.

This crash site could well be the most unintentionally visited site on the island as the aircraft crashed on the track, demolishing one of the electricity poles on the Snaefell Mountain Railway before crashing (this can be noticed as the pole was replaced with a wooden example whereas the originals are cast iron). Parts can be found on both sides of the path from the café at the railway terminus to summit of the hill, as well as by the railway tracks.

De Havilland Dragon Radpide G-AIUI: Hargreaves Airways Ltd. 10-06-1948
Map No.10
SC 223747 (1,350 ft), Cronk ny Arrey Laa, Dalby

Mr C.S.M. Herbert	Pilot	Killed
Mr A. Thorneywork	Pass	Survived
Mrs A. Thorneywork	Pass	Killed
Mstr J. Thorneywork	Pass	Killed
Mr C. Stagg	Pass	Survived
Mr W. Wearing	Pass	Killed
Mrs J. Perrigo	Pass	Killed
Mrs F. Povey	Pass	Killed

The aircraft had been chartered by Mr Thorneywork to fly his family and friends from Birmingham to Ronaldsway and having passed over the south of the island the pilot turned back and flew into the high ground while in cloud.

The site is marked by a fence post and a small scar containing a few fragments.

Handley Page Halifax C. Mk.8 G-AJNZ: World Air Freight Ltd. 28-09-1948
Map No.11
SC 225746 (1,350ft), Cronk ny Arrey Laa, Dalby

Capt J.F.G. Savage	Pilot	Killed
Nav Off R.L. Miller	Nav	Killed
Eng Off A.H. Noon	Flt Eng	Killed
Radio Off O.H.G. Hiscock	Radio Op	Killed

Alan Clark with part of the undercarriage from Halifax G-AJNZ on Cronk ny Arrey Laa, the aircraft first impacted on the ridge on the right hand edge of the photo.

The Halifax was being used to fly churns of milk from Northern Ireland to the mainland of the UK to relieve a shortage. The route being used was Nutts Corner to Speke, near Liverpool. While carrying out such a flight the aircraft struck the northern end of Cronk ny Arrey Lhaa and crashed a couple of hundred yards beyond, where much of the aircraft was destroyed by fire.

Very little remains where the aircraft burned out. There is a small bare patch with a few small pieces of aluminium and a single large piece from one of the undercarriage assemblies.

Alan Clark with burnt remains of Handley Page Hampden P1260 on the northern side of Snaefell.

Handley Page Hampden Mk.I P1260: No.7 Sqn, RAF. 01-01-1940
Map No.12
SC 392881 (1,500ft), Snaefell, Laxey

P/O H.M. MacGregor	Pilot	Killed
Sgt R.J. Bailey	Nav	Killed
Sgt T.O. Dennis	WO/AG	Killed
Cpl E. Brightmore	WO/AG	Survived

The crew were on a daytime cross-country navigation exercise from RAF Upper Heyford near Bicester in very poor winter weather. The crew became lost over the Irish Sea and while in a blizzard flew into Snaefell.

There is not much left at this site, there are only a few pieces of melted aluminium where the aircraft came to rest and was destroyed by fire, a few similar pieces can be found near the Snaefell Mountain Railway at SC 394881.

Hawker Hurricane Mk.IIB Z3253: No.133 Sqn, RAF.   08-10-1941
Map No.13
SC 409874 (850ft), Snaefell Mines, Laxey

P/O R.N. Stout	Pilot	Killed

This was one of fifteen Hurricanes being ferried from RAF Fowlmere in Cambridgeshire to RAF Eglinton in Northern Ireland for training; the flight was broken into stages with a stop at RAF Sealand near Chester and another at RAF Jurby-Andreas. Following the stop at RAF Sealand the flight left for the Isle of Man, nine arrived safely and two returned to Sealand due to the weather conditions. Four more crashed on the island, this aircraft being one of two on high ground, where both pilots had flown up valleys and into hills.

Nothing remains at this site which lies just above the old mine track, a few years ago there was surface wreckage but a landslide erased the entire site.

Hawker Hurricane Mk.IIB Z3677: No.133 Sqn, RAF.   08-10-1941.
Map No.14
SC 434894 (850ft), North Laxey Mines, Corrany

P/O H.H. McCall	Pilot	Killed

For general details see the previous entry.

No surface wreckage remains at this site and it has been located with the aid of period photographs. There is an ancient stone wall covered in vegetation running down the hill near the site and some parts have been found built into this wall, the site also lies within 100 yards of a the remains of an old Keeill.

Lockheed Hudson Mk.I N7337: No.1 OTU, RAF.   09-09-1941
Map No.15
SC 451910 (1,100ft), North Barrule, Corrany

Sgt J.B. Healey	Pilot	Killed
Sgt J.A. Moore	Pilot	Killed
Sgt N.E. Eggleton	WO/AG	Killed
Sgt R.J. Clarke	WO/AG	Killed

The crew was on a navigation exercise from RAF Silloth in Cumbria when the aircraft flew into the eastern end of North Barrule while in cloud.

Only a few tiny pieces remain in a scar which apart from the pieces of aircraft looks like it was created by natural erosion. One of the items is part of a window frame from the aircraft.

Above is the scar at the crash site of Lockheed Hudson N7337 on North Barrule.

Martin B-26C (AT-23) 41-35791: 449th BS / 22nd BG, USAAF. 04-07-1944
Map No.16
SC 224746 (1,400ft), Cronk ny Arrey Laa, Dalby

Maj C.W. Hoover	Pilot	Survived
Capt R.A. Schekzer	Co-pilot	Killed
1st Lt F.E. Swain	Nav	Killed
Maj D. MacConaghy	Pass	Survived
Maj H.M. Schull	Pass	Killed
Capt M.A. Cundiff	Pass	Killed
Capt R.E. Lowther	Pass	Killed
1st Lt R.C. Botsford	Pass	Killed

The aircraft was being ferried from Andrew's Field in Essex to Langford Lodge in Northern Ireland when it flew into high ground in cloud and broke up over a wide area.

Nothing remains where the aircraft first impacted, but a large scar is present where one wing burned, it is just to the south of the large cairn on the summit and to the seaward side of the footpath.

Vickers Wellington Mk.IC Z8424: No.8 FPP, ATA.   08-10-1941
Map No.17
SC 396878 (1,900ft), Snaefell, Laxey

1st Off K.M. Seeds (ATA)	Pilot	Killed

This crash occurred on the same day as the Hurricanes already recorded. The pilot was ferrying the aircraft from Vickers at Hawarden near Chester to Aldergrove near Belfast when it struck the Southern side of Snaefell just below the summit.

As with many of the sites on the island this has only a couple of fragments of surface wreckage and it is most easily located with the aid of period photographs, the best of which are on display at the museum at Ronaldsway.

Vickers Wellington Mk.XIII MF174: EANS, RAF.   22-12-1944
Map No.18
SC 251760 (1,100ft), South Barrule, Dalby

W/O J. Piasecki (PAF)	Pilot	Killed
F/Lt F.R. Riley	Co-pilot	Killed
F/O H.A. Hartland	Nav	Killed
W/O J. Cromarty	WO	Killed

The crew was on a cross-country navigation training flight from Shawbury in Shropshire when the aircraft crashed on South Barrule in poor visibility.

Many small parts of the aircraft can be found scattered across the lower north western slopes of the hill not far from the footpath up the hill from Round Table. This is not shown on most maps but is signed locally.

Chapter Eight

Scotland: Lowlands

The Scottish Lowlands, although not officially a geographical area of the country, has traditionally been used to describe the area from the English border up to and including the Central Belt, a term used to describe the area of highest population density in Scotland, stretching from Glasgow in the west to Edinburgh in the east. Despite the name, it is not really geographically central, but is in fact in the south of Scotland. Also somewhat misleading is the description of Lowlands, as there is a lot of high ground in this region and some even approaches 3,000ft above sea level. Although in comparison to the Highlands, to the north of the Central Belt, it may be considered lower ground. As in all areas, Scotland's unique landscape features are dictated by the underlying geology, which is unusually varied and complex for such a relatively small country. Many of the sedimentary rocks in the Lowlands area were formed on the bed of an ancient ocean and were pushed up and folded during a tectonic collision, as what is now Scotland and England came together. This collision also created further fault lines and was followed by sporadic periods of volcanic activity, which saw the formation of extensive granite intrusions, which were more resistant to later glacial erosion and are largely responsible for the area's higher peaks today.

Examination of this section's map quickly reveals that the crash sites in this section form distinct clusters, dictated by the region's areas of high ground and their proximity to airfields or frequently used flight paths. The largest of these groups represents the aircraft which crashed in the Dumfries and Galloway area, where the highest ground in the region is located. This was also close to a number of airfields, including the navigation training schools at Dumfries, West Freugh and Wigtown. Between them they account for most of the many Avro Ansons lost in the region, though there were a couple that originated from the Isle of Man and Cumbria. Other aircraft flying from stations further north, or en route from England to bases in Scotland were also lost on the mountains of Dumfries and Galloway. RAF Bomber Command aircraft, which feature prominently amongst the losses covered in other regions of the UK, account for only a handful in this area. An OTU Wellington crashed in the hills above Largs, a Liberator from an HCU crashed in the mountains of Dumfries and Galloway and the only operational Bomber Command loss was that of a Hampden on the northern end of the Cheviot. Post war, two fast jets from the USAF came to grief here as well, these being an RF-4C Phantom on a reconnaissance training flight from Alconbury in Cambridgeshire and an F-111 on a low level flight from Upper Heyford in Oxfordshire, illustrating the region's continued importance for aircrew training.

Another cluster of crash sites in the region is to be found on the Mull of Kintyre and although the Kintyre peninsula rises to over 1,000ft for most of its length, it was the Mull at its southern tip that proved the most dangerous obstacle. Frequent fog and low cloud from the Atlantic often shrouds it from view to aircraft approaching from the west and as it rises from sea level to 1,300ft in less than a mile from the coast, there is little warning of the impending danger. Of the aircraft lost on the Mull, perhaps the most well known due to widespread press coverage at the time of the crash, as well as on the subsequent controversy over responsibility, was the 1994 loss of an RAF Chinook helicopter and the lives of the twenty-nine passengers and crew. The majority of the remaining losses here were RAF Coastal Command aircraft, with a Whitley, Neptune and Wellington, all being lost in the area close to the Chinook crash site. Another passenger-carrying aircraft, which crashed on the Kintyre peninsular, was an RAF Liberator being operated by BOAC on a flight from Canada to the UK with among its passengers scientists and a Belgian Count.

The remaining Lowlands areas only feature a few, more scattered, crash sites and to the east, the aircraft involved were from more diverse origins than those on the west coast. These include; a *Luftwaffe* Ju88, which flew into a hill near Edinburgh while on a raid against the docks at Leith and further south, a Defiant night fighter from the OTU that was based at East Fortune, as well as a cold-war era Javelin all-weather fighter from RAF Leuchars in Fife. Also to the south are two aircraft, which crashed just on the Scottish side of the border, in the Cheviot, an area mostly covered in the Pennines section, as it is the northern most point of the Pennine Way. The northern boundary of the region is a little vague, so this section includes a few aircraft in the hills immediately to the north of the Central belt, with all except the USAF B-29 and Royal Navy Martlet, being on lower hills.

In common with all the areas covered in this book, the amount of material present today at many of the sites in this section has reduced since they were first recorded and in some cases only a small fraction remains of what could be found say 20 or even 10 years ago. The remoteness of the sites and difficult terrain, that prevented their original recovery at the time of the crashes and protected them for so long seems to no longer be such an obstacle to those dedicated to their recovery for restoration projects, museums and even private collections. Certainly, access to modern excavation equipment, all-terrain vehicles and even helicopters may well be a factor in a few cases, but perhaps the greatest influence has been the improvement in road networks, opening up once remote areas to countless visitors. Articles have appeared in aviation journals, on the internet and in enthusiasts' publications, lamenting the loss of material from these sites, often accompanied by comparison photographs graphically illustrating just how much has disappeared in many cases. Certainly organised recovery operations have accounted for a few sites, usually containing substantial sections of specific rare aircraft types. But a great many other sites seem to be gradually vanishing over long periods of time, indicating that it is most likely the work of hundreds, if not thousands of individuals, each wanting to take home their own 'souvenir' that is responsible. However on the positive side, it seems that more memorials are being placed at crash sites and existing memorials being restored, providing at least some lasting reminder. Certainly at more recent crash sites, it is likely that only memorials will be found, as modern accident investigation techniques usually requires the complete recovery of all remains and even when this is not the case, it is likely to be required by local authorities on environmental grounds.

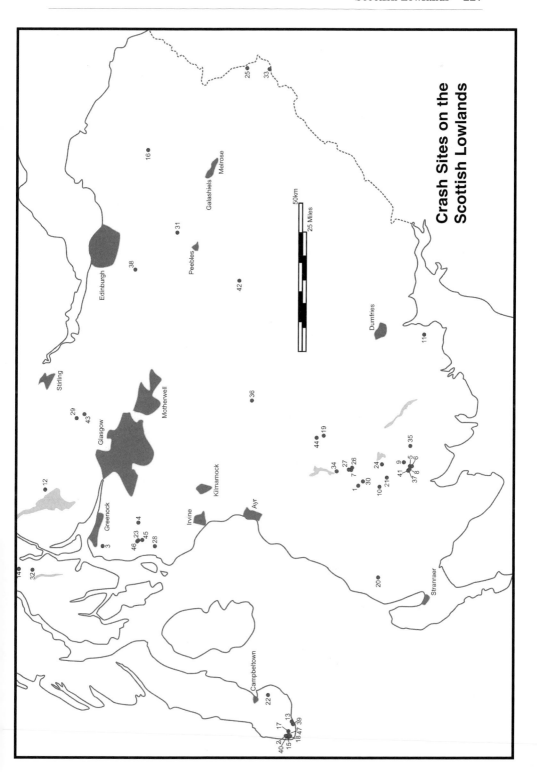

Crash Sites on the
Scottish Lowlands

Armstrong Whitworth Whitley Mk.V P5009: No.10 BGS, RAF. 27-11-1940
Map No.1
NX 444848 (1,625 ft), Loch Enoch, Dumfries & Galloway

P/O L. Szamrajew (PAF)	Pilot	Killed
Sgt J. Luszczewski (PAF)	Pilot	Killed
AC1 D. Barnes	–	Killed (Missing)

The Whitley departed from RAF Dumfries at 13:00, in order to fly to RAF West Freugh in Dumfries & Galloway and collect a group of RAF Officers. Owing to cloud cover at West Freugh the crew had been briefed to fly to the south of the direct route to the airfield. However, at 13:15 the Royal Observer Corps lost track of the aircraft around 4 miles west of Dalry, to the north of the direct route. Two weeks later wreckage from the aircraft was located by a Shepherd boy near to Loch Enoch. An RAF team climbed to the site the following day and determined that the aircraft had hit the mountain and exploded. No trace was found of AC1 Barnes, however, wreckage from the aircraft was scattered into Loch Enoch.

Small pieces of the aircraft can be seen in the water at the edge of Loch Enoch, while several sections of wing and fuselage lie in a boggy hollow to the east.

Armstrong Whitworth Whitley Mk.V P5041: No.502 Sqn, RAF. 23-01-1941
Map No.2
NR 599094 (1,100ft), Balmavicar, Mull of Kintyre, Argyll

F/Lt P.L. Billing	Pilot	Killed
F/O A.P.B. Holmes	Nav	Killed
Sgt A.R. Hooker	Obs	Killed
Sgt H. Pilling	Obs	Killed
Sgt D.J. Peter	WO	Killed

The crew was on a Convoy Escort flight from RAF Limavady near Londonderry in Northern Ireland when they became disorientated in poor weather and flew into the western side of the Mull of Kintyre, which rises very quickly from sea level to over 1,000ft.

The site is marked by a scar, beside a stream which runs down the hill, containing burnt fragments of the aircraft. Nearby is a single undercarriage leg and a collection of other fragments.

The scar and small number of fragments at the crash site of Whitley P5041 on the Mull of Kintyre.

Avro Anson Mk.I K6255 / M: No.269 Sqn, RAF.   26-07-1939
Map No.3
NS 238730 (875 ft), Dunrod Hill, Greenock, Inverclyde

Sgt Robson	Pilot	Survived
Mr H.J. Reynolds (CAG)	–	Died of Injuries 27-07-1939
LAC Ball	–	Survived
LAC Ward	–	Survived

Flying from RAF Abbotsinch in Renfrewshire, the aircraft was one of 15 Ansons on a formation cross-country training flight. While at low level the formation leader headed for a gap in a bank of cloud, but it began to fill as the aircraft flew through it and he instructed the formation to break. However, it appears Sgt Robson did not receive the instruction, entered the cloud and then flew into the hilltop.

At the site where the aircraft impacted, demolishing part of the stone boundary wall between Caldron Hill and No.1 Dam, there is no longer any wreckage. However, in the stream approximately 50 metres below the breach in No.1 Dam is the core from one of the Armstrong Siddeley Cheetah engines. The other engine is set into a concrete base in the nearby visitor centre car park at NS 247721.

Avro Anson Mk.I L7949: No.12 E&RFTS, RAF.   13-09-1938
Map No.4
NS 318606 (1,050ft), Lairdside Hill, Lochwinnoch, Renfrewshire

F/O J.H. Charsley	Pilot	Survived
H. Jordon	WO	Survived
P. Davidson	Pass	Survived
W. Nichol	Pass	Survived

The crew was on a cross country navigation flight from Prestwick when the aircraft
struck Lairdside Hill in cloud and overturned.

The site lies on the edge of a boggy area, where a large amount of the aircraft was
buried but has since been uncovered. The undercarriage and one of the aircraft's
Cheetah engines is still at the crash site, whilst the other engine lies some distance away
partially buried in the head of a stream at NS 319608.

Note: J.H. Charsley had previously served with the Royal Navy, though he spent some
time on temporary attachment to the RAF. He had reached the rank of Lt Cdr before
resigning his commission to begin service at the lower rank of F/O in the RAF Reserve.

*A large collection of panels and part from one of the undercarriage units at the crash
site of Anson L7949. Out of view to the right is one of the two Cheetah engines.*

Cheetah engine with complete propeller from Anson N9589.

Avro Anson Mk.I N9589: No.4 (O)AFU, RAF.   12-06-1944
Map No.5
NX 509667 (1,600 ft), Clints of the Spout, Cairnsmore of Fleet, Dumfries & Galloway

Sgt W.A. Edwards	Pilot	Killed
Sgt H.W.G. Rennison	Nav (u/t)	Killed
Sgt R.C. Beggs (RNZAF)	BA (u/t)	Killed
F/Sgt B.B. Hayton	WO/AG (Inst)	Killed
F/Sgt A.W. Wauchope (RAAF)	WO/AG (u/t)	Killed

Having taken-off from RAF West Freugh in Dumfries & Galloway for a night navigation and IR (Infra Red) bombing exercise, the aircraft flew into the mountainside, which was probably covered by cloud, while on a westerly track.

   The aircraft impacted on the rock face of Clints of the Spout, the wreckage then falling onto the slope below where some of it still remains. The two engines, each with the remains of their propeller unit still attached lie on the slope along with parts from the undercarriage assemblies and a few aluminium panels. The Anson from which this wreckage originated has been positively identified from the serial number discernable on one of the engines, as several Anson aircraft flew into Cairnsmore of Fleet and are recorded on a memorial stone at the summit.

Avro Anson Mk.I W2630: No.1 (O)AFU, RAF.   17-04-1942
Map No.6
NX 510669 (1,300 ft), Clints of the Spout, Cairnsmore of Fleet, Dumfries & Galloway

Sgt J.C.H. Allen	Pilot	Killed
Sgt E.C. Hirst	WO	Survived
Mr W. Paterson	Pass	Killed

During a night flying test from RAF Wigtown in Dumfries & Galloway the aircraft was flying at low level when it struck the side of the mountain. Mr Paterson was a civilian employed by Airwork Ltd.

On the slope, amongst the rocks and heather, there is a scar where the aircraft impacted. This contains many small parts from the aircraft, while resting on rocks immediately below is one of the engines, with most of the propeller unit attached. The other engine, with half of the propeller unit attached, lies at the base of the slope along with aluminium panels from the nose and engine nacelles. The Anson from which this wreckage originated has also been identified from the serial number on one of the engines. Please note that some references number this aircraft W2930.

Cheetah engine from Anson W2630 with its propeller succumbing to the elements and tailwheel remains in the foreground.

Avro Anson Mk.I DG787 / J: AN&BS, RAF.   23-10-1942
Map No.7
NX 497872 (2,550 ft), Corserine, The Rhinns of Kells, Dumfries & Galloway

Sgt J.G. Millinger	Pilot	Killed
Sgt C. Lunny	Nav (Inst)/WO	Killed
F/Lt V. Jellinek (Czech)	Nav (u/t)	Killed
Sgt P. Haas (Czech)	Nav (u/t)	Killed

This Anson flew into the mountain top during a night cross-country navigation exercise from Jurby on the Isle of Man. The wreck was located on 25 October 1942.

At the site tiny fragments of wreckage are scattered in a bare patch on the grassy slope, the only item of any size being one of the aircraft batteries. Low down on the south-western slopes of Corserine, however, are the remains of an Armstrong Siddeley Cheetah engine, assumed to be from this aircraft.

Avro Anson Mk.I EG485 / L1: No.10 (O)AFU, RAF.   22-02-1944
Map No.8
NX 498670 (2,125 ft), Cairnsmore of Fleet, Dumfries & Galloway

Sgt N.J. McLeod	Pilot	Survived
P/O P.J. Lalonde (RCAF)	Nav	Survived
P/O J.M. Cooley (RCAF)	BA	Killed
W/O J.J.M. Ward	WO/AG (Inst)	Killed
F/Sgt M.C. Simpson (RAAF)	WO/AG (u/t)	Killed

On the last phase of a night navigation and IR (Infra Red) bombing exercise, from RAF Dumfries in Dumfries & Galloway, the aircraft arrived over the Whithorn Range at 23:20. Due to poor visibility though, the planned IR bombing was abandoned and the aircraft repositioned over the West Freugh 'Occult' light. It then turned onto an easterly track to return to base, but subsequently failed to clear the mountain top. On investigation it was concluded that the aircraft had flown into strong air currents and lost altitude.

In an area of rocks there are a few pieces of steel framework and some aluminium panels. The Anson from which this wreckage originated has been positively identified, from an aerial photograph of the wreck taken for the investigation into the accident.

Avro Anson Mk.I EG693: No.2 (O)AFU, RAF.   06-12-1944
Map No.9
NX 523690 (1,450 ft), Craigronald, Dumfries & Galloway

F/Sgt C.P. Angus (RAAF)	Pilot	Killed
Sgt M. Schneider	Nav	Killed
Sgt J.W. Melhuish	BA	Killed
Sgt K.R. Ridehalgh	WO/AG	Killed

The aircraft flew into the mountainside while in cloud, during night navigation-exercise from RAF Millom in Cumbria. Sgt Schneider survived the impact but died later in the day on arrival at hospital.

One of the two Cheetah engines from Anson EG693 on Craigronald, with Loch Grannoch in the background.

Scattered on the rough slope at the site, are several aluminium panels from the engine nacelles, an oxygen bottle and one of the engine exhaust ducts. The two engines also remain, one with part of the propeller unit attached being obvious, while the other is almost completely buried in a boggy area slightly further up the slope.

Avro Anson Mk.I MG356: No.4 (O)AFU, RAF.   21-07-1944
Map No.10
NX 440773 (2,175 ft), Bennanbrack, Dumfries & Galloway

F/Sgt R.J. Crotty (RAAF)	Pilot	Killed
Sgt D.B. Northmore (RAAF)	Nav (u/t)	Killed
Sgt B.E.W. Becker	BA (u/t)	Killed
W/O P. Smith (RAAF)	WO/AG (Inst)	Killed
Sgt E.H.P. Greenwell	WO/AG (u/t)	Killed

While on a night navigation exercise, from RAF West Freugh, the aircraft flew into the cloud covered mountain top. On investigation it was thought that the aircraft had drifted to the east of the planned route during the flight. Therefore when the crew intercepted the West Freugh approach beam, they may have descended thinking they were in the vicinity of the airfield, when they were in fact over high ground.

Parts of the undercarriage assemblies, an engine exhaust duct, oxygen bottles and many small pieces of aluminium lie in a patch of rocky ground at the site, not far from the top of the ridge.

The rocky area at the crash site of Anson MG356 with the remains of an undercarriage assembly and oxygen bottles scattered about it.

Avro Anson Mk.I MG827: No.10 (O)AFU, RAF.   04-11-1944
Map No.11
NX 953621 (1,700 ft), Criffell, New Abbey, Dumfries & Galloway

F/O C.E. Johnson	Pilot	Survived
F/O H. Gunn	Nav	Survived
W/O N. Jackson	WO	Survived
W/Cdr N.A. Burt	Pass	Survived

This Anson flew into the hilltop while in cloud during a day cross-country training flight from RAF Dumfries. The aircraft remained relatively intact and the onboard radio equipment still functioned, so contact was made with base and a rescue party was dispatched. F/O Gunn decided to make his way down off the hill and was subsequently picked up by the rescue party. He then climbed back up the hill and assisted in locating the wreck, in poor visibility and winds of 75 mph. The other three survivors were then rescued.

One of the Armstrong Siddeley Cheetah engines from the aircraft remains in a peat grough at the site, along with the remains of the two undercarriage assemblies and a number of aluminium panels.

Avro Lancaster Mk.III PB456 SR-D: No.101 Sqn, RAF.   13-09-1944
Map No.12
NS 428930 (675 ft), Conic Hill, Loch Lomond, Stirling

F/O C.E. Brooks (RCAF)	Pilot	Killed
Sgt E. Foweather	Nav	Killed
Sgt F.A.W. Blerkom	Flt Eng	Killed
F/O L.G. Peardon (RCAF)	BA	Killed
F/Sgt V.J. Ward	WO	Killed
Sgt J.R. Stokes (RCAF)	AG	Killed
Sgt J. Watt (RCAF)	AG	Killed

The Lancaster hit the boggy hilltop while in an extremely steep dive at 22:10. Structural failure had occurred, with the tail unit breaking away, but it appears this happened after the aircraft had already entered the dive, as the tail unit came down close to the bulk of the wreckage. The aircraft had been on a night cross-country training flight from RAF Ludford Magna in Lincolnshire.

The patch of very soft and wet bog where the aircraft impacted still has small pieces of wreckage protruding from it. In 2006 members of the Dumfries and Galloway Aviation Museum used a mechanical excavator to extract two of the Rolls-Royce Merlin engines from the aircraft.

Avro Shackleton M.R. Mk.2 WB833 / T: No.204 Sqn, RAF.   19-04-1968
Map No.13
NR 647074 (460ft), Glenmanuilt Hill, Mull of Kintyre, Argyll

S/Ldr R.C.L. Haggett	Pilot	Killed
F/O D.R. Burton	Pilot	Killed
F/O M. Creedon	Pilot	Killed
Sgt J.R.F. Creamer	Eng	Killed
F/Lt R.J.D. Denny	Nav	Killed
F/Lt G.C. Fisken	Nav	Killed
F/Lt R. Hellens	AEO	Killed
F/Sgt T.F.A. Buttimore	AE Op	Killed
Sgt B.R. Dixon	AE Op	Killed
Sgt N.M. Duffy	Sig	Killed
M/Sig R.C. Stratton	Sig	Killed

The crew were on an early morning training flight from RAF Ballykelly near Londonderry in Northern Ireland. Dense sea mist covered the North Channel and Firth of Clyde that morning and the aircraft was flying in the mist. It was heard approaching Kintyre from the east and was seen exiting the top of the mist seconds before it impacted the hill just above the road to the southwest of Garvalt farm.

An obvious scar containing small fragments of the aircraft can be found to the left of the confluence of two streams above the 'Hissing Well'. At the time of writing plans are in place to have a memorial erected in the near future at the cemetery at Keil Point (NR 763077).

The tail gunners position from B-29 44-62276 is in fact far less intact than many previously published photographs appear to suggest – which is probably why it is still at the crash site!

Boeing B-29A 44-62276: 32nd BS / 301st BG, USAF.   17-01-1949
Map No.14
NN 161022 (1,550 ft), Succoth Glen, Lochgoilhead, Argyll

1st Lt S.C. Craigmyle	Pilot	Killed
1st Lt M.P. Barry	Co-pilot	Killed
1st Lt R.D. Klingenberg	Nav	Killed
1st Lt R.A. Fritsche	BA	Killed
16 Passengers	See Appendices	Killed

Flying to Keflavik in Iceland, where the aircraft was to refuel before continuing to its base in the United States, the aircraft departed from RAF Scampton at 08:05 and headed north-west towards Barra Head. At 09:20 the aircraft contacted Prestwick Air Traffic Control and obtained permission to change its cruise altitude from 8,500ft to 14,500ft. Around 30 minutes later, it dived into the ground and exploded. At the time a cold weather front lay across central Scotland and on investigation it was determined that heavy icing was almost certainly a factor in the accident. A disturbed area of ground indicated the aircraft had contacted a hilltop at 2,000ft before diving into the ground on the mountainside below.

A particularly large scar at the site contains much wreckage, including substantial sections of wing main spar, the two main undercarriage legs and the remains of at least two engines. A further badly damaged engine lies on the slope below the scar, close to a section of the tail unit, which includes the tail 'turret' and tail skid. Pieces of airframe are scattered over a wide area, part of which now has trees planted across it. In 1993 a memorial cairn, with a brass plaque set into it, was constructed by members of No.2296 (Dunoon) Air Training Corps Sqn and the Dumfries & Galloway Aviation Museum.

The crash site of B-29 44-62276 in the mountains of Argyll & Bute, the aircraft's engines, undercarriage and rear turret remain at the site. Overlooking this is a cairn and memorial plaque to the twenty crew and passengers who perished in the

Boeing Vertol Chinook H.C. Mk.2 ZD576: No.7 Sqn, RAF.   02-06-1994
Map No.15
NR 593087 (900ft), Beinn Na Lice, Mull of Kintyre, Argyll

F/Lt J.P. Tapper	Pilot	Killed
F/Lt R.D. Cook	Co-pilot	Killed
M/ALM G.W. Forbes	Ldm	Killed
Sgt K.A. Hardie	Crewman	Killed
25 Passengers	See Appendices	Killed

This accident has been one of the most widely debated in recent times. The helicopter was being used to fly personnel from the RUC, Army and SAS to a meeting at Fort George near Inverness. The flight began after sunset at Aldergrove in Northern Ireland and the aircraft headed east across the North Channel. It struck the western side of Beinn Na Lice at just over 850ft above sea level and was completely wrecked.

As with the other more recent accidents in this book, the site has been marked by a memorial to the crew and passengers. This is one of the few occasions where a visitor has to start from above the site to access it as the public road ends at The Gap nearly 200ft higher up the hill.

Boulton Paul Defiant Mk.I T4042: No.60 OTU, RAF.   29-08-1941
Map No.16
NT 573577 (1,500ft), Hunt Law, Lauder, Scottish Borders

     Sgt A.D.C. La Gruta   Pilot   Killed

The pilot was on a training flight from East Fortune, in East Lothian, when the aircraft dived into the hill.

    This is one of only a couple of crash sites where airmen remain buried and a gravestone has been placed here to mark this. Around this, there are many pieces of the aircraft, which presumably were dug out during attempts to recover Sgt La Gruta's body. He is also commemorated on the Runnymede Memorial.

Bristol Beaufighter T.F. Mk.X LZ455: No.2 OAPU, RAF.   30-10-1943
Map No.17
NR 615087 (1,250ft), Beinn Bhreac, Mull of Kintyre, Argyll

     F/O K.J. Nixon   Pilot   Killed
     Sgt A.B. Solari   Nav   Killed

The aircraft was being flown from Bristol's Filton works on a ferry flight to an unrecorded destination when it crashed on almost the highest point of Beinn Bhreac.

    The site is located in a depression just below the southern summit of Beinn Bhreac, and beside a fence running south-east to north-west towards the summit. It consists of a large collection of aluminium panels from the aircraft while partially buried in one corner are steel under-carriage parts and engine bearers.

Parts from Bristol Beaufighter LZ455 lie in a hollow on Beinn Bhreac.

Bristol Beaufort Mk.I N1180 / S: No.1 TTU, RAF.   02-09-1942
Map No.18
NR 598080 (1,275ft), Tor Mhor, Mull of Kintyre, Argyll

P/O L.P. Booker (RNZAF)	Pilot	Killed
Sgt A.A. Haydon (RNZAF)	Pilot	Killed
Sgt F.J.B. Griffin	Obs	Killed
Sgt T.H. Grasswick (RCAF)	WO/AG	Killed

The aircraft flew into Tor Mhor, not far to the north west of the transmitter station, while on a night navigation exercise from RAF Turnberry, though the aircraft was normally stationed at Abbotsinch.

The remains of this aircraft consist of engine cowling panels and sections of lagged pipework in a hollow near to the top of the hill above the car park at The Gap.

Bristol Blenheim Mk.IV P4848: Special Duties Flt Perth, RAF. 08-11-1939.
Map No.19
NX 615965 (1,250 ft), Ben Inner, Dumfries & Galloway

F/Lt K.N.M. Eyres	Pilot	Killed

P4848 flew into the hillside while en-route from RAF Perth in Perth & Kinross to St.Athan in the Vale of Glamorgan. The aircraft was fitted with an unknown installation, which required a special guard to be mounted at the site once the aircraft was found on 17 November 1939.

Parts from the undercarriage assemblies, aluminium panels and the remains of a Bristol Mercury engine lie in the tussock grass at the site.

Consolidated B-24M 44-50695: 713th BS / 448th BG, USAAF.   12-06-1945
Map No.20
NX 133778 (1,350ft), Goodman's Cairn, Ballantrae, Dumfries & Galloway

Capt J.G. Blank	Pilot	Killed
1st Lt J.K Huber	Co-pilot	Killed
1st Lt B.F. Pargh	Nav	Killed
1st Lt F.X. Pollio	BA	Killed
T/Sgt D.E. Marrow	Eng	Killed
T/Sgt M.L. Kanerak	Radio Op	Killed
S/Sgt W.T. Harriman	Gunner	Killed
S/Sgt C.C. King	Gunner	Killed
S/Sgt L.F. Menrad	Gunner	Killed
S/Sgt J.A. Wildman	Gunner	Killed
7 Passengers	See Appendices	Killed
3 Passengers	See Appendices	Survived

This is one of three B-24s which crashed while being ferried to the US following the end of the conflict in Europe (see the Highlands & Islands section of this book for details of the other two). The aircraft was being flown from Seething in Norfolk to Prestwick before its onward leg across the Atlantic. It crossed the Galloway coast in low cloud and a short while after it ploughed into the southern end of Beneraird.

A scar where the aircraft burnt out can be found close to the crest of the ridge the aircraft crashed on.

Consolidated Liberator Mk.II AL624: No.1653 HCU, RAF.   14-09-1942
Map No.21
NX 470748 (1,800 ft), Drigmorn Hill, Dumfries & Galloway

P/O I.H. Betts	Pilot	Killed
Sgt D.E. Warner	Co-pilot	Killed
Sgt J.C. Freestone	Obs	Killed
Sgt G.C. Boar	WO/AG	Killed
Sgt G.D. Calder (RAAF)	WO/AG	Killed
Sgt J.E.C.A. Steele-Nicholson	AG	Killed
Sgt V.F. Talley	AG	Killed
Sgt J. Bowrey	AG	Killed

Having taken-off from RAF Burn in Yorkshire at 11:00, on a cross-country training flight, the aircraft later flew into the side of the mountain while in cloud. It is likely the crew became uncertain of their position and decided to descend though the cloud in the hope of obtaining a visual position fix. The wreckage was located the day after the accident by a shepherd.

Pieces of airframe are scattered over quite a wide area, but no substantial items from the aircraft remain.

Parts from Liberator AL624 lie scattered around a stream on the slopes of Drigmorn Hill.

Consolidated Liberator Mk.I AM915: BOAC.   01-09-1941
Map No.22
NR 733158 (900ft), Arinarach Hill, Mull of Kintyre, Argyll

Capt K.D. Garden (BOAC)	Pilot	Killed
1st Off G.L. Panes (BOAC)	Pilot	Killed
Flt Eng C.A. Spence (RAFFC)	Flt Eng	Killed
Radio Off S.W. Sydenham (RAFFC)	WO	Killed
Lt Col L.H. Wrangham (RM)	Pass	Killed
S. Pickering (USN)	Pass	Killed
Count G. de Baillet-Letour	Pass	Killed
M. Benjamin	Pass	Killed
E. Taylor	Pass	Killed
Prof. Balmain	Pass	Killed

The aircraft was on an overnight transatlantic flight from Montreal to Ayr and on arrival, at about 08:00, the crew requested information to be able to proceed to Squires Gate rather than land at Ayr. However, Squires Gate was fog bound so the crew radioed their intention to land at Ayr. The aircraft was tracked by radio direction finding equipment flying in a north-westerly direction towards Kintyre before contact was lost at just after 10:00. The aircraft had flown into Arinarach Hill at a height of about 900ft and when located it was reported that the wreckage was spread over a considerable distance.

During a 2006 visit only a single piece of the aircraft, part of one of the engine exhaust stacks, was found on the edge of the forest which now covers the hill and a fence post with 'LIB' etched into it which marks the point where large sections of the wreckage were reported to have lain until the 1980s. There are reports of a metal cross in the forest where the aircraft impacted but the tree cover proved too thick to allow a full search.

De Havilland Devon C. Mk.1 VP969: MCCF, RAF.   03-06-1958
Map No.23
NS 258607 (1,425 ft), Box Law, Largs, North Ayrshire

F/Lt B.N. Barclay	Pilot	Survived
F/O Anderson	Nav	Survived

Having taken-off from Jurby in the Isle of Man at 09:40 the aircraft arrived in the vicinity of Renfrew, Glasgow and due to the poor visibility requested a QGH let down. This would have involved a ground controller instructing the aircraft to descend and turn based on Direction Finding fixes until it was established on the approach to the airfield. Renfrew Air Traffic Control instructed the aircraft to fly an NDB (Non-Directional Beacon) let-down instead, with the crew following a published procedure based on the indicated bearing to an NDB radio navigation aid. The crew, however, were unfamiliar with this type of approach and did not realise that the heights in the published procedure were actually the height to maintain above terrain, and not the altitude to fly at. As a result

The inverted centre section, complete with both wings attached and the two engines lying in the foreground from Devon VP969 on Box Law.

the aircraft descended too low while over high ground, and struck the hillside.

The inverted centre section with both wings attached remains at the site. The undercarriage legs are still attached to the centre section, while on the ground in front of the engine mounts are the two de Havilland Gipsy Queen engines. Lower down the slope is part of the nose, the tail planes, the fin and also the rudder.

De Havilland Dragonfly G-AEHC: The London Express Newspapers Ltd. 02-02-1937
Map No.24
NX 516766 (1,425 ft), Darnaw, Clatteringshaws Loch, Dumfries & Galloway

Mr L.T. Jackson	Pilot	Killed
Mr A.C. Phillpot	WO	Killed
Major H.J. Pemberton	Pass (Reporter)	Killed
Mr C. Wesley	Pass (Photographer)	Killed

Having taken-off from Renfrew, Glasgow at around 11:00, the aircraft flew south to survey an air route to Speke, Liverpool, which had been proposed for commercial flying by the Maybury Civil Aviation Committee. This was one of a number of routes being flown by the aircraft as groundwork for a series of articles to be published in the *Daily Express*. However, the aircraft later descended and flew into the hilltop while in cloud. The following day an air search was conducted but nothing was found due to cloud cover, and Anson K6252 of No.269 Sqn, RAF taking part in the search flew into a hilltop between Leadhills and Abington. The burnt-out wreck of the Dragonfly was discovered by a shepherd on the 4 February 1937.

A cairn with a stone plaque built into it stands on a rock outcrop at the site, and is marked as 'Meml' on Ordnance Survey 1:25000 scale maps. It was unveiled on the 14 February 1937 having been commissioned by the *Daily Express*.

The memorial at the crash site of the Daily Express DH Dragonfly on Darnaw.

De Havilland Mosquito N.F. Mk.II DD753: No.54 OTU, RAF.   12-12-1944
Map No.25
NT 850235 (1,725 ft),The Curr, The Cheviot Hills, Scottish Borders.

F/Lt H.J. Medcalf	Pilot	Killed
F/O R.E. Bellamy	Nav / Radar Op	Killed

Approximately 20 minutes after departing from RAF Charterhall in the Scottish Borders, on a night-interception exercise, the aircraft flew into the hillside.

There is a large scar on the slope where the aircraft impacted and then burned, while nearby are a couple of hollows where wreckage was buried following the accident. The remains of the undercarriage assemblies, sections of armoured plating and parts from the engine nacelles can still be seen at the site.

De Havilland Mosquito Mk.II DD795: No.60 OTU, RAF.   21-01-1944
Map No.26
NX 505870 (2,500 ft), Corserine, The Rhinns of Kells, Dumfries & Galloway

F/Sgt K. Mitchell	Pilot	Killed
F/Sgt J.J. Aylott	Nav	Killed

This aircraft flew into the mountain and disintegrated during a night cross-country training flight from RAF High Ercall in Shropshire. The following day No.2 Sqn, RAF conducted an air search but nothing was found, and the aircraft remained missing until a shepherd came across the wreckage on the 11 February 1944.

The site lies on a spur, adjacent to the Scar of the Folk, and parts from the undercarriage assemblies and small fragments of wreckage can still be found.

Undercarriage remains and other smaller parts are all that remains of Mosquito DD795.

Douglas Dakota D-896: Belgian Air Force.   10-04-1947
Map No.27
NX 498881 (2,400 ft), Carlin's Cairn, The Rhinns of Kells, Dumfries & Galloway

Capt R. Loyen	Pilot	Killed
Adjt A. Dierirks	Nav	Killed
Adjt F. Curtiss	Radio Op	Killed
Capt O. leJeune	Pass	Killed
Adjt A. Roderique	Pass	Killed
Adjt M. Cardon	Pass	Killed

This Dakota was flying from Brussels Evère in Belgium to Prestwick in South Ayrshire, where it was to be overhauled by Scottish Aviation Ltd. However, it appears that, during the latter stage of the flight, the pilot opted to take a direct route over Dumfries & Galloway and not follow the briefed routeing via Milleur Point on the coast. At 13:20 following a request from Prestwick Air Traffic Control, the aircraft reported its altitude as 2,000ft. It was immediately instructed to climb to 4,500ft, as had been previously requested, unless in visual contact with the ground. This instruction was not acknowledged though, and at around this time eye witnesses observed the aircraft flying in poor visibility up a valley near the mountain which it then struck. On impact the aircraft struck a rock outcrop, the wreckage falling onto the slope below and then catching fire.

Small pieces of airframe are strewn down the scree on the very steep slope below the

One of the largest remaining parts from the Belgian Air Force Dakota on Carlin's Cairn is this section of wing structure which lies in the forestry plantation below the crash site.

impact point. Near the base of the slope lies a propeller reduction gear unit. At NX 502882, in the plantation of trees, one of the Pratt & Whitney Twin Wasp engines from the aircraft can be found, while approximately 50 metres to the north there is a partially buried section of wing structure.

Fairey Firefly F.R. Mk.I DT977 / 4A: No.1770 Sqn, RN.   26-10-1944
Map No.28
NS 240550 (1,300ft), Blaeloch Hill, Largs, North Ayrshire

Sub Lt(A) J.H. Fairclough	Pilot	Killed
Sub Lt(A) A.J. King	Obs	Killed

The two crewmembers were carrying out a navigation exercise using wireless direction finding. The aircraft's wireless equipment failed and while flying in low cloud the aircraft struck Blaeloch Hill.

A large crater can be found on the slope where the aircraft hit the hill, this contains many parts from the aircraft's structure, undercarriage and on one edge is the propeller reduction gear and hub. The aircraft's Roll Royce Griffon engine can be found, slowly sinking into the soft ground, a short distance to the south-west of the main site.

Fairey Firefly F.R. Mk.1 PP566 / 208-AC: No.1830 Sqn, RN.   08-01-1950
Map No.29
NS 667822 (1,775 ft), Meikle Bin, Kilsyth Hills, Stirling

Lt J.A.M. Robertson	Pilot	Killed
NA J. Smith	-	Killed

It is understood that the aircraft had problems maintaining radio contact while on a local flight from Abbotsinch (HMS *Sanderling*) in Renfrewshire and after over-flying the airfield, entered cloud and subsequently struck the hill. The wrecked aircraft was located the following day.

A sizeable section of the port wing lies near the summit of the hill, while the Rolls-Royce Griffon engine lies lower down just above the edge of the plantation of trees at NS 665822. During the 1990s the rear fuselage of the aircraft was recovered by the South Yorkshire Aircraft Museum.

The remains of the port wing from Firefly PP566 on Mickle Bin, the main undercarriage oleo and steel cannon housings are still present.

General Dynamics F-111E 68-0003: 20th TFW, USAF.   19-12-1979
Map No.30
NX 458832 (1,925 ft), Craignaw, Dumfries & Galloway

Capt R.A. Hetzner	Pilot	Killed
Capt R.C. Spaulding	Nav	Killed

Airborne from Upper Heyford in Oxfordshire the aircraft had completed a bombing exercise before proceeding to Dumfries & Galloway to commence day low-level flying practice. The weather conditions were reasonable, but the aircraft subsequently flew into the snow covered hillside at high speed and exploded, scattering wreckage over a wide area.

A defile on a rock outcrop indicates the impact point, from where a trail of tiny fragments leads up the rocky slope for over 200 metres. On a wide ledge overlooking the impact point is a stone cairn, which has a memorial plaque set into it, erected in 1987 by members of the Auld Kilmarnock Hill Walking Club.

Gloster Javelin F.A.W. Mk.6 XA825 / A: No.29 Sqn, RAF.   21-11-1960.
Map No.31
NT 296475 (1,925ft), Emly Bank, Peebles, Midlothian

F/Lt V.L. Hill	Pilot	Killed
F/Lt J.M. Knight	Nav / Radar Op	Killed

The two crew were on a cross country training flight from RAF Leuchars in Fife. While flying west across the Moorfoot Hills the aircraft struck Emly Bank very close to its summit and broke up.

Wreckage from the aircraft is spread over a wide area. There are parts from the forward end of the aircraft, including the nose wheel, in the area where it first impacted, to the north of a recently installed wind turbine. Further parts are located in two gullies which lead off the hill to the north. The farthest scattered parts are the remains of the two engines, in the western of the two gullies in the region of NT 291474.

Grumman Martlet Mk.I AL251: No.802 Sqn, RN.   13-12-1940
Map No.32
NS 157974 (2,050 ft), Beinn Bheula, Lochgoilhead, Argyll

Lt (A) G.F. Russell	Pilot	Killed

Following assignment to No.802 Sqn the aircraft was on a ferry flight from Abbotsinch (HMS *Sanderling*) in Renfrewshire to Donibristle (HMS *Merlin*) in Fife, when it flew into the mountainside while in cloud. It is of interest that Martlet AL248, piloted by Sub Lt M.A. Birrell and on a ferry flight that involved the same routeing that day, is recorded as having put down in Loch Lomond.

Two sections of wing from the aircraft remain, one being a substantial portion of the starboard wing with roundel markings still discernable. Nearby is part of the bulkhead from the rear of the cockpit, and an undercarriage leg and engine from the aircraft.

One of the major wing sections from Martlet AL251 on Beinn Bheula.

Handley Page Hampden Mk.I L4063: No.50 Sqn, RAF.   17-03-1940
Map No.33
NT 847158 (1,675ft), Windy Rig, Cocklawfoot, Borders

F/O V.H. Ayres	Pilot	Killed
P/O P.A.F. Addie	Obs	Killed
Sgt G.A. Rowling	WO/AG	Killed (Missing)
LAC A.V. Wallace	WO/AG	Killed (Missing)

The crew had been carrying out a night patrol over the North Sea from their base at Waddington in Lincolnshire. While trying to return to Waddington the crew had contacted their base to ask for QDMs to lead them safely back to Lincolnshire. At around this time it was reported by the crew that they had sighted a large estuary which they believed to be the Humber. The QDMs they were given indicated that they should turn onto a southerly course which the pilot did. A short time later the aircraft impacted the northern side of Windy Gyle where much of the aircraft was consumed by an intense fire. It is reported that no trace was found of Sgt Rowling and LAC Wallace, which led to them being listed as missing.

For many years parts from the aircraft remained at the site but these were recovered during the late 1980s/early 1990s to aid in a rebuild project. As part of this recovery a memorial was constructed at the site, this has a white cross on top of a stone plinth with plaque.

Hawker Hurricane Mk.IV LD594: No.439 Sqn, RAF.   18-03-1944
Map No.34
NX 490921 (950 ft), Loch Doon, Dumfries & Galloway

P/O R.M. MacTavish (RCAF)   Pilot   Killed

This Hurricane dived into the ground at high speed, either as a result of the pilot being overcome following an oxygen system failure, or mechanical failure resulting in loss of control. The aircraft had been one of eleven Hurricanes flying in formation, during a ferry flight from RAF Ayr in South Ayrshire to RAF Hurn in Dorset, as part of a Squadron move.

Within a firebreak in the forest there is a pile of wreckage from the aircraft, including small sections of wing structure, the propeller hub and the remains of the engine radiator unit. The badly damaged Rolls-Royce Merlin engine lies nearby in the trees bordering the firebreak.

Under tree cover, and a good layer of pine needles, near Loch Doon is the Rolls Royce Merlin engine from Hurricane LD594.

Hawker Typhoon Mk.IB JR439: No.440 Sqn, RAF.   18-03-1944
Map No.35
NX 583670 (450 ft), Dunharberry, Dumfries & Galloway

    P/O K.O. Mitchell (RCAF)   Pilot   Killed

As with Hurricane LD594, while on a ferry flight as part of a Squadron move from RAF Ayr in South Ayrshire to RAF Hurn in Dorset, the aircraft dived into the ground while on the first stage of the flight, en-route to RAF Woodvale in Lancashire where it was expected to refuel.

    Part of the propeller reduction gear unit from the aircraft is mounted on a stone cairn, marked on Ordnance Survey 1:25000 scale maps, just off the track that runs parallel to the disused railway line, west of where the Little Water of Fleet Viaduct once stood. The actual site of the accident is nearby on the edge of the forest, where wreckage can be seen beside the track. A few sections of armoured plating and many small pieces of airframe remain.

Hawker Typhoon Mk.IB MN532 / FA-E: No.56 OTU, RAF.   27-03-1945
Map No.36
NS 729214 (1,625 ft), Stony Hill, East Ayrshire

    F/O R.S. Bellis (RCAF)   Pilot   Killed

While on a cross-country training flight from RAF Milfield in Northumberland and having flown around 20 miles off the planned route, it appears the pilot descended to obtain a visual position fix and hit the cloud-covered hillside.

    Several pieces of airframe and small sections of armoured plating lie in the grass around a shallow depression in the slope.

Heinkel He111H-4 / 5J+SH: I/KG4, *Luftwaffe*.   09-08-1940
Map No.37
NX 497673 (2,125 ft), Cairnsmore of Fleet, Dumfries & Galloway

Lt A. Zeiss	Pilot	Killed
Uffz W. Hajesch	–	Killed
Uffz G.F. VonTurckheim	–	Killed
Uffz W. Mechsner	–	Killed

This Heinkel flew into the rocky mountain top and burned out at 01:30. The aircraft had flown from Soesterberg in Holland and is thought to have been tasked with dropping mines off the coast of Northern Ireland near Belfast.

    An area of rocks at the site is strewn with small bits of melted aluminium. There are no substantial pieces of wreckage left today, as the tail and wing sections that remained following the crash were removed in the 1970s, forty years after the accident. On 8 August 1980 a memorial stone, recording the aircraft accidents on Cairnsmore of Fleet, was unveiled at the summit of the mountain. This was arranged by the Dumfries & Galloway Aviation Museum, with the 2½ tonne inscribed granite block being airlifted onto the summit by an HH-53 helicopter from the USAF.

Junkers Ju88A-14 144537 / E3+HM: KG 6, *Luftwaffe*. 25-03-1943
Map No.38
NT 170621 (1,400ft), Hare Hill, Balerno, Mid-Lothian

Olt F. Forster	Pilot	Killed
Ogf H. Kristall	–	Killed
Ufz H. Bluhm	–	Killed
Gfr W. Euler	–	Killed

This aircraft was one of a number that were taking part in a raid against the Central Belt of Scotland, which according to the records of No.63 MU was the first enemy activity in the area since 1941. The raid was conducted at low level, which caused this aircraft and three others on the raid to come to grief on the high ground of Southern Scotland, with fatal consequences for the crews.

The site of the crash is marked by a post with a memorial plaque bearing the names of the four unfortunate crewmen and numerous small fragments of the aircraft.

A small collection of wreckage gathered around the simple wooden memorial on Hare Hill near Edinburgh marks the spot where a Ju88 ploughed into the hill in March 1943.

Lockheed Hudson Mk.III AE640: OADF, RAF. 25-07-1941
Map No.39
NR 639071 (230ft), Feorlan, Mull of Kintyre, Argyll

F/Lt K.F. Arnold DFC	Pilot	Killed
Sgt P. Keast	Obs	Killed
Mr W. Bratherton (CTC)	WO	Killed

The crew were ferrying the brand new aircraft from Lockheed's factory at Burbank in California to St Eval in Cornwall via Ayr. The aircraft flew into the hill whilst heading west, presumably after being directed to fly in that direction as part of the let-down procedure that was in place at Ayr. Normally in poor weather aircraft were guided to Ayr and allowed to fly directly overhead and ordered to fly east for 2-3 minutes before being brought back over the airfield. The crews were then directed to fly on a bearing of 250°

for 3 minutes and then to turn through 180⁰ and descend though cloud until the sea was visible before making a visual approach to the airfield.

Despite this being one of the lowest crash sites in the region, access is difficult due to the road being single track with no parking and the area between the road and the site can only be easily crossed early or very late in the year when there is no bracken. The site itself is in the woodland between the house at Feorlan and the river in the gorge below. To reach it leave the road just above the house and follow the boundary fence until it turns to go up hill at its southern most point. At this point the site should be visible through the trees on a flat area below a number of large boulders, where there is a bare patch containing hundreds of small burnt fragments of the aircraft and melted aluminium left by the post crash fire.

Lockheed Neptune M.R. Mk.1 WX545: No.36 Sqn, RAF.   10-10-1956
Map No.40
NR 598092 (1,200ft), Balmavicar, Mull of Kintyre, Argyll

F/Lt G. Finding	Pilot	Killed
F/O J.A. Campbell	Co-pilot	Killed
Sgt C. Armstrong	Flt Eng	Killed
F/O G. Rishton	Nav	Killed
F/Sgt R. Fox	RO	Killed
F/Sgt R.M. Noble	Sig	Killed
Sgt E. Honey	Sig	Killed
Sgt B.E. Lynn	Sig	Killed
Sgt R.V. Smith	Sig	Killed

The crew were taking part in a combined forces exercise and were an aspect of the anti-submarine section. The aircraft was flying south along the coast of the Kintyre peninsular at about 1,000ft above sea level but drifted slightly to the east and struck a rise causing the aircraft to break up into several large pieces.

Much of the wreckage lies where it came to rest following the crash as little effort was made to clear up the site. The only major part, which has been moved, is the

Tail section from Neptune WX545 on the Mull of Kintyre.

complete tail fin, which initially sat on the rise that the aircraft first hit but can now be found at its base. A Wright Cyclone engine, the undercarriage and large pieces of the wings remain, though the fuselage was almost entirely destroyed by fire, but what little was left can also be seen here. A memorial was placed at the southern end of the site in 1998 and this stands out when approaching from below as a regular shape on the skyline.

McDonnell Douglas RF-4C 68-0566: 1st TRS, 10th / TRW, USAF. 28-03-1979
Map No.41
NX 493674 (1,850 ft), Cairnsmore of Fleet, Dumfries & Galloway

| Capt T. Seagren | Pilot | Killed |
| Lt R. Spalding | WSO | Killed |

The aircraft hit the mountain during a night radar sortie, while flying on a north-easterly track, creating a deep scar in the rocky ground and scattering wreckage over the shoulder of the mountain near Eastman's Cairn.

A few fragments of wreckage lie in the impact scar, just below a small cairn, while other small pieces are scattered over a wide area.

North American Harvard Mk.IIB FT401: No.22 FTS, RAF.   16-01-1953
Map No.42
NT 133260 (1,775 ft), Little Knock, Tweedsmuir, Scottish Borders

| Msm N.C. Wadham (RN) | Pilot | Killed |

The pilot had taken off from RNAS *Anthorn* on the southern side of the Solway Firth in Cumbria, on a daytime solo aerobatic and QGH practice flight. He had been due to return after one hour, but 40 minutes after taking off the aircraft was seen flying low along the Tweed valley near Tweedsmuir, between 75 and 100ft above the ground. The witness then saw the aircraft turn up one of the glens towards Great Knock, which was in cloud and a short time later a crash was heard. The accident report for the aircraft stated that a friend of the pilot lived 'at the point where the aircraft turned off starboard into the small valley'.

The largest remaining part from the aircraft is one of its wings, located a short distance from a pit containing further parts. Parts also remain where the aircraft first hit on the northern side of the hill.

Percival Prentice Mk.1 G-AOLR: Finance & General Company Hire Ltd. 30-07-1961
Map No.43
NS 682793 (1,025 ft), Kilsyth Hills, North Lanarkshire

| Mr C.H. Bonson | – | Killed |
| Mr N.M. Cameron | – | Killed |

This aircraft flew into the cloud-covered hillside while inbound to Renfrew, Glasgow. It is thought to have been delivering spare parts for an airliner that had been grounded at Renfrew due to radio failure.

Several pieces of airframe still remain, including sections of wing spar and a fuel tank.

A section of main spar from the Percival Prentice on the Kilsyth Hills.

Supermarine Spitfire Mk.VB AD540 / 'Blue Peter': No.242 Sqn, RAF.   23-03-1942
Map No.44
NX 604992 (1400 ft), Craigenrine, Cairnsmore of Carsphairn, Dumfries & Galloway

P/O D.G. Hunter-Blair	Pilot	Killed

The Spitfire dived into the ground after the pilot lost control while on an operational patrol from RAF Ayr in South Ayrshire, probably due to oxygen failure. P/O Hunter-Blair baled out at low altitude and did not survive.

Exactly 51 years after the accident members of the Dumfries & Galloway Aviation Museum finally located the site, following several attempts and much research, and subsequently excavated a significant quantity of wreckage from the aircraft, including the Rolls-Royce Merlin engine, which was recovered using an RN Sea King helicopter. A memorial plaque was later placed on a rock at the site, while a second plaque was placed on a rock where P/O Hunter-Blair came down on Dugland Hill at NS 606005.

Vickers Viking Mk.1B G-AIVE / 'Vestal': BEA.   21-04-1948
Map No.45
NS 261592 (1,475 ft), Irish Law , Largs, North Ayrshire

Capt J. Ramsden	Pilot	Survived
1st Officer D.P. Clifton	Co-pilot	Survived
Mr A.H. Lloyd	Radio Officer	Survived
Mr C. Moroney	Steward	Survived
16 Passengers	See Appendices	Survived

At 19:12 the aircraft departed Northolt, London on a scheduled passenger service to Renfrew, Glasgow arriving over the airfield around 2 hours later. However, having requested permission to make a beam approach, it is understood that radio contact with Renfrew Air Traffic Control was lost. The aircraft flew out to the west-south-west, presumably to hold while the crew attempted to re-establish radio contact, but flying in cloud it hit the hillside at 21:35. The aircraft remained relatively intact, but after having skidded to a halt it caught fire, with the crew and passengers having to evacuate immediately. Capt Ramsden and Mr Watt then set off for, arriving in Largs in the middle of the night. The other crew and passengers subsequently obtained assistance and descended off the hill the following morning.

Some salvageable equipment from the aircraft was recovered using a helicopter the week after the crash, but a significant quantity of wreckage is still on site. The two engine nacelles remain where the aircraft burned out, one having the retracted

Engine nacelles from Viking G-AIVE remain where the aircraft burned out, one with its Bristol Hercules engine still attached.

undercarriage assembly with main wheel and tyre inside it and the Bristol Hercules engine attached. The nacelles also have sections of the inboard wings attached in which the internal geodetic framework is visible. In a patch of bog lower down the slope is part of the tail, while in the col to the west of the site the two propeller hub and reduction gear units can be found.

Vickers Wellington Mk.IC R1164: No.20 OTU, RAF.   25-01-1941
Map No.46
NS 257609 (1,450 ft), Box Law, Largs, North Ayrshire

F/O J.F.M. Millar	Pilot	Killed

The Wellington flew into hill top while in cloud and disintegrated. The aircraft was on a ferry flight from RAF Kirkbride in Cumbria to RAF Lossiemouth in Moray.

A peat-filled scar contains the bulk of the wreckage, consisting mainly of small fragments with the largest item being one of the propeller reduction gear units.

Vickers Wellington Mk.VIII LB137: No.6 OTU, RAF.   02-12-1943
Map No.47
NR 601087 (1,275ft), Beinn na Lice, Mull of Kintyre, Argyll

F/O H.O. Dransfield	Pilot	Killed
Sgt J.A. Duddridge	Co-pilot	Killed
F/O C.C Cooper (RAAF)	Nav	Killed
F/Sgt R.J. Wardrop (RNZAF)	WO/AG	Killed
F/Sgt V.F. Suttor (RAAF)	WO/AG	Killed
F/Sgt R.F. Canavan (RAAF)	WO/AG	Killed

The crew, stationed at Silloth in Cumbria, was carrying out a practice 'Square Search' in the sea area off the Isle of Mull. The Court of Inquiry concluded that the aircraft must have suffered a wireless failure at about 15:00hrs as it had been in regular contact until that point. It was observed by radar and the ROC flying west over Campbeltown at 16:00. At some point after this while flying east or south-east the aircraft flew into the seaward side of Beinn na Lice not far below its summit.

Only a few small pieces of geodetic framework from the aircraft can still be found at the crash site.

Chapter Nine

Scotland: The Highlands and Islands

D ividing the United Kingdom up geographically into manageable and logical areas for the purpose of this publication was always going to involve some degree of compromise. Scotland, by virtue alone of the sheer size of the area covered, in relation to the other parts of the country featured, would by rights require several separate sections – but each featuring only a mere handful of sites. Therefore the authors decided to divide it only into two sections, 'Highlands and Islands' and 'Lowlands', with the dividing line being approximately the northern edge of the Central Belt, to simplify the arrangement of the accompanying maps. The geology of this region illustrates the range and complexity of Scotland's rocks. Along the western-most areas we find some of the oldest rocks in the British Isles and indeed Europe at some 3,000 million years old, as well as some of the youngest at 60 million years old. The dramatic mountainous landscape is the result of a turbulent geological past. The Northwest Highlands formed from ancient sedimentary rocks being uplifted by thrust faulting from the east and weathered into mountain ranges, as well as prolific volcanic activity forming yet further mountain groups in the Grampians and on some of the islands. Metamorphism and faulting caused by tectonic collision accounts for almost all the remaining areas of high ground. Additionally, Scotland has over 790 islands, divided into four main groups: Shetland, Orkney, and the Inner Hebrides and Outer Hebrides.

Including the Islands, the area covered in this section alone is almost as large as the whole of England, stretching some 300 by 200 miles. The terrain that can be experienced varies enormously from gentle rolling heather moorland of the Moray coast to windswept boggy islands and the blanket bogs of Caithness to the highest and most remote mountains in the British Isles, including Ben Nevis, the highest peak at 4,406ft. Obviously many of the areas covered here are not likely to be visited by casual walkers and correct equipment and a degree of experience is essential before venturing into such wild and remote areas. The authors strongly suggest that careful, thorough planning is required when attempting to reach many of the sites listed, with extra consideration given to the changeable weather, as snow is common on the higher peaks even in summer. In fact, some of the highest crash sites on north facing slopes may remain buried in snow for most of the year.

In common with other areas, the majority of the aircraft losses in the region date from the Second World War period, with RAF aircraft making up most of these and with a fairly even mix of operational and training flights being involved. Typically many of the operational flights taking place over the area during wartime involved long flights over the sea, such as anti-submarine patrols or convoy escort duties and it seems that crews were especially vulnerable as they returned from such duties, probably tired or unsure of their exact position until they sighted land. With the added difficulties of frequent poor weather conditions reducing visibility, as well as the need for night operations, it is perhaps unsurprising that so many aircraft came to grief, with the ever present high ground seemingly always ready to catch out the unwary or lost. Almost all of the USAAF (later USAF), aircraft losses in the Highlands & Islands were on ferry flights, with Prestwick being one of the major staging posts for long distance ferry flights across the Atlantic in both directions. Combat also played a role with inclusion of the very first German aircraft to crash on land, after being shot down by UK forces, in this case anti-aircraft fire and a raider which crashed whilst attempting a forced landing, after being disabled by fighter action, a little over a year later. Post war there have been a many more crashes and they seem to continue to occur at a rate of at least one per year, though today any wreckage is soon removed in its entirety for the UK Air Accidents Investigation Branch (AAIB) to examine. Most have been civilian light aircraft, though as the area still serves as an important training area for NATO forces there have been further military losses, with a number of these being included.

Due to the nature of the terrain, most of the airfields in the region are concentrated on the flatter areas of the east coast, though there were also Coastal and Fighter Command stations on a number of the Islands. There were only two air stations on the west coast that saw operational service during wartime, excluding Machrihannish which falls within the area covered by the Scottish Lowland section. These comprised Connel near Oban, a small grass strip (now paved), which was used by a detachment from No.516 Squadron for Combined Forces training, as well as in emergencies for occasional American aircraft inbound on the North Atlantic air ferry route. At least one B-24 and a B-17 overran the runway here attempting to land on what must have been a barely adequate runway for this purpose. No.516 Sqn lost an entire flight of three Hurricanes in February 1944 and two of these are covered in this section, the third crashed on low lying ground near Alloa. The second air station was the busy major flying boat base at Oban itself, which suffered a small number of losses on the islands, but most of their accidents were over water.

With a relatively large number of crash sites still containing substantial sections of aircraft in this region, it is not surprising that many sites attracted the attention of enthusiasts right from the earliest days of interest in wartime aircraft remains. Obviously the very factors of terrain, inaccessibility and the weather conditions, that meant recovery at the time of the original crashes was so difficult, continued to protect sites for some time. But over recent years more and more has disappeared, as tracks have been improved and modern all-terrain vehicles and even helicopters etc have been brought in to aid recovery operations. Official bodies and amateur organisations have recovered many major parts of often now extinct aircraft to aid rebuild and restoration projects and other large sections have been removed to be placed in museums as exhibits in their own right – ultimately this is probably the only way to ensure the long term survival of these parts for future generations, as the nature of the metals used in aircraft construction makes them highly susceptible to corrosion and the elements eventually take their toll, especially once the last vestiges of protective paint weather away or are burnt off by moorland fires, exposing the bare metal. Many sites listed here still contain major remains, partly because of their inaccessibility or in a few cases due to the protection of individual landowners, but often because the aircraft type involved

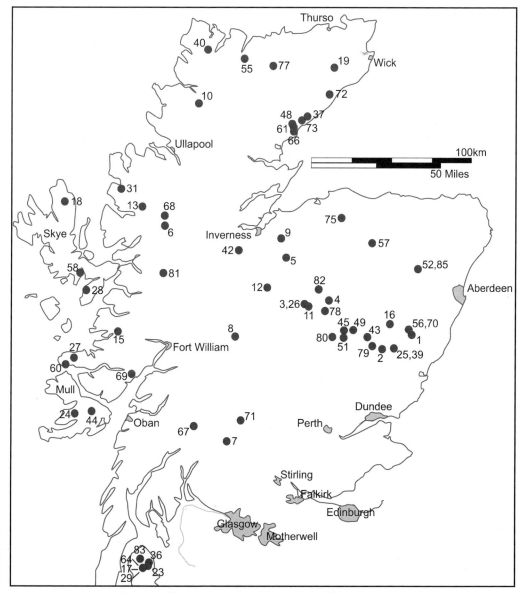

Crash Sites on the Scottish Highlands

is not particularly rare or the parts have weathered to the point that any use in a restoration project is no longer viable. Left alone they will naturally deteriorate further and eventually corrode away, but it will be a slow process and they should remain as memorials and be visible to walkers for many years to come. However if parts from sites are removed piecemeal for souvenirs and the engines and larger sections subjected to hacksaws, chisels etc. they will all too soon disappear.

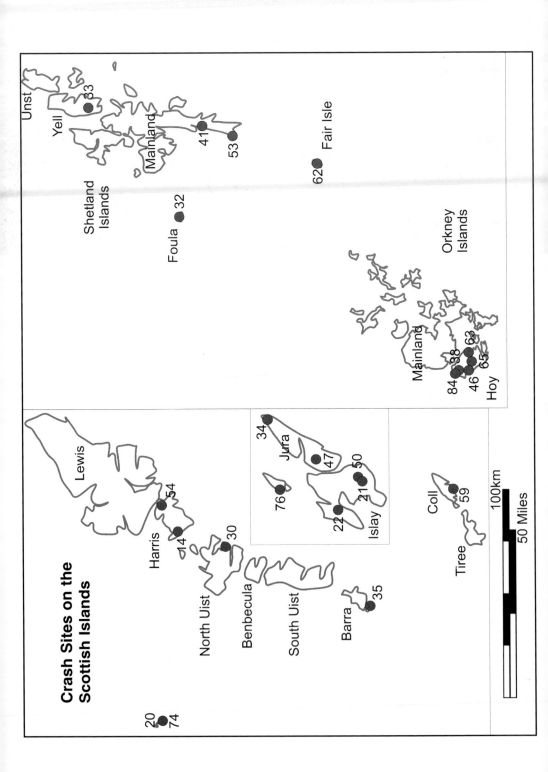

Crash Sites on the
Scottish Islands

Sections of wing spar and various panels from Oxford N6438 lie hidden amongst the heather in a gully.

Airspeed Oxford Mk.II N6438: No.2 FIS, RAF.   03-09-1942
Map No.1
NO 628819 (1,650ft), Meluncart, Grampian Mountains, Aberdeenshire

P/O J. Keddie	Pilot	Killed
P/O W.F. White	Pilot	Survived

During a training flight from RAF Montrose in Angus, the aircraft flew into the hill in poor visibility. P/O White was seriously injured and only rescued after lying in the open for 28 hours.

Several sections of wing spar and many aluminium panels are gathered together in a shallow gully close to the crash site.

Airspeed Oxford Mk.I DF448: No.2 FIS, RAF.   26-10-1944
Map No.2
NO 427731 (1,900ft), Little Hill of Donald Young, Grampian Mountains, Angus

F/Sgt J.P. Waters	Pilot	Survived
Sgt W. Shuttleworth	Pilot	Survived

While on a beam approach training flight from RAF Montrose in Angus, the aircraft was following a QDM to the airfield when it struck a cloud-covered hilltop. The aircraft bounced and flew on briefly, before crash landing on another hilltop.

The undercarriage assemblies, sections of the main spar from the wing and a couple of fuel tanks lie at the site. There are also many burnt fragments in two small scars and it appears rather than remove the airframe the salvage team burned the wreckage on site.

Small fragments from Oxford DF448 lie in a small bare patch on the heather covered hillside at Little Hill of Donald Young.

Airspeed Oxford Mk.I HM724: No.19 (P)AFU, RAF.   12-10-1943
Map No.3
NH 962000 (3,950ft), Braeriach, Cairngorm Mountains, Aberdeenshire

F/O E.W. Hutchins	Pilot (Inst)	Survived
F/O J. Turner	Pilot (u/t)	Survived
F/O G.C. Vaudrey (RAAF)	Pass	Survived
F/O R. McGregor (RNZAF)	Pass	Survived

HM724 flew into a downdraught and stalled onto the mountain top during a training flight from RAF Dalcross in the Highlands. The crew all survived with the aircraft remaining relatively intact. However, lying on the upper slopes of the third highest mountain in Great Britain and far from the nearest access track, salvaging even the easily removable equipment from the aircraft proved difficult. Therefore No.56 MU obtained permission to abandon the bulk of the wreck and it was burnt on site.

On the path up Braeriach, close to the top of the ridge, can be found a small pile of steel framework and pieces of melted aluminium, surrounded by stones to prevent them being scattered by the wind. A few small sections of wing structure also remain nearby, but there appears to be no trace of the two engines from the aircraft.

Airspeed Oxford Mk.I PH404: No.311 Sqn, RAF.   10-01-1945
Map No.4
NJ 111026 (3,550ft), Stob an t-Sluichd, Cairngorm Mountains, Moray

S/Ldr K. Kvapil (Czech)	Pilot	Killed
W/O R. Jelen (Czech)	Pass (Pilot)	Killed
F/O L. Linhart (Czech)	Pass (Pilot)	Killed
F/O J. Vella (Czech)	Pass (Pilot)	Killed
F/O V. Kauders (Czech)	Pass (WO/AG)	Killed

Having taken-off from RAF Tain in the highlands the aircraft failed to arrive at the intended destination of RAF Hornchurch in Greater London. On 19 August 1945 the wrecked aircraft was found by hill walkers on the remote mountain top.

An area strewn with pieces of steel framework and burnt fragments can be found at the site where the salvage team burned the bulk of the wreckage from the aircraft. The two Armstrong Siddeley Cheetah engines lie nearby along with a section of the main spar from the wing, which has the mounts for the undercarriage assembly attached. In 2005 a granite plaque was fixed to a large rock above the site, commemorating all the aircrew killed in the Cairngorm Mountains.

Armstrong Whitworth Whitley Mk.V N1498: No.19 OTU, RAF. 06-01-1942
Map No.5
NH 844290 (2,000ft), Carn a Choire Moire, Tomatin, Highland

Sgt D. Pike	Pilot (Capt)	Survived
P/O J.G. Irvine (RNZAF)	Pilot	Killed
P/O J.G. Castling (RNZAF)	Pilot	Killed
Sgt C.M. Edgehill	Obs	Survived
Sgt C.S. George DFM	WO/AG	Killed
Sgt C.W. Green	WO/AG	Killed
Sgt E.F. Kane	WO/AG	Survived

The aircraft was returning to RAF Kinloss from a cross-country training flight when the aircraft struck snow-covered high ground at 2,000ft above sea level. The aircraft radio equipment had failed during the flight removing one of the most useful navigation aids to the crew.

Until 2003 large sections of the aircraft remained at the site, but these were recovered by the Midlands Aircraft Recovery Group. Only small pieces of the aircraft are still at the site along with a memorial cairn close to the summit of the hill.

Since the recent recovery of the remains of Whitley N1498, only a few scattered parts and the memorial plaque close to the summit are now to be seen at this site.

Armstrong Whitworth Whitley Mk.V P4996: No.78 Sqn, RAF.   27-02-1941
Map No.6
NH 084486 (2,100ft), Sgurr nan Ceannaichean, Glen Carron, Highland

W/Cdr, G.T. Toland,	Pilot	Killed
Sgt, G.A. Forsyth,	Pilot	Killed
P/O, D.H. Gates,	Obs	Killed
Sgt, G.R. Armstrong,	WO/AG	Killed
Sgt, N.L. Lane,	WO/AG	Killed

The crew had been taking part in a raid against Koln from RAF Dishforth, in Yorkshire. During the return flight the crew became hopelessly lost and flew into the summit of Sgurr nan Ceannaichean.

Small pieces of the aircraft can be found scattered down the north-western side of the mountain from about 2,100ft with most being quite low down towards Coire an t-Seilich. There is no defined impact point, only the widely spread small pieces of wreckage.

Armstrong Whitworth Whitley Mk.V P5090 / YG-L: No.502 Sqn, RAF.   24-11-1940
Map No.7
NN 476172 (2,100ft), Fathen Glinne, Balquhidder, Stirling

Sgt W.J. Barnfather	Pilot	Killed
Sgt J.J. Westoby	Pilot	Killed
P/O J. Whitsed	Obs	Killed
Sgt J.G. Curtis	WO/AG	Killed
Sgt J. Perfect	WO/AG	Killed
Sgt W.S. Hamilton	AG	Survived

The crew was on a night-time convoy escort sortie from RAF Limavady in Northern Ireland and during the flight their radio equipment failed. With no navigation aid other than dead reckoning the crew became lost and subsequently flew into high ground.

The site still has very evident sections of the aircraft's undercarriage and pieces of wing structure remaining. The bulk of the wreck was recovered by the 1980s, this included a near complete wing and the engines. The eventual fate of these parts and reason for them being recovered is unknown, however it is known that the wreck was reported as a possible new crash by more than one passing aircraft so this may have been at least part of the reason. Until the mid 90s a propeller was mounted on a plinth at Strathyre but after enquiring in the local area this too was found to have been removed.

Armstrong Whitworth Whitley Mk.V LA877 / ZV-W: No.19 OTU, RAF.   03-07-1943
Map No.8
NN 527806 (1,725ft), Meallan Odhar, Kinloch Laggan, Highland

Sgt D.C. Hunt	Pilot	Killed
Sgt E.A. Deacon	Nav	Killed
F/Sgt D.J. Gillies (RCAF)	BA	Killed
Sgt R.N. Cowie	WO/AG	Killed
Sgt K.P. Gemmel (RCAF)	AG	Killed

The crew was on a training flight from Kinloss when their aircraft was seen to crash by an ROC post. It was suspected that there had been an in flight fire before the aircraft dived into the ground.

Many parts from the aircraft are scattered around the crash site and for a short distance to the south-east of the site.

Armstrong Whitworth Whitley Mk.V BD295 / UO-N: No.19 OTU, RAF. 17-05-1943
Map No.9
NH 811408 (1,800ft), An Riasgach, Cawdor Moor, Highland

F/Lt R.W.P. Macfarland	Pilot	Survived
Sgt K.J. Sampson	Pilot	Killed
F/O A.C. Barrie	Nav	Killed
Sgt R. Hartley	BA	Killed
F/Sgt A.T. Hawkins	WO/AG	Killed
Sgt R.A. Hartwell	WO/AG	Died of Injuries 19-05-1943
Sgt Padley	AG	Survived

The crew was on a practice bombing sortie, while trying to locate the bombing range the aircraft flew into rising ground of Cawdor Moor in cloud.

The site lies on heather covered moorland where quite a few parts of the aircraft can be found gathered together close to a shooting butt.

Avro Anson Mk.I N9857: No.19 OTU, RAF.   13-04-1941
Map No.10
NC 294232 (2,125 ft), Imir Fada, Ben More Assynt, Highland

F/O J.H. Steyn DFC	Pilot	Killed
P/O W.E. Drew	Obs (Inst)	Killed
Sgt C. M. Mitchell	Obs (u/t)	Killed
F/Sgt T.B. Kenny	WO (Inst)	Killed
Sgt J.Emery	WO/AG (u/t)	Killed
Sgt H.A. Tompsett	WO/AG (u/t)	Killed

During a night cross-country navigation exercise, from RAF Kinloss in Moray, the aircraft encountered heavy snow showers. After turning onto a southerly track over Cape Wrath the pilot attempted to climb above the clouds, but minutes later the aircraft transmitted the message 'Icing up…lost power in port engine…losing height…descending through three thousand feet.' The aircraft then remained missing until a shepherd came across the wreck on the 25 May 1941. The following day RAF personnel climbed to the scene and decided to bury the bodies of the crew on site, the graves being covered by a mound of peat and a stone cairn.

In 1985 the stone cairn at the site was rebuilt by No.2489 (Bridge of Don) Air Training Corps Sqn, with a plaque being set into it and a tall metal cross placed on top. Scattered on the boggy plateau around this memorial are the remains of the aircraft. The two Armstrong Siddeley Cheetah engines, both main undercarriage assemblies with wheels and tyres, several fuel tanks, pieces of fuselage framework and aluminium alloy panels are to be seen. The site is indicated as 'grave' on current Ordnance Survey 1:25000 scale maps.

Cheetah engine from Anson N9857 on Ben More Assynt.

Small fragments from Anson DJ106 incorporated into the memorial cairn on Ben MacDui.

Avro Anson Mk.I DJ106: No.19 OTU, RAF.   21-08-1942

Map No.11

NN 986992 (4,100ft), Ben MacDui, Cairngorm Mountains, Aberdeenshire

Sgt J Llewelyn	Pilot	Killed
F/Sgt G. Fillingham	Obs	Killed
P/O W. Gilmour (RCAF)	Obs	Killed
F/Sgt K.E. Carruthers	WO/AG	Killed
Sgt J.B. Robertson	WO/AG	Killed

The Anson struck the mountain while in cloud, during a navigation exercise from RAF Kinloss in Moray. The aircraft remained missing for several days, the wreckage being located on 24 August 1942.

At the site, on the upper slopes of the second highest mountain in Great Britain, there is a cairn and plaque commemorating the crash, marked as 'Meml' on Ordnance Survey 1:50000 and 1:25000 scale maps. A few small fragments of wreckage are built into the cairn, but the bulk of the remaining wreckage is scattered to the north, down the stone covered slope into Coire Mór. One of the Armstrong Siddeley Cheetah engines and the remains of an undercarriage assembly lie near the top of the slope. The remains of the other undercarriage assembly, sections of steel framework and a number of aluminium alloy panels are gathered together lower down, while a few pieces of wreckage including the core of the other engine lie in the Allt a' Choire Mhóir at the bottom of the slope.

Large remains of Lancaster PD259 are still to be found at the main crash site and scattered around the nearby moorland.

Avro Lancaster Mk.I PD259 / JO-G: No.467 Sqn, RAAF.   31-08-1944
Map No.12
NH 728107 (2,300ft), Carn Icean Duibhe, Monadhliath Mountains, Highland

F/O R.H. Beddoe (RAAF)	Pilot	Killed
F/Sgt F.M. Walker (RAAF)	Nav	Killed
W/O G.H. Middleton	Flt Eng	Killed
F/Sgt T.R. Dent (RAAF)	WO	Killed
F/Sgt D.H. Ryan (RAAF)	BA	Killed
F/Sgt S.A. Abbott (RAAF)	AG	Killed
F/Sgt B.M. Glover (RAAF)	AG	Killed

While on a night cross-country training flight, from RAF Waddington in Lincolnshire, the aircraft crashed on the hillside at around 23:15. The Accidents Investigation Branch was called in to determine the cause of the accident, but the results of the investigation are not known. It is apparent from the spread of wreckage though, that sections of the aircraft broke away before it hit the ground.

A significant quantity of wreckage from the aircraft still remains at the site, in part due to the remote location, but also as a result of the Balavil Estate owners' desire for the bulk of the wreckage to remain where it was. The removal of two propellers for use as memorials has been approved though, one being placed in the graveyard at Balavil House and the other in the station memorial garden at RAF Waddington.

Avro Lancaster G.R. Mk.3 TX264 / BS-D: No.120 Sqn, RAF.   14-03-1951
Map No.13
NG 944601 (3,100ft), Triple Buttress, Beinn Eighe, Torridon, Highland

F/Lt H.S. Reid DFC	Pilot	Killed
Sgt R. Clucas	Co-pilot	Killed
F/O R. Strong	Nav	Killed
F/Sgt G. Farquhar	Flt Eng	Killed
F/Lt P. Tennison	Sig	Killed
F/Sgt J. Naismith	Sig	Killed
Sgt W.D. Beck	Sig	Killed
Sgt J.W. Bell	Sig	Killed

Approximately 6½ hours after taking-off from RAF Kinloss in Moray, on a night navigation training flight, the aircraft reported to flying control that it was 60 miles north of Cape Wrath, but no further updates were then received from the aircraft and it failed to return to base. The following morning an air search was commenced, but nothing was found. Then on the 17 March 1951 RAF Kinloss received reports of a red flash being seen in the Torridon Mountains the night the aircraft had gone missing. An aircraft was immediately dispatched to conduct an air search of the mountains and

Rolls-Royce Merlin engine from Lancaster TX264 lies at the base of Beinn Eighe and overlooking Loch Coire Mhic Fhearchair.

spotted the partially burned out wreck on Beinn Eighe. However, due to the position of the wreck on the snow covered mountain, a prolonged period of poor weather and the equipment available, it was the 30 March 1951 before the RAF Kinloss Mountain Rescue Unit reached the impact point and began to recover the bodies of the crew. A task not completed until 5 months after the accident when the last patches of snow on the mountain finally melted. As a result of the difficulties the Mountain Rescue Unit experienced in dealing with the accident, there were significant changes in the RAF Mountain Rescue Service.

The point where the aircraft impacted lies on a rock strewn slope, dangerously close to the top of a rock face on Triple Buttress. However, the bulk of the wreckage from the aircraft lies on the scree slope below the rock face, having fallen down a gully, known by climbers as 'fuselage gully', in which parts of the aircraft, including a propeller assembly, are wedged. Quite high up on the scree slope can be found another propeller assembly, which has a memorial plaque attached to one of its blades, while lower down are several large sections of wing structure and the shattered remains of two Rolls-Royce Merlin engines. The other two engines, one main undercarriage assembly with wheel and tyre and the other separated wheel and tyre lie near the base of the slope in Coire Mhic Fhearchair. There is also another memorial commemorating the accident, consisting of a propeller assembly mounted on a cairn, but this is within the base at RAF Kinloss.

Avro Shackleton A.E.W. Mk.2 WR965 / 65 'Dylan': No.8 Sqn, RAF.   30-04-1990
Map No.14
NF 998907 (500ft), Maodal, Isle of Harris, Western Isles

W/Cdr S.J. Roncoroni	Pilot	Killed
F/O C. Hudson-Burns	Co-pilot	Killed
W/Cdr C.F. Wrighton	Nav	Killed
S/Ldr J.A. Lane	Nav	Killed
F/Lt A.D Campbell	Nav	Killed
Sgt G.A.R. Miller	Flt Eng	Killed
F/Lt K.S. Forbes	Ftr Controller	Killed
M/AEOp R.A. Scutt	AE Op	Killed
F/Sgt K.P. Ricketts	AE Op	Killed
Cpl S.J. Boulton	Technician	Killed

The Shackleton flew into the cloud-covered hillside after discontinuing a visual approach to Benbecula in the Western Isles, when visibility fell below the required minima. Operating from RAF Lossiemouth in Moray, the aircraft was making the approach as part of crew continuation training during a gap in a multi phase maritime exercise off the Western Isles. It is understood the aircraft had been observed well to the north of where it was expected to be while making the approach.

On the slope where the aircraft disintegrated only a few tiny fragments of wreckage remain. However, on top of the hill a few small parts are placed around a memorial, consisting of a plaque set against a stone cairn on which the 'Orange Harvest' Radar Warning Receiver from the aircraft is mounted at NF 997904.

Avro Shackleton M.R. Mk.3 XF702: No.206 Sqn, RAF.   21-12-1967
Map No.15
NM 793836 (600ft), Creag Bhan, Lochailort, Highland

S/Ldr M.C. McCallum	Pilot	Killed
F/O T.C. Swinney	Co-pilot	Killed
F/O D.J. Evans	3rd Pilot	Killed
F/Lt B.G.W. Mackie	1st Nav	Killed
F/O R.J. Fonseca	2nd Nav	Killed
Sgt M.A. Jones	Eng	Killed
Sgt K.B. Hurry	Sig	Killed
F/O J.V. Young	AEO	Killed
F/Sgt D.J. Harris	AE Op	Killed
Sgt M.B. Bowen	AE Op	Killed
Sgt C.P. Matthews	AE Op	Killed
S/Ldr H. Harvey	Pass (AEO)	Killed
P/O I.C. MacLean	Pass (Sec)	Killed

The crew was on the outward leg of a training flight from RAF Kinloss near Inverness. The aircraft suffered from severe icing in cloud while at 8,000ft and it was tracked flying in a South-westerly direction at ever decreasing ground speeds. Eventually the aircraft lost too much airspeed, stalled and dived into the ground. Despite the power from the four Rolls Royce Griffon engines the pilots had been unable to maintain their speed. This aircraft was also fitted with a pair of Viper turbojet engines in the rear of the outboard engine nacelles. These had been fitted solely for use on take-off as they seriously affected the fatigue life of the airframes. Their operation while in flight was strictly forbidden under the instructions in the pilot's manual. One recommendation from the Court of Inquiry was that this rule be disregarded in similar circumstances as losing some of an aircraft's useful life was regarded as better than losing an aircraft and its crew altogether.

The site is marked by a large scar, which runs diagonally across the hill. In this is a memorial plaque that was laid in May 2007 consisting of a small cairn and a few small fragments of the aircraft.

The scar caused by the crash of Shackleton XF702 in 1967, showing evidence of the two wing-tip fuel tanks having exploded on impact, can be seen from quite a distance.

Avro Vulcan B. Mk.1A XH477: No.50 Sqn, RAF.   12-06-1963
Map No.16
NO 492884 (2,250ft), Hill of St.Colm, Aboyne, Aberdeenshire

F/Lt D.A. Blackmore	Pilot	Killed
F/O D.G. Faulke	Co-pilot	Killed
F/Lt A.D. Roper	Nav (Plotter)	Killed
F/Lt J.B. Ross	Nav (Radar)	Killed
F/Lt J.R. Chapman	AEO	Killed

While attempting to follow a low-level profile in poor visibility, as part of a routine training flight from RAF Finningley in South Yorkshire, the aircraft struck the hill and disintegrated.

Small bits of airframe wreckage are scattered in a peat grough at the site, a few bearing traces of the white 'anti-flash' paint scheme applied to the RAF 'V-Bomber' nuclear deterrent force. The only trace of the four Bristol Olympus engines appears to be a few scattered compressor blades and fragments of casing.

Boeing B-17G 42-97286: 560th BS / 388th BG, USAAF.   10-12-1944
Map No.17
NR 956399 (2,300ft), Beinn Nuis, Brodick, Isle of Arran, North Ayrshire

Capt J.N. Littlejohn Jnr.	Pilot	Killed
2nd Lt R.N. Stoaks	Co-Pilot	Killed
2nd Lt W.J. Frey	Nav	Killed
1st Lt R.W. Rosebasky	Nav	Killed
2nd Lt L.W. Bond	BA	Killed
Cpl J.A. Payne	Eng	Killed
Cpl A.E. Thomas	Radio Op	Killed
Maj J.R. Bell	Pass	Killed
2nd Lt J.D. Merkley	Pass	Killed
M/Sgt C.S. Brown	Pass	Killed
S/Sgt W.D. Kriner	Pass	Killed

The aircraft was on a cross-country flight from Knettishall in Suffolk to Prestwick on the Ayrshire coast. The crew had strayed slightly off course in cloud and struck the eastern face of Beinn Nuis.

The point of impact is on a near vertical cliff and is inaccessible. However shattered sections of the wing spars, undercarriage and a broken up engine remain in the rocks on the slope below where the aircraft impacted. Smaller pieces also remain at the base of the cliff.

Boeing B-17G 44-83325: Project 91116-R, USAAF.   03-03-1945
Map No.18
NG 456631 (1,600ft), Beinn Edra, Trotternish, Isle of Skye, Highland

1st Lt P.M. Overfield	Pilot	Killed
2nd Lt L.E. Cagle	Co-pilot	Killed
2nd Lt C.K. Jeanblanc	Nav	Killed
Cpl H.D. Blue	Eng	Killed
Cpl A.W. Kopp	Radio Op	Killed
Cpl H.A. Fahselt	Eng / Gunner	Killed
Cpl J.H. Vaughan	Gunner	Killed
Cpl G.S. Aldrich	Gunner	Killed
Cpl C.D. Wilkinson	Gunner	Killed

On the final stage of a transatlantic ferry flight, the aircraft was flying from Meeks Field in Iceland to Valley on Anglesey, but drifted off track and while in cloud hit the eastern escarpment of Beinn Edra.

The impact point lies on a rock face, only accessible with suitable climbing equipment. However, the bulk of the remaining wreckage lies on the slope below the escarpment. On the scree below a gully are the main undercarriage legs, parts from the Wright Cyclone engines and a section of wing structure. Lower down on boggy ground at NG 458632 is more wreckage from the aircraft, including the engine manifolds.

Boeing Fortress Mk.IIA FL455 / Z9-A: No.519 Sqn, RAF.   01-02-1945
Map No.19
ND 142448 (475ft), Blar nam Faoileag, Rangag, Highland

F/Lt F.K. Humphries AFC	Pilot	Survived
F/O G.H. Pullan	Co-pilot	Survived
F/O T.G. Wrigley	3rd Pilot	Survived
F/Sgt W.H. Payne	Flt Eng	Killed
F/Sgt E.A. Wood	Nav	Died of Injuries 12-02-1945
Sgt D.A. Pressley	Met Obs	Died of Injuries 03-02-1945
F/Sgt K.A.I. Day	WO/AG	Killed
F/Sgt G.A.F. Panzer	WO/AG	Killed
Sgt A.P. Beatson	WO/AG	Killed

The crew was a weather reconnaissance flight from Wick, coded Recipe 1. During the return leg of the flight the aircraft encountered extremely bad winter weather with icing that caused the failure of two engines, following which it crashed on a near flat bog to the west of Wick. During the crash the aircraft broke into two sections.

Two of the aircraft's engines and some fairly large pieces of structure still remain on the surface at the site.

One of the most remote sites in this book, the view from the crash site of Beaufighter LX798 overlooks the neighbouring island of Boreray.

Bristol Beaufighter T.F. Mk.X LX798: No.304 FTU, RAF.   04-06-1943
Map No.20
NA 101002 (1,225ft), Conachair, St.Kilda

Sgt W. Duxbury	Pilot	Killed
Sgt S.A. Thornton	Nav	Killed

The Beaufighter departed from RAF Port Ellen on the Isle of Islay in Argyll at 20:11, the purpose of the flight being to complete a night navigation exercise and also assess fuel consumption. After approximately 4 hours the aircraft had diverged from the planned route and was flying on a north-westerly track when it struck the steep slope close to the summit of Conachair on St.Kilda. On impact most of the wreckage travelled up the slope and then fell over the highest sea cliffs in Great Britain. The aircraft remained missing until late August when the wreckage that had not gone into the sea was finally spotted by the pilot of a Beaufighter from No.304 FTU.

An engine exhaust duct, part of an undercarriage assembly and a propeller hub and reduction gear unit with the remains of two blades attached, lie on the slope where the aircraft impacted.

Bristol Beaufighter T. F. Mk.X LX946: No.304 FTU, RAF.   12-09-1943
Map No.21
NR 389520 (850ft), Maol Mheadhion, Bowmore, Isle of Islay, Argyll & Bute

F/O K.B. Thomas (RCAF)	Pilot	Killed
P/O J.R. Waldron	Nav	Killed

The aircraft crashed shortly after take-off from Port Ellen airfield on the island. It was speculated that the pilot was distracted by the burning wreck of another Beaufighter which had crashed close to the airfield only 5 minutes before LX946 took off.

A large collection of panels and sections of the airframe remains on the grassy hillside close to a 'track' which runs up to a hut beside Loch Beinn Uraraidh. On the opposite side of the hill, again beside a track, at NR 389522 lies a stripped engine and a fuel tank.

Bristol Beaufighter T. F. Mk.X NE309: No.304 FTU, RAF.   01-01-1944
Map No.22
NR 251638 (300ft), Sunderland Hill, Port Charlotte, Isle of Islay, Argyll & Bute

F/O A.N. Book (RCAF)	Pilot	Killed
F/O F.E. Osbaldeston	Obs	Survived

The aircraft struck fairly level moorland while carrying out local flying from RAF Port Ellen, the aircraft was burned out following the crash.

Only a couple of small pieces remain on top of a small heather covered rise on the very boggy low moorland, less than 100m on a bearing of approximately 240° from the wall/stream junction at NR 252409.

Bristol Beaufort Mk.I L4479: No.5 OTU, RAF.   30-08-1942
Map No.23
NR 986408 (1,500ft), Goat Fell, Brodick, Isle of Arran, North Ayrshire

F/Sgt L.O. Glay (RCAF)	Pilot	Killed
F/Sgt J.O. MacLean (RCAF)	Obs	Killed
F/Sgt J.W. Leyland (RCAF)	WO/AG	Killed

The crew was on a night time cross-country navigation flight from RAF Turnberry on the Ayrshire coast, when the aircraft flew into the mountain.

The site is marked by a bare patch on the edge of the hill above Glen Rosa containing many burnt fragments of the aircraft. Pieces of the wing spars are scattered over a larger area, one section can be found next to a stream back towards the path from Brodick Castle.

Bristol Beaufort Mk.I L9803 / Y: No.5 OTU, RAF.   02-09-1942
Map No.24
NM 525335 (2,000ft), Ben More, Isle of Mull, Argyll & Bute

F/Sgt R.A.E. Lutes (RCAF)	Pilot	Killed
Sgt C.D. Hammond	Nav	Killed
F/Sgt B.D. Francis (RCAF)	WO/AG	Killed
F/Sgt J.B. Hargreaves (RCAF)	WO/AG	Killed

During a night cross-country navigation exercise from RAF Abbotsinch in Renfrewshire the aircraft drifted off track and hit the mountain at 23:00.

Pieces of airframe wreckage are scattered down the mountain from the site, with the largest remaining parts lying on a grassy ledge between two lines of rock outcrops.

Mark Sheldon with one of the larger pieces of Beaufort L9803 on a wet and windy day on the Isle of Mull.

Engine from Blenheim Z7356 against the dramatic backdrop of the Cairngorm Mountains.

Bristol Beaufort Mk.I AW242: No.217 Sqn.   08-03-1942
Map No.25
NO 515740 (2,000ft), Hill of Wirren, Bridgend, Angus

Sgt R.W.G. Stephens	Pilot	Killed
Sgt C Tofield	Obs	Killed
Sgt J. Hayhurst	WO/AG	Killed
Sgt L.F. Humphrys	WO/AG	Killed

Having taken-off from RAF Leuchars in Fife for a positioning flight to RAF Wick in the Highlands, the aircraft struck the hillside while flying in cloud.

A pit on the steep heather covered slope contains a significant quantity of airframe wreckage and parts from the undercarriage assemblies.

Bristol Blenheim Mk.IV Z7356: No.526 Sqn, RAF.   22-03-1945
Map No.26
NN 963999 (3,775ft), Braeriach, Cairngorm Mountains, Aberdeenshire

W/O C.H. Fletcher	Pilot	Killed
F/O J.E. Shaw	Nav	Killed
F/O S.C. Gale	WO/AG	Killed
Cpl J. Michie	Pass	Killed
LAC A.M. Fulton	Pass	Killed
LAC A.V. Bryce	Pass	Killed

This Blenheim descended through cloud, during a transit flight from RAF Digby in Lincolnshire to RAF Longman in the Highlands, and struck the mountainside.

Sections of airframe are scattered north from the point of impact toward the col between Braeriach and Sròn na Lairige with one engine remaining at NH 963001. Other sections of airframe lie lower down the mountain in Coire Ruadh including the other engine, which is in the stream close to the rough path down from the col into the Lairig Ghru.

Cessna 206 Skylane EI-BGK: 16-06-1989
Map No.27
NM 518677 (1,250ft), Beinn an Leathaid, Ardnamurchan, Highland

Mr C. Petersen	Pilot	Killed

The pilot operated a business flying fish and shellfish from Northern Scotland and the islands to England and Continental Europe and was undertaking such a flight from Benbecula to Glasgow when his aircraft struck the eastern side of Beinn an Leathaid just below and to the north of the summit.

At the site where the aircraft crashed the only remaining piece is the aircraft's battery. Just below the crash site the hill drops away steeply into a series of crags and scree slopes and at the base of these crags there are parts from the aircraft, including sections of wing spar and a seat frame.

Consolidated B-24H 41-29369: 2nd Ferry Group, ATC, USAAF. 23-07-1945
Map No.28
NG 592091 (280ft), Ach na Cloiche, Tarskavaig, Isle of Skye, Highland

1st Lt W.H. Bell	Pilot	Killed
1st Lt T.E. Lundell	Co-pilot	Killed
1st Lt A.L. Harmonay	Nav	Killed
T/Sgt S.E. Hansen	Eng	Killed
S/Sgt R.R. Bisbing	Radio Op	Killed
2nd Lt A.A. Vogel	Pass	Killed
Flt Off G.W. Baker	Pass	Killed
Flt Off E.E. Eads	Pass	Killed
Flt Off M. Fleak	Pass	Killed
Flt Off E. Grzesiek	Pass	Killed
Flt Off E.J. Ruszala	Pass	Killed
Flt Off N.D. Stanley	Pass	Killed
Flt Off W.L. Titus	Pass	Killed

The aircraft was being flown back to the USA and while to the south of Skye the port outer engine caught fire. The outboard wing section and engine eventually broke off striking the tail causing this to separate as well. The main bulk of the aircraft fell onto a hill near Ach na Cloiche with the other pieces being widely scattered.

The main crash site is marked as a fenced enclosure on maps (or a building on the 1:50000 maps) and the remains of this can still be found. Within this enclosure there is a bare patch containing numerous small fragments from the aircraft, though no remains are believed to be present at the locations where the other sections fell.

Consolidated B-24D 42-41030: Knox Prov Grp, USAAF.   20-08-1943
Map No.29
NR 957395 (2,300ft), Beinn Nuis, Brodick, Isle of Arran, North Ayrshire

2nd Lt W.M. Connelly	Pilot	Killed
Flt Off F.J. Chew	Co-pilot	Killed
2nd Lt A.T. Spindle	Nav	Killed
2nd Lt R.J. Hartl	BA	Killed
S/Sgt F.W. Brantner	Flt Eng	Killed
S/Sgt J.B. Moore	Radio Op	Killed
Sgt R.F. Daub	Gunner	Killed
Sgt G.H. Peyton	Gunner	Killed
S/Sgt C.E. Cislo	Pass	Killed
Sgt L.S. Golis	Pass	Killed

The aircraft was being ferried from Gander to Prestwick, while descending through cloud towards its destination it flew into the western side of Beinn Nuis close to the summit.

The crash site is marked by a section of wing which lies partially buried close to where the aircraft first impacted. This is to the west of the footpath from Brodick and at the head of the stream running up Corie Nuis. Some sections from the forward part of this aircraft can also be found on the eastern side of the mountain, not far from the crash site of B-17 42-97286 (Map No.17) already mentioned.

After the crash B-24D 42-41030 was broken up by a team from No.63 MU, they partially buried this large section of wing with one of the main undercarriage oleos still attached.

Consolidated B-24D 42-72851: Bridges Prov Grp, 8th USAAF.   15-09-1943
Map No.30
NF 929665 (625ft), North Lee, Lochmaddy, North Uist, Western Isles

2nd Lt M.E. Salway Jr	Pilot	Killed
2nd Lt F.G. Zeigenbusch	Co-pilot	Killed
2nd Lt W.A. Moore	Nav	Killed
2nd Lt E.F. Colburn	BA	Killed
T/Sgt E.N. Busch	Eng	Killed
Sgt R.J. Fischer	Eng	Killed
S/Sgt C.W. Plog	Radio Op	Killed
Sgt P.H. Lambert	Radio Op	Killed
Sgt J.E. Wallace	Gunner	Killed
Sgt C.L. Balzer	Gunner	Killed

Flying from Meeks Field in Iceland to Nutts Corner in County Antrim, the aircraft was on the final stage of a transatlantic ferry flight. It flew into the hillside in poor visibility at around 13:15, having descended below the briefed minimum altitude for the flight.

Following the accident No.63 MU dismantled the wreck, with parts, including the four Pratt & Whitney Twin Wasp engines, then manhandled down the hill to the nearby shoreline. A raft was improvised from telegraph poles and four 50-gallon drums to move the salvaged parts across the sea loch to Lochmaddy. This operation took over four months to complete, mainly due to prolonged periods of bad weather. Not all the wreckage was removed though and in a scar where the aircraft burned out there is a section of wing and one main undercarriage leg. Further wreckage is scattered down the slope below the site, the largest part being a propeller reduction gear unit with two propeller blades still attached. There is also a memorial stone and plaque at the site, on the slope adjacent to the scar.

Consolidated B-24H 42-95095: 66th BS / 44th BG, USAAF.   13-06-1945
Map No.31
NG 808711 (525ft), Lochan Sgeireach, Gairloch, Highland

1st Lt J.B. Ketchum	Pilot	Killed
1st Lt J.H. Spencer	Co-pilot	Killed
2nd Lt R.J. Robak	Nav	Killed
T/Sgt H.L. Cheek	Flt Eng	Killed
T/Sgt J.C. Stammer	Radio Op	Killed
S/Sgt R.E. Davis	Gunner	Killed
S/Sgt E.J. Gilles	Gunner	Killed
S/Sgt A.L. Natkin	Gunner	Killed
S/Sgt H. Riefen	Gunner	Killed
S/Sgt E. Einarsen	Pass	Killed
S/Sgt J.B. Ellis Jnr.	Pass	Killed
S/Sgt R.J. Francis	Pass	Killed
S/Sgt J.H. Hallissey	Pass	Killed
S/Sgt J.D. Harvey	Pass	Killed
S/Sgt A.W. Hastings	Pass	Killed

This accident occurred in almost identical circumstances to the loss of B-24H 41-29369. The aircraft was ferrying from Warton in Lancashire via Prestwick to Meeks Field in Iceland where it was due to proceed onward to the USA. A fire in one or more engines caused eventual structural failure and loss of control.

Large pieces of the aircraft, including its undercarriage and engines remain scattered at the crash site which straddles the lochan, along with a memorial to the crew and passengers, which is marked on recent OS maps. Further remains are submerged in the lochan and out of reach to anyone without getting rather wet!

Wreckage from B-24H 42-95095 overlooks the Lochan where many parts of the aircraft remain submerged. A Pratt & Whitney Twin Wasp engine can be seen resting on a rock to the left of the island and a propeller blade is protruding from the water near the shore in the foreground.

Consolidated Canso 11062: No.162 Sqn, RCAF.   29-07-1944.
Map No.32
HT 961392 (775ft), Hamnafield, Isle of Foula, Shetland

F/O A.R. Hildebrand (RCAF)	Pilot (Capt)	Killed
F/O W.H. Lloyd (RCAF)	Pilot	Killed
F/O G.G. Bradshaw (RCAF)	Nav / BA	Killed
W/O J.H. Knight (RCAF)	Flight Engineer	Survived
F/Sgt R.W.E. Townsend (RCAF)	Flight Engineer	Killed
P/O J.E. Bowler (RCAF)	WO	Killed
P/O E.C. Watson (RCAF)	WO	Killed
W/O R.D. Harvey (RCAF)	WO/AG	Killed

The crew was on an anti-submarine patrol between Iceland and Scotland, while flying from Reykavik, landing at Wick where the Squadron had a detachment. Wick was closed due to weather so the crew was instructed to divert to Stornaway while over the Shetland Islands. While flying south-west away from the main islands the aircraft struck the high ground on the island of Foula.

Parts of the aircraft are scattered over a wide area around the crash site, though little remains where it actually struck the hill. Lower down are the two engines, partially buried fuselage and wing sections and the remains of the aircraft's undercarriage.

Consolidated Catalina Mk.I Z2148: No.240 Sqn, RAF. 19-01-1942.
Map No.33
HU 481853 (300ft), Willa Mina Hoga, Isle of Yell, Shetland

F/Lt H. Goolden	Pilot	Killed
F/O A. Helme	Co-pilot	Survived
P/O L.G. Schell (RCAF)	Obs	Killed
Sgt S. Irvine	Flt Eng	Killed
Sgt A.O. Pitcher	Flt Eng	Killed
Sgt E. Henowy	WO/AG	Killed
Sgt L.A. Rowe	WO/AG	Killed
Sgt A.R. Breakspear	WO/AG	Killed
F/Sgt D.E.C. Lockyer	Radio/Elec Eng	Survived
AC R. Richmond	Flt Mech	Survived

Having flown to RAF Invergordon in the Highlands, from RAF Castle Archdale in County Fermanagh where No.240 Sqn were then based, the flying boat refuelled before departing in the early hours. The crew had been tasked with conducting a long duration patrol off the coast of Norway, in search of the German battleship *Tirpitz*. However, while on the outbound route one of the engines failed and difficulty was experienced in maintaining altitude on the remaining engine, due to icing and turbulence. The aircraft diverted to RAF Sullom Voe in the Shetland Isles, but on arrival the aircraft had to hold while the flare path, required for a night landing, was lit and adjusted for the prevailing wind. It appears though, that while holding off the coast, the aircraft drifted and on commencing its approach to Sullom Voe flew into the hill on the nearby Isle of Yell.

A bare patch of peat remains on the moorland where the aircraft burned out, strewn with tiny fragments of wreckage and the remains of the two Pratt & Whitney Twin Wasp engines. Adjacent to the scar is the starboard wing, with many of the upper surface panels missing from it. Slightly further up the gentle slope is a tall stainless steel Celtic style cross, marked as 'Meml' on Ordnance Survey 1:25000 scale mapping, which was erected in 1991. A further memorial to the crew, comprising a propeller blade and plaque mounted on a plinth, is located outside the 'Old Haa' in Burravoe at HU 520795.

A partly burnt out wing of Catalina Z2148 on the desolate moorland of Yell marks the site where seven airmen died.

Consolidated Catalina Mk.I AH533 / DA-G: No.210 Sqn, RAF. 15-07-1941
Map No.34
NR 687985 (700ft), Cruch na Seilcheig, Kinuachdrachd, Isle of Jura, Argyll & Bute

S/Ldr P.S. Hutchinson	Pilot	Killed
P/O E.R. Pinches	Pilot	Killed
Sgt E.C. Graham	WO/AG	Killed
LAC C.A. Kew	-	Killed
AC1 R. Fearnley	-	Killed
Cpl T. Simner-Jones	-	Killed
Cpl J.C. Kinniard	-	Killed
AC J. Kelly	-	Survived

The aircraft was being flown to No.210 Sqn's base at Oban from Helensburgh following an overhaul. After an attempted landing at Oban in poor weather the aircraft sustained some damage and took to the air again. The pilot headed south, either to attempt a second landing at Oban or a forced landing at sea to await better weather. While still in low cloud the Catalina struck high ground on the northern end of the island of Jura where it was destroyed by fire.

Fairly corroded parts can be found at the crash site, while some larger pieces of structure were dumped in a wooded area down the hill from the crash site. This site, as with a number of others in the Highlands & Islands is within an estate where deerstalking takes place and during these times it is recommended to contact the Ardlussa Estate.

Consolidated Catalina Mk.IVB JX273: No.302 FTU, RAF.   12-05-1944
Map No.35
NL 637959 (475ft), Theiseabhal Beag, Isle of Vatersay, Western Isles

W/O D.J.R. Clyne	Pilot	Killed
Sgt E. Kilshaw	Co-pilot	Survived
Sgt P. Lee	Nav	Survived
Sgt R. Beavis	Flt Eng	Survived
Sgt R. Whiting	Flt Mech	Survived
Sgt P.W.N. Hine	Flt Mech /AG	Killed
Sgt F.J. Bassett	WO/AG	Killed
Sgt R. Anstey	WO/AG	Survived
Sgt G. Calder	WO/AG	Survived

Airborne from RAF Oban in Argyll, on a night training flight, the aircraft was on the outbound route flying at 200ft when the radar failed. However, the aircraft remained at low altitude and continued towards the next turning point in the planned route, at Barra Head in the Western Isles, on a westerly track. As the aircraft approached the turning point the navigator then realised the aircraft was off track to the north, the pilot's compass having been a few degrees out of alignment. A climb was immediately

Some of the larger parts from Catalina JX273 on the island of Vatersay, dumped by the recovery team from No.56 MU.

commenced but it was too late and the aircraft flew into the hill.

A few small pieces of wreckage remain at the site, near to the top of the hill. However, No.56 MU tasked with salvaging the aircraft, cut it up and dragged the wreckage down the hill and then piled it up and weighted it down with stones, in a gully between the road and the sea at NL 641957, where much of it still remains. The tail planes along with sections of the wings and fuselage are still identifiable, as is the pylon that mounted the wing onto the fuselage, which is lying lower down on the rocky shore line. Adjacent to the gully there is a standing stone with a plaque attached to it commemorating the accident.

Consolidated LB-30A Liberator AM261: ATFERO, RAF.   10-08-1941
Map No.36
NR 993425 (2,400ft), Mullach Buidhe, Corrie, Isle of Arran, North Ayrshire

Capt E.R.B. White (BOAC)	Pilot	Killed
Capt F.D. Bradbrooke (ATA)	Co-pilot	Killed
20 Passengers	See Appendices	Killed

The crew was flying a reverse ferry flight across the Atlantic from RAF Heathfield at Ayr to Gander in Newfoundland with ferry pilots and radio operator as passengers so they could then ferry new aircraft across the Atlantic to the UK. The aircraft took off and climbed away on course but failed to gain enough height to avoid the high ground of Arran which it struck while in cloud.

Only very small items of this aircraft remain lodged under rocks where the crash occurred. There are some slightly larger pieces in one of the gullies to the east of the crash site.

Consolidated Liberator Mk.V BZ724: No.59 Sqn, RAF.   18-08-1944
Map No.37
NC 973153 (1,475ft), Beinn Mhealaich, Helmsdale, Highland

P/O J. Lloyd (RNZAF)	Pilot	Survived
F/O R.H. Legrow (RCAF)	Co-pilot	Killed
P/O R. Seigler (RCAF)	1st Nav	Killed
Sgt H.F.J. Newell	2nd Nav	Killed
Sgt E.N. Lowe	Flt Eng	Killed
P/O A.J. McLay (RAAF)	WO	Killed
Sgt G.A. Grill	WO/AG	Killed
Sgt D. Pratt	WO/AG	Killed
Sgt A.W. Christie	WO/AG	Killed
Sgt T.H.M. Instone	WO/AG	Killed

The aircraft crashed while the crew was returning from an anti-submarine patrol from Ballykelly in Northern Ireland. The Liberator had taken off during the evening of 17 August and while in flight had been ordered to land at Tain. The crew had been in radio contact with Skitten near Wick and then Tain before contact was lost at just after 04:30 when the aircraft, flying south along the coast, struck the high ground near Helmsdale.

A crater containing pieces of the aircraft can be found on the hill, while other pieces are in a nearby gully. There is also a second collection of wreckage approximately 100m to the north of the main crash site.

Consolidated Liberator Mk.V FL949 / PP-Y: No.311 Sqn, RAF. 01-01-1945
Map No.38
HY 208030 (1,250ft), Cuilags, Isle of Hoy, Orkney

W/O O. Bures (Czech)	Pilot	Killed
F/Sgt M. Bodlak (Czech)	Co-pilot	Killed
F/Sgt O. Mandler (Czech)	Nav	Killed
F/Sgt Z. Launer (Czech)	Flt Eng	Killed
F/Sgt A. Bednar (Czech)	WO/AG	Killed
F/Sgt I.K. Englander (Czech)	WO/AG	Killed
F/Sgt J. Zapelal (Czech)	WO/AG	Killed
Sgt M. Dorniak (Czech)	WO/ AG	Killed

The crew was on an operational anti-submarine flight from RAF Tain, on the northern edge of the Moray Firth. While returning in extremely bad wintry weather the aircraft struck the upper part of the Cuilags at 1,250ft.

Parts of the aircraft, including two of the engines and several pieces of radio equipment, are scatted for a long distance from where the aircraft crashed to the bottom of the hill at HY 214026. This is due to the recovery crew from No.56 MU attempting to clear the site by dragging the remains off the high ground so they could be buried in deeper soil at the base of the hill.

Alan Clark with some of the remaining wreckage from FL949 on the sub-arctic hilltop of the Cuilags.

Consolidated Liberator Mk.VI KG857 / LL-S: No.547 Sqn, RAF. 17-10-1944
Map No.39
NO 521733 (1,875ft), Hill of Wirren, Bridgend, Angus

F/Lt H.R. Ellis	Pilot	Survived
F/O J.R. Menzies (RCAF)	2nd Pilot	Killed
F/O H.C. Wheeler	3rd Pilot	Survived
Sgt J.G. Lee	Nav/BA	Killed
F/O D.N. Edwards	Nav	Killed
Sgt A.J.L. Lee	FE	Killed
F/Sgt R.M. McGregor	WO/Flt Mech/AG	Killed
Sgt R.C. Daynes	WO/AG	Killed
Sgt C.E. Townshend	WO/AG	Killed
Sgt W.J. Murray (RCAF)	AG	Survived
Sgt G.J.V. Berryman	AG	Survived

The crew had taken off from Leuchars for a night time anti-submarine patrol to the north of Cape Wrath. After only 20 minutes the aircraft struck the southern side of Wirren and was completely destroyed.

A burnt out section of wing and other pieces of the aircraft lie scattered on the upper slopes of the Hill of Wirren.

De Havilland Mosquito Mk.IV DZ486: No.618 Sqn, RAF.   05-04-1943
Map No.40
NC 350560 (2,000ft), Cranstackie, Durness, Highland

F/O D.L. Pavey	Pilot	Killed
Sgt B.W. Stimson	Nav/BA	Killed

The aircraft flew into the upper part of the mountain while the crew was on a bombing exercise from Skitten at Killimster near Wick.

Many of the metal components from the largely wooden Mosquito can be found at the site. Sections of the undercarriage, one of the elevators and the pilot's seat back armour lie spread across the slope. The only large items that are not present are the aircraft's two Merlin engines, though there are a number of shattered pieces from them, which suggest they were all but destroyed by the crash.

De Havilland Mosquito B. Mk.IV DZ642 / AZ-H: No.627 Sqn, RAF. 22-11-1944
Map No.41
HU 392284 (625ft), Royl Field, Clift Hills, Shetland

F/Lt J.A. Reid	Pilot	Killed
F/O W.D. Irwin (RCAF)	Nav	Killed

Having taken-off from RAF Woodhall Spa in Lincolnshire the aircraft was tasked with releasing target markers for a bombing raid on the U-Boat pens at Trondheim in Norway. During the return to base the aircraft requested permission to divert and land at Scatsta in Shetland as fuel reserves were running low. Due to cloud cover the aircraft was provided with steers, in order to position for an approach to the airfield, and was following these when it then crashed into the hillside, possibly having run out of fuel.

A granite memorial with a bronze plaque commemorates the two crew lost in this crash and nearby wreckage is scattered across the hillside, including both Roll-Royce Merlin engines, the engine mounts, a propeller hub and reduction gear unit with parts of the propeller blades attached, sections of armoured plating, a steel weapons carrier, plus the remains of the undercarriage assemblies, wheels and tyres.

One of the propeller reduction gear and hub units from Mosquito DZ642 on the lonely western side of the Clift Hills of Shetland.

De Havilland Mosquito P.R. Mk.IX MM244: No.544 Sqn, RAF. 25-11-1943
Map No.42
NH 550325 (1,100ft), Corryfoyness, Drumnadrochit, Highland

F/O N.M. Burfield (RAAF)	Pilot	Survived
Sgt A. Barron	Nav	Survived

The crew was on a high altitude cross-country navigation flight from RAF Benson in Oxfordshire. While at 30,000ft the aircraft suffered from the fuel supply cutting persistently. When both engines failed at 12,000ft the aircraft was abandoned by its crew and crashed on open hill, though this is now within a forestry plantation.

The site which is at the end of a fire break is marked by a water-filled crater with a small collection of metal fragments on one bank.

De Havilland Mosquito Mk.VI G-AGGF: BOAC.   17-08-1943
Map No.43
NO 351806 (2,575ft), Drumhilt, Auchronie, Angus

Snr Capt L.A. Wilkins	Pilot	Killed
F/Sgt H. Beaumont	WO	Killed

The crew was flying the aircraft on a scheduled service from Leuchars to Stockholm to deliver freight and diplomatic mail, carrying just over 600kg of freight. When the aircraft was 155 miles off Scotland, the pilot turned back to Leuchars, however, in radio transmissions he never stated the reason. The wrecked aircraft was found by a gamekeeper on 7 September 1943. It had crashed with the undercarriage down and both engines running under power.

A scar containing the burnt remains of the aircraft can still be found. The largest remaining items are the undercarriage units, still locked in the down position.

Douglas Dakota Mk.IV KK194: No.45 Grp, RAF.   01-02-1945
Map No.44
NM 628354 (1,600ft), Ben Talaidh, Glen Forsa, Isle of Mull, Argyll & Bute

F/O F. Bishop	Pilot	Killed.
P/O T.B.M. Alexander	Nav	Survived
WO G. Nichols	Radio Op	Survived
S/Ldr A.E. Alderton	Pass	Killed
S/Ldr D.B. Auchinvole	Pass	Survived
F/Lt J.D.L. Gammie	Pass	Survived
F/Lt B. Miller	Pass	Survived
F/O H. Ellis	Pass	Killed.

The newly built aircraft was being used to transport passengers and equipment across the Atlantic, from Dorval in Canada. The aircraft had taken off after a stop in Iceland for the onward leg to Prestwick. While flying in very bad weather the aircraft hit the north-eastern side of Ben Talaidh.

One of the main undercarriage units, still complete with wheel and tyre lies partially buried in the gully where the bulk of the remains of Dakota KK194 was dumped.

Not much remains where the aircraft actually crashed. The Maintenance Unit responsible for the clear up, No.63, dumped almost the entire aircraft into Allt nan Clar where the crumpled and now partly buried remains can still be found today. A propeller and hub, which lay at the base of the mountain in Glen Forsa has since been mounted on a plinth as a memorial at NM 617377.

English Electric Canberra B. Mk.2 WJ615: No.35 Sqn, RAF.   22-11-1956
Map No.45
NO 207846 (3,300ft), Carn an t-Sagairt Mór, Braemar, Aberdeenshire

| F/O A.A. Redman | Pilot | Killed |
| F/O A.A. Mansell | Nav | Killed |

On a night diversion exercise from RAF Upwood in Cambridgeshire the aircraft conducted a QGH let down to RAF Kinloss in Moray, a ground controller instructing the aircraft to descend and turn based on Direction Finding fixes until it was established on the approach to the airfield. On reaching 300ft the aircraft commenced a missed approach and climbed away. It then turned onto a southerly track to return to base, but failed to climb to a safe height. Approximately 10 minutes later the aircraft flew into the mountain top and disintegrated.

Although a few parts were removed using a helicopter, for the investigation into the accident, the bulk of the wreckage was left strewn across the mountain top. A scar and a few pieces of airframe remain where the aircraft impacted at the northern edge of the

The almost complete, and upturned, outer sections of the port wing from Canberra WJ615 close to the summit of Carn an t-Sagairt Mór.

summit plateau. Only 10 metres away on the plateau one of the tail planes is partially buried, and from here a trail of tiny fragments can be followed south to where more sizeable pieces of wreckage lie in hollows on the western edge of the summit plateau. Scattered further on are the compressor, combustion and turbine stages from the Rolls-Royce Avon engines and the main wheel units, one of which still has the tyre on. The furthest wreckage from the impact point is at approximately NO 207841. On impact the outer wings from the aircraft broke away and the port wing with engine nacelle and jet pipe attached lies north-east of the summit cairn at NO 208845, while the starboard wing is partially buried at NO 210843.

Fairey Albacore Mk.II BF592: 817 Sqn, RN.   26-06-1942
Map No.46
ND 210978 (800ft), Mel Fea, Isle of Hoy, Orkney

     Sub Lt (A) J. Leggat (RN)   Pilot   Killed

The pilot was ferrying the aircraft from the Naval Air Station at Evanton, on the Cromarty Firth north east of Dingwall, to RNAS Hatson near Kirkwall on Mainland Orkney. The aircraft struck the seaward side of Mel Fea on the western coast of Hoy above the formidable 600ft high sea cliffs of Rack Wick Bay.

The site is located above the cliffs at Rackwick where the aircraft's fourteen cylinder Taurus engine and sections of the wings and undercarriage lie, along with hundreds of smaller fragments. The substantially complete tail structure was recovered in the 1990s by the Fleet Air Arm museum to aid in their Albacore rebuild project.

Fairey Barracuda Mk.II LS391: No.815 Sqn, RN.   02-01-1945
Map No.47
NR 496746 (1,800ft), Beinn an Oirr, Isle of Jura, Argyll & Bute

Lt Cdr D. Norcock	Pilot	Killed
Sub Lt (A) W.M. Moncrieff	Obs	Killed
PO L.W. Gurden	WO/AG	Killed

The aircraft, flying from Machrihanish (HMS *Landrail*) in Argyll struck the mountainside at dusk, but the circumstances under which the accident occurred are not known.

In 2000 a substantial quantity of wreckage was recovered from the site for the Fleet Air Arm Museum, including sections of wing and fuselage, the tail unit and the Rolls-Royce Merlin engine. Only smaller parts now remain, amongst the scree below the point of impact. This area is difficult to search though, as the scree covering the steep slope consists of large pieces of rock. The site lies within the Inver Estate.

Fairey Barracuda Mk.III PM870: 818 Sqn, RN.   14-07-1945
Map No.48
NC 888105 (1,525ft), Col-bheinn, Brora, Highland

Sub Lt(A) D. Allen	-	Killed
Sub Lt(A) J. Hirst	-	Killed

The crew was flying from RNAS Fearn, HMS *Owl*, near Tain when they flew into the southern side of Col-bheinn.

A large, though badly damaged, portion of the aircraft's main spar with much of the wing structure still attached can be found at the crash site.

Substantial remains of Albacore BF592, including large sections of the wings and in the background the Bristol Taurus engine.

Most of Fairey Firefly Z2108 still lies scattered at the crash site including its Rolls-Royce Griffon engine shown here.

Fairey Firefly T. Mk.I Z2108 / 245-LM: No.766 Sqn, RN.   16-05-1949
Map No.49
NO 264850 (2,900ft), Cuidhe Crom, Lochnagar, Aberdeenshire

Lt R.M. Osborne	Pilot	Killed
Lt A.A. Dowell	Pilot	Killed

On an instrument training flight from Lossiemouth (HMS *Fulmar*) in Moray, the aircraft flew into the mountain in bad weather. Following an intensive search the wreck was located by the RAF Kinloss Mountain Rescue Unit on the 18 May 1949.

Virtually all the wreckage from the aircraft still remains at the site, and can be seen from several miles away due to the yellow paint scheme applied to the aircraft for its role as a dual-control deck landing trainer. At the edge of a boulder field is a scar, where the aircraft partially burned out. The scar contains several quite sizeable pieces of airframe, including the main spar from the centre section of the wing. Immediately below the scar is the fuselage from aft of the rear cockpit with squadron markings, roundel and aircraft serial number clearly discernable. Next to the fuselage section is the starboard outer wing. The port outer wing lies higher up the slope along with one of the main undercarriage legs. Slightly further down the slope from the scar are the Rolls-Royce Griffon engine, the engine supercharger, the propeller reduction gear unit and the other main undercarriage leg. A trail of smaller parts then runs down the rocky slope for another hundred metres or so to where the rudder from the aircraft can be found.

Fairey Firefly A. S. Mk.5 WB336: No.719 Sqn, RN.   25-09-1951
Map No.50
NR 407542 to NR 412541 (1,400ft), Beinn Uraraidh, Bowmore, Isle of Islay, Argyll & Bute

P4 D.J. Slater (RAN)	Pilot	Killed
Ob 4 E.J. Edmonds (RAN)	Obs	Killed

The two man Australian crew was participating in a 'controlled anti-submarine exercise' having taken off from Eglinton in Northern Ireland. The crew had been ordered to begin a search task in the area to the south-west of Islay which they duly acknowledged, but this was the last time they were in contact with their base. The wreckage was later found scattered in a line running ESE to WNW on the eastern side of Beinn Uraraidh.

Much of the wreckage still lies where it came to rest in 1951 and when visiting the site walkers are likely to encounter the aircraft's Rolls Royce Griffon engine first, this is at the WNW end of the wreckage trail. From there to the last major section, the tail unit still bearing the faded station code for Eglinton, there are many large sections including the remains of the starboard wing and complete port wing, undercarriage and carrier arrestor gear.

Fairey Swordfish (Identity Not Positively Determined):
Map No.51
NO 204801 (2,400ft), Glen Callater, Braemar, Aberdeenshire

Crew – Name(s) not known Pilot (plus 2?)   Killed?

The identity of the Swordfish that crashed in Glen Callater has not been positively determined, however, it is thought that it might be Swordfish L9730 and that it came down in the Glen during a flight from Arbroath in Angus.

The steel framework from the wings and fuselage and many small fire-damaged parts

Looking north across the high ground of Islay towards the Paps of Jura. A wing from Firefly WB336 lies on the hillside where it crashed. The remainder of the aircraft is scattered over a wide area of the hill.

Framework of the wings of the as yet unidentified Swordfish lies amongst the rocks in Glen Callater.

lie in an area of rocks on a steep slope. Other pieces of wreckage are scattered down the valley from the site, including the crumpled engine cowling ring.

Gloster Meteor F. Mk.8 WA882: No.222 Sqn, RAF. 12-02-1952
Map No.52
NJ 663220 (1,425ft), Bennachie, Alford, Aberdeenshire

P/O J.B. Lightfoot	Pilot	Killed

Approximately 20 minutes after departing from RAF Leuchars in Fife, on a low-level day cross-country training flight, the aircraft was flying in overcast conditions when it hit the snow-covered hillside.

Several pieces of airframe wreckage remain in a hollow amongst the heather, below a track running around the hillside and just upslope of a firebreak in a plantation of fir trees. On the hilltop at NJ 662222 there is a stone cairn, and a few further parts from the aircraft lie beside it.

Handley Page Halifax Mk.II R9438: No.35 Sqn, RAF. 31-03-1942
Map No.53
HU 346135 (925ft), Fitful Head, Sumburgh, Shetland

F/Sgt J.B. Bushby	Pilot	Killed
Sgt A.J. Peach	Co-pilot	Killed
Sgt R. Meredith	Flt Eng	Killed
Sgt G.N.E. Powell	Nav	Killed
F/Sgt J.P.B. Buckley (RCAF)	WO/AG	Killed
P/O M.L. Usher (RCAF)	WO/AG	Killed
Sgt J.A. Wood	AG	Killed

The crew had taken part in a raid from Kinloss against the German battleship *Tirpitz*, which was at anchor in Faettenfjord. On the return leg the aircraft flew directly into the cliffs at Fitful Head, oddly while flying east, possibly attempting to land at Sumburgh. Only two bodies were recovered from the site and another two were found but due to their position on the cliff it was impossible to recover them. The other three bodes were never found.

The crash site itself is inaccessible, there is however a granite memorial above the crash site at the summit of Scantips.

Handley Page Halifax G.R. Mk.II Srs.Ia JP165 / D: No.58 Sqn, RAF. 09-04-1945
Map No.54
NG 128983 (925ft), Beinn nan Leac, Isle of Harris, Western Isles

F/O W.J. Richardson DFC DFM	Pilot	Survived
F/Sgt E. Lack	Co-pilot	Survived
F/Lt R.A. Shrubb	Nav / BA	Killed
W/O J. M. Stitt	Flt Eng	Survived
F/Sgt T.M. Gledhill	WO/AG	Died of injuries 14-04-1945
F/Sgt L. R. Griffiths	WO/AG	Survived

Having taken-off from RAF Stornoway in the Western Isles at 09:00 for a bombing and radar exercise, the aircraft was contacted by flying control and instructed to conduct local sector flying instead, due to poor weather approaching off the Atlantic. The crew decided to fly through the 'Tarbert Gap' on Harris, from East Loch Tarbert to West Loch Tarbert, but while flying inbound entered broken cloud, drifted south of the intended route and hit the hillside.

On impact the aircraft caught fire and the scar where it burned out, on a steep slope, is strewn with lumps of melted aluminium alloy. At the base of the slope are many pieces of airframe wreckage, sections of armoured plating, pieces of the wood from the propeller blades and other interesting parts including the mounting and drive motor for the H2S radar scanner. The four Rolls-Royce Merlin engines from the aircraft were recovered from the site in the 1980s using an RAF helicopter.

Handley Page Hampden Mk.I P2118 / Z9-D: No.519 Sqn, RAF. 25-08-1943
Map No.55
NC 583498 (1,600ft), Sgor Chaonasaid, Ben Loyal, Highland

F/Lt H.R.M. Puplett DFC	Pilot	Killed
P/O G.W. Ritchie	Nav	Killed
F/O C. A. Faulks	WO	Survived
F/Sgt T.R.T Hudson-Bell	WO/AG	Killed

The Hampden departed from RAF Wick in the Highlands at 16:14 to conduct a search for Hampden P5334, which had transmitted a mayday call at 13:38, after reporting an engine fault while on a long range meteorological reconnaissance and anti-submarine sortie. However, nothing was found, and as the aircraft reached its prudent limit of endurance, the search had to be abandoned. While returning to base the aircraft flew off track and at 23:59 struck the mountainside. On impact it caught fire and was spotted by local men who immediately climbed to the site and rescued F/O Faulks.

Many parts from the aircraft are scattered down the steep slope below the impact point, including one of the main undercarriage assemblies. Lower down the mountain at NC 586502 is a section of framework from the centre section of the aircraft and an engine cowling ring, while in a boggy hollow slightly further east are two fuel tanks and further airframe wreckage.

Hawker Audax Mk.I K7376: No.8 FTS, RAF.   05-05-1939
Map No.56
NO 607852 (1,600ft), Cairn of Edendocher, Grampian Mountains, Aberdeenshire

(A)P/O Lenahan	Pilot	Survived
(A)P/O Atkinson	Pass	Survived

During a training flight from RAF Montrose in Angus the aircraft flew into the hill in poor visibility at 08:50. On impact (A)P/O Atkinson was thrown clear of the aircraft suffering minor injuries, while (A)P/O Lenahan became trapped in the wreckage. Unable to extract his colleague (A)P/O Atkinson set off to obtain assistance and made his way to Balblythe farm, where at 12:00 he was found in a collapsed state. A search for the wreck was then mounted, but it was 04:00 the following morning before it was located and (A)P/O Lenahan rescued.

A significant proportion of the fuselage framework, including the engine firewall, still remains at the site along with some wing framework and a fuel tank.

The upturned fuselage framework from Audax K7376.

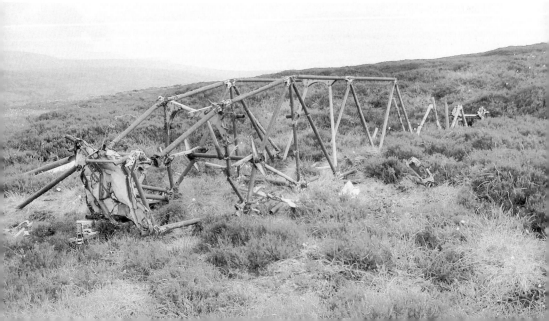

Hawker Hunter F.G.A. Mk.9 XG261 / J: No.2 TWU, RAF.   28-05-1980
Map No.57
NJ 367368 (1,550ft),The Scalp, Dufftown, Moray

     F/O M.C. Longstaff   Pilot   Survived

After taking-off from RAF Lossiemouth in Moray the aircraft engaged in combat manoeuvring practice with another Hunter. Recovering from a wingover manoeuvre the pilot selected full power and dived in pursuit of the other aircraft, however, the flaps had been previously selected to an intermediate setting to improve low-speed handling and as the aircraft accelerated it pitched increasingly nose down. As the airspeed exceeded 300 kts the flaps had to be retracted for the dive to be recoverable. Not realising the flap setting was the issue and unable to pull out of the dive the pilot ejected as the aircraft passed through 11,000ft, leaving it to dive into the hilltop.

    The crater made by the aircraft has been filled in, but a slight depression can still be discerned and tiny fragments of wreckage are still scattered over the surrounding area.

Hawker Hunter F.G.A. Mk.9 XK151: No.2 TWU, RAF.   12-02-1980
Map No.58
NG 559192 (1,025 ft), An Carnach, Isle of Skye, Highland

     F/Lt R.D. Green   Pilot   Killed

This Hunter departed from RAF Lossiemouth in Moray in order to assess the weather conditions in the low flying areas that No.2 TWU planned to use during training flights that day. Over the west coast of Scotland the weather deteriorated and while flying at low level in poor visibility the aircraft struck the mountain top and exploded.

    A wooden cross in memory of F/Lt Green has been placed at the rock outcrop the aircraft struck on the top of the mountain to the south of the triangulation pillar. Only a few fragments of wreckage remain, with most being scattered on a rise approximately 100 metres west-south-west of the impact point.

Hawker Hurricane Mk.IIC LF180: No.516 Sqn, RAF.   06-02-1944
Map No.59
NM 203544 (25ft), Hyne Farm, Arinagour, Isle of Coll, Argyll & Bute

     W/O J.E. Stephen   Pilot   Killed

The pilot was one of three on a 'Combined Operations' exercise from Connel near Oban when the flight ran into poor weather. Two of the flight came to grief on the west coast, the third aircraft Hurricane LF160 was force landed by its pilot, P/O C.L.D. Figgis, near to Alloa on the east coast near Stirling. W/O Stephen attempted to make a 'wheels down' forced landing on the island of Coll but struck a rock outcrop and overturned.

    The remains of the aircraft's engine can be seen at the site on very boggy ground at only 25ft above sea level, while not far away from the engine and a little way to the east close to a ditch is a single undercarriage leg.

The small remains from Hurricane LF207, gathered behind a small enclosure, are quite hard to spot from below as the front of the enclosure is covered by moss and heather.

Hawker Hurricane Mk.IIC LF207: No.516 Sqn, RAF.   06-02-1944
Map No.60
NM 465638 (650ft), Druim na Gearr Leacainn, Ardnamurchan, Highland

  F/Lt A.J. Woodgate (RNZAF)   Pilot   Killed

The pilot of this aircraft was leading the formation in which Hurricane LF160 was flying. When the formation became separated in poor weather this aircraft flew into high ground in cloud.

 Small pieces of the aircraft remain in a small, well concealed, stone enclosure. A plaque commemorating this and the crash of LF160 can be found attached to a rock outcrop on Beinn na Seilg at NM 460640.

Hawker Sea Hawk F.G.A. Mk.4 WV845: AWTF, RN.   04-09-1957
Map No.61
NC 890080 (900ft), Creag an Lochain Deirg, Brora, Highland

  Sub Lt F.G. Maguire (RN)   Pilot   Killed

The pilot was on a live firing exercise using the range on the former airfield at Tain, when one of the rockets misfired. Sub Lt Maguire flew out to sea to attempt to clear the hung up ordnance. Some time after the aircraft flew into high ground just inland from Brora.

 The site lies on the northern side of the hill, where small pieces of the aircraft can be found scattered on the gently sloping hillside and there is a collection of fragments of skinning and of the self-sealing fuel tanks.

Heinkel He111-H2 2645 / T5+EU: Wekusta 1, *Luftwaffe*.   17-01-1941
Map No.62
HZ 213717 (150ft), Vaasetter, Fair Isle, Shetland

Lt K-H. Thurz	Pilot	Survived
Gfr G. Nentwig	Eng	Killed
Ufz B. Lıking	Eng	Survived
Fw J. Wohlfahrt	Radio Op	Survived
Wd Insp L. Gburek	Met Obs	Killed

Having taken off from Oldenberg in Germany, on a meteorological observation sortie, the aircraft was detected by radar approaching the Shetland Isles and was subsequently intercepted by two Hurricanes from No.3 Sqn, RAF, flown by P/O Berry and F/O Watson. The aircraft flew into cloud to evade the fighters, but had already been hit several times, with both engines being damaged. The crew prepared to abandon the aircraft but then spotted Fair Isle and decided to force land. However, the aircraft hit the ground hard on touching down, killing Gfr Nentwig and Wd Insp Gburek, before it slid to a halt and then caught fire.

The two fire damaged and badly corroded Junkers Jumo engines from the aircraft still remain at the site, while in a gully to the east is a sizeable section from the tail unit.

Junkers Ju88   / 4D+EK: 1/KG 30, *Luftwaffe*.   17-10-1939
Map No.63
ND 296977 (0ft), Pegal Burn, Isle of Hoy, Orkney

Olt W. Flaemig	Pilot	Killed
Ofw Faust	Obs	Killed
Ufz Attenburger	WO/AG	Killed
Ufz F. Ambrocious	WO/AG	Survived

The crew was one of a number which carried out a daylight attack on the Royal Navy's fleet anchorage in Scapa Flow. After attacking the anchored ships the crew attempted to escape via the western side of the Flow only to come under fire from anti-aircraft guns on the small island of Rysa Little, just off Hoy. The ground fire found its mark and the Ju88 burst into flames, the only survivor of the crew baled out shortly before it impacted and he landed in the sea close to the crash site. He was severely injured by the fire and his hasty departure from the aircraft at low level.

This is one of only two aircraft in this book which lie at sea level. Parts of the aircraft can be found at the mouth of Pegal Burn where the action of the tide uncovers small pieces. The aircraft had dived into the ground at the mouth of the river and burned out.

Lockheed C-60A 42-56014: 17th Fy Grp, USAAF.   30-09-1943
Map No.64
NR 955401 (2,300ft), Beinn Nuis, Brodick, Isle of Arran, North Ayrshire

1st Lt J.R. MacKenzie	Pilot	Killed
2nd Lt R.H. Riddle	Co-pilot	Killed
S/Sgt J.G. Johnson	Eng	Killed
PFC B.T. Boone	Eng	Killed
Pvt W. Silberg	Radio Op	Killed
Maj L.C. Goldsmith	Pass	Killed
S/Sgt J.M. Fantasky	Pass	Killed

The aircraft was being flown from Prestwick, near Ayr, to Stornoway in the Outer Hebridies. When the aircraft failed to arrive at Stornoway it was reported missing; the wreck being discovered on the 2 October. The pilot had taken off and was heading west to avoid the higher mountains to the north but had not gained sufficient height to pass safely over Arran.

Pieces of the aircraft can be found forming a trail of wreckage from where it impacted high in a gully and down into the corrie beneath. These are mainly small airframe and engine parts.

Lockheed Hudson Mk.I N7310: No.220 Sqn, RAF.   19-03-1941
Map No.65
ND 252962 (1,025ft), Withi Gill, Isle of Hoy, Orkney

Sgt R.D. Harris	Pilot	Killed
Sgt G.E. Towe	Co-pilot	Killed
Sgt H.C. Street	WO/AG	Killed
Sgt W. Wood	WO/AG	Killed

The crew was on an anti-submarine and convoy protection flight from RAF Wick. While returning the crew attempted to get navigational assistance from Wick by radio. Around this time the aircraft flew into the hillside on the southern edge of Withi Gill and was destroyed by fire.

Large sections of the aircraft can be found at the site which is at a little over 1,000ft. The port wing lies inverted and fairly complete close to the burnt out starboard wing. There are scattered smaller items were the aircraft impacted on the hill and a section of the rear fuselage is located some distance away down the hill at ND 270960. An aileron from the aircraft can be seen along with other artifacts from the island in the Scapa Flow museum beside the ferry slipway at Lyness.

Lockheed Hudson Mk.III T9292 / UA-P: No.269 Sqn, RAF.   01-05-1941
Map No.66
NC 891063 (500ft), Socach Hill, Brora, Highland

F/Sgt N. Child	Pilot	Killed
Sgt Marshall	Nav	Survived
P/O A.J.M. Adolphus	WO/AG	Killed
Sgt A.V. Summers	WO/AG	Killed

The substantial wreck of Lockheed Hudson N7310 on Withi Gill, the starboard wing lies close by but gutted by fire.

The crew was returning to Wick from convoy escort duties and was unable to descend safely through low cloud and abandoned the aircraft when fuel became dangerously low. Two of the three killed drowned when they landed in the sea just off Brora, the third either struck part of the aircraft while baling out or his parachute failed.

Very little of the aircraft remains where it crashed, with only a few small fragments being located recently.

Lockheed Hudson Mk.III T9432 / ZS-B: No.233 Sqn, RAF.   15-04-1941
Map No.67
NN 270260 (3,000ft), Ben Lui, Tyndrum, Stirling

F/Sgt D.E. Green	Pilot	Killed
Sgt F.V.N. Lown	Co-pilot	Killed
Sgt L.A. Aylott	Nav	Killed
Sgt W.A. Rooks	WO/AG	Killed

The aircraft was based at RAF Aldergrove in Northern Ireland and was on convoy escort duties. In wintry weather the crew became lost while trying to return to their base and flew into Ben Lui somewhere not far south of the summit. The aircraft continued over the ridge and crashed down the south eastern flank of the mountain coming to rest next to a gully high up on the mountain.

This is one of the largest sites, in terms of remaining wreckage, in the country, with both wings and engines being present along with the undercarriage and a large section of the rear fuselage still bearing much of its painted finish including the serial number visible on the side. All of this lies in a broad gully, which drops away very steeply not far to the south of the wreckage. There are also a few other parts lower down the mountain.

Among the most intact wrecks in the British Isles is Hudson T9432 on Ben Lui. Lying scattered along the gully is the complete airframe with the exception of the forward fuselage. The rear fuselage shown here is slowly being crushed by winter snows, with the wings just visible in the background.

Being such a substantial wreck, we felt a second photo was warranted in this case and shown here is one of the well preserved engines from Hudson T9432.

Martin B-26C 41-34707: 455th BS / 322nd BG, USAAF.   03-06-1943
Map No.68
NH 087542 (1,900ft), Beinn na Feusaige, Glen Carron, Highland

1st Lt M.E. Young	Pilot	Killed
2nd Lt R.A. Anderson	BA	Killed
S/Sgt V. Bravo	Eng	Killed
S/Sgt M.R. Miller	Radio Op	Killed
M/Sgt L.M. Cross	Gunner	Killed

This B-26 was being ferried to Prestwick on the Ayrshire coast from Meeks Field in Iceland when it struck high ground in low cloud and was completely burnt out.

The remains of the aircraft lie in a scar, which is about 8 x 15ft and although this contains a reasonable amount of burnt wreckage, the only large pieces are a short section of wing spar and a burnt section of a fuel tank cover.

McDonnell F-101C 56-0013: 78th TFS / 81st TFW, USAF.   07-05-1964
Map No.69
NM 882579 (2,575ft), Maol Odhar, Strontian, Highland

Capt M.H. Reed	Pilot	Killed

The pilot was on a low level cross-country exercise from RAF Bentwaters in Suffolk with a number of other aircraft. While flying in cloud the aircraft struck the northern side of the mountain.

A large amount of the aircraft, including both J57-13 engines, remains at the head of Allt Coire nam Frithallt, though very little of it is at the point where the aircraft impacted. Other pieces of the aircraft were flung over the lip of the Coire and can be found scattered around the summit of Maol Odhar.

Miles Master Mk.I T8684: No.8 FTS, RAF.   09-10-1941
Map No.70
NO 616850 (1,225 ft), Cairn of Finglenny, Strachan, Aberdeenshire

LAC G.W. Hogben	Pilot (u/t)	Killed

LAC Hogben flew into the cloud covered hillside, during a navigation exercise from RAF Montrose in Angus.

Quite a few pieces of airframe lie scattered at the site, the paintwork on several of the panels being in good condition. The Rolls-Royce Kestrel engine and the propeller hub from the aircraft can be found up the slope at NO 615849, where it appears an attempt to salvage them was abandoned.

The Rolls Royce Kestrel engine from Miles Master T8684.

A piece from the forward fuselage of the USAF F-101C that crashed near Strontian, clearly visible is the 'AIR' of US AIR FORCE stencilled on it.

Panavia Tornado G.R. Mk.1A ZG708: No.13 Sqn, RAF. 01-09-1994
Map No.71
NN 559285 (975ft), Glen Ogle, Killin, Stirling

F/Lt P.P. Harrison	Pilot	Killed
F/Lt P.J.M. Mosley	Nav	Killed

The crew was on a low-level reconnaissance training flight from RAF Marham in Norfolk. They had completed the reconnaissance objectives and were beginning the low level part of their flight. During the turn into Glen Ogle the aircraft struck the ground with its port wingtip at around 400 knots and was completely destroyed.

The deaths of the two airmen are commemorated by a memorial at the lower end of the crash site, this is beside a now tarmac cycle way and close to a parking area off the A85. The location of this is marked on present Ordnance Survey 1:50000 and 1:25000 scale maps.

Short Sunderland Mk.III W4026 / DQ-M: No.228 Sqn, RAF. 25-08-1942
Map No.72
ND 111284 (675 ft), Eagles Rock, Berriedale, Highland

F/Lt F.M. Goyen	Pilot (Capt)	Killed
Wg/Cdr T.L. Moseley	2nd Pilot	Killed
F/O S.W. Smith (RAAF)	3rd Pilot	Killed
P/O G.R. Saunders	Obs	Killed
Sgt L.E. Sweett	Flt Eng	Killed
F/Sgt W.R. Jones	Flt Mech/AG	Killed
F/Sgt C.N. Lewis	Flt Mech	Killed
Sgt A.R. Catt	WO/AG	Killed
Sgt E.F. Blacklock (RNZAF)	WO/AG	Killed
F/Sgt E.J. Hewerdine	AG	Killed
Sgt A.S.W. Jack	AG	Survived
Air Cdre HRH The Duke of Kent KG, KT, GCMG & GCVO	Pass	Killed
P/O The Hon. M. Strutt (RCAF)	Pass (AG)	Killed
Lt J.A. Lowther MVO (RNVR)	Pass (Private Sec)	Killed
LAC J.W. Hales	Pass (Batman)	Killed

The large monument on Eagles Rock where the Sunderland carrying the Duke of Kent crashed.

Transporting Air Cdre HRH The Duke of Kent and his entourage to Iceland, the aircraft departed from RAF Invergordon in the Highlands at 13:10. Approximately 30 minutes later it flew into the cloud covered high ground while on a northerly track, having diverged from the planned route. Sgt Jack the sole survivor made his own way off the hill, arriving at a croft the following morning. As a result the local men who arrived at the site in the hours after the accident thought there were no survivors.

At the site there is a tall, white, stone cross commemorating the accident, marked as 'Meml' on Ordnance Survey 1:25000 & 1:50000 scale maps. When it came to the salvage of the wreck, special instructions were issued, that every piece of wreckage was to be cleared from the site. However, a few tiny pieces were overlooked.

Short Sunderland Mk.III DP197 / S: No.4 OTU, RAF.   15-08-1944
Map No.73
NC 936117 (900ft), Creag Riabhach, Lothbeg, Highland

F/O R.S. Rowson (RCAF)	Pilot (Capt)	Killed
F/Lt R.L. Mercer (RCAF)	2nd Pilot	Killed
F/O A.N. Unser (RCAF)	3rd Pilot	Killed
F/Lt W.B. Sargent (RCAF)	Nav	Killed
P/O P.A. Whyte (RCAF)	Flt Eng	Killed
F/Sgt R.C. Norton	Flt Mech / AG	Killed
F/Sgt A. DiPesa (RCAF)	WO/AG	Killed
P/O R.W. Fulton (RCAF)	WO/AG	Killed
W/O1 L.H. Ludington (RCAF)	WO/AG	Killed
P/O V.C. Stordy (RCAF)	WO/AG	Killed
F/O T.B. Wood (RCAF)	WO/AG	Killed
F/Sgt N. Dlusy (RCAF)	WO/AG	Killed
W/O R.E. Jackson (RAAF)	-	Killed
Sgt W. Komer (RCAF)	AG	Killed
Sgt D.R. Trask	AG	Killed

This Sunderland flew into the hilltop in poor visibility and burned out. Flying from RAF Alness (formerly Invergordon) in the Highlands the aircraft was on a night training flight, to practise using the onboard radar in an anti-submarine role. The accident occurred 1½ hours into the flight, after the aircraft had been recalled to base by flying control as a result of deteriorating weather conditions.

Wreckage is scattered over the hilltop for approximately 100 metres, with the remains of the four engine-cowling rings and a section of fuel tank being amongst the largest remaining pieces. Where the aircraft burned out, on a rise, there is a large scar containing many small fire damaged fragments.

Short Sunderland Mk.III ML858: No.302 FTU, RAF.   08-06-1944
Map No.74
NF 086992 (750ft), Gleann Mor, St.Kilda

W/O C.C. Osborne (RNZAF)	Pilot (Capt)	Killed
F/O R.D. Ferguson (RNZAF)	2nd Pilot	Killed
F/O W. Thompson (RNZAF)	Nav	Killed
Sgt R. Lewis	Flt Eng	Killed
W/O J.R. Lloyd (RNZAF)	WO/AG	Killed
F/Sgt B. Bowker	WO/AG	Killed
F/Sgt O.G. Reed (RNZAF)	WO/AG	Killed
Sgt D.J.C. Roulston (RNZAF)	AG	Killed
Sgt F.M. Robertson (RNZAF)	AG	Killed
Sgt J.S. Thomson	AG	Killed

Having taken-off from RAF Oban in Argyll at 22:00, the crew was on the last training flight of their course at No.302 FTU. The planned route was to take the aircraft to St.Kilda, via Colonsay and Barra Head, before returning to base. However, flying in poor visibility the aircraft later crashed in Gleann Mor on St.Kilda, while flying on a southerly track. Due to cloud cover the following day it was the 10 June 1944 when the wreckage was spotted by overflying aircraft. A high speed launch was immediately dispatched to the island and identified the wreckage, but it was three days later, when an RAF team was landed on the island, that the bodies of the crew were recovered and then committed to the sea off nearby Boreray. On the 10 July 1944 a salvage team was landed on the island to dispose of the wreckage, thereby preventing it from being reported again by overflying aircraft. An attempt to break-up the airframe with explosives proved ineffective so it was cut up, the smaller parts being buried in several pits while the larger sections were weighted down with stones and then either covered by peat or painted brown.

Despite the work of the salvage team a considerable amount of wreckage can still be found strewn down Gleann Mor. On the slope where the aircraft impacted are scattered the four Bristol Pegasus engines, three propeller hubs with the remains of several blades attached, sections of wing structure and a few small parts. Lower down the valley in the Abhainn a' Ghlinne Mhòir are more sections of airframe, including the remains of the tail unit and rear gun turret, while on the western side of the valley near Airigh Mhòr pieces of wreckage lie amongst stones. In village bay there is memorial plaque to the aircrew killed on St.Kilda, situated inside the Kirk.

Supermarine Seafire Mk.15 SW826: No.766 Sqn, RN.   05-07-1948
Map No.75
NJ 189532 (800ft), The Drum, Bridge of Shougle, Moray.

      PO R.P. Walker (RN)   Pilot   Survived

The pilot was on an exercise from RNAS Lossiemouth with another, Seafire SW904. The two aircraft collided in mid air, SW904 went out of control and crashed in a barley field killing its pilot. SW826 was also badly damaged in the collision but its pilot was able to bale out before the aircraft plunged to earth.

Small pieces of the aircraft remain in a small scar in the heather where the aircraft fell to earth.

Supermarine Sea Otter (Identity Not Positively Determined): RN?
Map No.76
NR 342918 (0ft), Ardskenish Beach, Isle of Colonsay, Argyll & Bute.

      Crew – Name(s) not known   Pilot (plus 1?)   Survived?

Very little is known of this accident other than the aircraft type and that it had landed at sea and was driven ashore by waves and wrecked. It has been reported that there was a crew of two in the aircraft and that they both survived the incident.

A section of undercarriage damper, two propeller blade bosses, a piece of corrugated aluminium with Saunders Roe marked stainless steel brackets (these markings being in the form of SR inspection stamps with the aircraft type number prefixing the main part numbers) and the heavily corroded remains of two cylinders from the aircraft's engine remain amongst the seaweed. The undercarriage damper and prop bosses are in a near circular hollow in the rocky shoreline.

This site can only be accessed at lower states of the tide and even then is never fully dry.

Vickers Wellington Mk.I L4348: No.20 OTU, RAF.　　　　　05-12-1941
Map No.77
NC 759457 (875ft), NW of Meall Ceann Loch Strathy, Tongue, Highland

F/Sgt H.S.D. Goss	Pilot	Killed
Sgt A.R. McCoy	Obs	Killed
Sgt A. Flint	Obs	Killed
Sgt A.J. Wilson (RNZAF)	WO	Killed
Sgt M.E. Kent (RAAF)	WO/AG	Killed

The aircraft crashed, after possibly diving into the ground, and burned out while the crew was on a cross country navigation exercise from Lossiemouth.

There is a distinct crater at the crash site, which is visible in aerial photographs and contains some sizable pieces, including the core of an engine and sections of geodetic framework.

Vickers Wellington Mk.IA L7775: No.20 OTU, RAF.　　　　　23-10-1940
Map No.78
NO 090965 (2,850ft), Bruach Mhor, Braemar, Aberdeenshire

P/O D.V Gilmour	Pilot	Survived
P/O H.M. Coombs	2nd Pilot	Killed
Sgt A.W. Milroy	-	Survived
Sgt K.W. Bordycott	Nav	Survived
Sgt G.R. Lyon	-	Survived
Sgt F. Hutson	WO/AG	Killed
Sgt J.A. Sparks	AG	Survived

While on a night cross-country navigation exercise the aircraft struck Bruach Mhor close to its summit.

Parts from the aircraft are still scattered at the crash site. However there are no longer any large sections present, as during 1986 the complete wings and tail section that remained here were recovered from the site. The wings can now be seen at the Lincolnshire Aviation Heritage Centre at East Kirkby, whilst the tail section is on display at the Wellington Aviation Museum at Moreton-in-Marsh, Gloucestershire.

Vickers Wellington Mk.IC L7845 / ZT-Z: No.20 OTU, RAF.   09-08-1942
Map No.79
NO 382762 (2,600ft), Muckle Cairn, Grampian Mountains, Angus

F/Sgt A.G.W Keene (RCAF)	Pilot	Killed
Sgt A. Kirby (RCAF)	Obs	Killed
Sgt J. Weatherson	Obs	Killed
Sgt O.K.L. Jensen (RCAF)	WO/AG	Killed
Sgt Holman	AG	Survived

Airborne from RAF Elgin in Moray the aircraft was on a day cross-country training flight when a section of the port engine cowling detached in flight, damaging the propeller assembly and in turn the engine. The aircraft subsequently stalled, crashed onto the hilltop and caught fire. Sgt Holman was rescued after being spotted by Flt Capt Huxley, an ATA pilot ferrying a Defiant, who was drawn to the scene by the smoke from the fire. A gamekeeper who had witnessed the aircraft crash, also made his way to the scene, but not realising there was a survivor, set off to report the accident while Flt Capt Huxley was orbiting over the wreck.

A significant quantity of wreckage, including the two Bristol Pegasus engines and several sections of geodetic framework from the wings and fuselage, are scattered around a scar where the aircraft burned.

Vickers Wellington Mk.IC R1646 / JM-D: No.20 OTU, RAF.   19-01-1942
Map No.80
NO 136803 (2,450ft), Dubh-choire, Braemar, Aberdeenshire

F/O J.W. Thomson DFC (RNZAF)	Pilot (Inst)	Killed
Sgt R.J. Jackson (RCAF)	Pilot	Killed
Sgt M.H.J. Kilburn	Pilot	Killed
F/Sgt H.J. Kelley (RCAF)	Obs	Killed
Sgt J.B. Riley	WO/AG	Killed
Sgt B.C. Dickson (RAAF)	WO/AG	Killed
Sgt R.A. Milliken (RAAF)	WO/AG	Killed
Sgt W.M. Greenbank	AG	Killed

This Wellington flew into the mountain during a cross-country training flight from RAF Lossiemouth in Moray. The aircraft remained missing for a month before a gamekeeper spotted the wreckage on the snow covered slope.

At the impact point there is a patch of bare peat containing small parts from the aircraft. While scattered on the slope below is much more wreckage, comprising many small sections of geodetic framework. In 1999 the two engines from the aircraft were recovered using an RAF Sea King helicopter and in 2006 one was unveiled as a memorial to the crew in Braemar, above the west bank of the river at NO 151914.

A section of geodetic framework from Wellington R1646 lying high up in Dubh-choire above Glen Clunie.

Vickers Wellington Mk.IC T2707 / JM-Z: No.20 OTU, RAF.   13-02-1942
Map No.81
NH 076193 (1,075ft), Alltbeithe, Glen Affric, Highland

Sgt C. Handley	Pilot	Survived
5 crewmembers - Names not known	–	Survived

During a cross-country training flight, from Lossiemouth in Moray to the Isle of Tiree, the starboard propeller assembly separated from the aircraft. Flying on a single engine in icing conditions the aircraft became uncontrollable, and the crew baled out. The aircraft then dived into the ground on the lower slopes of Mullach Fraoch-choire in Glen Affric and was completely destroyed.

   The impact point is marked by a scar in the rocky ground, strewn with shattered pieces of geodetic framework from the wings and fuselage and other wreckage. One of the Bristol Pegasus engines is recognisable, but the cylinder heads are detached. These lie scattered nearby with those from the other completely shattered engine. A propeller hub and reduction gear unit with most of one blade attached, oxygen bottles and the oil cooler from an engine also remain.

The shattered remains of Wellington T2707 in Glen Affric. One of the aircraft's Pegasus engines and remains of a propeller assembly are visible.

Vickers Wellington Mk.III HF816 / A: No.20 OTU, RAF.   14-08-1944
Map No.82
NJ 048095 (2,450ft), An Lurg, Aviemore, Highland

P/O P.L.B. Paterson	Pilot	Killed
Sgt J.M. Downey	Nav	Killed
Sgt H. Todhunter	2nd Nav	Killed
Sgt S. Fraser	BA	Killed
P/O D.H. Rankin	WO	Killed
Sgt R.A.G. Bailey	AG	Killed

The crew had taken off on a cross-country navigation exercise from RAF Lossiemouth from which they failed to return. The aircraft was reported to have 'exploded in the air' prior to crashing close to the summit of An Lurg. The crew positions in the No.20 OTU record book for two of the crew are different to those recorded by the CWGC.

Today, broken sections of geodetic framework, oxygen bottles, armour plate and shattered engine parts can be found at the crash site.

Vought Chespeake Mk.I AL941: No.772 Sqn, RN.   22-07-1943
Map No.83
NR 935451 (1,425ft), Gleann Diomhan, Catacol, Isle of Arran, North Ayrshire

Sub Lt (A) A.J.A. Buchanan (RNVR)	–	Killed
Sub Lt (A) H.W. Smith (RNVR)	–	Killed

The two crew were on a training flight from HMS *Landrail*, Machrihanish, near Campbeltown when their aircraft hit the side of Beinn Tarsuinn, one of many hills of that name on Arran, in poor weather.

The largest remaining item is a section of wing more than 12ft long, which lies next to the river in the bottom of the glen at NR 936455 at 1,100ft. Spread from there to where the aircraft impacted are other pieces, including the two main undercarriage legs, engine and cockpit framework.

Vought Corsair Mk.II JT461 / 7C: No.1841 Sqn, RN.   11-07-1944
Map No.84
HY 197040 (800ft), Enegers, Isle of Hoy, Orkney

Sub Lt (A) E. de A. Hewetson (RNZNVR)	Pilot	Killed

The pilot was on a training flight from RNAS Hatson near Kirkwall to the aircraft carrier HMS *Formidable* when the aircraft struck the hillside at Enegers completely destroying the aircraft.

Both of the distinctive wing roots which give the Corsair its gull winged appearance and the pilot's armoured headrest can be found at the site. More parts can be seen spread over a fairly wide area and these are mainly concentrated in the northern of two gullies which descend the steep hillside.

The distinctive gull-wing shaped wing-root structure from Corsair JT461 on Hoy.

Westland Wallace Mk.II K6028: No.1 AOS, RAF.   03-09-1939
Map No.85
NJ 668215 (1,200ft), Bruntwood Tap, Bennachie, Aberdeenshire

P/O E.A. Cummings	Pilot	Killed
LAC A.R.R. Stewart	Obs	Killed

Following disbandment of No.1 AOS, the aircraft was being ferried to RAF Evanton in the Highlands, when it flew into the hillside in poor visibility.

Sections of wing and fuselage framework, a few crumpled aluminium alloy panels and parts from the undercarriage struts are scattered down the heather covered slope.

Wreckage from Westland Wallace K6028 on Bennachie, a reasonably large amount of this aircraft remains at the site.

Chapter Ten

Ireland

Although divided into two states, geographically Ireland is an island in the north Atlantic, featuring a large central lowland plain of limestone covered with glacial deposits, forming a landscape of widespread bogs and lakes, surrounded by a ring of coastal mountains, the highest peak of which is Carrauntoohil at 3,414ft above sea level. These mountain ranges vary in geological structure, with uplifted sedimentary rocks, including old red sandstones to the south. While to the north volcanic activity is responsible for the granite peaks to the north-west and basalt to the north-east. Politically, the majority of the island consists of the state of the Republic of Ireland and to the north-east is Northern Ireland, a constituent country forming part of the United Kingdom and covering approximately one sixth of the island's total area. For the purposes of this book, the authors have decided to treat Ireland as a whole.

As with all areas, most of the aircraft losses in Ireland date from the WW2 period, during which the Irish Republic (Eire) remained neutral, so officially at least, few Allied aircraft were operating over this part of the country. An exception was the 'Donegal Corridor', where an agreement between the British and Irish governments permitted aircraft to overfly the few miles of land separating Northern Ireland from Donegal Bay. Officially the route was to be used for air/sea rescue flights and exercises, but it greatly increased the effectiveness of allied patrols over the Atlantic and was in regular use by flying boats from bases on Lower Lough Erne and several crashed in the area. Interestingly survivors from such flying boat losses were declared to be mariners and not subject to internment and so were returned across the border by the Irish authorities. As for the rest of the republic, despite its neutrality, it was regularly overflown by both sides, whether intentionally or not, often by meteorological reconnaissance and anti-shipping or anti-submarine patrol aircraft from both the RAF and *Luftwaffe*. As these aircraft were generally heading out to, or returning from long range patrols over the Atlantic, it is hardly surprising that a number of them came to grief on the mountains along the west coast of Ireland.

At the outbreak of WW2 the strategic importance of Northern Ireland to the British, with its ship building industry and ports was already obvious, yet there was only one operational RAF airfield to protect the area! Ireland's declared neutrality in the conflict made the British authorities nervous and for a time it was feared that the republic might be seen as a weakness, providing a 'back door' route for a German inavsion. Also the importance of Belfast, with its shipyards and nearby Shorts aircraft factory had also been spotted by the Germans who launched air raids on the area. Soon numerous airfields began to be built, to provide protection against potential invasion and fighter cover for potential air raid targets. Additionally, as the importance of the North Atlantic convoys grew, Northern Ireland became a base for the escorts that protected them, as well as for the long-range patrol aircraft already mentioned. Air traffic over the area further increased with the arrival of the USAAF in 1942, when the aircraft maintenance depot at Langford Lodge opened, initially to provide for repair of American aircraft operated by British forces, but it soon became one of the three primary air depots in the UK for the assembly, repair and maintenance of US operated aircraft. By the end of the conflict there were nearly thirty airfields in Northern Ireland, including eight used by the USAAF.

As on the British mainland, a few crash sites have, over the years, attracted the attention of those intent on the recovery of the metal simply for its scrap value, a notable example being the Ju52 in County Wicklow, which was almost completely cleared. The actions of the military authorities also led to some sites being either systematically stripped for intelligence purposes, or deliberately burnt to destroy largely intact aircraft. The activities of locals also often depleted crash sites, with parts from aircraft finding new uses, though in some cases this has actually preserved remains and they can still be seen close by, with sections of aircraft having been incorporated into fences or even used for roofing buildings in a couple of cases. As with other areas, major parts have also been recovered in more recent years for museum exhibits or by private individuals. There also appears to be a strong interest in maintaining the memory of past events, and at many sites locals have been responsible for erecting memorials, which will mark them long after the last pieces of wreckage have disappeared.

Access to the moors and mountains in the Republic of Ireland is not covered by any Right to Roam and there is no official Open Access Land as in the UK. However, walking and rambling trails in Ireland have become very popular in recent times, leading to a number of schemes for walking route development resulting in an increasing number of established paths. Most walking areas or access to these walking tracks is still via farmland which is private property. Although the rights of walkers and ramblers are specified in legislation, which includes 'recreational user' as a category of users of privately-owned lands, it is important to remember that such access is made through the goodwill and tolerance of farmers and landowners. So when crossing farmland, walkers need to ensure that their presence is unobtrusive and does not interfere with farming activities. In the few areas where landowners do not tolerate walkers accessing the hills and mountains across their farmland, there are generally signs to indicate this.

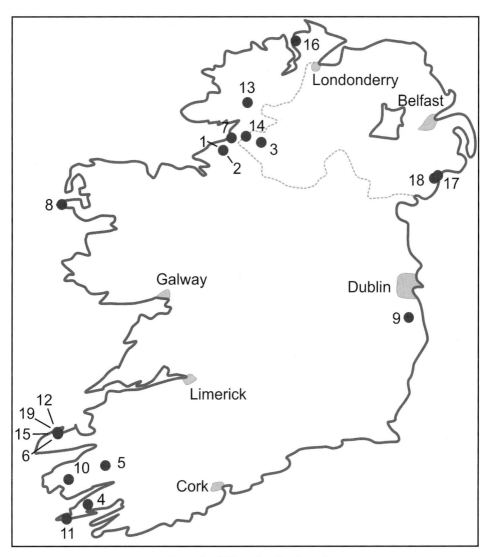

Crash Sites in Ireland

Boeing B-17G 42-31420: Chambers Prov Grp, USAAF.   09-12-1943
Map No.1
G-767497 (1,950ft), Tievebaun Mountain, County Sligo

2nd Lt R.C. Walch	Pilot	Survived
2nd Lt W.M. Orim	Co-pilot	Survived
2nd Lt W.M. Wallace	Nav	Killed
2nd Lt R.E. Fox	BA	Killed
S/Sgt M.I. Mendosa	Eng	Survived
S/Sgt R.A. Smith	Radio Op	Survived
Sgt W.H. G. Vincent	Gunner	Survived
Sgt E.C. Drake	Gunner	Survived
Sgt C.W. Williamson	Gunner	Survived
Sgt A.J. Latecki	Gunner	Killed

Having taken-off from Reykjavik in Iceland, on the final leg of a transatlantic ferry flight, the aircraft was en route to Prestwick in North Ayrshire when adverse winds resulted in fuel reserves running low. The aircraft was diverted to RAF Nutts Corner in County Antrim, but descended below the cleared altitude and flew into the hilltop while in cloud.

A section of wing and the two main undercarriage oleos remain on the boggy hilltop. The four Wright Cyclone engines from the aircraft were recovered from the site in 2006.

One of the largest remaining parts left of B-17G 42-31420 is this section of wing with the main undercarriage mount and engine turbo charger.

The crash site of Consolidated Catalina AM265 is marked by this simple memorial.

Consolidated Catalina Mk.II AM265 / BN-A: No.240 Sqn, RAF. 21-03-1941
Map No.2
G-776491 (800ft), Glenade, County Leitrim

P/O H.L. Seaward	Pilot	Killed
F/O A.E. Whitworth	Co-pilot	Killed
F/O C.P. Davidson	Obs	Killed
Sgt R.H. Oldfield	Obs	Killed
Sgt H.H. Newbury	WO/AG	Killed
Sgt F.R.A. Chalk	AG	Killed
Sgt H. Dunbar	AG	Killed
Sgt G.H. Slack	AG	Killed

The aircraft flew into the hillside and burned out only minutes after taking-off from RAF Castle Archdale in County Fermanagh, on an Atlantic patrol sortie.

A few small fragments remain in a scar and a wooden memorial cross is located by an adjacent fence.

Consolidated Catalina Mk.IVA JX242 / P: No.202 Sqn, RAF.   20-11-1944
Map No.3
H-053563 (1,100ft), Loch-na-Laban, Magho, County Fermanagh

F/Lt G. Forbes-Lloyd	Pilot	Killed
Sgt G.F. Tribble	2nd Pilot	Killed
W/O C. H. Moore	3rd Pilot	Survived
P/O W.J. Sharp (RAAF)	Nav	Killed
W/O E. Slack	Nav / BA	Killed
Sgt J.W. Geldert	Flt Eng	Killed
Sgt P.B. Marshall	WO / Mech/AG	Killed
Sgt F.J. Deem	WO/AG	Killed
Sgt D.W. Nater	WO/AG	Killed
F/Sgt C.W. Bowater	-	Survived

This Catalina descended into high moorland (now within the Lough Navar Forest), South of Lower Lough Erne, while returning to RAF Castle Archdale in County Fermanagh, from an anti-submarine patrol.

Small sections of wreckage lie by Loch-na-Laban, where a memorial plaque is attached to a post. An identical plaque on a stone can be found by the viewpoint over Lower Lough Erne at H-062576.

Consolidated Liberator G.R. Mk.V BZ802 / V: No.86 Sqn, RAF. 27-08-1943
Map No.4
V-695516 (1,300ft), Gowlane, Caha Mountains, County Cork

F/O R.M. Kildea	Pilot	Killed
F/O D.W. Roberts	Co-Pilot	Killed
F/O C.F. Cropper	Nav/BA	Killed
F/Sgt E.B.H. Wells	Flt Eng	Killed
F/Sgt J.S. Ripon	WO/AG	Killed
Sgt G.L. Plume	WO/AG	Killed
Sgt W.H. Harris	WO/AG	Killed

Twelve hours after taking-off from RAF Aldergrove in County Antrim for an anti-submarine patrol in the Bay of Biscay, the aircraft arrived over the South West coast of Ireland, having flown off track while returning to base. It is reported that the aircraft began circling in the vicinity of Castletownbere in County Cork and then flew into the cloud covered hillside.

Sections of main undercarriage and a few small pieces of wreckage remain at the site where two stone memorial plaques were placed in 1983. The crankshaft from one engine lies lower down the slope.

Remains of one of the engines from Liberator BZ802 is little more than the crankshaft and pistons holding a few cylinder liners still in place.

Douglas C-47A 43-30719: 437th TCG, USAAF.   17-12-1943
Map No.5
V-835843 (2,950ft), Cummeenapeasta, Macgillycuddys Reeks, County Kerry

2nd Lt J.L. Scharf	Pilot	Killed
2nd Lt L.E. Goodin	Co-pilot	Killed
2nd Lt F.V. Brossard	Nav	Killed
S/Sgt W.T. Holstlaw	Eng	Killed
Sgt A.A. Schwartz	Radio Op	Killed

Having taken-off from Port Lyautey in French Morocco, with four other C-47s on the final leg of a transatlantic ferry flight, the aircraft was en route to RAF St. Eval in Cornwall. It appears though that the aircraft missed a scheduled turning point, and deviated off the planned route, after separating from the formation. Arriving over the south-west coast of Ireland several hours before dawn the aircraft descended and having turned onto a south-easterly track flew into the mountain. The aircraft then remained officially missing until the 3 February 1944 when local authorities were informed of the wreck.

Small fragments of melted aluminium alloy in the steep boulder field mark the impact point, below which is a trail of wreckage including parts of the undercarriage. The remains of an engine lie further down the mountain amongst rocks at V-832844, while a section of wing with 'star and bar' insignia can be seen in Lough Cummeenapeasta at V-836846. A small memorial plaque is attached to a rock near the section of wing, while two other memorial plaques are located on a wall in Cronin's Yard at V-837873.

Engine from Douglas C-47A 43-30719 remaining near the crash site.

Focke-Wulf FW200 Condor – / F8+KH: III/KG40, *Luftwaffe*.   20-08-1940
Map No.6
Q-473117 (2,250ft), Faha Ridge, Brandon Mountain, County Kerry

Olnt K. Mollenhausen	Pilot	Survived
Ofw R. Beumer	Co-pilot	Survived
Fw L. Wochner	Nav	Survived
Dr E. Kruger	Meteorologist	Survived
Ufz H. Bell	Gunner	Survived
Gfr K. Kych	Gunner	Survived

Following an engine fault, during a meteorological reconnaissance sortie off the west coast of Ireland, the aircraft attempted to return to base, at Bordeaux in France. However, the fault became critical, and with fog over the nearby land it was decided to ditch the aircraft. Descending to the west, the aircraft had entered cloud when the pilot saw the mountainside directly ahead. Impact was inevitable, but the pilot pitched the aircraft nose up, and it stalled into the steep slope, coming to rest relatively intact. The crew became the first *Luftwaffe* airmen to be interned by the Irish Government.

A large barren rocky area containing fragments of wreckage remains where the aircraft was burned out. Lower down the mountain lie a main undercarriage assembly and one engine, while there is a section of wing near the Pilgrim's Path up Mount Brandon at V-477115. One of the engines removed from the mountain can be seen in the car park of the bar in the village of Cloghane. On the wall outside the bar there is also a plaque recording all four air crashes on Mount Brandon.

One of the BMW radial engines from Focke-Wulf Condor F8+KH.

Handley Page Halifax Mk.V LK704 / A: No.518 Sqn, RAF. 23-01-1944

Map No.7

G-827603 (50ft), Tullan Strand, Bundoran, County Donegal.

W/O L.J. Upshall (RCAF)	Pilot	Killed
Sgt F.C.E. Hussey	Flt Eng	Killed
F/O V. Adamic (RCAF)	WO/AG	Killed
W/O F. Ash	WO/AG	Killed
F/O F.E. Dawson (RCAF)	WO/AG	Killed
F/O N.G. Gzowski (RCAF)	–	Killed
F/O C.L. Scott (RCAF)	–	Killed
Sgt D.P. Hewitson	Met Obs	Killed

This aircraft had taken-off from Isle of the Tiree in Argyll for a meteorological reconnaissance flight, codenamed Mercer, that required flying west over the Atlantic for up to 700 miles, before returning to base. After more than 12 hours in the air, while flying in poor visibility, the aircraft hit the cliff top and disintegrated. The rear fuselage fell into the sea and the bodies of F/O Gzowski and F/O Scott were swept away. The RAF investigation concluded that fuel reserves were running low and the pilot was trying to force land.

There is no wreckage on the cliff-top where the aircraft crashed, but in 2002 a memorial was placed by the nearby cliff top road. In the 1990s some wreckage was uncovered on the beach below the crash site.

The memorial at Tullan Strand commemorating the crash of Halifax LK704.

Handley Page Halifax G.R. Mk.6 RG843 / Y3-O: No.202 Sqn, RAF. 16-06-1950
Map No.8
F-566059 (1,650ft), Croaghaun, Achill Island, County Mayo

F/O E.G. Hopgood	Pilot	Killed
F/O M.W. Horsley	Co-pilot	Killed
F/O J.K. Browne	Nav	Killed
Eng1 H. Shaw	Eng	Killed
Sig1 C.J. Rogan	Sig	Killed
Sig1 B.H. deS. McKenna	Sig	Killed
Gn1 M. Gilmartin	AG	Killed
LAC J.C. Lister	Met Obs	Killed

On a long-range meteorological flight, with the pilot flying on instruments in poor visibility at relatively low level to facilitate obtaining observations, the aircraft struck high ground on Achill Island and burned out. It is understood that the aircraft was on the planned route, but possibly further along track than the navigator thought, and had not climbed to the required safety altitude before reaching the coast.

Engines, undercarriage and pieces of airframe are strewn across the rocky slope from the impact point.

Junkers Ju52 (AAC-1) 1429 / 46 B: French Air Force (on loan). 12-08-1946
Map No.9
O-178097 (2,075 ft), Djouce Mountain, County Wicklow

Capt C. Habez	Pilot	Survived
Mr M. Tourret	Co-pilot	Survived
Mr G. Biagioni	Nav	Survived
Mr D. Duran	WO	Survived
Ms A. de Brimont	Stwd	Survived
21 Passengers	See Appendices	Survived

Flying from Le Bourget, Paris to Collinstown, Dublin the aircraft flew into the hill, while in cloud, on a westerly track. Having bounced over a rise it came to rest reasonably intact, minus undercarriage and engines. The twenty-one French Girl Guides onboard were on their way to a summer camp at Powerscourt in County Wicklow.

Nothing is immediately obvious at the site, but a few pieces, not salvaged for scrap, remain in the area.

Junkers Ju88A-5 771 / DE+DS: Wekusta 2, *Luftwaffe*. 26-12-1941
Map No.10
V-548735 (150ft), Inny Valley, Waterville, County Kerry

Ufz B. Hullmann	Pilot	Survived
Ufz R. Beckmann	Eng	Survived
Ufz W. Kipp	Radio Op	Survived
Wd Insp A. Klanke	Met Obs	Survived

Unable to return to base in northern France after losing fuel, during a meteorological observation sortie off west coast of Ireland, the aircraft force landed on the peat bog.

Small lumps of melted aluminium alloy remain, the Irish Air Corps having burned the virtually intact aircraft rather than salvage it.

Junkers Ju88D-1 430030 / D7+DK: Wekusta 2, *Luftwaffe*. 23-07-1943
Map No.11
V-522404 (500ft), Ballynacarriga Hill, Dursey, County Cork.

Ufz H. Auschner	Pilot	Killed
Ogfr J. Kuschidlo	Eng	Killed
Gfr G. Dümmler	Radio Op	Killed
Reg Rat B. Noth	Met Obs	Killed

The Ju88 flew into cloud obscured headland, while on a north-westerly course, and disintegrated while on a meteorological observation sortie off the west coast of Ireland.

German ammunition cases can be found close to where the aircraft impacted, and other fragments have been found scattered on the lower part of the ridge to the north-west. A memorial plaque is located on a section of wall near the car park at V-509428.

Short Sunderland Mk.III DD848 / N: No.201 Sqn, RAF. 22-08-1943
Map No.12
Q-475136 (1,300ft), Macha-an-Mhil, Brandon Mountain, County Kerry

F/Lt C.S. Grossey	Pilot (Capt)	Killed
F/Lt A.C. Griffin	2nd Pilot	Killed
P/O G.N. Wilkinson	3rd Pilot	Killed
F/Sgt N.B. Pickford	Nav	Killed
F/Sgt J.R. Coster	WO/AG	Killed
Sgt G.F.W. Tilt	WO/AG	Killed
F/Sgt J.W. Burton	WO/AG	Killed
F/Sgt W.N. Pitts	AG	Killed
F/Sgt W. Maclean	AG	Survived
Sgt G.W. Davies	AG	Survived
Sgt J.S. Applegate	AG	Survived

During an anti-submarine patrol, from RAF Castle Archdale in County Fermanagh, the aircraft diverged from the planned route and while flying in cloud it struck the mountain, disintegrated and partially burned out.

A scar remains where part of the aircraft burned out, containing pieces of airframe and one of the Bristol Pegasus engines. The other three engines remain nearby, two lying slightly lower down the slope, above an area of bog where further pieces of airframe can be found.

Note: Depth charges have been noted to be still present at, or close to this site – unfamiliar items must obviously not be touched!

Short Sunderland Mk.III DW110: No.228 Sqn, RAF.   31-01-1944
Map No.13
G-954898 (2,000ft), Bluestack Mountains, County Donegal

F/Lt H.C.S. Armstrong DFC	Pilot (Capt)	Killed
F/O M.V. Wareing	2nd Pilot	Killed
F/Lt M.L. Gillingham	3rd Pilot	Killed
F/O J.G. Trull	Nav	Survived
W/O J.B. Richardson	Flt Eng	Survived
F/Sgt F.T. Copp	Flt Eng	Killed
Sgt C.S. Hobbs	Flt Mech/AG	Survived
F/Sgt J.E. Parsons	WO/AG	Killed
Sgt C.R. Greenwood	WO	Killed
F/Sgt F.G. Green (RCAF)	AG	Killed
F/Sgt A. Gowans	AG	Survived
F/Sgt J.K. Gilchrist	AG	Survived

Airborne from RAF Pembroke Dock in Pembrokeshire, on an anti-submarine patrol, the aircraft was signalled to divert on its return to RAF Castle Archdale in County Fermanagh. Having acknowledged the instruction and subsequently provided an ETA, the aircraft was descending through cloud while nominally on track to Lower Lough Erne, when it struck the mountain, disintegrated and burned out.

Wreckage is scattered across the mountain from the impact point, including the four engines, tail section and large pieces of fuselage & wing. A memorial plaque is fixed to a rock outcrop below the impact point.

Mark Sheldon with a large section from the fuselage of Sunderland DW110 in the Bluestack Mountains.

Short Sunderland Mk.III NJ175 / T: No.422 Sqn, RCAF.   12-08-1944
Map No.14
G-943615 (325ft), Cashelard, Belleek, County Donegal

F/Lt E.C. Devine (RCAF)	Pilot (Capt)	Killed
F/O M.A. Platsko (RCAF)	2nd Pilot	Survived
F/O R.T. Wilkinson (RCAF)	3rd Pilot	Killed
F/O G.W. Allen (RCAF)	Nav	Survived
P/O B. Parker (RCAF)	Nav/BA	Survived
Sgt H.R. Jeal (RCAF)	Flt Eng	Survived
Sgt J.F.S. Clark	Flt Mech/AG	Survived
F/Sgt J.R. Forrest (RCAF)	WO/AG	Killed
P/O A.L. Locke (RCAF)	WO/AG	Survived
Sgt D.V. Oderkirk (RCAF)	WO/AG	Survived
Sgt C.L. Singer (RCAF)	AG	Survived
Sgt G.A. Colburne (RCAF)	AG	Survived

Approximately 10 minutes after taking off from RAF Castle Archdale in County Fermanagh, for an anti-submarine patrol, the starboard outer propeller unit separated from the engine and struck the float under the wing. Despite jettisoning the weapons load (depth charges) and dumping fuel, the aircraft was unable to maintain altitude and a crash landing was attempted. On touching down the aircraft struck a small rise, turned over and broke into two. The forward section caught fire and burned out.

In 2000 a memorial stone was unveiled at the site, adjacent to a track across the peat bog.

Short Sunderland Mk.III G-AGES: BOAC.   28-07-1943
Map No.15
Q-468127 (2,000ft), Macha-an-Mhil, Brandon Mountain, County Kerry

Capt T. Allitt	Pilot	Killed
2nd Off J.H. Slater	Co-pilot	Survived
Nav Off E.W. Vincent	Nav	Survived
Radio Off C.M.P Phillips	Radio Op	Survived
Radio Off F.T.J. Parr	Radio Op	Survived
Eng Off V. Rawlinson	Eng	Survived
Eng Off R.B. Lawes	Eng	Survived
8 Passengers	See Appendices	Survived
10 Passengers	See Appendices	Killed

Flying the second stage of BOAC service 20W223 (Lagos in Nigeria to Foynes in Ireland) the aircraft had taken-off from Lisbon in Portugal on 27 July 1943 with eighteen passengers onboard. Having flown overnight, at first light the aircraft reported it was overhead the Shannon Estuary at 6,000ft. It appears the intention was then to hold for 45 minutes, allowing visibility to improve before alighting, as the aircraft turned onto a westerly heading to fly out towards the sea. After approximately 20 minutes a descent through the cloud was commenced, however, the aircraft had drifted south and although the captain suddenly saw the ground and attempted to climb, the aircraft struck the mountain side and skidded up the slope into an area of boulders, where it caught fire.

Two of the Bristol Pegasus engines and small pieces of melted aluminium alloy remain amongst the boulders where the aircraft burned out, while the tail unit and other large pieces lie at Q-468124. The other two engines and a wing float are displayed at the Foynes Flying Boat Museum.

This stone memorial has been erected at the crash site of Sunderland NJ175.

The base of the tail from the BOAC operated Sunderland, G-AGES, on Brandon Mountain.

Vickers Wellington Mk.VIII W5653: No.221 Sqn, RAF.   11-04-1941
Map No.16
C-297414 (700ft), Urris Hills, Inishowen, County Donegal

F/O A.P Cattley	Pilot	Killed
P/O J.L. Montague	Co-pilot	Killed
Sgt J.W.H. Bateman	Obs	Killed
Sgt F.K.B. Whalley	WO/AG	Killed
Sgt B.F. Badman	WO/AG	Killed
Sgt F.G. Neill	WO/AG	Killed

Eight hours after taking off from RAF Limavady in County Londonderry, on an Atlantic convoy escort patrol, the aircraft returned. Attempting to let down through cloud cover, following a QDM bearing to the airfield, the aircraft flew into the western slopes of the Urris Hills and burned out.

A scar on the steep rock strewn hillside, above the shore of Lough Swilly, contains a few lumps of melted aluminium alloy and one of the undercarriage assemblies. A wooden memorial cross has been erected at the site, and there is also a memorial plaque on the wall of the old forge in the village of Lenankeel.

Vickers Wellington Mk.III X3599: No.57 Sqn, RAF.   16-03-1942
Map No.17
J-363293 (925ft), Thomas's Mountain, Mourne Mountains, County Down

F/O H.E. Hunter	Pilot	Killed
F/O J.W. Elliott	Obs	Killed
Sgt W.S. Taylor	WO/AG	Killed
S/O B.K. Blakiston-Houston (WAAF)	Pass	Killed
Sgt Henderson	-	Survived

This Wellington flew into the hill in poor visibility and burned out while on a cross-country training flight from RAF Feltwell in Norfolk to RAF Aldergrove in County Antrim.

Pieces of melted aluminium alloy remain in an area of bare gravel at the site. In 1984 the Ulster Aviation Society recovered both engines from the site.

Vickers Wellington Mk.IC X9820: No.105 (Transport) OTU, RAF. 12-09-1943
Map No.18
J-343286 (2,300ft), Slieve Commedagh, Mourne Mountains, County Down

F/Sgt J.S. Price (RNZAF)	Pilot	Killed
Sgt H.T.A. Walters	Nav	Killed
Sgt T. Brewin	WO/AG	Killed

The aircraft hit the mountain top, while flying in cloud, during a navigation exercise from RAF Bramcote in Warwickshire.

A scar on the grassy slope marks the impact point, a short distance north of the Mourne Wall, where a few pieces of wreckage are scattered.

The crash site of Wellington X3599 from No.57 Sqn is marked by this rock strewn scar.

Geodetic structure and a turret mounting ring from Wellington HF208 on Brandon Mountain.

Vickers Wellington Mk.XIV HF208: No.304 Sqn, RAF.   20-12-1943
Map No.19
Q-472132 (1,775ft), Macha-an-Mhil, Brandon Mountain, County Kerry

F/Sgt K. Adamowicz (PAF)	Pilot	Killed
Sgt S. Czerniowski (PAF)	Co-pilot	Killed
Sgt N.H. Kuflik (PAF)	Nav	Killed
Sgt P. Kowalewicz (PAF)	WO	Killed
Sgt W. Pietrzak (PAF)	AG	Killed
Sgt K. Lugowski (PAF)	AG	Killed

Airborne on an anti-submarine patrol from RAF Predannack in Cornwall the crew requested permission from flying control to discontinue the patrol and return to base, as the radio equipment used for direction finding was malfunctioning. Minutes later the aircraft flew into the cloud-covered mountain top.

Wreckage is scattered across the slope where the aircraft disintegrated, including both Bristol Hercules engines, with one lying in a stream. Following this stream down the mountain there is a trail of pieces all the way to where parts of the tail planes and rear turret lie in the stream at Q-477133.

Appendix A

Passenger Lists

WALES
Boeing B-17G 44-8639: 511th BS / 351st BG, USAAF.   08-06-1945
　　　　Craig Cwm Llywd, Barmouth, Gwynedd

1st Lt R.E. Higley	Pass	Killed
S/Sgt T.O. Smith	Pass	Killed
Sgt C.F. Devaney	Pass	Killed
Cpl C.G. Pool	Pass	Killed
Sgt J.D. Leasure	Pass	Killed
T/sgt P. Lucyk DFC	Pass	Killed
T/Sgt M. Lemewski	Pass	Killed
Sgt E.R. Birtwell	Pass	Killed
Sgt S.R. Coons Jr	Pass	Killed
Sgt B.P. Dobbs	Pass	Killed

Douglas Dakota EI-AFL / 'St Kevin': Aer Lingus.   10-01-1952
　　　　Cwm Edno, Dodwydelen, Conwy

Mr N.G. Aston	Pass	Killed
Mrs R. Aston	Pass	Killed
Miss Belton	Pass	Killed
Mr J. Benson	Pass	Killed
Mr T.J. Carroll	Pass	Killed
Dr D.J. O'Donovan	Pass	Killed
Mr G.T. Fitzgerald	Pass	Killed
Dr J.C. Gaffney	Pass	Killed
Mr W.M. Good	Pass	Killed
Miss J. Kiely	Pass	Killed
Capt N. Laker (Pilot)	Pass	Killed
Mrs D. Laker	Pass	Killed
Miss M. Laker	Pass	Killed
Mr W.A. Lynch	Pass	Killed
Miss P.M. Noakes	Pass	Killed
Mr H.C. Richardson	Pass	Killed
Mr J.F. Stacpoole	Pass	Killed
Mr E.D. Stone	Pass	Killed
Miss L. Wenman	Pass	Killed
Mr A.H. Whiteside-Thwaite	Pass	Killed

PEAK DISTRICT

Douglas DC-3 Dakota GAHCY: British European Airways.   19-08-1948
        Wimberry Stones, Mossley, Greater Manchester

Mr R.F. Ashton	Pass	Survived
Mr W. Ashton	Pass	Killed
Ms S.M. Baird	Pass	Killed
Mrs E.H. Barclay	Pass	Killed
Miss J.M. Barclay	Pass	Killed
Mr C. Beanstock	Pass	Killed
Miss D.M. Brimelow	Pass	Killed
Mr D.H. Clarke	Pass	Killed
Mr M. Davis	Pass	Killed
Mr H. Evans	Pass	Survived
Mrs R. Evans	Pass	Survived
Master R.A. Evans	Pass	Killed
Master S. Evans	Pass	Survived
Miss B.A. Farrell	Pass	Killed
Mr G.S. Gisby	Pass	Killed
Miss I.G. Jones	Pass	Killed
Mr H.S. Lea	Pass	Killed
Miss K. McMahon	Pass	Survived
Mr H.B. Prestwich	Pass	Killed
Mrs J. Prestwich	Pass	Killed
Miss E.A. Prestwich	Pass	Killed
Miss J.C. Prestwich	Pass	Killed
Master M. Prestwich	Pass	Survived
Mrs E. Schofield	Pass	Killed
Mrs B.E. Sydall	Pass	Killed
Mr A.J. Vickery	Pass	Survived
Mrs E. Vickery	Pass	Killed
Master D. Vickery	Pass	Killed
Mr C. Watt	Pass	Survived

PENNINES

Bristol 170 Freighter Mk. 21E G-AICS: Silver City Airways.   27-02-1958
        Winter Hill, Lancashire

Mr T. Adams	Pass	Killed
Mr J.C. Bridson	Pass	Killed
Mr N.H. Brown	Pass	Killed
Mr R. Caine	Pass	Killed
Mr W.R. Cain	Pass	Killed
Mr T.A. Callow	Pass	Survived
Mr T.E. Christian	Pass	Killed
Mr E.R. Clague	Pass	Killed
Mr R.H. Corkill	Pass	Killed
Mr D.C. Corlett	Pass	Killed

Mr G.W. Corlett	Pass	Killed
Mr W.N. Corlett	Pass	Killed
Mr L.A. Cowin	Pass	Killed
Mr D. Craine	Pass	Killed
Mr J.W. Crellin	Pass	Killed
Mr J.J. Crennell	Pass	Killed
Mr J.A. Cretney	Pass	Killed
Mr T.J. Crosbie	Pass	Survived
Mr W.N. Ennett	Pass	Survived
Mr J.W. Fargher	Pass	Killed
Mr T.J. Gilbertson	Pass	Killed
Mr A.L. Gleave	Pass	Killed
Mr W. Harding	Pass	Killed
Mr D. Harding	Pass	Killed
Mr D.M. Howarth	Pass	Killed
Mr F. A. Kennish	Pass	Survived
Mr L.S. Kneale	Pass	Killed
Mr G.W.S. Lace	Pass	Killed
Mr F. Leece	Pass	Killed
Mr J.H. Lindsay	Pass	Killed
Mr V.J. McMahon	Pass	Killed
Mr W.R. Moore	Pass	Killed
Mr J.B. Parkes	Pass	Killed
Mr E. Partington	Pass	Died of Injuries
Mr C.E. Staley	Pass	Killed
Mr W.A Tonkin	Pass	Killed
Mr T.A. Watts	Pass	Killed
Mr T.W. Williams	Pass	Killed
Mr H. Williamson	Pass	Survived

Consolidated B-24J 42-100322: 714th BS/448th BG, USAAF.   02-01-1945
Burn Fell, Forest of Bowland, Lancashire

1st Lt J.E. Fields	Pass	Killed
2nd Lt J.B. Brown	Pass	Survived
2nd Lt O.O. Casto	Pass	Killed
2nd Lt R. Seymour	Pass	Survived
S/Sgt B.O. Chernow	Pass	Survived
S/Sgt M.J. Hill	Pass	Survived
S/Sgt E.E. Lyons	Pass	Killed
T/Sgt F. Louthan	Pass	Survived
T/Sgt P. Mazzagatty	Pass	Killed
Sgt R.M. Brandon	Pass	Survived
Sgt J.C. Jacobs	Pass	Survived
Sgt J.J. Madden	Pass	Survived
SgtM.S. Thomas	Pass	Survived

ISLE OF MAN

Boeing B-17G 43-38856: 534th BS / 381st BG, USAAF.   23-04-1945
North Barrule, Corrany, Isle of Man

Cpl E.S. Ammerman	Pass	Killed
Cpl E.G. Bailey	Pass	Killed
Pvt A.R. Barbour	Pass	Killed
Cpl T.P. Flaherty	Pass	Killed
T/Sgt W.E. Geist	Pass	Killed
M/Sgt E.Z. Gelman	Pass	Killed
S/Sgt R.L. Gibbs	Pass	Killed
T/Sgt J.L. Grey	Pass	Killed
Cpl H.C. Gupton Jr	Pass	Killed
Sgt I.R. Hargaves	Pass	Killed
1st Lt W.W. Hart	Pass	Killed
1st Lt J.M. Hinkle	Pass	Killed
Sgt M.J. Kakos Jr	Pass	Killed
S/Sgt W.M. Manes	Pass	Killed
Sgt J.M. Martinez	Pass	Killed
S/Sgt A.M. Mata	Pass	Killed
Cpl L.H. Maxwell	Pass	Killed
T/5 W.A. McCullough	Pass	Killed
1st Lt L.E. McGehey	Pass	Killed
T/4 A. Piter Jr	Pass	Killed
PFC A. Quagliariello	Pass	Killed
Cpl M.L. Ramsowr	Pass	Killed
T/Sgt J.W. Sullivan	Pass	Killed
Cpl H. Super	Pass	Killed
Sgt E.C. Ullmann	Pass	Killed

SCOTLAND: LOWLANDS

Boeing B-29A Superfortress 44-62276: 32nd BS / 301st BG, USAF. 17-01-1949
Succoth Glen, Lochgoilhead, Argyll

M/Sgt W.W. Baker	Pass	Killed
S/Sgt M.W. Bovard	Pass	Killed
Pfc R. Brown Jr	Pass	Killed
Sgt A.V. Chrisides	Pass	Killed
T/Sgt D.E. Cole	Pass	Killed
Pfc F.N. Cook	Pass	Killed
T/Sgt F.M. Dobbs Jr	Pass	Killed
Pfc J.L. Heacock	Pass	Killed
Sgt C.W. Ross	Pass	Killed
Sgt C.G. Jones	Pass	Killed
Sgt P.W. Knight	Pass	Killed
Pfc B.J. Krumhols	Pass	Killed

T/Sgt J.B. Lapicca	Pass	Killed
Sgt R.W. Mangum	Pass	Killed
M/Sgt H.P. Prestoch	Pass	Killed
T/Sgt R.G. Taylor	Pass	Killed

Boeing-Vertol Chinook H.C. Mk.2 ZD576: No.7 Sqn, RAF. 02-06-1994
Beinn na Lice, Mull of Kintyre, Argyll

Maj R. Allen (Army)	Pass	Killed
DCI D.S. Bunting (RUC)	Pass	Killed
Col C.J. Biles OBE (Army)	Pass	Killed
DCS D.P. Conroy QGM BEM (RUC)	Pass	Killed
DS P.G. Davidson (RUC)	Pass	Killed
DI S.A. Davidson (RUC)	Pass	Killed
Maj C.J. Dockerty (Army)	Pass	Killed
Mr J.R. Deverell CB MBE (HMG)	Pass	Killed
Mr M.G. Dalton (HMG)	Pass	Killed
Asst Chf Con J.C.B. Fitzsimons MBE (RUC)	Pass	Killed
DS R.P. Foster (RUC)	Pass	Killed
DS W.R. Gwilliam (RUC)	Pass	Killed
Lt Col R.L. Gregory-Smith (Army)	Pass	Killed
Mr J.S. Haynes MBE (HMG)	Pass	Killed
Maj A.R. Hornby MBE (Army)	Pass	Killed
Mrs A.C. James (HMG)	Pass	Killed
DI K.M. Magee (RUC)	Pass	Killed
Mr M.B. Maltby (HMG)	Pass	Killed
DCS M.M. Neilly (RUC)	Pass	Killed
DS J.T. Phoenix (RUC)	Pass	Killed
Maj R. Pugh (Army)	Pass	Killed
Mr S.L. Rickard (HMG)	Pass	Killed
Maj G.P. Sparks (Army)	Pass	Killed
Lt Col J.W. Tobias MBE (Army)	Pass	Killed
Lt Col G.V.A. Williams MBE QGM (Army)	Pass	Killed

Consolidated B-24M 44-50695: 713th BS / 448th BG, USAAF. 12-06-1945
Goodman's Cairn, Ballantrae, Dumfries & Galloway.

Lt Col H.H. Thompson	Pass	Killed
Capt H.L. Earmart	Pass	Killed
T/Sgt R. Pokorny	Pass	Survived
S/Sgt S.G. Arrons	Pass	Killed
S/Sgt A.D. Good	Pass	Killed
S/Sgt J.R. May	Pass	Survived
Sgt A.W. Lindsey	Pass	Killed
Cpl E.C. Fortin	Pass	Killed
PFC G.T. Gafney Jr	Pass	Killed
Sgt K. Nelson	Pass	Survived

Vickers Viking Mk.1B G-AIVE / 'Vestal': BEA.   21-04-1948
     Irish Law , Largs, North Ayrshire

Mr G. Davies	Pass	Survived
Mr A. Hems	Pass	Survived
Mr E. Hopper	Pass	Survived
Mr B. Goldwater	Pass	Survived
Mr T. Molland	Pass	Survived
Mr H. Moore	Pass	Survived
Mrs M. Most	Pass	Survived
Mrs H. Most	Pass	Survived
Mr Sejersted	Pass	Survived
Mrs Sejersted	Pass	Survived
Mrs J. Sheville	Pass	Survived
Mr H.D. Watt	Pass	Survived
Mrs E. Wighton	Pass	Survived
Mr J.H. Wilson	Pass	Survived
Mr J. Young	Pass	Survived
Mrs Young	Pass	Survived

SCOTLAND: HIGHLANDS & ISLANDS

Consolidated LB-30A Liberator AM261: ATFERO, RAF.   10-08-1941
     Mullach Buidhe, Corrie, Isle of Arran

Capt J.J. Anderson (RAFFC)	Pass	Killed
Capt D.J. Duggan (RAFFC)	Pass	Killed
Capt G.T. Harris (RAFFC)	Pass	Killed
Capt H.R. Judy (RAFFC)	Pass	Killed
Capt W.M. King (RAFFC)	Pass	Killed
Capt J.E. Price (RAFFC)	Pass	Killed
Capt H.C.W. Smith (RAFFC)	Pass	Killed
Capt J. Wixen (RAFFC)	Pass	Killed
1st Off J.J. Rouleston (RAFFC)	Pass	Killed
F/Eng E.G. Reeves (RAFFC)	Pass	Killed
Radio Off R.B. Brammer (RAFFC)	Pass	Killed
Radio Off J.B. Drake (RAFFC)	Pass	Killed
Radio Off H.S. Green (BOAC)	Pass	Killed
Radio Off W.G. Kennedy (RAFFC)	Pass	Killed
Radio Off G. Laing (RAFFC)	Pass	Killed
Radio Off W.K. Marks (RAFFC)	Pass	Killed
Radio Off H.C. McIntosh (RAFFC)	Pass	Killed
Radio Off A.A. Oliver (ATA)	Pass	Killed
Radio Off G.H. Powell (ATA)	Pass	Killed
Radio Off H.D. Rees (ATA)	Pass	Killed

IRELAND
Short Sunderland Mk.III G-AGES: BOAC.   28-07-1943
    Macha-an-Mhil, Brandon Mountain, County Kerry

Sgt R.E. Bertram	Pass	Survived
Sgt K.J. Devall (RAFVR)	Pass	Killed
Sgt A.B. Dupree (RNZAF)	Pass	Survived
Mr L.G. French	Pass	Survived
Mr O. Frith	Pass	Survived
Capt D.J. Hartigan (Royal Artillery)	Pass	Killed
Mr W.S. Hebden	Pass	Survived
P/O L. King	Pass	Survived
Mr R.F. Larche	Pass	Survived
Col A.F.R. Lumby CIE OBE (Army)	Pass	Killed
Mr L. Milner	Pass	Killed
Col S.L. Pullinger (Royal Engineers)	Pass	Killed
Mr M.A. Roth	Pass	Killed
Sgt V.F.E. Simmons	Pass	Survived
Gp/Capt D.W. Stannard (RAF)	Pass	Killed
Mr T.W. Thomson	Pass	Killed
Mr I.K. Thorn	Pass	Killed
Mr H. Tristram	Pass	Killed

Junkers Ju52 (AAC-1) 1429 / 46 B: French Air Force (on loan). 12-08-1946
    Djouce Mountain, County Wicklow

Ms J. Alexandre	Pass	Survived
Ms F. Béchet	Pass	Survived
Ms G. Bétrancourt	Pass	Survived
Ms A. Bonnet	Pass	Survived
Ms M. Bourdeauducq	Pass	Survived
Ms J. Conort	Pass	Survived
Ms C. de Geuser	Pass	Survived
Ms C. de Vitry	Pass	Survived
Ms A. Emo	Pass	Survived
Ms N. Jacques-Léon	Pass	Survived
Ms A. Laporte	Pass	Survived
Ms O. Lecoquière	Pass	Survived
Ms A. Lemonnier	Pass	Survived
Ms E. Lemonnier	Pass	Survived
Ms L. Levy-Bruhl	Pass	Survived
Ms G. Martin	Pass	Survived
Ms A. Nattier	Pass	Survived
Ms M. Noyer	Pass	Survived
Ms S. Ostrowetsky	Pass	Survived
Ms O. Stahlberger	Pass	Survived
Ms M. Ygouf	Pass	Survived

Appendix B

Manufacturers' Stamps

The following manufacturers' inspection stamps have all been noted by the authors on pieces of wreckage still to be found at the crash sites listed in this book. Please note, they do not provide definitive proof of identification for the type of aircraft a piece may originate from, but do identify the manufacturer of the section, revealing an insight into the sub-contracting system used to build aircraft during WW2. For further information on identifying aircraft types, please see the following Part Numbers section.

Airspeed
Oxford, Consul

Armstrong Whitworth
Lancaster, Lincoln, Meteor, Whitley

Avro
Anson, Audax, Canberra, Lancaster, Shackleton, Tutor, Vulcan

Avro Yeadon
Anson

Blackburn
Botha, Skua, Sunderland

Boulton Paul
Barracuda, Defiant

Bristol
Beaufighter, Beaufort, Blenheim, Wayfarer and all aircraft fitted with Bristol engines

Canadair
Sabre

Canadian Car & Foundry Corporation
Hurricane

Curtiss
Tomahawk

De Havilland
Devon, DH-60, Domine, Dragon, Dragonfly Dragon Rapide, Hornet, Mosquito, Oxford, Sea Vixen, Tiger Moth, Vampire, Venom

Douglas
B-17, B-24, Boston, C-47, C-54, DC-3

English Electric
Canberra, Halifax, Hampden, Vampire

Fairey
Albacore, Barracuda, Battle, Firefly, Halifax, Swordfish

Ford
B-24

Gloster
Henley, Hurricane, Javelin, Meteor, Typhoon

Handley Page
Canberra, Halifax, Heyford

Hawker
Hart, Hind, Hunter, Hurricane, Sea Hawk, Typhoon

Lockheed
C-60, Hudson, Neptune, P-38, Ventura

London Aircraft Production Group
Halifax

Production Group

Morris Motors
Tiger Moth

Noorduyn
Harvard, UC-64

North American
Mustang

Phillips & Powis
Hawk Trainer, Martinet, Master, Oxford

Republic
P-47

Rootes Securities
Blenheim, Halifax

Saunders Roe
Sea Otter

Shorts
Stirling, Sunderland

Supermarine
Spitfire

Vega
B-17

Vickers / Vickers Armstrong Viking, Vildebeast, Warwick, Wellington, Lancaster

Vickers Blackpool
Wellington

Vickers Castles Bromwich
Spitfire

Vickers Chester
Wellington

Westland
Hector, Lysander, Seafire, Wallace

Appendix C

Part Number Prefixes

A common find at most crash sites are pieces with part numbers stamped into them. Some of these number sequences, but by no means all, can be related directly to the aircraft type by means of their number/letter prefixes.

The combination of a part number with an appropriate prefix and a company inspector's stamp can be the key to identifying an aircraft wreck, or at least provide an indication as to what type of aircraft has been found, so further inquiries can be made. The recording of such evidence at crash sites has been used to aid in the identification of a number of the aircraft in this book.

However, Some companies did not often stamp parts and others used systems that, without a parts catalogue cannot be linked to a particular type. An example of a company that used a numbering system, which does not reference the aircraft type, is the Hawker Siddeley group which from the mid 1930s included Hawker, Avro and Gloster. Most parts produced by these companies followed a standard format of a letter followed by five or six numbers or a combination of letters and numbers. Most of the stamped sequences that can be linked to an aircraft type use the aircraft's type number as their prefix, for example both de Havilland and Vickers used this principle for their part numbering, as did a few others. The following part number prefixes have all been noted by the authors on pieces of wreckage still to be seen at the crash sites listed in this book.

Manufacturer	Type	Prefix	Example
Airspeed	Oxford	10	102591
Armstrong Whitworth	Whitley	SP	SP85864
Blackburn 18 B	Botha	190	HE190 15B 1K, EHE190
Consolidated	B-24	32	32W2004 10412
Consolidated	Catalina	28	-
Curtiss	Tomahawk	75, 87	75 69 439, 87 03 084
De Havilland	Devon	4 (104)	-
De Havilland	DH60X Moth	60	-
De Havilland	Dominie	89	-
De Havilland	Dragon	84	-
De Havilland	Dragon Rapide	89	-
De Havilland	Dragonfly	90	-
De Havilland	Hornet	3 (103)	3FC549
De Havilland	Mosquito	98	L982100
De Havilland	Sea Vixen	10 (110)	-
De Havilland	Tiger Moth	82	-
De Havilland	Vampire	0 (100)	B06545A
English Electric	Canberra	EA3	EA3 10 525 1AXN
Gloster	Javelin	GA5	GA5 14 0024 2
Grumman	Martlet	71	-
Handley Page	Halifax	57	57277B38
Handley Page	Hampden	52	-
Handley Page	Heyford	38, 50	-
McDonnell	F-101	20	20-30155-8
North American	P-51 / Mustang	102	102-310227-54
North American 101	Sabre	151, 170	151 610157, 170 14006
Republic	P-47	89	89F11180
Short	Stirling	29	4291292
Supermarine	Sea Otter	309	30908/1049
Supermarine	Spitfire / Seafire	300 to 390	30065 61 5D SS
Vickers	Warwick	462	-
Vickers	Wellington	285	28557 852

Appendix D

Air Crew Positions

Ast Crew Chf	Assistant Crew Chief
AEO	Air Electronics Officer
AE Op	Air Electronics Operator
AG	Air Gunner
Air Eng	Air Engineer
BA	Bomb Aimer / Bombardier
(Capt)	Aircraft Captain
Crew Chf	Crew Chief
Co-pilot	Co-pilot
Dpr	Dispatcher
Elec Eng	Electrical Engineer
Eng	Engineer
Fitter (II)	Fitter (Class II)
Flt Eng	Flight Engineer
Flt Mech	Flight Mechanic
Gnd Eng	Ground Engineer
(Inst)	Instructor
Ldm	Loadmaster
Met Obs	Meteorological Observer
Nav	Navigator
Obs	Observer
Ord Op	Ordnance Operator
Photo Advr	Photographic Advisor
Pilot	Pilot (2nd / 3rd as applicable)
Pass	Passenger
Radar Op	Radar Operator
Radio Op	Radio Operator
Sec	Secretary
Sig	Signaller
Stwd	Steward / Stewardess
Sup	Supernumerary
(u/t)	Under Training
WO	Wireless Operator
WSO	Weapons Systems Operator

Appendix E

Aircraft Type Designations

A.	Assault / Attack
A.S.	Anti-Submarine
A.S.R.	Air Sea Rescue
B.	Bomber
B-	Bomber
C.	Cargo
C-	Cargo
F.	Fighter
F-	Fighter / Photo Reconnaissance
F.A.W.	Fighter All Weather
F.B.	Fighter Bomber
F.G.A.	Fighter Ground Attack
F.R.	Fighter Reconnaissance
G.R.	General Reconnaissance
	(Also Ground Attack Reconnaissance - Tornado & Jaguar)
H.C.	Helicopter Cargo
M.R.	Maritime Reconnaissance
N.F.	Night Fighter
P-	Pursuit
P.R.	Photo Reconnaissance
R-	Reconnaissance
T.	Trainer
T.F.	Torpedo Fighter
UC-	Utility Cargo

Bibliography

The following books have been selected as their content specifically includes details of crash sites and memorials in the UK. Most concentrate on specific geographical areas or go into greater historical detail on a few selected incidents. No responsibility can be taken for the accuracy of the historical information contained in these works, some are excellent, others far from it. Though it should be remembered that many of the archive sources now available to aviation historians have only recently become so. Grid references are included in many of the books listed, though in some cases only partial references are given and again their accuracy cannot be vouched for. From experience, if planning a trip to such a site, verifying its location (or in some cases, its existence!) from more than one source is recommended.

Many of these works are now out of print and many were only printed in limited numbers in the first place, making them difficult to get hold of today. For this reason, several early, self published, works have been omitted, particularly as the information they contained was repeated in later publications. If you do wish to consult a book but encounter difficulties obtaining a copy, your local public library requests service should be able to help.

Boylan, M. S. *A Moorlands Dedication, An account of the 40 military aircraft accidents in the Leek area of North Staffordshire during World War Two*, William H. Beech, 1992, ISBN 0952055805.

Clark, P. *A Border Too High: A Guide to Wartime Crashes in the Border Hills*, Glen Graphics, 1999, ISBN 1900038307

Collier, R. and Wilkinson R., *Dark Peak Aircraft Wrecks 1*, Leo Cooper Ltd, 1997, ISBN 0850524751.

Collier, R. and Wilkinson R., *Dark Peak Aircraft Wrecks 2*, Leo Cooper Ltd, 1998, ISBN 0850523362.

Doyle, P.A. *Aviation Memorials of Essex: A Gazetteer of the Memorials to Feats of Aviation in the County*, Forward Airfield Research Publishing, 2006, ISBN 0952562499

Doylerush. E. *Fallen Eagles, A Guide to Aircraft Crashes in North-East & Mid-Wales*, Midland Counties Publications, 1993, ISBN 0904597660.

Doylerush, E., *No Landing Place, A Guide to Aircraft Crashes in Snowdonia*, Midland Counties Publications, 1985, ISBN 0904597571.

Doylerush, E. *No Landing Place Volume 2, More Tales of Aircraft Crashes in Snowdonia*, Midland Publishing Ltd, 1999, ISBN 1857800907.

Doylerush, E., *Rocks in the Clouds: High-Ground Aircraft Crashes of South Wales*, Midland Publishing Ltd, 2007, ISBN 1857802810.

Doylerush, E. *The Legend of Llandwrog, The story of an airfield and the birth of the RAF Mountain Rescue Service*, Midland Counties Publications, 1994, ISBN 0904597881.

Earl, D. W. *Hell on High Ground, A Guide to Aircraft Hill Crash Sites in the UK and Ireland*, Airlife Publishing Ltd, 1995, ISBN 1853105694.

Earl, D. W. *Hell on High Ground Volume 2, World War II Air Crash Sites*, Airlife Publishing Ltd, 1999, ISBN 1840370823.

Gardner, J. *Aviation Landmarks, After the Battle*. 1990, ISBN 0900913665

Hill, T. R. *Down in Wales, Visits to some wartime air crash sites*, Gwasg Carreg Gwalch, 1994, ISBN 086381283X.

Hill, T. R. *Down in Wales 2, Visits to more wartime crash sites*, Gwasg Carreg Gwalch, 1996, ISBN 0863814018.

Hill, T. R. *Final Descent, Air Crashes in Wales And The Borders*, Leo Cooper Ltd, 1999, ISBN 0850526590.

Hurst, M. J., *Air Crashes In The Lake District*, Airlife Publishing Ltd, 1997, ISBN 185310874X.

Ingham, M. J., *Air Force Memorials of Lincolnshire*, Midland Publishing Ltd, 2006, ISBN 1857800354

MacCarron, D. *Landfall Ireland, The story of Allied and German aircraft which came down in Eire in World War Two*, Colourprint Books, 2003, ISBN 1904242030.

Mason, J. D. *Circular Walks to Peak District Aircraft Wrecks*, Walk & Write Ltd, ISBN 0907496946.

Merrill, J. N., *Dark Peak Aircraft Wreck Walks*, Walk & Write Ltd, 2001, ISBN 1903627044

Merrill, J. N., *White Peak Aircraft Wrecks Walks*, Walk & Write Ltd, 2004, ISBN 1903627494.

Poole, S. *Rough Landing or Fatal Flight, A History of Aircraft Accidents On, Over and Around the Isle of Man*, Amulree Publications, 1999, ISBN 190150803.

Roberts, W. J. L., *Aircraft Crash Sites and the Stories Behind Them*, Brecon Beacons National Park Service, 1996.

Sloan, R. *Aircraft Crashes: Flying Accidents in Gwynedd, 1910-1990*. Gwasg Carreg Gwalch. 1990 ISBN 0863812813

Smith, D. J. *Britain's Aviation Memorials and Mementoes*, Patrick Stephens Ltd, 1992, ISBN 185260395X

Smith, D. J. *High Ground Wrecks and Relics, Aircraft Hulks on the Mountains of the UK and Ireland*, Midland Publishing Ltd, 1997, ISBN 1857800702.

Smith, P. J. C. *Flying Bombs Over The Pennines, The story of the V-1 attack aimed at Manchester on December 24th 1944*, Neil Richardson, 1988. ISBN 1852160292

Sources of Information

The following list includes many sources consulted during the preparation of this work, but is by no means intended to be a comprehensive listing. Many other works and additional published and unpublished sources have been consulted over the years, including; newspapers, journals, diaries and oral accounts from eyewitnesses. It does however, provide the reader with some suggested starting points for further research.

Brew, A., *The Defiant File*, Air-Britain (Historians) Ltd, 1996, ISBN 0851302262.

Chorley, W. R., *Royal Air Force Bomber Command Losses Volume 1, 1939-1940*, Midland Counties Publications, 1992, ISBN 0904597857.

Chorley, W. R., *Royal Air Force Bomber Command Losses Volume 2, 1941*, Midland Counties Publications, 1993, ISBN 0904597873.

Chorley, W. R., *Royal Air Force Bomber Command Losses Volume 3, 1942*, Midland Counties Publications, 1994, ISBN 090459789X.

Chorley, W. R., *Royal Air Force Bomber Command Losses Volume 4, 1943*, Midland Counties Publications, 1996, ISBN 0904597903.

Chorley, W. R., *Royal Air Force Bomber Command Losses Volume 5, 1944*, Midland Counties Publications, 1997, ISBN 0904597911.

Chorley, W. R., *Royal Air Force Bomber Command Losses Volume 6*, 1945, Midland Counties Publications, 1998, ISBN 090459792-.

Chorley, W. R., *Royal Air Force Bomber Command Losses Volume 7, Operational Training Units 1940-1947*, Midland Publishing, 2002, ISBN 1857801326.

Chorley, W. R., *Royal Air Force Bomber Command Losses Volume 8, Heavy Conversion Units and Miscellaneous Units 1939-1947*, Midland Publishing, 2003, ISBN 1857801563.

Cummings, C., *The Price of Peace: A Catalogue of RAF Aircraft Losses Between VE-Day and End of 1945*, Nimbus Publishing, 2004, ISBN 0952661950. (Note: this is one of a series of titles by this author that details postwar RAF losses)

Halley, J. J. M.B.E., *Broken Wings, Post-War Royal Air Force Accidents*, Air-Britain (Historians) Ltd, 1999, ISBN 0851302904.

Hamlin, J. F., *The Oxford, Consul & Envoy File*, Air-Britain (Historians) Ltd, 2001, ISBN 0851302890.

Holmes, H., *Avro Lancaster, The Definitive Record*, Airlife Publishing Ltd, 1997, ISBN 1853107212.

Lake, A., *Flying Units Of The RAF, The Ancestry, Formation and Disbandment of all Flying Units from 1912*, Airlife Publishing Ltd, 1999, ISBN 1840370866.

McNeill, R., *Royal Air Force Coastal Command Losses of the Second World War, Volume 1*, Aircraft and Crew Losses 1939-1941, Midland Publishing, 2003, ISBN 1857801288.

Morgan, E.B. and Shacklady, E., *Spitfire: The History*, 2nd Revised edition, Key Books Ltd, 2000, ISBN 0946219486.

Norman, Bill, *Broken Eagles: Luftwaffe Losses Over Yorkshire*, Pen & Sword Books Ltd, 2001, ISBN 0850527961.

Norman, Bill, *Luftwaffe Losses Over Northumberland and Durham 1939-1945*, Pen & Sword Books Ltd, 2002, ISBN 0850529131.

Oliver, D., *British Military Aircraft Accidents, The Last 25 Years*, Ian Allan Ltd, 1990, ISBN 0711017867.

Sturtivant R. and Burrow, M., *Fleet Air Arm Aircraft 1939 to 1945* Air-Britain (Historians) Ltd, 1995, ISBN 0851302327.

Sturtivant R., *Anson File*, Air-Britain (Historians) Ltd, 1988, ISBN 0851301568

Sturtivant R. Burrow, M. and Howard, L., *Fleet Air Arm Fixed-Wing Aircraft Since 1946*, Air-Britain (Historians) Ltd, 2004, ISBN 0851302831.

Webb, D. C., *UK Flight Testing Accidents 1940-71*, Air-Britain (Historians) Ltd, 2002, ISBN 0851303311.

Note: Air-Britain (Historians) Ltd. Have published many research orientated works, including the 'Register' series, listing aircraft of the Royal Air Force in serial order and giving details of each aircraft, the units which flew it and its final fate. Also their 'File' series, a few examples of which are listed here, deal with many individual aircraft types in detail, including the fate of each example built.

Online database Sources:
American Battle Monuments Commission: **www.abmc.gov** (Follow links to search ABMC Databases).
Armed Forces Memorial: **http://www.forcesmemorial.org.uk** (follow links to search the post WW2 Roll of Honour).
Auckland War Museum: **http://www.aucklandmuseum.com** (follow link to search the Cenotaph Database).
Australian War Memorial: **www.awm.gov.au** (follow links to search the Roll of Honour).
Australian World War Two Nominal Roll: **www.ww2roll.gov.au** (Contains information from the service records of some one million individuals who served in WW2).
Commonwealth War Graves Commission: **www.cwgc.org** (commemorates those who died up to 31st December 1947).

Archive Sources:
The following list features the main archives likely to be used when researching aircraft losses, together with the main categories of documents likely to be consulted. The inclusion of each archive's URL does not indicate that the actual documents required are available online, though online application for copies of documents may be available.
National Archives of Australia: **http://www.naa.gov.au**
      RAAF Personnel Service Records
      RAAF Personnel Casualty Files (A705)
National Archives, UK: **www.nationalarchives.gov.uk**
      Squadron Operations Record Books (AIR 27/xx)
      Station Operations Record Books (AIR 28/xx)
      Misc Units Operations Record Books (AIR 29/xx)
      Accident Investigation Branch Reports (AVIA 5/xx)
      Board of Trade Accident Files (BT 217/xx + BT 233/xx)

Civil Aviation Authority Records (DR 11/xx)

Luftwaffe Casualties Intelligence Files (AIR 16/xx + AIR 22/xx)

Royal Air Force Museum, Department of Research and Information Services, **www.rafmuseum.org**

Air Ministry Form 78, Aircraft Movement Cards

Air Ministry Form 1180, Aircraft Accident Cards

United States Air Force Flight Safety Center, Kirtland AFB, New Mexico, **www.kirtland.af.mil**

Post 1955 USAF Accident Records

United States Air Force Historical Research Agency, Maxwell AFB, Alabama, **www.maxwell.af.mil/au/afhra/**

Pre 1956 USAAF / USAF Accident Records

Note: There are a couple of commercial sources providing copies of USAAF / USAF / USN records, that may be more convenient and cost effective than the official sources listed above. Accident-Report.com, run by Mike Stowe at: **www.accident-report.com** can supply:

Pre 1956 USAAF / USAF Accident Reports

Pre 1956 US Navy Accident Cards

USAAF Missing Air Crew Reports

USAAF Individual Aircraft History Cards

Abbreviations

ADG	Air Depot Group
AFC	Air Force Cross
AFSC	Air Force Service Command
AGS	Air Gunners School
AN&BS	Air Navigation and Bombing School
ANS	Air Navigation School
AOS	Air Observer School
ARC	American Red Cross
ASG	Air Service Group
ATA	Air Transport Auxiliary
ATFERO	Atlantic Ferry Organisation
ATG	Air Transport Group
AACU	Anti Aircraft Co-operation Unit
AWTF	Air Weapons Training Flight
BAD	Base Air Depot
BCCF	Bomber Command Communications Flight
BEM	British Empire Medal
BG	Bombardment Group
BGS	Bombing & Gunnery School
BOAC	British Overseas Airways Corporation
BS	Bombardment Squadron
BU	Base Unit
CAG	Civil Air Guard
CB	Companion of the Order of the Bath
CCCS	Coastal Command Communications Squadron
CNS	Central Navigation School
(C) OTU	(Coastal) Operational Training Unit
CTC	Civilian Technical Corps
CWGC	Commonwealth War Graves Commission
DFC	Distinguished Flying Cross
DFM	Distinguished Flying Medal
DRS	Depot Repair Squadron
DSO	Distinguished Service Order
EANS	Empire Aerial Navigation School
EFTS	Elementary Flying Training School
E&RFTS	Elementary & Reserve Flying Training School
ETA	Estimated Time of Arrival
FPP	Ferry Pilots' Pool
FBW	Fighter Bomber Wing
FFAF	Free French Air Force
FG	Fighter Group
FIS	Flying Instructors School
FLR	Fleet Reserve
FS	Fighter Squadron
FTG	Fighter Training Group
Ftr	Fighter
FU	Ferry Unit
Flt	Flight
FTS	Flying Training School
FW	Fighter Wing
GCMG	Knight Grand Cross of the Order of St Michael and St George
GCVO	Knight Grand Cross of the Royal Victorian Order
Grp	Group

HCU	Heavy Conversion Unit
Hon	Honourable
IFR	Instrument Flight Rules
ITS	Initial Training School
KG	*Kampfgeschwader* (Bomber Wing)
Jr	Junior
KG	Knight of the Garter
KT	Knight of the Thistle
Kts	Knots (Nautical Miles Per Hour)
MBE	Member the Order of the British Empire
MCC&FF	Maintenance Command Communication and Ferry Flight
Mk	Mark
MU	Maintenance Unit
MVO	Member of the Royal Victorian Order
N/A	Not Applicable
NATO	North Atlantic Treaty Organisation
NDB	Non Directional Beacon (Nav Aid)
OADF	Overseas Aircraft Dispatch Flight
OADU	Overseas Aircraft Dispatch Unit
(O)AFU	(Observer) Advanced Flying Unit
OAPU	Overseas Aircraft Preparation Unit
Ob Grp	Observation Group
OCU	Operational Conversion Unit
OPRON	Operations Squadron
OTU	Operational Training Unit
PAF	Polish Air Force
PFFNTU	Path Finder Force Navigation Training Unit
Prov	Provisional
PRG	Photographic Reconnaissance Group
PRS	Photographic Reconnaissance Squadron
(P)AFU	(Pilot) Advanced Flying Unit
QDM	(magnetic course to steer)
QGH	(descent procedure based on direction finding fixes)
QGM	Queen's Gallantry Medal
RG	Reconnaissance Group
RFS	Reserve Flying School
RAF	Royal Air Force
RAFVR	Royal Air Force Volunteer Reserve
RAAF	Royal Australian Air Force
RAFFC	Royal Air Force Ferry Command
RAN	Royal Australian Navy
RAuxAF	Royal Auxiliary Air Force
RCAF	Royal Canadian Air Force
RCNVR	Royal Canadian Navy Volunteer Reserve
RN	Royal Navy
RNAS	Royal Naval Air Station
RNZAF	Royal New Zealand Air Force
ROC	Royal Observer Corps
RRE	Radar Research Establishment
RS	Radio School
SAC	School of Army Co-operation
SAF	Singapore Armed Forces
SFTS	Service Flying Training School

SGR	School of General Reconnaissance
SPTU	Staff Pilots Training Unit
Sqn	Squadron
Srs	Series
Stn Flt	Station Flight
TCG	Troop Carrier Group
TCS	Troop Carrier Squadron
TCU	Transport Conversion Unit
TFPP	Training Ferry Pilots Pool
TFS	Tactical Fighter Squadron
TFW	Tactical Fighter Wing
Tng	Training
TRS	Tactical Reconnaissance Squadron
TRW	Tactical Reconnaissance Wing
TTU	Torpedo Training Unit
TWU	Tactical Weapons Unit
USAF	United States Air Force
USAAF	United States Army Air Force
USN	United States Navy
VB	Bombing Squadron
VFR	Visual Flight Rules

Air Crew Ranks

(A)	(Acting) RAF / (Aviation) RN
1st Lt	1st Lieutenant
1st Off	1st Officer
2nd Lt	2nd Lieutenant
2nd Off	2nd Officer
ACRM1c	Aviation Chief Radioman 1st Class
Adjt	Adjutant
Air Cdre	Air Commodore
AMM3c	Aviation Machinist's Mate 3rd Class
AOM	Aviation Ordnanceman
ARM3c	Aviation Radioman 3rd Class
AC1	Aircraftman 1st Class
AC2	Aircraftman 2nd Class
Ast Chf Con	Assistant Chief Constable
Capt	Captain
Cdr Sgn	Commander Surgeon
Cdt	Cadet
Cpl	Corporal
CPOA	Chief Petty Officer Airman
CWM	Commissioned Ward Master
DCI	Detective Chief Inspector
DCS	Detective Chief Superintendent
DI	Detective Inspector
DS	Detective Superintendent
Eng 1	Engineer 1
Eng Off	Engineering Officer
Esn	Ensign

F/Lt	Flight Lieutenant
F/O	Flying Officer
F/Sgt	Flight Sergeant
Flt Capt	Flight Captain
F/Eng	Flight Engineer
Flt Off	Flight Officer
Fw	*Feldwebel*
Grp Capt	Group Captain
Gfr	*Gefreiter*
Gnr 1	Gunner 1
LAC	Leading Aircraftman
LAM	Leading Airman
Lt	Lieutenant
Ltn	*Leutnant*
Lt Cdr	Lieutenant Commander
Lt Col	Lieutenant Colonel
Lt JG	Lieutenant Junior Grade
Maj	Major
M/ALM	Master Air Loadmaster
M/AEOp	Master Air Electronics Operator
M/Sgt	Master Sergeant
M/Sig	Master Signaller
Msm	Midshipman
Nav Off	Navigating Officer
Ob 4	Observer 4
Ofw	*Oberfeldwebel*
Ogfr	*Obergefreiter*
Oltn	*Oberleutnant*
P/O	Pilot Officer
PO	Petty Officer
P2	Pilot 2
P4	Pilot 4
PFC	Private First Class
Pvt	Private
Radio Off	Radio Officer
Reg Rat	*Regierungs-Rat* (Gov't Official)
SBA	Sick Berth Attendant
S/Ldr	Squadron Leader
S/Sgt	Staff Sergeant
Sgt	Sergeant
Sig 1	Signaller 1
SM 2	Signalman 2nd Class
Snr Flt Eng	Senior Flight Engineer
S/O	Section Officer
Sub Lt	Sub Lieutenant
T/4	Technician 4th Grade
T/5	Technician 5th Grade
T/Sgt	Technical Sergeant
Ufz	*Unteroffizier*
Wd Insp	*Wetterdienstinspektor* (Met Obs)
W/Cdr	Wing Commander
W/O	Warrant Officer